# Controversial Issues
# in the Social Studies:
# A Contemporary Perspective

# Contributors

James L. Aldrich

James A. Banks

Anne M. Blackburn

Charles Bloomstein

John F. Cuber

Martha Tyler John

Raymond H. Muessig

William A. Nesbitt

James B. Parsons

Anne R. Peterson

David D. Stafford

Jo A. Cutler Sweeney

Kenrick S. Thompson

*Illustrations Courtesy*
*The Hirshhorn Museum and Sculpture Garden*
*Smithsonian Institution*

# Controversial Issues
# in the Social Studies:
# A Contemporary Perspective

**Raymond H. Muessig,** *Editor*

**45th Yearbook • 1975**

**NATIONAL COUNCIL FOR THE SOCIAL STUDIES**
1201 Sixteenth Street, N.W. Washington, D. C. 20036

# NATIONAL COUNCIL FOR THE SOCIAL STUDIES

## Officers for 1975

THE NATIONAL COUNCIL FOR THE SOCIAL STUDIES is the professional organization of educators at all levels—elementary, secondary, college and university—who are interested in the teaching of social studies. Membership in the NATIONAL COUNCIL FOR THE SOCIAL STUDIES includes a subscription to the Council's official journal, *Social Education,* a copy of the Yearbook, and a periodic newsletter. In addition, the Council publishes bulletins, curriculum studies, pamphlets, and other materials of practical use for teachers of the social studies. Membership dues are $15.00 a year. Applications for membership and orders for the purchase of publications should be sent to the Executive Director, 1201 Sixteenth Street, N.W., Washington, D. C. 20036.

TO

RICHARD E. GROSS

*A distinguished NCSS President*
*who has long supported dealing with controversial issues*

# A Brief Expression of Appreciation

*This Yearbook is the product of many incisive heads,
sensitive hearts, and capable hands. Steadfast
officers, devoted directors, and loyal
members-at-large of the National Council for the Social
Studies have provided advice and encouragement
throughout the project. The Publications
Board has played a role in developing and fostering
this endeavor, and its special representative,
Robert Beery, has been exceptionally
courteous and willing to help. The confidential readers
who reacted to this manuscript warrant recognition.
Members of the NCSS editorial staff,
Daniel Roselle, Willadene Price, and Mary Anne Joda,
have guided typewritten matter into concrete
type. Professional writers and publishers
have been generous in granting permission to use enriching
quotations. Yet, the heroic figures in this undertaking
are the Yearbook authors, for they have shouldered
the burdens of their chapters on top of already staggering
loads, met almost impossible deadlines with saintly
dispositions, and suffered the slings and
arrows of others' red pencils with noble forbearance.*

RAYMOND H. MUESSIG

# Foreword

WITH the Watergate debacle etched on every mind, with disputes over school textbooks providing many pages of copy for newspapers, and with nations continuing to tear at each other's boundaries, teachers of social studies have been living closely with controversy. In fact, people everywhere seem to be holding strong views on a whole continuum of issues, and they express their commitments in a variety of ways. How one arrives at this point of commitment becomes increasingly important in a democracy.

Citizens in such a political environment must be able to think critically and rationally about issues of broad public concern. This posture is not assumed overnight at the times when one votes. If it is to happen at all, these skills must be learned while still in school. In that setting, there is the time and the laboratory for those experiences which will develop the skills of critical thinking and problem-solving. During the school years, the student's belief in freedom of speech, sensitivity to humanitarian problems, and respect for variations in customs and opinions can be strengthened by encouraging the pursuit of solutions and viable alternatives within the framework of democratic action. The study of controversial issues is a valuable means to this end.

The social studies teacher bears a great responsibility for seeing that the student has the right to hear, to read, to discuss and to reach judgments about a great variety of societal issues. This process protects freedom. Without the maintenance of a spirit of free inquiry and impartiality in the classroom, the student's education must be judged delinquent no matter how extensive the cornucopia of experiences.

In teaching about controversial issues the social studies teacher needs to be prepared to assume certain obligations. The issues to be studied must be selected carefully, and, during the class study, the teacher must see that all viewpoints are considered. Prior to this, however, it is imperative that an adequate setting for such study be developed by social studies teachers, the school administration, and the school board representing the community.

All too often, such a setting does not exist. As a result, in spite of the dissent of the 1960s, Vietnam, and proliferating energy crises, some social studies classrooms have ignored all aspects of controversy. Perhaps in fear, or because of feelings of inadequacy about coping with volatile issues, they have ignored the critical examination of contemporary events. As one observer of the current social studies scene commented, "Better the artifacts than the actualities of the present."

The National Council for the Social Studies is on record in support of the study of controversial issues and presents this Yearbook as evidence of its convictions. It is concerned that social studies teachers face up to controversy and that they assume special responsibilities to teach students *how* to think, not *what* to think. Every student must be assured the right to confront and study controversial issues without penalty. To accomplish this, the teacher guards the openness to discuss different points of view at all times and assumes the obligation to approach such issues with critical inquiry, not advocacy.

The *NCSS Statement on Academic Freedom* has this to say, "It is the prime responsibility of the schools to help students assume the responsibilities of democratic citizenship. To do this, education must impart the skills needed for intelligent study and orderly resolution of the problems inherent in a democratic society. Students need to study issues upon which there is disagreement and to practice analyzing problems, gathering and organizing facts, discriminating between facts and opinions, discussing differing viewpoints, and drawing tentative conclusions. It is the clear obligation of schools to promote full and free contemplation of controversial issues and to foster appreciation of the role of controversy as an instrument of progress in a democracy."

It is singularly appropriate in this age of controversy for the National Council for the Social Studies to present this Yearbook to its members. Anything less in a time of societal conflict would be irresponsible.

The National Council for the Social Studies is deeply indebted to Raymond H. Muessig for carrying the editorial responsibility for this Yearbook and to the contributors who have made the publication a reality. It is our belief that their presentation can only advance the democratic way of life by encouraging the free exchange and examination of ideas.

JEAN TILFORD, *President*
*National Council for the Social Studies*

# The Illustrations

The illustrations in this Yearbook focus on unique works of
sculpture in the Hirshhorn Museum and Sculpture Garden,
Washington, D. C., a new and unusual museum
of contemporary art under the administration of the Smithsonian
Institution. Their publication in this volume reflects
the conviction that there is a close and significant
relationship between the social studies and the arts.
The purpose of the Hirshhorn Museum and Sculpture Garden,
according to S. Dillon Ripley, Secretary of the
Smithsonian Institution, is "to remind us
all that life is more than usual, that the human mind in its
relentless diversity is capable of seeing life subjectively,
and being stirred by objects into new and positive
ways of thought. . . ." How appropriate, then, that these works
of art appear in a book on
Controversial Issues in the Social Studies: A Contemporary Perspective!

# Contents

xi

# PART ONE

*Some Theoretical and Practical Aspects of Dealing with Controversial Issues*

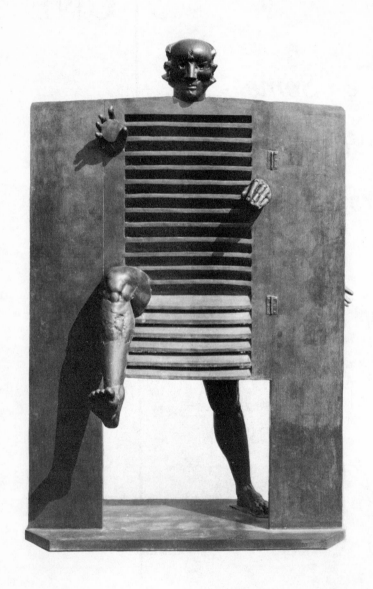

*"Humankind cannot be restrained
from the search for truth."*

# 1

# Some Thoughts
# on Controversial Issues

Raymond H. Muessig

## Introduction

ALTHOUGH this is the introductory chapter to the 1975 Yearbook of the
National Council for the Social Studies, it is not intended to represent a
consensus of thought among the diverse authors represented here. The
fine people who have generously contributed manuscripts to this publication agree on a number of points in general, but they represent contrasting
perspectives with respect to many specifics.

For example, one can infer logically from their participation in this
endeavor that they all believe that controversial issues cannot and should
not be ignored, but they are not unanimous in their feeling that the entire
focus of the social studies program should be on contemporary value
conflicts. They all assume that it requires a substantial amount of time
for an individual to acquire understandings, skills, appreciations, attitudes, and values that would help him or her to become a more critical,
reflective thinker, yet some of the writers are uncertain about whether a
K-12 approach is indicated, whether very young children ought to and
are able to grapple with personal-social concerns. There are professionals
represented in this project who fervently desire each student to take action
on individual and cultural problems, as contrasted with fellow educators
who calmly hope to teach a learner to examine his or her beliefs and to
decide for himself or herself whether he or she will implement his or her
commitments, and, if so, which ones. A few individuals involved in the
evolution of this Yearbook maintain that a teacher should be Black to

*RAYMOND H. MUESSIG is Professor of Social Studies Education,
Faculty of Humanities Education, College of Education, The Ohio State
University, Columbus, Ohio.*

lead a study of problems affecting that minority group, that a teacher ought to be female to guide an analysis of controversies related to women's rights, and the like. Most publication participants, however, hold that this would lead to inordinate restrictions in too many areas for innumerable informed, competent, fair, empathetic teachers, and these Yearbook associates would agree with the essence of Dick Gregory's conclusion that, "just being Negro doesn't qualify you to understand the race situation any more than being sick makes you an expert on medicine."[1]

This Yearbook contains built-in controversies, which should attract added attention. The Yearbook editor has attempted to protect, preserve, and respect the convictions and the integrity of independent authors, not to gloss over disputes. As a case in point, he has decided that Chapter 1 should be *his* offering and that he ought to be responsible solely for its contents. As did Abraham Lincoln, one of his favorite heroes, the author likes to listen to, to tell, and to adorn and invent stories to try to buttress and vivify certain points. He has simply labeled these homely illustrations as "Items" in this paper.

Chapter 1 attempts to treat the nature of controversial issues, the importance of dealing with controversial issues, some earlier efforts and publications concerned with the teaching of controversial issues, and some arguments against and for handling controversial issues.

## The Nature of Controversial Issues

"What is food to one man may be fierce poison to others," observed Lucretius (c. 95-55 B.C.). And so it is with what are called "controversial issues." Something easily, readily, or automatically accepted by one person or group may be highly debatable to others.

**Item:**

Otto N. Thuziast is a traveling salesman. He owns a Mercedes 220D (the "220" signifies the smallest four-door model available when he purchased it, and the "D" indicates a diesel engine). A badge on the automobile's grill indicates that Mr. Thuziast has already driven this vehicle over 100,000 kilometers. This is his second Mercedes, and he has been an active member of the Mercedes-Benz Club of America for five years. When he is not on the road, he attends the monthly meeting of the local M-B club chapter in the major city in which he resides. One such session, featuring a short film from the Mercedes factory, has just concluded. As the evening is still young, Otto and some other members decide to remain a bit longer just to share features they like especially about the car that wears the three-pointed star. The group is heterogeneous, including a now-retired Army nurse who bought a 230 while stationed in Germany, a college student who is restoring an older

190 SL, a classroom teacher wno balked at the initial price of his 220, but who expects it to "last longer than I will," a physician who was attracted by the classic lines of his 280 SE, and a mechanic employed by the local M-B dealer who was trained in Stuttgart. The following are random excerpts from their discussion:

> I'm convinced that the Mercedes diesel engine—with its overhead camshaft, five main bearings, and fuel injection that eliminates the conventional car's ignition system—is one of the best engines ever designed. It may not have a lot of "pep," but it almost runs forever; and it usually averages better than twenty-three miles-per-gallon.

> My "baby" is a product of the oldest motor car manufacturing firm in the world. Mercedes concentrates on steady engineering improvements instead of getting caught up in the latest design fads.

> Mercedes has had sturdy construction, safety door locks, recessed door handles and controls, a breakaway rearview mirror, fully independent suspension, an anti-sway bar, and four-wheel disc brakes that dissipate heat and thus resist fading. We've got two teenage drivers in our family, and I feel better about their driving our car than any other one I can think of.

> My wife and I like the dual heating controls on our 250. She can turn up the heat on her side, and I can turn it down on my side—sooo, we're both comfortable. Oh, and we really go for the fully adjustable, front reclining bucket seats, designed to orthopedic standards. Sometimes, we just pull into a rest stop, drop back the seats, and take a nap on a long trip.

> My M-B has a thirty-six foot turning circle. It can make a "U" turn in less space than most compacts. It has lots of passenger space on the inside, but it isn't a mile long on the outside.

> I can't get over how well a Mercedes holds its value. Mine has depreciated less than any other car I've ever owned.

Thus, we see that Otto and the others with whom he has interacted would all respond with an immediate, resolute, affirmative answer to the relatively simple quesion: "Should a person own a Mercedes-Benz automobile?" There is no controversy in this situation.

Now, let us turn to another individual and his associates for whom this same question has highly emotional properties.

Kom U. Nitty belongs to the Cougar's Club of Center City, Iowa, a civic-service-minded men's group which has a luncheon meeting weekly. Following the thumping of a huge oak gavel on a cross-section from a tree stump, the flag salute, a prayer, introductions of members and guests, fines for minor, humorous "offenses" to get quarters out of some of the Cougars for the treasury, a talk by the local fire chief, and a consideration of several potential fund-raising projects, there is time for Mr. Nitty and a few stalwarts to sit around and "jaw" about various things.

Kom just happens to mention a friend of his in Chicago who went to Germany, picked up a new "Mersa*deez*" diesel, toured parts of Europe, and had the car shipped back to the United States. Nitty's comment stimulated reactions such as these:

I've never even heard of a "Mersa*deez*," and I sure wouldn't want some off-breed car in my garage!

We otta keep American dollars at home! I don't see why people take vacations in foreign countries when there are so many things to see in this great country of ours. And, I sure don't like it when a fella buys a car that ain't American when we got people outta work in *D*etroit!

What happens if you take a long trip in one of them "Mersa*deez*" things, and it breaks down in the middle of nowhere? I hear a lotta guys who own foreign cars have trouble with parts and service!

We hadta fight them Krauts in two World Wars. Why should we do anathin' to help 'em, like buying stuff they make?

I'll betcha have trouble startin' one of them diesels in the middle of winter! You'd probly hafta get fuel at truck stops, so the wife and kids would hafta use the dirty Johns!

Whether we like it or not, controversy surrounds almost all of us— regardless of our age, sex, race, religion, political affiliation, place of residence, socio-economic status, amount of formal education, etc.

**Item:**

Younger children sometimes "play a game," albeit macabre, where queries similar to those below can provoke an altercation:

Would ya rather have a nail pounded inta your head or get stomped on by a elephant?

Would ya rather have a big, slimy snake bite ya or get hit by a car?

Would ya rather hafta eat garbage or mud?

Old people, on the other hand, might bring up disputable matters in this vein:

Should you contribute parts or all of your body to a medical center or be cremated?

Should there be an open- or closed-casket ceremony at a funeral home?

Should a married woman be buried with her engagement and wedding rings, or should the rings go to a loved one?

Although controversy usually is regarded as a situation involving two or more people who hold different points of view and who may possess different facts, one person can also construct his or her own dialogue.

**Item:**

M. I. Marriageable, a college student, faces a personal controversial issue if he queries, "Should I ask Sutcha Dahl to marry me?" Going for a long walk across the campus, he could silently or audibly [This might arouse certain suspicions regarding his mental health!] have this form of exchange between two of his "selves":

*First Self:* I really feel good when I'm with Sutcha.

*Second Self:* Yes, but would you feel the same way five, or ten, or twenty, or forty years from now?

*First Self:* I don't know, but Sutcha and I have a lot of laughs together, and we've only argued a few times.

*Second Self:* But you've dated only five months! It's usually great at first, but you don't really know much about each other and about disagreements that could come up in the future.

*First Self:* I'm twenty-one years old! I'm a man! I can make my own decisions and get married without my parents' consent!

*Second Self:* Easy does it, old man! You've got two quarters left before you complete your bachelor's degree in history. Your mom and dad are putting you through. Sutcha has four or five quarters left. If you and Sutcha get married soon, will your folks and hers continue to help each or both of you? Or, after you receive your B.A., will you have to get some sort of job so Sutcha can finish? What type of work are you prepared for? Could you support *two* people? Have you thought about graduate work in history, or something else—like law? Would Sutcha work to put you through more college? What if you and Sutcha get married and then have a baby before he or she is planned? What if you, or Sutcha, or the baby should require expensive medical care?

*First Self:* You know, you really ask a lot of irritating questions! Maybe I should talk with Sutcha about stuff like this. And my mom and dad too. They can be a drag, but they've lived longer than I have, and they have helped me a lot in many ways. I should get to know Mr. and Mrs. Dahl too. I've only been with them briefly on two occasions. After all, they might become my in-laws! I've got to think more about all of this, I guess. It's all so confusing!

An initially bland contact involving two people—even though they may not know each other—can move easily into a disagreement.

**Item:**

Oliver Lawes Verry, Professor Emeritus of Political Science at James Madison State University, was home alone, as usual on a Thursday evening, as his wife was with her weekly bridge group. At 7:50 he was summoned to the front door by the hideous sequence of chimes Mrs. Verry had ordered installed recently. Dr. Verry found himself both startled and amused when he was greeted by a woman about his age who looked like a Gilbert Stuart painting of George Washington—white hair, firm jaw, and all. As it was a cold winter night, the kindly professor asked the woman to come into the warm living room.

The stately woman introduced herself as Miss Apree Henshun; said that she and her sister—also a "Maiden Lady"—lived with their ninety-one-year-old mother in a house just a block over; announced proudly that she was selling bumper stickers to raise funds for the Society of America's Protection and Solidarity; and asked Professor Verry if he would purchase one. Verry examined the bumper sticker, which was red, white, and blue, had an American flag at one end and an eagle at the other, and carried this message: "Once Upon a Time We Had a Constitution."

A reasonable facsimile of the dialogue that took place follows:

> *Dr. Verry:* May I ask, please, what this bumper sticker statement means to you?
>
> *Miss Henshun:* That should be obvious! Our Society believes that the Founding Fathers, God bless them, knew what they were doing and drafted a noble Constitution with which no one should tamper! We support a *strict* interpretation of the original document as it was passed in 1776, without any further monkey business by communists, egghead liberals, hippies, and such trash!
>
> *Dr. Verry:* Well now, was it 1776 when the original Constitution became the law of the land or 1788?
>
> *Miss Henshun:* What?
>
> *Dr. Verry:* And, are you and all of the members of your Society saying that the Constitution should never have been amended?
>
> *Miss Henshun:* I should say so!
>
> *Dr. Verry:* Do you believe in the "Bill of Rights," Miss Henshun?
>
> *Miss Henshun:* Of course I do!
>
> *Dr. Verry:* Are you aware that the "Bill of Rights" consists of the first ten *Amendments* to the Constitution, proposed in 1789 but not put in force until 1791?
>
> *Miss Henshun:* Ahh . . . I, err . . .
>
> *Dr. Verry:* Do you vote and cherish that right?
>
> *Miss Henshun:* Certainly!
>
> *Dr. Verry:* It was the 19th *Amendment* to the Constitution in *1920* that gave women that right. You see, Miss Henshun, the Constitution is a *living* document. The scope and application of the framers' original words have had to change over the years as conditions have changed.
>
> *Miss Henshun:* I assume all of this means that you do not wish to purchase a bumper sticker.
>
> *Dr. Verry:* Your assumption is correct. I'm sorry that I cannot support your Society, but I believe that we still have a Constitution which must be further improved. Our initial Constitution was originated by *men* (*women* being excluded)—a few of whom were brilliant

and dedicated and many of whom were intelligent and sincere—
who, nevertheless, were fallible human beings, with personal and
sectional interests, who could not create a perfect, permanent
instrument. They were men of *property* who had merchants and
manufacturers among their friends and constituents, men from the
Deep South who wanted to continue the slave trade, New Eng-
landers who desired to secure as much sea-borne business as possible for Yankee shippers. . . . It is possible that the Constitution
did not represent the needs and wishes of a majority of the American people, even at that time.

*Miss Henshun:* But wasn't Prohibition an Amendment that turned out
to be a mistake that occurred because people meddled with the
Constitution?

*Dr. Verry:* The 18th Amendment of 1919 probably created more problems than it alleviated; however, we both recall, don't we, that it
was repealed by the 21st Amendment in 1933. Errors can be made
by altering the Constitution, but they can also be undone. That's
the beauty of a flexible document, Miss Henshun.

*Miss Henshun:* Well, thank you for your time. Good evening.

*Dr. Verry:* You are welcome, and a good evening to you too.

Having established something of a more general backdrop germane
to the nature of controversial issues, the author would like now to present three "Items" concerned specifically with classroom teaching situations. The first is a case which tries to demonstrate that a teacher can
inadvertently touch on a subject which is viewed as controversial by a
single individual who may be a "power figure" in a community. The
second illustrates a response by a "special interest" or "pressure" group
in a community. The third shows how a broader segment or all of a
community might be aroused.

### Item:

Mr. Pence L. Pusher was the Coordinator of Field Experiences for a small
liberal arts college rather remotely located in a Southwestern state. He
placed a student teacher in a neighboring community for the fall semester.
The student teacher was getting along beautifully until a boy in her third-
grade class asked innocently how, when, and where she was going to cele-
brate Christmas, which was less than two weeks away.

The young woman indicated that she was a Jew and that she would be
in another state for part of *Hanukkah*, not Christmas. This stimulated class
interest and various questions which the student teacher answered. She explained that *Hanukkah*, the Feast of Lights, consisted of eight successive
ceremonial days tied to the ancient Hebrew calendar; that each of the eight
nights was an occasion for gaiety; that there were often small gifts for
children each evening; that special foods (*latkes,* etc.) were served; that
songs such as *"Maoz Tzur"* were sung; that the nine-branched *Menorah*

consisted of the *shamosh,* the helping candle, which the family's father used to ignite successive candles each night; and that *Hanukkah* commemorates a triumph of courage and faith in the long struggle for religious freedom and a renewed dedication.

Although the student teacher's class was attentive and appreciative, Mr. Pusher received an angry phone call the next day from Mr. Watt A. Biggott, the Superintendent of Schools in the neighboring community, asking Pusher why he had a "foreigner" student teaching in *his* (Biggot's) district who had planted doubts in the minds of young, impressionable children about Christmas. The superintendent indicated strongly that there were enough "fundamentals" to be "covered" at the elementary level so that there was no time to get into unnecessary things that would only upset people.

Pusher expressed considerable surprise—though he attempted, as long as he could, to be calm, nondirective, and diplomatic—when Biggott told Pusher that candidates applying for teaching positions in Biggott's area were expected to affirm their Christian faith as one condition of their employment. Biggott hastened to assure Pusher, however, that teachers were free, of course, to attend the church of their choice (all Protestant). They were not *required* to teach Sunday school, though it was hoped that they would. The superintendent concluded that Pusher would have to select preservice "visitors" more carefully if they were to be allowed in the district.

**Item:**

Mr. Pedant Offen was a teacher in a fairly large senior high school. He was well-grounded in American history—in which he usually had a full teaching assignment—and experienced in traditional textbook-centered instruction.

One year Mr. Offen "got stuck" with a single elective section in government at various levels. He decided to begin with a brief look at municipal government. The students in his class were intelligent, energetic, and resourceful. They secured a list of items being discussed by their city council, one of which was the possible installation of parking meters along the main street of the central business district.

Since the matter appeared to motivate the group and to be of an innocuous nature, Offen relaxed and followed the path suggested by a few of the "natural leaders" in the section. As an after-school homework assignment, the student leaders recommended that the pros and cons of parking meters be investigated at a grassroots level. On their own, then, various learners talked with their friends, parents, other relatives, and neighbors; chatted with shoppers entering and leaving stores; met with a person associated with the Chamber of Commerce; contacted some store owners; interviewed two of the council members; and even held a phone conversation with the mayor.

As they accumulated facts and opinions, the creative class assembled a "PRO" bulletin board and a "CON" bulletin board. The group divided itself into "for" and "against" camps, held a lively debate, eventually came out in favor of the parking meters, and wrote a joint letter to the city council calling for affirmative action.

Shortly thereafter, Pedant found a man, Mr. Groop Conn Serned, waiting outside the door of his (Offen's) classroom after the last bell for the day had rung. Serned loudly demanded, and got, an immediate conference with Pedant, even though the teacher had hoped to grade some American history examinations before calling it a day. Serned announced that he was President of the Businessmen United for Growth (BUG), whose *prominent members* he represented. *His* views were *their* views.

Serned talked about the nature of his own business—and the operations of other members of his group—which demanded a high volume; said that parking meters would be a "damned nuisance" for customers and that the meters might further encourage patrons to head for a shopping center going up less than a mile away where there would be abundant *free* parking; made it clear that he and his fellow businessmen "got soaked plenty for taxes" and resented teachers—who were "paid public servants"—getting into things which should not concern them; expressed a desire to see Offen "canned"; and made it clear that he was going to see the principal and phone a friend of his on the school board.

Mr. Offen tried to get Mr. Serned to read the two bulletin boards and to show Groop that there *were* a number of arguments against the installation of parking meters listed on the "CON" display that included Serned's points. But Serned was not to be assuaged.

The following week, Pedant's principal, Mr. Seymour Pressures, asked Offen to submit a written report on "everything that had happened" in preparation for a conference. Pedant complied with the request and later met with Pressures after school in the principal's office. Seymour began by saying that he was "sorry that this mess must be brought up"; that Pedant had "done a solid job as an American history teacher without any previous complaints"; and that Offen had been a "loyal faculty member."

Pressures indicated that he had met over lunch with Mr. Serned, the Executive Committee of the Businessmen United for Growth, and a school board member; that he had defended Pedant as a "dependable, tenured teacher"; that he had admitted that "things can get out of hand occasionally in even the best-run classrooms"; and that he was sure that "Mr. Offen will watch it in the future and stick to the textbook." The principal felt that "it will all blow over in time." He asked Offen if the teacher had any comments or questions.

Pedant apologized for the trouble he had caused his principal, thanked Seymour for trying to smooth things over, expressed his willingness to be cautious, and asked for permission to be excused.

**Item:**

Nigh Eva Tay was a young, pretty, eager, well-meaning, first-year high school social studies teacher. She was born, raised, and educated in a state other than the one in which—after sending out many letters to school districts in various parts of the country, filling out application forms, securing recommendations, having set after set of confidential papers dispatched, and driving in her terribly tired, tiny Toyota for interviews—she was finally able to secure a position.

Miss Tay was a comprehensive social studies major in her university. In terms of quarter-hours, she completed 25 credits in sociology (which she enjoyed), 20 in geography (which was a convenient subject to schedule), 18 in political science (which was becoming too "behavioristic" for her tastes), 15 in history (which was merely a matter of memorization), 6 in anthropology (which was "pretty remote and weird at times"), and 6 in economics (which she abhorred). Her three 5-hour history courses were entitled "Medieval Europe," "England in the 18th Century," and "The History of Russia from 1801-1914."

The daily teaching assignment given to Nigh consisted of two periods of "World History," one section of "Principles (not *"Problems"*!) of Democracy," one session of "American History," a general study hall, and a course called "Mini-Courses in History" (an offering being tried out for the first time and consisting of topics selected by the individual teacher which would be studied for about two to four weeks each).

Miss Tay asked the Chairman of the Social Studies Department for suggestions regarding possible topics for the "Mini-Courses in History" and got this answer:

> Well . . . this addition to the program was the idea of two other social studies teachers—not mine. I had never heard of "mini-" anything before they brought it up. I don't know any more about what to do than you do, I'm afraid. Perhaps things such as "A History of Inventions" or, ahhh, "The Presidents of the United States" or "Important Treaties" or, errr, "Immigration" or, mmmm, "Industrialization" would be appropriate.

For no particular reason, Nigh decided to start with "The Presidents of the United States." Lacking a better idea for getting her "unit" underway, she dug up a list of all of the Presidents and wrote the name of each Chief Executive on a separate 3" x 5" card. In front of the class, she dropped the cards into a paper bag, shook the bag, walked from one student to the next, and told each learner to "pick a card." She asked her charges, please, not to argue or to complain about the person they had drawn, or to start trading cards, or that sort of thing. There were some grumbles as pupils found that they were saddled with William Henry Harrison, John Tyler, James K. Polk, Zachary Taylor, Millard Fillmore, Franklin Pierce, James Buchanan, and the like, and one student remarked that they would have to leave out some men—perhaps some of the most interesting ones—because there were more Presidents of the United States than there were class members; but the neophyte pedagogue asserted that they would just "move along with the project."

Miss Tay announced that there would be some supervised study time in class; that two or three sets of encyclopedias would be wheeled into the classroom; that a limited number of students would be given passes to work in the school library; that some preparation would be regarded as a homework assignment; and that every learner would give an oral report on his or her President to the entire group.

The first three oral reports were, in a word, *deadly!* Nigh thought that she might have to discontinue this approach—due to inattention and lack of involvement in discussion. However, the next "volunteer" to come to the front of the room was Dan D. Brane, who, unknown to Miss Tay, was the brightest student in the class. Here is what Dan said:

> My report is on Warren G. Harding, the 29th President of the United States, from 1921-1923.
>
> I started out just to get stuff about Harding from encyclopedias. I read *The World Book Encyclopedia* in class, like most of you have. Oh, and I used *Encyclopaedia Britannica* in the school library and an *Encyclopedia of American History,* edited by Morris, in our neighborhood library. But I couldn't get too turned on to this project.
>
> My uncle Frank—he's my dad's only and younger brother, and he puts siding on houses—is a kinda history "nut" and reads a lotta stuff, especially biographies. Anyway, my family and I were over at his house playing *Tripoley* with his family, and I mentioned that I had to give an oral report on President Harding. He got all excited and hauled out two books he made me take home. One was *The Memoirs of Herbert Hoover: 1920-1933,* and in it I read what Hoover remembered about his contacts with Harding. The other book was *The Shadow of Blooming Grove: Warren G. Harding in His Times* by Francis Russell. Russell's biography is really interesting. I read quite a bit of it, some of which I've included in this report.
>
> Warren Gamaliel—I'm not sure how you pronounce his middle name—Harding was born on November 2, 1865 near what is now Blooming Grove, Ohio. He died in San Francisco, California on August 2, 1923. He was the seventh President from Ohio.
>
> Harding went to school longer than Presidents like Andrew Johnson, but he was not well-educated like Woodrow Wilson and others. Harding attended Ohio Central College from 1879-1882 and studied law briefly. During his life, he read little good literature and didn't have much appreciation for other arts. He liked to play poker and golf and to trade jokes.
>
> Harding became the owner and editor of the *Marion Star,* which became a pretty successful newspaper. From 1900-1904, he was a State Senator. He was the Lieutenant Governor of Ohio from 1904-1906 and a U.S. Senator from Ohio from 1915-1921.
>
> While he was in the U.S. Senate, Harding voted for the Prohibition Amendment and said in a speech that the Prohibition laws should be enforced strictly, but this didn't seem to keep him from buying and drinking quite a bit of liquor himself. Senator Harding opposed the League of Nations, though President Harding later supported the World Court and Disarmament Conference.
>
> Harding's Presidential campaign was pushed and managed by Harry

M. Daugherty, an Ohio political boss, who probably contributed around $50,000 of his own money in the effort to get Harding elected.

At the Republican national convention in Chicago in 1920, Harding was finally nominated on the *tenth* ballot. The delegates were hot, tired, and anxious to go back home, so they settled on Harding—not one of the original top contenders—as a compromise candidate. Harding was a handsome, solidly built man who *looked* like a President to many people. He was a kindly, friendly man who liked to be liked and tried to avoid making enemies. He was popular with a lot of Senators. He was from an important state. He had an appealing speaking voice, though he was not a good debater. He seems to have found it hard to take a stand on issues and to make decisions—putting them off as long as possible. It was anticipated that he would follow the lead of Congress. As a newspaperman, he got along pretty well with the members of the press.

Harding had a low-powered, "front porch" campaign, like the approach used by McKinley. He promised a "return to normalcy" to a public that wanted to take it easy after World War I, and he was elected by a landslide vote.

Harding made some good Cabinet appointments with Herbert Hoover, Charles Evans Hughes, and the elder Henry Wallace, and he named William Howard Taft as Chief Justice of the U.S. Supreme Court. However, he rewarded personal and political friends with offices too. Some of these people were not intelligent or morally strong enough to handle their complex assignments and demanding responsibilities. Harding made Daugherty his Attorney General, a decision that was criticized immediately. He let Will H. Hays have the spot as Postmaster General. Making Albert B. Fall the Secretary of the Interior and Edwin Denby the Secretary of the Navy turned out to be a bad move.

I'm sorta getting ahead of myself, I guess, but I hafta put this in someplace. Harding was eventually betrayed by his friends—the same kind of thing that happened to President Ulysses Simpson Grant. Either shortly before or during a big speaking tour, Harding found out that news of corruption in his administration was coming to the surface. The President might even have had a hunch that he could be impeached in time.

Anyway, while traveling, Harding became ill and died on August 2, 1923. Some friends felt that "heartbreak" was the reason that he passed away, but doctors listed the cause as "cerebral hemorrhage." Harding's Vice-President, Calvin Coolidge, was sworn in as President on August 3rd in Plymouth, Vermont.

Early in 1924, Congressional committees started looking into rumors of graft and corruption during the Harding administration. There were scandals in the departments of Justice, Navy, and Interior and in the Veterans' Bureau and the Office of the Alien Property Custodian.

In the spring of 1921, Albert B. Fall, the Secretary of the Interior, had persuaded President Harding to sign an order that permitted

Edwin Denby, the Secretary of the Navy, to transfer to the Department of the Interior the administration of U.S. Navy oil reserves at Teapot Dome, Wyoming and Elk Hills, California. In 1922, Fall had secretly leased the Teapot Dome reserves to Harry F. Sinclair, an oil operator, and the Elk Hills fields to Edward L. Doheny, another petroleum man. In 1929, Fall was convicted of bribery, sentenced to one year in prison, and fined $100,000.

Colonel Charles R. Forbes, who had been Chief of the Veteran's Bureau and who had resigned in 1923, was indicted for fraud, conspiracy, and bribery. He was sentenced to two years in a federal penitentiary and fined $10,000 in 1925. The Alien Property Custodian, Colonel Thomas W. Miller, was sent to prison in 1927 on charges of conspiring to defraud the government. Harry M. Daugherty, the Attorney General, was investigated for failing to prosecute for graft in the Veterans' Bureau and for receiving payments from Prohibition violators. He was tried for conspiracy in 1927 but was acquitted. He resigned from the Cabinet in 1924 at the request of President Coolidge.

Ohhh, in the book by Mr. Russell, it says that Warren G. Harding fell in love with Carrie Fulton Phillips, a thirty-year-old, attractive woman, in 1905. Mr. and Mrs. Harding and Mr. and Mrs. Phillips were friends in Marion for a number of years and made some trips together. Russell reports that Warren's affair with Carrie lasted until 1920 and that the correspondence over the long period included a number of love letters, some of which were rather long ones from Harding. *The Shadow of Blooming Grove: Warren G. Harding in His Times* also mentions Nan Britton, a woman much younger than Mrs. Phillips, who wrote a book after Harding's death called *The President's Daughter,* in which Miss Britton claimed to have become Harding's mistress when she was twenty years old, to have received love letters and money from Harding, to have met with him in various cities, and to have had a daughter, Elizabeth Ann, by the President.

It is not possible to make a *final* judgment about the 29th President— or any person, I suppose. There were documents that were destroyed by his wife; and others that are available and that have not been studied carefully yet; that are still to be released; and that may be found in one place or another for years to come.

Harding, however, seems to be regarded as one of the "weak" Presidents. I don't think that even he thought he was sufficiently intelligent, decisive, courageous, and creative to handle that job. But I believe that he had considerable respect for the office of the President of the United States; that he wanted a lot to become a bigger and better man and to measure up to the high honor bestowed on him; and that he desired to accomplish things that would endear him to the people during his time and in the future. It appears that he was not a corrupt President but that he used bad judgment in trusting certain people who were dishonest. Grant's second term was probably marred more by corrupt appointees than was Harding's only term, and *maybe* President Nixon's second term, with the Watergate scandal and all, will make the administrations of Grant and Harding look like Sunday school picnics.

Gosh, this was longer than I thought it would be. You must be getting "antcy," so I'll get this report over.

In October, following Harding's death, the Harding Memorial Association was incorporated to raise funds for a permanent resting place for the dead President. A lot of money came pouring in from the children and adults of America, and an impressive tomb was finally built. The Harding home at 380 Mount Vernon Avenue in Marion was formally dedicated as a National Historic Landmark in the Sixties. The house has been restored and furnished so it looks just about the way it did when Mr. and Mrs. Harding lived there.

Do you have any questions or something you want to talk about?

As oral reports go in many social studies classes, it might be concluded that Dan D. Brane did a pretty good job. In countless school districts throughout the nation, a report such as this would not attract the slightest attention from the general public. Nigh Eva Tay could continue the procedure she devised, ask for the remainder of the reports, and go on to something else unscathed.

However, there are *some* communities (in this particular *imaginary* case, one *might* anticipate that Marion\* *could* be one of them) in America where a teacher, such as Miss Tay, *could* arouse the ire of many local citizens. *Perhaps* residents living in and/or around Mount Vernon, Virginia (George Washington), Quincy, Massachusetts (John and John Quincy Adams), Monticello, Virginia (Thomas Jefferson), Hermitage, Tennessee (Andrew Jackson), Springfield, Illinois (Abraham Lincoln), Greenville, Tennessee (Andrew Johnson), Galena, Illinois (Ulysses S. Grant), Oyster Bay, New York (Theodore Roosevelt), West Branch, Iowa (Herbert Hoover), Hyde Park, New York (Franklin D. Roosevelt), etc. in particular *might* be especially "touchy" about *their* Presidents. In general, there are Americans who hold that all of the Chief Executives should be "honored" and "glorified" and that nothing "unfavorable" or "disrespectful" should be brought out in schools about any of our Presidents.

Again, for the purpose of illustration, let us suppose that Dan D. Brane's oral report is delivered in a community where controversial issues may be handled and that Miss Tay (or the class) suddenly sees some possibilities inherent in what Dan has said. There are a number of questions that might

---

\* As a history "buff," the author of this Chapter has visited the homes and tombs of some of the Presidents. He has been to Marion once as a "tourist," but he does not know that community. At The Ohio State University in Columbus, he taught some good undergraduate students from Marion and a few fine master's candidates employed there as teachers. In the past, on several social occasions, through mutual friends, he has met and talked with one of President Harding's relatives, whom he liked as a person and respected as an intelligent man. Nothing in this *fictitious* example is intended to offend *anyone* who lives in Marion, who hallows the memory of the 29th President, or who is related to Warren G. Harding.

emerge out of this kind of beginning and that could be examined. The following are suggested:

Should all documents related to a person's activities while he or she is an elected, paid official be the property of the public or should they belong to him or her? If they are personal property, should they be sold or contributed? If contributed, should they be allowed as an income tax deduction?

Should every activity of a President and his or her family be regarded as public information, or should a President and his or her family have a private life, as human beings, which is not violated or subjected to national or even worldwide scrutiny?

Should any individual closely associated with a President—personally and/or politically—ever reveal information that was acquired through a confidential relationship?

Should any of the documents related to the personal and political life of a President be destroyed to protect his or her memory and/or the honor of our country or the reputations of other people associated with or related to him or her who are themselves innocent of any wrongdoing?

In an investigation which might lead to indictment or impeachment proceedings, should a President be legally required to release evidence (transcripts of meetings, memoranda, tapes, etc.) which might violate his or her concept of confidentiality, national security, etc.?

To what extent, if any, should a President be held responsible for the behavior of members of his or her Cabinet and others whom he or she has appointed? Should the President be expected to resign if persons he or she has named to some official position are found guilty of immoral and/or illegal acts, or should a President be compelled to answer in other ways for misconduct on the part of people whom he or she has selected?

Should the Party system be changed or eliminated?

Should there be political campaigns? If so, why? If not, why? If campaigns are continued, should the way in which they are conducted be changed? For example, should campaign funds be identical for competing candidates and be provided through public taxation or some other system?

Should all public servants be career employees who have trained for offices and been advanced according to their competencies? Should the "spoils system" be continued in any form?

Should men or women be investigated thoroughly, required to furnish complete financial statements, etc. before they are permitted to run for office, before they are appointed to some position at the pleasure of someone in office, before they are sworn in, after they have assumed some responsible role in government, etc.?

Should Americans draw some distinction between the *office* of the President of the United States and the *person* who occupies that office at a given time? That is, should they always respect the Presidency whether they esteem the man or woman who is the President? Should the people of this nation hold to higher ethical, moral, and legal standards for the President than for any other person in the land? Should a President who is guilty of some form of wrongdoing be punished *more* or *less* than the "average citizen"?

Should it be expected that the various roles customarily assigned to the Presidency (including, for example, ceremonial functions) be performed by a single individual, or should there be a group of people serving as President*s*, each of whom is uniquely qualified for a particular duty?

Should the President be limited to one six-year term (as Warren G. Harding and others have proposed)—or some arrangement other than the one we now have (a four-year term with the possibility of a second four-year term)—to reduce campaign expenditures, give the Chief Executive more time to try to implement his or her programs, eliminate the advantages an incumbent eligible for a second term has with respect to political patronage, etc.? Or, should we have an executive or group of leaders, serving at the pleasure of a legislature, who can be replaced at any time? Etc.

## The Importance of Dealing with Controversial Issues

A generous number of quotations have been assembled for this portion of the chapter with a clear purpose in mind.

**Item:**

The best automotive mechanic is the one who *understands* thoroughly *why* and *how* things work in a car *before* he reaches for a wrench or a screwdriver. He has *grasped the principles* of the internal combustion engine *prior to* doing a tune-up job. He *comprehends the concept* of polarity *previous to* clipping red-and-black jumper-cables between two batteries, seeing the necessity for connecting positive to positive and negative to negative.

**Item:**

I have heard it said that pharmacists are "over-trained these days when *all* they do is to put little pills into bottles." However, there are instances— admittedly infrequent, but nonetheless critical—when *well-grounded* druggists, aware of the nature of drugs, their potential side effects, etc., have prevented serious consequences for their customers.

Some druggists know more about particular pharmaceuticals than busy general practitioners who have prescribed them.

A patient may be going to more than one physician. A competent, conscientious pharmacist maintains a complete record of *all* the medicines a patron has taken, is using, and may be consuming and may have a fairly good overall picture of the illnesses for which the customer has been and is being treated. The druggist possessing *beforehand* awareness of "drug interaction" problems (the adverse reaction of one medication on another) may spot potential dangers in combined drugs. A client, for instance, may be taking a pill ordered by a psychiatrist to combat severe depression. The same consumer may be going to another doctor who has prescribed Reserpine (widely used as an effective anti-hypertension agent), which, if used excessively, can increase depression. Dilantin (an anti-convulsant) has an adverse effect in diabetic patients, as it reduces insulin secretion from the pancreas. Tetracyclines (antibiotics) are less effective if taken with milk or in conjunction with iron preparations for anemia. Butazolidin Alka (for anti-inflammatory treatment) can cause gastro-intestinal disturbances unless taken with milk or on a full stomach.

**Item:**

Gott Grate Paine suffered for several years from a severe pain in his lower back. He sought out an orthopedic surgeon who conducted an examination, had X-rays taken, ran a series of tests, and then asked Mr. Paine, "Do you think you need surgery?"

Gott returned the doctor's question with a question: "If *you* don't know, how do you expect *me* to know?"

The physician apparently lacked a sufficient *theoretical grasp* of the situation to engage in *practical action* which was supported well.

Unless elementary and secondary teachers and college and university professors are *immersed deeply* in reflective theory and until such time as they *really understand* why and how they should deal with controversial issues, we could face some rough weather ahead and make some serious mistakes. This Yearbook provides many, though by no means all, of the insights necessary for *mindful* instruction.

Through the use of "quotable quotes" and related comments, Chapter 1 hopes to demonstrate that dealing with controversial issues is far more important than many people in social studies education have yet to realize. Without intending to overstate the case, a crucial facet of the future of children and youth, of education, of our own society, and of the world is at stake here. One cannot predict how much time is left to develop reflective persons who can attempt to improve the human condition and to save mankind, but it is apparent that we must be engaged seriously *now* in this crusade.

Euripides (c. 484-406 B.C.) was one of the early thinkers to perceive a prominent essence of the spirit of reflection where a significant dispute is involved. "In a case of dissension," he observed, "never dare to judge until you have heard the other side." With areas of disagreement, there is always at least one other side, and there may be numerous dimensions. The teacher who endeavors to bring out as many view-points as possible in a fair manner is less likely to "get into trouble" than the instructor who permits a biased discussion to take place. He or she may even have to serve as a "devil's advocate" and to introduce facts and opinions that have escaped notice, to take the position of those with whom he or she may disagree personally so alternatives are added to the mix, to invite resource persons with divergent leanings, and to use a host of contradictory instructional materials. If a problem is worth investigating, it is worth investigating well.

Before one "buys" reflection and decides that dealing with contro-versial issues is important enough to assume the risk, he or she has to con-sider the extent to which he agrees with Socrates (c. 470-399 B.C.) that "The unexamined life is not worth living" and with Cicero (106-43 B.C.) that "To think is to live." There is a high price attached to the belief that reflection *is* life, a pervasive process wedded to daily exist-ence—not just a device that is summoned on occasion.

"By identifying the new learning with heresy, you make orthodoxy synonymous with ignorance," wrote Desiderius Erasmus (c. 1465-1536). As a person—contrary to what he was taught during his early Sunday-school years—the writer has serious doubts about whether the *meek* should inherit the earth. As an educator, he is frightened that the *stupid* have already taken over or that they soon will! Meek people, by definition, are mild, soft, spiritless, docile, resigned, long-suffering, passive, yielding, submissive, manageable, etc. Stupid persons are dense, dull, imperceptive, empty-headed, unreasoning, simple-witted, tedious, inane, shallow, wooden, etc. Those who are meek are fearful of fresh, different, challenging ideas, while stupid individuals are unable to deal with original proposals. The meek are vulnerable to authoritarianism and even totalitarianism; the stupid lack the vision and motivation neces-sary to construct a better tomorrow. A reflective citizenry could be neither meek nor stupid. It would consist of people who would be open-minded, ideational, speculative, contemplative, analytic, deliberative, considerate, sensible, sensitive, autonomous, variegated, courageous, alive, involved, responsible, inventive, enterprising, productive, alert, clear-eyed, farsighted, etc. Reflective persons would embrace "new learning" and shun "orthodoxy." They would heartily agree with Spinoza (1632-1677) that "True virtue is life under the direction of reason."

Individuals who have studied and accepted reflective philosophy (pragmatism, instrumentalism, experimentalism, etc.) would not be surprised or disturbed by Samuel Butler's (1612-1680) assertion that "The course of true anything never does run smooth." They expect that there will always be difficulties of one kind or another. A given concern may be put to rest only to be replaced by one or more new perplexities. Some problems may continue over long periods of time or may seem beyond resolution. However, reflective people choose to face and to deal with quandaries, not to "cop out" or "drop out."

Philip Dormer Stanhope, Fourth Earl of Chesterfield (1694-1773), aphorized, "Our prejudices are our mistresses; reason is at best our wife, very often needed, but seldom minded." Reflective educators do not assume that man is innately rational, yet they maintain that man can be taught to become increasingly thoughtful regarding his commitments and actions. They agree with David Hume (1711-1776) that "A wise man proportions his belief to the evidence" and feel that well-considered instruction can produce more wise men. They support Thomas Jefferson's (1743-1826) position that "Error of opinion may be tolerated where reason is left free to combat it" and are dedicated to preserving and nurturing freedom of the mind. They recognize, as Thomas Carlyle (1795-1881) did, that "Every new opinion, at its starting, is precisely in a minority of one" and defend minority expressions and the rights of minorities to become majorities through rational, open, orderly, evolutionary processes. Henri Frédéric Amiel (1821-1881) wanted "Truth above all, even when it upsets and overwhelms us!" Reflective educators share in Amiel's desire. They attach great importance to what Ralph Waldo Emerson (1803-1882) wrote: "Nothing is at last sacred but the integrity of your own mind."

Another insight into reflection which underlines the importance of dealing with controversial issues in the social studies classroom has been provided by Friedrich Wilhelm Nietzsche (1844-1900): "A very popular error—having the courage of one's convictions: rather it is a matter of having the courage for an attack upon one's convictions." Every belief is tentative. It must be considered throughout one's lifetime. It may be confirmed, and thus strengthened, again and again. It could be moved up or down in one's hierarchical value structure in the light of current circumstances. It may be abandoned if it does not produce satisfactory waves of consequences. The reflective teacher is not an iconoclast, bent on destroying cherished values just because he or she enjoys breaking images. But he or she cannot accept, on an *a priori* basis, any commitment—even such a generally venerated "tenet of democracy" as "the dignity and worth of the individual human personality." "Democracy" and "human dignity and worth" are likely to be esteemed by many Americans, but they cannot be embraced before they have been warranted. According to Oscar Wilde (1854-1900), "Man is a reasonable animal who always loses his temper when he is called upon to act in accordance with the dictates of reason." Wilde's perspective would have to be altered by a reflective educator. Man *can* become a more reasonable animal; during the most trying situations he needs even more to act in accordance with the dictates of reason.

Oliver Wendell Holmes, Jr. (1841-1935) said, "Every year, if not every day, we have to wager our salvation upon some prophecy based upon imperfect knowledge." One rarely has the time or energy to muster all of the data and proposals necessary to warrant fully a belief regarding a controversial issue. Yet he must give as thorough a consideration as possible to the stand he will take and hope for the best. Also, "A man must not swallow more beliefs than he can digest," a warning issued by Havelock Ellis (1859-1939). It is better for one to hold a smaller number of values which he has contemplated than an army of commitments which he has not pondered.

F. Scott Fitzgerald (1896-1940) once opined that "The cleverly expressed opposite of any generally accepted idea is worth a fortune to somebody." The reflective person knows that he cannot possess the whole "truth" and nothing but the "truth." He courts ideas that differ from his own and the company of those who disagree with him, for that is a way of correcting errors in his thinking and a means of facilitating his growth. He concurs with Alfred North Whitehead (1861-1947) that "A clash of doctrines is not a disaster—it is an opportunity." And, he is likely to be in accord with George Santayana's (1863-1952) perception that "Life is not a spectacle or a feast; it is a predicament."

Many American children and youth are struggling to tell us in various ways that our schools can no longer afford to ignore critical problems that are dividing individuals, families, groups, organizations, communities, states, regions, our nation, and other countries. We cannot attempt to wait until our young men and women reach their eighteenth birthdays before they are allowed or welcomed to engage in the study and analysis of the vital concerns that touch their lives.

### Some Earlier Efforts and Publications Concerned with the Teaching of Controversial Issues

Madison Avenue advertising agencies have enjoyed considerable success in their campaigns designed to persuade Americans that "new" is "better," that the "latest" good or service can be equated with an "improvement." However, experience has taught more than one consumer that "new" processed foods may not have the flavor or contain the natural nutrition that "old" staples did; that "new" appliances and automobiles may not perform as well initially or last as long as did "old" hardware; that "new" selling, accounting, billing, and adjustment systems—involving computers and all—are not as personal and satisfying as "old" ways of fulfilling the special needs of a customer.

It is not certain who first coined the expression "The *New* Social Studies," but he or she probably confused or misled more people than he or she enlightened or guided in a helpful manner. A scholar with a broad background in the history, philosophy, psychology, and sociology of education is likely to conclude that there are few completely "new" ideas with respect to theories of instruction. Those who have promoted and succumbed to one fad after another in social studies education since Sputnik (launched by the U.S.S.R. in 1957) have included the uninformed, the suggestible, the insecure, the opportunistic, the modish, and the lazy. Fine old wine has been poured hastily into garish new bottles; standard vocabulary used carefully by learned professional educators has been replaced hurriedly by "buzz words" so vague that even given latecomers into the field who have coined them are hard-pressed to provide operational definitions; and some of the "young (and a few older) Turks" leading the "Revolution" in the social studies have had such a deficient background in the foundations of education that they have rediscovered fire and reinvented the wheel.

Reasoning about personal-social concerns can hardly be viewed as a "recent trend," for it can be traced back to Protagoras and Socrates; on through Abélard, Montaigne, Sir Francis Bacon, Thomas Jefferson, John Stuart Mill, and Thomas Henry Huxley; to Charles S. Pierce, William James, John Dewey, Max Otto, and Boyd H. Bode; thence to H. Gordon Hullfish and Alan F. Griffin; and on to Robert E. Jewett, Lawrence E. Metcalf, Donald W. Oliver, and many others.

John Dewey's *How We Think,* which first appeared in 1910 and was revised in 1933 as *How We Think: A Restatement of the Relation of Reflective Thinking to the Educative Process,* must be cited as one of the most significant pioneer works leading to the development of this Yearbook.

*Modern Educational Theories,* published in 1927, was Boyd H. Bode's very readable endeavor to clarify and amplify Dewey's philosophy for those who desired to make education more relevant.

In the 1920s and 1930s, Harold Rugg was one of the well-known reformers in the field of social studies education. The series of school textbooks which he developed correlated information from history and the social sciences and directed its attention to contemporary controversial issues. It unleashed a storm of protests from conservative laymen on the one hand, because it revealed problems and flaws in "the American way of life." It brought criticism from liberal educators on the other hand, for it tried to spur youth into bringing about certain kinds of preordained reforms and treated some complex matters in a superficial way.

In 1936, *Education* published an article entitled "Teaching Controversial Issues in the Classroom" by R. W. Hatch. Even the famous educational psychologist, Edward L. Thorndike, got into the act and delivered the 1937 Inglis Lecture, published by the Harvard University Press as *The Teaching of Controversial Subjects.* "Teachers and Controversial Questions" by Alex Meiklejohn appeared in the June, 1938 issue of *Harper's.* In November of that same year, *The American Journal of Sociology* printed "The Problem of Teaching Social Problems" by Richard C. Fuller. Charles E. Guilford discussed "Presenting Controversial Issues" in the May, 1941 copy of *The Social Studies.*

Although many doctoral dissertations end up on university library shelves suffering from dry rot and are ultimately decorated with cobwebs and green mold, this was not to be the fate of one Ph.D. thesis, *A Philosophical Approach to the Subject-Matter Preparation of Teachers of History,* completed by Alan F. Griffin at The Ohio State University in 1942. Griffin had an exceptional and early grasp of reflective social studies instruction. His dissertation is still read widely today, and his teaching has had considerable influence on those who have elected to deal with human beings' problems. In 1942 as well, the Thirteenth Yearbook of the National Council for the Social Studies, edited by Howard R. Anderson, concentrated on *Teaching Critical Thinking in the Social Studies,* and John H. Haefner penned "The Historical Approach to Controversial Issues" for October's *Social Education.*

Ronald B. Edgerton asked, "Do Pupils Want Teaching of Controversial Issues?" in *The Clearing House* for February of 1944. Richard E. Gross asserted that "Teaching Controversial Issues Can Be Fun" in the October, 1948 issue of *Social Education.* And, W. C. Throw treated "Teaching of Social Issues" for *Phi Delta Kappan,* published in January, 1949.

The NCSS reaffirmed its commitment to *The Teaching of Contemporary Affairs* in 1951 with the Twenty-First Yearbook, which John C. Payne edited. The Committee on Academic Freedom of the National Council for the Social Studies took a stand on "The Treatment of Controversial Issues in the Schools" that same year in the May issue of *Social Education.* One of the most important, concise, practical, and enduring publications offered by the NCSS has been "How To Handle Controversial Issues," authored by Richard E. Gross as Number 14 in the *How To Do It Series,* which was introduced in 1952 and then revised in 1961 and 1964. One should also mention *What Policies Should Guide the Handling of Controversial Issues?,* a 1954 booklet produced by the Committee on Tenure and Academic Freedom of the National Education Association.

Social studies methods texts are legionary, of course. With respect to this Yearbook, however, the 1955 issuance of *Teaching High School*

*Social Studies* by Maurice P. Hunt and Lawrence E. Metcalf must be acknowledged as something of a hallmark. This penetrating work was
well-received by many social studies educators and influenced the
thoughts and actions of a number of preservice and inservice teachers.
(It is available in a 1968 second edition, *Teaching High School Social
Studies: Problems in Reflective Thinking and Social Understanding.*)

In 1961, the National Education Association released *Controversial
Issues in the Classroom* and Dodd, Mead and Company printed *Reflective Thinking: The Method of Education* by H. Gordon Hullfish and
Philip G. Smith. Although *Reflective Thinking: The Method of Education* is not a "social studies" book, *per se,* and may seem a trifle "dated"
to the fashionable, it is one of the most lucid treatises when it comes to
wedding experimentalism and pedagogy. The neophyte who wishes to
apprehend and apply reflection should find this source beneficial.

Again, in the methods book genre, *Teaching Public Issues in the
High School* (1966) by Donald W. Oliver and James P. Shaver comes
to mind.

It is fitting to conclude this section on some earlier efforts and publications concerned with the teaching of controversial issues with three
offerings available from the National Council for the Social Studies.
There are insights to be gained from *Effective Thinking in the Social
Studies,* the 37th Yearbook, edited by Jean Fair and Fannie R. Shaftel
and published in 1967, from *Values Education: Rationale, Strategies, and
Procedures,* the 41st Yearbook (1971), which Lawrence E. Metcalf
edited, and from *Problem-Centered Social Studies Instruction: Approaches to Reflective Teaching,* Curriculum Series Number 14, 1971,
with Richard E. Gross and Raymond H. Muessig functioning as editors.

## Some Arguments Against and For Handling Controversial Issues

"Should controversial issues be handled?" is, itself, a controversial
issue with many sub-issues—a few of which will be treated cursorily,
with some representative cons and pros, due to the length limitations
imposed on this chapter.

### Should the Social Studies Teacher Allow Pupils To Examine
### Traditional, Widely-Held Community Values?

SOME NEGATIVE ARGUMENTS. It has been said that the man who
pays the piper calls the tune. Many taxpayers view teachers as parental
surrogates and expect local customs, opinions, and beliefs to be trans-
mitted faithfully and reinforced complacently. These are especially
confusing, tense, troubled times for a host of Americans, and there
seems to be an increasing hunger for stability, tranquility, and the

reassurance of "eternal verities" associated with an idealized reminiscence of "the good old days," "the way things were." There may be more and more citizens who will seek relaxing activities and turn their backs on the nagging, disconcerting items that are so much a part of the daily news. There is an "oversupply" of social studies teachers, which may mean that the bland conformist will be hired in preference to the individual who announces an intention to face up to problems with students and/or that a teacher new to a district who has been concentrating on current dilemmas will be denied tenure and replaced by a Pollyanna who will not rock the boat. The public's support of schools all over the nation has waned in recent years, which could be due in part to constituents' feelings that teachers have failed to do what is expected of them with respect to underscoring and exemplifying provincial folkways and mores.

One may form the impression that there is less interest in general education as an overall goal and in teaching learners to think as a specific aim. Gone are the golden days of Project Social Studies, and the meager funds that are available for program development are being diverted into career, vocational, and technical education. In short, there is a reduced concern regarding preparing well-rounded, incisive human beings and an increased absorption with training youth for jobs.

The "accountability" movement—with its "behavioral objectives" or "performance criteria"—may force teachers to forsake high-level understandings, difficult to evaluate, and to turn to mundane skills, easy to measure.

There is also the possibility that more of the social studies curriculum will be mandated along subject-centered lines with overt and covert forms of indoctrination required by school boards, city councils, and state legislatures mirroring local temperaments, and that teachers will become less active, autonomous professionals and more passive, subservient laborers.

SOME POSITIVE ARGUMENTS. Alexander Pope observed that "The most positive men are the most credulous." Although increased numbers of Americans reside in and around cities, too many of them might still be called "mentally rustic." They hold stubbornly to oft-repeated, parochial, archaic, "common sense" "Truths" based upon insufficient, unsophisticated, antiquated evidence or no tested data whatsoever. The answer to this condition is not its antithesis, nihilism, a complete disbelief in anything: for every individual needs some sense of purpose in order to go on. In *The Challenge of the Passing Years: My Encounter with Time,* R. M. MacIver presents a balanced, mature point of view:

Man lives by his values. Without them no society could endure. But values, too, are subject to the test of time. They must meet the challenge of changing conditions and changing needs. Societies that cannot adjust their values to the challenge lose out in the race and are eroded away. . . .[2]

Boyd H. Bode expresses a similar idea in *Modern Educational Theories:*

A person cannot live intelligently and effectively without convictions of some sort. But neither can he live intelligently and contribute to the betterment of things if he is incapable of changing his convictions. . . .[3]

In *Education and Human Relations,* Ashley Montagu adds that

. . . [It] is a good practice, from time to time, to hang a question mark on the beliefs we take most for granted, for those beliefs may in fact be wholly or partly erroneous. Many of our most entrenched beliefs, when subjected to such questioning, are found to be so encrusted with age and fortified by rationalization that they have become impervious to any but the most critical examination. . . .[4]

W. Somerset Maugham contributes this thought in *The Summing Up:* ". . . Experience has shown that the prevalence of a belief, no matter for how long it has been held, is no guarantee of its truth. . . ."[5]

And, in *The Democratic Way of Life,* T. V. Smith and Eduard C. Lindeman hold that ". . . To tell a man what to think is in every long run the working equivalent of telling him not to think at all. . . ."[6]

When the author of this Chapter read Walter Lippmann's *The Public Philosophy*[7] in 1955, he was struck by an idea that he has considered and reconsidered on numerous occasions. Lippmann disagrees with Jeremy Bentham's position that *the people* is simply a collection of living persons; that the interests of the community are nothing more than the expressed needs of its members at a point in time; and that a legislator ought to keep in mind only those things which would increase the happiness and security of his immediate constituents. For Lippmann, the people is a much broader concept, for it is composed of the generations of human beings who are no longer present, those who are currently alive, and those who are yet to be born.

The author is solely responsible for the interpretation (or misinterpretation) of what he gleaned from Lippmann's book and for the educational application he is now going to make. An important subissue, it seems, is "What public, if any, should the social studies teacher attempt to serve?" Should the public be

the articulate parents of Shees A. Bratte, who are in constant contact with the teacher, making frequent demands, voicing endless complaints, issuing threats of one kind or another? What about the separated mother and father of Nee Glecktedd, who never interact with the teacher?

fifty per cent plus one of the parents of students in each class? Of pupils in all of the teacher's classes? Of all the learners in a single school? Of all children and youth in a district? A state? The nation? The world?

all registered voters, including some parents, at one level or more? The bills they support? The representatives they elect?

past, present, and future participants of all ages in isolated societies or the total family of man?

the "wisest" and the "best" thinkers and humanitarians in government? Philosophy? The arts? Science? History and the social sciences? Education in general? Social studies education in particular? Other areas? A combination of fields?

whatever the individual social studies teacher decides it ought to be?

**Item:**

At various times over the years, the author of this Chapter has been required by policies to participate in decisions regarding the screening, admission, and retention of undergraduates seeking places in preservice teacher education programs and, in rare instances, the continuation of student teachers having serious difficulties. He believes in quality instruction in the abstract, but he does not like to "play God" in concrete cases. It is hard, and usually upsetting, to have to inform a person that he or she probably should not try to become a teacher or that he or she does not seem to have the potentialities for continued professional growth. The better one knows an individual—his or her background, motivations, sacrifices, disappointments, efforts, strengths, commitments, etc.—the more painful it is to say "No" to him or her. All of this is so subjective anyway! Yet, one elementary teacher—guiding the all-day learning activities of 25-35 pupils for 40-45 years in the self-contained classroom—could come in contact with 1,000-1,575 children, and a secondary teacher—working with 150-200 students a day for a similar period—might be with 6,000-9,000 youth! The greater responsibility of the university educator of teachers, it appears, should be to all of those learners rather than to the given preservice candidate.

If the preceding item provides the basis for an acceptable analogy, the social studies teacher may have to take a broad view of the public which encompasses the most people over the longest possible sweep of time. Thus, even though a few, many, or most of his or her surrounding and current constituents are opposed to teaching children and youth to reflect on controversial issues, the social studies instructor might operate on the basis of what is necessary to meet greater mankind's persistent past, present, and anticipated future need to think about quandaries, their hoped for resolution, and the process of intellectualizing itself. In time, with enough steadfast social studies teachers, a more comprehensive concept of the public might be considered by existing people to the point where they would support value clarification philosophically and financially.

## Should the Social Studies Teacher State His or Her Beliefs Associated with a Controversial Issue?

SOME NEGATIVE ARGUMENTS. There are those who feel that dealing with controversial issues is a *privilege,* given *conditionally* to the *responsible* social studies teacher, which can be withdrawn if abused. The social studies teacher could take advantage of his or her frequent access to a captive audience and might reward acceptance or punish rejection of his or her beliefs on a particular concern. Therefore, the instructor should be absolutely neutral, serve only as the moderator for an objective discussion, and express no personal opinions whatsoever. He or she would be permitted to introduce various facts and contrasting views of different individuals and groups, but his or her own judgments on data and perspectives would be withheld. As a *private citizen,* the teacher might act on his or her own convictions; but as a *professional,* he or she must be noncommittal.

SOME POSITIVE ARGUMENTS. With the possible exception of a person who has played a great deal of poker, it is unlikely that an individual can mask his or her emotions entirely about things of importance to him or her. Through verbal cues and gestures, he or she reveals leanings in one direction or another. The teacher who tries to appear dispassionate may impress his or her class ultimately as being insincere or as being a robot which does not care about crucial conflicts, their value components, and their possible amelioration. It is better for the teacher to be himself or herself, a real, live, feeling, fallible, involved human being; to seek warranted beliefs with his or her learners; to state unequivocally his or her present commitments; to encourage learners to question his or her assertions just as they do all others; and to change his or her posture when it does not stand the test of open scrutiny.

## Should the Social Studies Teacher Risk Increasing the Frustrations of Children and Youth by Asking Learners To Think about Controversial Issues?

SOME NEGATIVE ARGUMENTS. Many people feel that the unexamined life is happier and smoother; that "ignorance is bliss"; and that "what you don't know won't hurt you." The pupil who looks carefully at himself or herself may not like all of what he or she sees and could become confused, vacillating, anxious, insecure, depressed to an increased degree. By reflecting on controversial issues, he or she might become aware of personal-social concerns that did not bother him or her before and of dilemmas, dichotomies, inconsistencies, frailties, hypocrisies, and corruptions which had previously escaped his or her notice. He or she could end up trading answers for questions, sureties for doubts, conclusions for hypotheses to the point where he or she might lose fixed values that have formerly guided his or her decisions and relationships with others; question the statements and actions of persons in positions of authority; and even become cynical, anomic, alienated, or rebellious.

SOME POSITIVE ARGUMENTS. Although a rebuttal might have been developed by drawing upon a number of fields, this treatment will be restricted to literary, psychological, and educational viewpoints.

*A literary perspective.* The central character, Yakov Bok, in Bernard Malamud's novel *The Fixer* asks, ". . . [What] choice has a man who doesn't know what his choices are? . . ." [8]

In *The End of the Road,* a novel by John Barth, we read:

. . . [One] of the hardest and most essential things is to be aware of all the possible alternatives to your position.

\* \* \*

. . . Choosing is existence: to the extent that you don't choose, you don't exist. . . .

\* \* \*

. . . [If] we were ever going to end our trouble we'd have to be extra careful not to make up any versions of things that would keep us from facing the facts squarely. If anything, we had to do all we could to throw ourselves as hard as possible against the facts, and as often as possible, no matter how much it hurt. . . .[9]

*In the Country of the Young* John W. Aldridge, an essayist, stresses the point that ". . . [Life] is something more than a bubble of contentment drifting between the security of the nursery and the perfection of the grave." [10]

*A psychological perspective.* Albert Ellis and Robert A. Harper both hold Ph.D. degrees and are psychotherapists and marriage counselors. This quotation is from their book *A Guide to Rational Living:*

. . . We would contend . . . that truly rational thinking almost inevitably leads to pleasant emotions of varying degrees of intensity. And, perhaps even more importantly, we particularly hold that once human reason is properly maximized and utilized to rid people of their disorganizing and disruptive feelings—that is, of their severe emotional blockings caused by many dreadful kinds of anxiety and anger—only *then* can highly pleasurable and productive feelings consistently exist. We say, in other words, the more reason, the more emotion—of a fortunate and joy-evoking kind.[11]

In *Gestalt Therapy Verbatim,* compiled and edited by John O. Stevens, Frederick S. Perls has this to say:

. . . You will probably be amazed that I am using the word frustration so positively. Without frustration there is no need, no reason to mobilize your resources, to discover that you might be able to do something on your own. . . .[12]

The best seller *I'm OK—You're OK: A Practical Guide to Transactional Analysis* by Thomas A. Harris contains these pertinent words:

. . . [Transactional Analysis] is realistic in that it confronts the patient with the fact that he is responsible for what happens in the future no matter what has happened in the past. Moreover, it is enabling persons to change, to establish self-control and self-direction, and to discover the reality of a freedom of choice.

* * *

. . . Teen-agers are confronted with big and little decisions. Yet, often they seem to have to wait for circumstances to make their decisions for them, because they are not really free to decide for themselves. Their brain is nearing its prime development. Their body is mature. But legally and economically they are dependent, and their attempts at emancipated action are frequently undercut by the realization that they can't really make their own decisions anyway, so what's the use of making good decisions. They feel they may as well drift along through adolescence and wait for the light to turn green. The Adult does not develop under these circumstances. Suddenly when they are legally emancipated they feel adrift, they don't know what they want to do, and many of them pass time hoping something will happen, someone will come along, somehow something will turn them on. Yet, at this point, one-fourth of their life has passed.[13]

*An educational perspective.* Alan F. Griffin concentrated on "Community Pressures and Education" in Chapter 8 of *Educational Freedom in an Age of Anxiety,* the Twelfth Yearbook of the John Dewey Society, edited by H. Gordon Hullfish. This passage is from Griffin's chapter:

The person who wants a child to think must stimulate doubt, must challenge unexamined ideas, must generate some degree of concerned perplexity. His intent, of course, is to help the child work his way back to security again, by a process which both extends the range of his knowledge and increases his willingness to *rely* upon his own thinking as a means of resolving doubts when they arise in the future. . . .[14]

This eloquent paragraph from *Reflective Thinking: The Method of Education* by H. Gordon Hullfish and Philip G. Smith provides a fitting conclusion to the line of argument the writer has been pursuing:

The fact that it is possible for an individual to reconstruct his standards disturbs those persons who fear that this act may have as its consequence the abandonment of certain codes or taboos which have long been established and respected in the culture. Such fears are well grounded. The fact cannot be denied that thinking is, in this sense, dangerous. Education always involves a degree of disintegration of, as well as a reconstruction of, personalities. *Education is, in fact, a remaking of individuals, and thus of the culture.* But the greater danger for both the individual and the culture is the denial to any of the opportunity to develop the ability and inclination to think.[15]

### Should the Social Studies Teacher Develop the "Minds" Instead of the "Hearts" of Students?

SOME NEGATIVE ARGUMENTS. Above all other aphorisms contained in Blaise Pascal's *Pensées,* readers tend to recall and to repeat, "The heart has its reasons, which reason does not know. . . ."[16] Numerous persons draw a distinction between the "mind" and the "heart." They separate the "cognitive" from the "affective" domain. They divide mankind into two stereotyped groups, composed of those who "think" and those who "feel."

The people who *think* are objective, dispassionate, critical, subtle, aloof, formal, cool, pessimistic, serious, tense, etc.

The individuals who *feel* are subjective, passionate, complimentary, open, gregarious, informal, warm, optimistic, whimsical, relaxed, and the like.

Opponents to developing the "minds" instead of the "hearts" of learners might offer assertions such as those appearing after the subheadings identified below.

*Thinking makes people unhappy.* ". . . [Those] who have the best stomachs are not the best thinkers," observed Voltaire, who may have been suffering from indigestion when he penned those words. John Keats felt, ". . . [To] think is to be full of sorrow. . . ." "Rob the average man of his life-illusion," said Henrik Ibsen, "and you rob him of his happiness at the same stroke." According to Malcolm de Chazal, "The man who can make others laugh secures more votes for a measure than the man who forces them to think." And, Donald R. P. Marquis reached this conclusion: "If you make people think they're thinking, they'll love you. If you really make them think, they'll hate you." If happiness is the real purpose of life, as multitudes have held, then reflection on controversial issues may undermine that aim.

*Thinking is impossible for most individuals.* A cerebral person himself, Herbert Spencer admitted, "Opinion is ultimately determined by the feelings, and not by the intellect." "To the vast majority of mankind nothing is more agreeable than to escape the need for mental exertion. . . . To most people nothing is more troublesome than the effort of thinking," James Bryce declared. Not exactly a prominent intellectual himself, Henry Ford observed, "Thinking is the hardest work there is, which is the probable reason why so few people engage in it." This comment from H. L. Mencken, one of America's most acerbic and brilliant writers, was published after his death:

. . . [The] average man never really thinks from end to end of his life. . . . The mental activity of such people is only the mouthing of clichés. What they mistake for thought is simply repetition of what they have heard. My guess is that well over eighty per cent of the human race goes through life without ever having a single original thought. That is to say, they never think anything that has not been thought before and by thousands.[17]

If most of his or her pupils cannot think, the teacher is wasting his or her time and that of the students in struggling vainly to promote this activity.

*Thinking encourages frivolity.* Even John Dewey, the patron saint of reflection in education, seems to have slipped a minute in *Reconstruction in Philosophy* and to have contributed something to this argument.

. . . When the scientific man appears to observe aimlessly, it is merely that he is so in love with problems as sources and guides of inquiry, that he is striving to turn up a problem where none appears on the surface: he is, as we say, hunting for trouble because of the satisfaction to be had in coping with it.[18]

Many Americans are *doers,* rather than *thinkers.* They would agree with this warning from Isaac Watts:

> For Satan finds some mischief still
> For idle hands to do.

And, they would find it difficult to comprehend and accept Victor Hugo's utterance in *Les Misérables:* "A man is not idle because he is absorbed in thought. There is a visible labour and there is invisible labour."

**Item:**

A perennial burden that college and university professors must bear is that the public in general and legislators and trustees in particular fail to see how these savants "earn their salt." If the higher education instructor teaches *only* six to fifteen hours a week, what on earth does he or she do with *all* of the rest of the time? Admittedly, there could be some justification in being paid to prepare for classes, to grade papers, to advise students, to work on committees, and a few other *necessary* things. Reluctantly, a lesser number of constituents might see a place for a certain amount of reading and attendance at a few meetings to keep up on one's field; limited research to advance knowledge; and restricted writing, speaking, and consulting to disseminate information. But time spent *just* to *sit* and *THINK* is too intangible an enterprise to support, even if the professor is putting in 50-70 hours a week!

When pupils have too much free time on their hands, they just get into trouble! They should be kept busy learning immediately useful, specific facts and skills, working at their desks with their heads down and their pencils flying! They can play around with potentially impractical, frothy, abstract ideas on their own! Thinking is usually inefficient, and the school should be an efficient institution!

*Thinking develops untrustworthy persons.* In Shakespeare's *Julius Caesar* we find this pointed warning:

> Yond Cassius has a lean and hungry look;
> He thinks too much: such men are dangerous.

There seems to be a general tendency in this country to distrust the "oddball" who thinks too soon, too long, too seriously, and too differently.

**Item:**

The recent war in Vietnam might serve as an illustration.

An individual who questioned American involvement at the early stages and who was way ahead of the later and widespread public disenchantment did his thinking "too soon" and was regarded as premature, suspect, and even unpatriotic.

A person who engaged in anti-war protests continuously was a harper and a malcontent who kept at it "too long."

Dalton Trumbo, who on January 3, 1970 penned these portions of the "Addendum: 1970" for the Introduction of *Johnny Got His Gun*, was *obviously* a writer who thought "too seriously" about the war:

. . . Numbers have dehumanized us. Over breakfast coffee we read of 40,000 American dead in Vietnam. Instead of vomiting, we reach for the toast. Our morning rush through crowded streets is not to cry murder but to hit that trough before somebody else gobbles our share.

An equation: 40,000 dead young men = 3,000 tons of bone and flesh, 124,000 pounds of brain matter, 50,000 gallons of blood, 1,840,-000 years of life that will never be lived, 100,000 children who will never be born. . . .

*  *  *

If the dead mean nothing to us . . ., what of our 300,000 wounded? Does anyone know where they are? How they feel? How many arms, legs, ears, noses, mouths, faces, penises they've lost? How many are deaf or dumb or blind or all three? How many are single or double or triple or quadruple amputees? How many will remain immobile for the rest of their days? How many hang on as decerebrated vegetables quietly breathing their lives away in small, dark, secret rooms? [19]

And William Eastlake thinks "too differently" when he describes two American soldiers in Vietnam in his book *The Bamboo Bed:*

. . . [Oliver and Elgar] were pacifists fighting a war. . . . They were pacifists in fact rather than theory because Oliver and Elgar simply never killed anybody. . . .

*  *  *

. . . Oliver and Elgar no longer believed in war. They had become completely uncivilized. They no longer wanted to kill their own kind.[20]

*Some Positive Arguments.* To some, whether the social studies teacher ought to enlarge the "minds" rather than the "hearts" of learners is a rhetorical, specious, factitious kind of issue. It can be dismissed on at least neurobiological, emotive, and aesthetic grounds.

*A neurobiological viewpoint.* Some of the content about to be presented here was drawn and adapted from a January 14, 1974 *Time* cover story, "Exploring the Frontiers of the Mind," by Associate Editor Peter Stoler.[21] The author of this Chapter also talked with a young physician specializing in neurosurgery at The Ohio State University Hospital to check out some statements he had read elsewhere and wanted to make. The Chapter author must be held accountable for still other remarks.

As a reflective person, this author perceives the brain as the most important, wonderful part of the human body. The heart, although it is essential and amazing in its own right, is a pump. For him, one is dead when his or her brain ceases to function, when he or she cannot reason for himself or herself.

The brain is divided down the middle. Its two cerebral hemispheres are anatomically separate, but they are *cross-wired*. One side of the brain regulates the opposite side of the body. The left cerebral hemisphere has been associated with speech and hearing and certain analytical functions; it is dominant in most people. (Leonardo Da Vinci, "Babe" Ruth, Charlie Chaplin, Cole Porter, "Harpo" Marx, Olivia de Havilland, Danny Kaye, F. Lee Bailey, Rod Laver, Rock Hudson,[22] and Raymond H. Muessig are notable exceptions.) The right side handles spatial perception, the synthesis of ideas, and aesthetic appreciations. Just how, when, and why the pair of cerebral hemispheres *interact* is not understood fully. But the heart—St. Valentine's Day and countless other events and attendant myths notwithstanding—is not the locus of our feelings and is not even shaped as popular artists have been wont to draw it.

Whatever man has been, is, and may become as a unique animal who can recall his experiences and those of others, try to fathom who he is and where he is going, and attempt to chart his tomorrow, is a result of his brain.

*An emotive viewpoint.* Disagreeing with Pascal, Bruno Bettelheim writes, "No longer can we be satisfied with a life where the heart has its reasons, which reason cannot know. Our hearts must know the world of reason, and reason must be guided by an informed heart. . . ."[23]

Ellis and Harper, quoted earlier, ask, ". . . But whoever said that well-organized, rational thinking was incompatible with intense emotion?"[24]

In an article in *Theory Into Practice,* entitled "Logical Reasoning: An Educational Goal," Alan R. Osborne and Gerald M. Reagan, two of this author's colleagues at The Ohio State University, assume this posture:

. . . The opposite of the rational is the irrational, not the emotional. And the opposite of the emotional is the non-emotional which may be either rational or irrational. The emotional may be irrational, but it need not be. And the rational may be non-emotional, but it is not necessarily so. In brief, a commitment to foster logical reasoning as an educational goal does not commit one to a goal of producing nonfeeling, insensitive human beings. Indeed many of us would hold that thoughtful human beings are less likely to become insensitive than are those who choose to reject reason.[25]

The reflective person does not always regard the *cognitive* domain (facts, concepts, generalizations, etc.) as separate and distinct from the *affective* realm (opinions, appreciations, attitudes, beliefs, values, etc.). There is a merger when one *studies* his *opinions, considers* his *appreciations, examines* his *attitudes, thinks about* his *beliefs, reflects on* his *values.* Facts, concepts, generalizations, etc. from history and the social sciences can be *contemplated* where *commitments* are at stake.

". . . Genuine thinking winds up, in short, with an appreciation of new values," [26] Dewey concluded in *How We Think: A Restatement of the Relation of Reflective Thinking to the Educative Process.*

In *Education for a New Morality,* Agnes E. Meyer reasoned,

No scientist or scientific philosopher would claim that intelligence, reason, and the scientific approach to problems will ever wholly dominate the course of history. For the elements of chance, the unforeseen events, the pressures and passions of group life can never be wholly eliminated from human activities. . . .

* * *

. . . [We] must achieve a humanism that is truly scientific and a science that is truly humane. . . .[27]

The reflective person may want to be just as happy as other people who are not devoted to a reasoned existence. However, he sees that happiness as the supreme goal of life is too amorphous, too contextual, too much a personal matter to exalt above all other aims for all time. He learns through experience and contemplation that there are moments, periods, when he will choose other objectives above happiness, that he will define happiness in different ways from day to day, year to year, and that what pleases him may displease others and vice versa. He can also defer immediate gratification for a more mature, refined, complete happiness at a later time.

*An aesthetic viewpoint.* The author of this Chapter is going to rely solely on John Dewey and on one "Item" of his own for the condensed treatment under this sub-heading.

In *The Quest for Certainty: A Study of the Relation of Knowledge and Action,* Dewey opines,

. . . Without the intervention of thought, enjoyments are not values but problematic goods, becoming values when they re-issue in a changed form from intelligent behavior. . . .

* * *

. . . Expertness of taste is at once the result and the reward of constant exercise of thinking. . . .[28]

A book that deserves to be read by all of us in social studies education, *Experience and Nature,* contains these pertinent ruminations of Dewey:

. . . Science is an instrumentality of and for art because it is the intelligent factor *in* art. . . .

*  *  *

Thinking is pre-eminently an art; knowledge and propositions are the products of thinking, are works of art, as much so as statuary and symphonies. . . .

*  *  *

. . . [Delightfully] enhanced perception or esthetic appreciation is of the same nature as enjoyment of any object that is consummatory. It is the outcome of a skilled and intelligent art of dealing with natural things for the sake of intensifying, purifying, prolonging and deepening the satisfactions which they spontaneously afford. . . .

*  *  *

. . . Cultivated taste alone is capable of prolonged appreciation of the same object; and it is capable of it because it has been trained to a discriminating procedure which constantly uncovers in the object new meanings to be perceived and enjoyed. . . .

*  *  *

. . . In esthetics, there are the goods of an undeveloped or perverted taste and there are the goods of cultivated taste. . . .[29]

**Item:**

For many years, and for reasons unknown to, and unconsidered by him, the author of this Chapter had always "liked" the paintings of the Impressionists and Post-Impressionists. For that matter, he had never analyzed why he "enjoyed" going to art museums at all, let alone why he "preferred" the work of Manet over Gauguin, Renoir over Toulouse-Lautrec, Seurat over Cézanne.

In Paris, in the spring of 1971, with a few Ohio State University students, he visited the small Jeu de Paume Museum, which contains Impressionist and Post-Impressionist paintings of the Louvre. It had been arranged that Mademoiselle Marguerite Prinet, an art historian, would guide us. The graying, dignified, urbane, beautiful Mademoiselle was a superb teacher and a marvelous human being. She knew more about her beloved subject than anyone this author has met before or since. He and Mademoiselle Prinet never mentioned pedagogy, but she was a "natural" at *induction, inquiry,* and *reflection.* As she invited us to look long and hard at the paintings she had selected carefully, she requested that we verbalize our thoughts and feelings. She pointed here and there, asking heuristic questions, encouraging us along the tour to try to frame our own generalizations, challenging us to probe our own values.

Why do you suppose Manet put this touch of sunlight here?

What seems to happen when Renoir puts these two vivid, glowing colors next to each other?

Can you come up with some reasons for Seurat's use of sparkling dots and dashes of unmixed color in this canvas?

Do you want to make any guesses about Van Gogh's emotional state when he painted this? Have you ever felt this way?

Does the position of the figure in this Degas have any meaning for you or evoke any feelings?

What do you perceive as the central mood of this Gauguin?

Do you believe that Toulouse-Lautrec admired the woman shown here? Why, or why not?

In this Cézanne, do you see the light right here as direct or reflected? From what direction might it have come? Was the source of the light close or far away? Does any of this make a difference to Cézanne. To you?

How many explanations can you offer why Monet—and others in this period—painted the same subject? Was this a waste of time, energy, talent?

Are there shadows in this picture? No? Why not, do you suppose? How about this one? Yes? What *colors* are the shadows? Aren't shadows just gray or black?

How would you describe the underlying spirit of Impressionism and Post-Impressionism—what the artists were trying to do?

Do you appreciate the work of these painters *more* or *less* as a result of our dialogue? Why?

Discussing our experience later, we could not believe the many insights we had gained through Mademoiselle Prinet's skillful guidance. The writer of this Chapter has been reading about Impressionism and Post-Impressionism ever since, and he has viewed additional paintings from this period in museums in Europe and the United States.

An early, undeveloped, solely "gut-level" response to Impressionism and Post-Impressionism is growing into an aesthetic gratification, enriched by further thought and emotion.

## Conclusion

With a mixture of reluctance and relief, this author must conclude this treatment of the nature of controversial issues, some earlier efforts and publications concerned with the teaching of controversial issues, and some arguments against and for handling controversial issues. But, like a dying character in a play by Shakespeare, the author has some parting words. Endeavoring, to the last, to remain faithful to the ethos of reflection, he would like to close with both some pessimistic and optimistic comments germane to the possible future of teaching students to grapple with controversial issues.

## SOME PESSIMISTIC COMMENTS

Although H. L. Mencken wrote this years ago, there are many who would agree with him today:

According to American theory, all power is in the hands of the plain people, and according to American legend they always exercise it wisely. The theory, of course, is almost as absurd as the legend. The plain people, in fact, can only exert their power through agents, and in the election of those agents they seldom face a clear choice between a good candidate and a bad one, or a wise idea and a foolish one. In the normal case both candidates are frauds and both ideas are idiotic. . . .[30]

The author of this Chapter delayed his writing of this Conclusion to read a gloomy, but perhaps realistic, new book, *An Inquiry into the Human Prospect,* by Robert L. Heilbroner. With considerable reluctance, Heilbroner deduces that

. . . We have become aware that rationality has its limits with regard to the engineering of social change, and that these limits are much narrower than we had thought. . . .

\* \* \*

. . . The outlook for man, I believe, is painful, difficult, perhaps desperate, and the hope that can be held out for his future prospect seems to be very slim indeed. Thus, to anticipate the conclusions of our inquiry, the answer to whether we can conceive of the future other than as a continuation of the darkness, cruelty, and disorder of the past seems to me to be no; and to the question of whether worse impends, yes.[31]

Probably a diminishing number of American adults, and an even smaller body of their progeny, could agree with poor Doctor Pangloss in Voltaire's *Candide,* written in 1758, that this is "the best of all possible worlds." Things *do* seem to be getting *worse*—not *better*—in innumerable areas of life. Old and young alike find it increasingly difficult to see even a glimmer of light at the end of the tunnel, to cope, to do anything to remedy personal-social ills. Even if one learns to reason for himself or herself about value conflicts, to formulate warranted beliefs, to submit tenable alternative resolutions, how can he or she influence The Bureaucracy, The Establishment, The Power Elite? Why contemplate what may wait ahead when one can barely make it through each day? What good is a developed capacity to think and to feel when it may atrophy from lack of exercise?

## SOME OPTIMISTIC COMMENTS

As Samuel Adams put it, "Our contest is not whether we ourselves shall be free, but whether there shall be left to mankind an asylum on earth for . . . liberty." We social studies people have a very real obligation to our children and youth and to their offspring to protect and magnify intellectual freedom.

Although he died over a century ago, Jean Louis Rodolphe Agassiz knew then that "The time has come when scientific truth must cease to be the property of the few—when it must be woven into the common life of the world." Our task is to inspire every learner to seek the "true" and the "beautiful" constantly. If we allow this quest to die, all is lost.

Friedrich Wilhelm Nietzche, who was not exactly the eternal optimist, proclaimed, "On the mountains of truth you can never climb in vain; either you will reach a point higher up today, or you will be training your powers so that you will be able to climb higher tomorrow." However depressed some of us may become at times with current conditions, we cannot throw in the towel. The "Dark Ages" cost us a great deal in terms of human progress, and a similar period cannot be afforded now.

In *A Common Faith,* Dewey wrote, ". . . . Men have never fully used the powers they possess to advance the good in life, because they have waited upon some power external to themselves and to nature to do the work they are responsible for doing. . . ." [32] The Chapter author's father, who is in his eighties and who was an automotive mechanic for almost sixty years, used to have a sign over his workbench. It read: "It ain't often that opportunity comes your way; it generally looks like work!" The opportunity is ours! The work is up to us and those who follow us!

The author of this Chapter agrees heartily with Herbert A. Thelen's statement in *Education and the Human Quest* that ". . . The school testifies to our faith that man and society can be improved, and that the way to improvement is through the trained use of intelligence." [33]

John Steinbeck's *The Winter of Our Discontent* contains this question: ". . . Can a man think out his life, or must he just tag along?" [34] For the reflective social studies teacher, the answer is obvious: A man *must* think out his life; he cannot afford to just tag along!

Over five years ago, the editor of this Yearbook penned this passage which still represents his feelings:

. . . G. K. Chesterton, a late and enthusiastic convert to Catholicism, supposedly remarked that Christianity had not failed, for it had never really been tried. In a similar fashion, a reflective approach has never been tested on a comprehensive, continuous basis. To my knowledge, there are no students who have had a fully reflective experience throughout their entire secondary schooling, let alone on a K-12 basis or from kindergarten through college. It gives me pleasure to contemplate what might be achieved in our nation and our world if we were to raise an entire generation capable of applying the method of intelligence to human concerns. . . .[35]

The author can think of no more fitting close than this statement, ending with a challenging question, by John W. Gardner in *The Recovery of Confidence:*

Teachers are right to demand that young people re-examine the received beliefs of childhood. That is a part of growing up as a thinking person. But after the shakeup, the individual must reconstruct a framework of values that is right for him and relevant to his time. And available evidence indicates that most individuals are not well equipped for the search. Can we help them? [36]

# FOOTNOTES

[1] Dick Gregory with Robert Lipsyte, *Nigger: An Autobiography* (New York: Pocket Books, Inc., 1968), p. 155.

[2] R. M. MacIver, *The Challenge of the Passing Years: My Encounter with Time* (New York: Pocket Books, Inc., 1963), p. 113.

[3] Boyd H. Bode, *Modern Educational Theories* (New York: Vintage Books, 1927), p. 262.

[4] Ashley Montagu, *Education and Human Relations* (New York: Grove Press, Inc., 1958), p. 124.

[5] W. Somerset Maugham, *The Summing Up* (New York: Pocket Books, Inc., 1967), p. 200.

[6] T. V. Smith and Eduard C. Lindeman, *The Democratic Way of Life* (New York: The New American Library of World Literature, Inc., 1951), p. 52.

[7] Walter Lippmann, *The Public Philosophy* (New York: The New American Library, Inc., 1955), p. 35.

[8] Bernard Malamud, *The Fixer* (New York: Dell Publishing Co., Inc., 1968), p. 32.

[9] John Barth, *The End of the Road* (New York: Bantam Books, Inc., 1969), pp. 62, 83, and 122, respectively.

[10] John W. Aldridge, *In the Country of the Young* (New York: Perennial Library, 1971), p. 119.

[11] Albert Ellis and Robert A. Harper, *A Guide to Rational Living* (Englewood Cliffs: Prentice-Hall, Inc.), p. 16.

[12] Frederick S. Perls, in John O. Stevens, compiler and editor, *Gestalt Therapy Verbatim* (Lafayette, California: Real People Press, 1969), p. 32.

[13] Thomas A. Harris, *I'm OK—You're OK: A Practical Guide to Transactional Analysis* (New York: Harper & Row, Publishers, 1969), pp. xiv and 176-177, respectively.

[14] Alan F. Griffin, "Community Pressures and Education," Chapter 8 in H. Gordon Hullfish, editor, *Educational Freedom in an Age of Anxiety,* Twelfth Yearbook of the John Dewey Society (New York: Harper & Brothers, Publishers, 1953), p. 164.

[15] H. Gordon Hullfish and Philip G. Smith, *Reflective Thinking: The Method of Education* (New York: Dodd, Mead & Company, 1961), pp. 58-59.

[16] Blaise Pascal, *Pensées* and *The Provincial Letters* (New York: Random House, Inc., 1941), p. 95.

[17] H. L. Mencken, *Minority Report: H. L. Mencken's Notebooks* (New York: Alfred A. Knopf, 1956), p. 10.

[18] John Dewey, *Reconstruction in Philosophy* (New York: The New American Library of World Literature, Inc., 1952), p. 119.

[19] Dalton Trumbo, *Johnny Got His Gun* (New York: Bantam Books, Inc. [Published by arrangement with Lyle Stuart, Inc.], 1970), pp. unnumbered.

[20] William Eastlake, *The Bamboo Bed* (New York: Simon and Schuster, 1969), pp. 39-40.

[21] Peter Stoler, "Exploring the Frontiers of the Mind," *Time* 103 (January 14, 1974): 50 and 55.

[22] Michael Barsley, *The Other Hand: An Investigation into the Sinister History of Left-Handedness* (New York: Hawthorn Books, Inc., 1967).

[23] Bruno Bettelheim, *The Informed Heart: Autonomy in a Mass Age.* (Glencoe: The Free Press, 1960), p. viii.

[24] Ellis and Harper, *op. cit.,* p. 16.

[25] Alan R. Osborne and Gerald M. Reagan, "Logical Reasoning: An Educational Goal," *Theory Into Practice* 12 (December, 1973): 264.

[26] John Dewey, *How We Think: A Restatement of the Relation of Reflective Thinking to the Educative Process* (Boston: D. C. Heath and Company, 1933), p. 101.

[27] Agnes E. Meyer, *Education for a New Morality* (New York: The Macmillan Company, 1957), pp. 43-44 and 5, respectively.

[28] John Dewey, *The Quest for Certainty: A Study of the Relation of Knowledge and Action* (New York: G. P. Putnam's Sons, Capricorn Books Edition, 1960), pp. 259 and 262, respectively.

[29] John Dewey, *Experience and Nature* (New York: Dover Publications, Inc., 1958), pp. 367, 378, 389, 399, and 402, respectively.

[30] Mencken, *op. cit.,* pp. 283-284.

[31] Robert L. Heilbroner, *An Inquiry into the Human Prospect* (New York: W. W. Norton & Company, Inc., 1974), pp. 17 and 22, respectively.

[32] John Dewey, *A Common Faith* (New Haven: Yale University Press, 1934), p. 46.

[33] Herbert A. Thelen, *Education and the Human Quest* (New York: Harper & Brothers, 1960), p. 29.

[34] John Steinbeck, *The Winter of Our Discontent* (New York: Bantam Books, Inc., 1962), p. 39.

[35] Raymond H. Muessig, "My Pedagogic Creed: A Statement of Personal Beliefs Regarding Secondary Social Studies Education," *Southwest Journal of Social Education* 1 (Fall, 1970): 63.

[36] John W. Gardner, *The Recovery of Confidence* (New York: W. W. Norton & Company, Inc., 1970), p. 89.

# 2

# Teacher Preparation
# and Models for Teaching
# Controversial Social Issues

## Jo A. Cutler Sweeney and James B. Parsons

### Things Teachers Need To Think About
### Concerning Social Issues

THIS SECTION of the chapter deals with questions which teachers need to consider when presenting controversial issues. Several general areas are included.

First, the teacher should engage in a self-reflective process. Since the study of controversial issues involves the analysis of values; and, since this analysis of values can only be successful if students' values are deemed important by the teacher, the teacher must be sure that he or she is willing to listen openly to student views.

Some teachers state that students do not have the aptitude, desire, or maturity to decide what issues they should study in school. In the study of controversial issues, it is important that the students contribute their unique values to the class. If a teacher feels that students, for whatever the reason, should not have the right to input into their own curriculum or play an active role in the classroom, then it does not seem plausible that this teacher could direct a study of controversial issues.

A second question that teachers should consider is whether they are willing to have their own values open to testing. A teacher must analyze

JO A. CUTLER SWEENEY *is Associate Professor of Curriculum and Instruction, School of Education Faculty, The University of Texas, Austin, Texas.*
JAMES B. PARSONS *is Graduate Student, Curriculum and Instruction, School of Education Faculty, The University of Texas, Austin, Texas.*

the implications of studying a particular issue of controversy. If, for example, a teacher feels very strongly against racism, he or she should decide how he or she will react to a student who, after using a model like the Social Issues Model, still maintains a strong racist attitude. If there are teachers who feel that their background makes them too biased to lead an impartial and non-threatening discussion on a particular controversial issue, those teachers should consider not dealing with that issue in their classrooms. If some teachers feel that it is important that their personal values about a particular controversial issue remain private, they should not attempt to deal with that controversial issue in their classrooms.

Third, controversial issues are only controversial if values are in conflict. It may be that the controversy lies only in the mind of the teacher. What the teacher may see as an important controversial issue, the students may feel is a moot point. If students do not feel the importance of examining a particular issue, a teacher will probably not be successful by forcing the students to examine it. This might mean that the teacher needs to find some method to discover and measure students' interests. The method may be a few carefully-placed questions, a paper-pencil poll, or a well-conditioned ear to the classroom conversation.

Fourth, the teacher must consider the amount of time that he or she is willing to spend. Is the teacher willing to spend the time necessary to prepare materials carefully? It is always wise to be well-prepared. If the teacher is going to have the students work through a model, the teacher should be familiar with the model. The teacher should develop a sound intellectual defense for the inclusion of controversial material. The discussion of controversial issues is not the place for spur-of-the-moment decisions. This does not mean that the direction of the discussion is determined in advance, but rather that the material to be used and the manner of presentation should be considered in advance.

Fifth, the teacher may need to ask if he or she is willing to spend the effort needed to go beyond the boundaries of his or her own classroom. Experience indicates that it is wise for the teacher to get interested people involved in the classroom. Parents, community groups, and administrators should be treated as positive sources of support instead of probable resisters. The administration should be involved from the outset. The classroom should be open to parents. Various segments of the community should be included in the classroom activities if possible. Generally, there should not be a "back room" feeling about the discussion of the controversial issue. If the teacher cannot justify his or her actions, he or she should not act.

Sixth, teachers may need to reconsider what their role as classroom leaders should be. Social issues do not contain single right solutions.

The students will not benefit very much if social issues discussions substitute "their facts" for the facts regularly dealt with in the social studies classroom.

Seventh, and perhaps the most important teacher ingredient for the examination of controversial issues, is establishing the emotional climate of the classroom. It is critical that the teacher establish rapport in a class where controversial issues are going to be discussed. There must be mutual confidence that the students can and will supply important information to the discussions. The students must have faith that the teacher can moderate an open and honest discussion of the materials. If the teacher has a bias, the students must be confident that the teacher will show it as a bias.

In summation, the teacher who is dealing with controversial issues should be willing to consider seriously the following questions.

## QUESTIONS I NEED TO ASK MYSELF

(1) Am I willing to engage in a self-reflective process?

(2) Am I willing to publicly allow my own values to be examined and not necessarily accepted?

(3) Am I willing to allow students to have input into the selection of classroom content?

(4) Am I willing to spend the time necessary to prepare and plan carefully?

(5) Am I willing to go beyond my own classroom to open the doors to other segments of the community?

(6) Am I willing, if necessary, to learn new techniques of classroom procedures and not to see my role as giving the right answers?

(7) Do I want to establish a classroom where students and the teacher can openly discuss serious societal conflicts?

This does not mean that these are the only questions which teachers need to consider; however, the deliberate avoidance of serious factors at the beginning might prejudice lesson success.

If the teacher feels that the learnings to be gained by the students are important enough to justify some possible additional effort on his or her part, he or she might also find informative the criteria suggested by Richard E. Gross for handling controversial issues discussion. In the National Council for the Social Studies' *How To Do It Series,* Richard E. Gross in "How to Handle Controversial Issues" lists seven criteria in the selection of controversial issues for class study. They are:

(1) *Is this issue beyond the maturity and experience level of the pupils?*

Gross states that teachers are wise to select those issues which the students are ready to deal with both in terms of background and maturity. This selection does not limit the study of controversial issues to those problems easily solved, Gross states. Chronic problems of society that no one can adequately solve should be studied. Even if no action on these problems is possible, the students should be aware of and grapple with them.

(2) *Is this issue of interest to the pupils?*

Students who are not interested in or who are lukewarm to an issue will not be enthused to examine it, Gross states. His inclusion of this criterion supports the importance of considering student involvement as suggested in the previous question, "Am I willing to allow my students an active role in the selection of classroom content?"

(3) *Is this issue socially significant and timely for this course and grade level?*

Gross states that one of the big problems in the study of a controversy is knowing what materials and issues to include and which ones to exclude. Teachers involved should be in communication with other teachers to provide reinforcement or enlargement when necessary and to prevent needless repetition.

(4) *Is this issue one which the teacher feels he or she can handle successfully from a personal standpoint?*

Central to this question, Gross states, is how a teacher should take a stand. Gross contends that the teacher should not set himself or herself up as an authority figure. He or she should not seek to indoctrinate or to have the students submit to his or her powerful leadership position.

Gross states that a teacher needs to examine constantly the extent to which he or she is influencing the students. If the teacher allows the students to express their values and opinions on an equal basis with his or her own; and, if the students see that the teacher's values and opinions are as subject to question as their own, the teacher can feel free to interject his or her values and opinions during the discussion of a controversial issue. This criterion ties in with the importance of self-reflection plus a willingness to examine one's own values.

Gross states that it is wise, in many cases, for the teacher to refrain from stating his or her values. However, the authors of this chapter feel that it is almost impossible for teachers to do this. It is unrealistic to think that a teacher can remain perfectly neutral.

Gross does state that some teachers feel it is best to reserve their statements until the end of the discussion of a controversy. Caution should be exercised, however, since saving teacher statements until the end of the discussion might give the students the impression that the teacher is trying to elicit the "right answer" and that the teacher's eventual statement is the correct response that the students should have logically arrived at. This is an important consideration since students might want to please the teacher more than express their own ideas.

(5) *Is this issue one for which adequate study materials can be obtained?*

Teachers, Gross contends, should conduct a conference with the school librarian. Materials should be selected with the reading and maturity levels of the students in mind. Materials should be selected that present both sides of the issue. When these materials are not available, Gross states, the teacher has an obligation to point this out to the students and to present the other less popular side. Teachers should take care, however, that the students do not interpret this presentation as the teacher's viewpoint, Gross warns.

(6) *Is this issue one for which there is adequate time to justify its presentation?*

Gross states that some issues cannot be justifiably handled in a short period of time and that the teacher should be sensitive to this possibility.

(7) *Is this issue one which will clash with community customs and attitudes?*

Gross states that some issues, in some communities, may be too hot to handle and that the teacher may be cutting his or her own throat by venturing into those areas.

Several things should be said concerning this criterion. If the teacher has tried to work with the community and administration before problems arise, chances of success are enhanced. Many principals will support their teachers if they have knowledge of a teacher's anticipated actions and justifiable reasons for those actions. It is *never* wise to proceed behind people's backs. If support is not forthcoming, the teacher should weigh the potential implications of his or her actions. If teachers believe they must continue against the wishes of the community and the administration, they should be prepared to accept the implications of their actions. A genuine commitment to openness might allow more opportunity to consider a variety of issues.

## Social Issues Model

The next obvious concern is how the teacher presents controversial issues. Teacher questions might include: Are there certain skills involved? Where do I go for guidance? This section deals with a Social Issues Model which can be used by classroom teachers.

The phases of the model are explained. Sample materials or questions to be used during each phase of the model are included for the teacher.

Some actual examples of classroom dialogue are provided for certain phases of the model to help with clarity.

Creative thinking and intelligent decision-making skills do not come mechanically from following directions or recipes. However, at the other extreme, simply giving students materials and expecting them to haphazardly arrive at rational decisions is expecting too much of the learners. Models are important because they add direction to materials presented in a working curriculum.

The Sweeney, Parsons' Social Issues Model is presented as a tool. It provides procedures that should help students develop decision-making skills. It should not be presented as a set of explicit directions. The model should not become more important than the student's education. The model should help the teacher organize and utilize materials effectively.

## SWEENEY, PARSONS' SOCIAL ISSUES MODEL

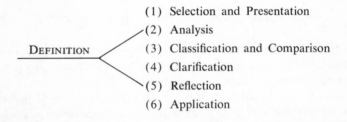

DEFINITION

(1) Selection and Presentation
(2) Analysis
(3) Classification and Comparison
(4) Clarification
(5) Reflection
(6) Application

A particular strength of this Social Issues Model is that it helps students engage in activities that deal with their own feelings and values. To use the model in the way that it is intended, the teacher must value rationality and the public communication of value decision-making. The teacher should, at the outset, appraise these criteria in the light of their implications.

The model encourages students to synthesize school "disciplines" in a natural way. The student can draw information from history, biology, English, or any other subject field. The decisions made by working through the model are real-life decisions; and, as real-life decisions, do not distinguish social studies from science from English. The student draws from each discipline to provide an integrated understanding of human behavior.

The model allows the student an open-ended device for looking at social controversy. This particular model was created because we believe that students have the right, the desire, and the aptitude to reach decisions concerning their own education. The students are helped by

## SWEENEY, PARSONS' SOCIAL ISSUES MODEL

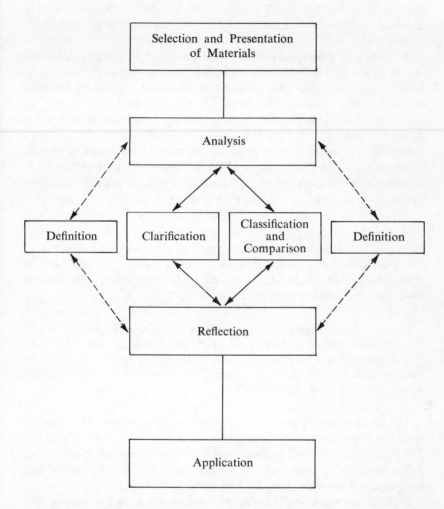

the teacher through the model; but, the value decisions reached by the individual students are not those predetermined by the teacher. The teacher is more concerned with the thoughtful examination of decisions and the decision-making process than judging whether the specific value decisions that the student reaches are "right" or "wrong."

The teacher's task is that of facilitating the flow of classroom activity. Duties include keeping the class from bogging down by sensing when activities need to be changed, moving the class from one step in the model to the next, serving in a heuristic capacity in questioning both language and rationality, acting as a moderator and devil's advocate in classroom discussions to assure that all sides of a controversy are given a free forum, functioning as an organizer to analyze the discussion in terms of the discrete values involved, and performing as a resource person.

A strength of the model is that a wide variety of inexpensive materials can be adapted to it. Materials can come from newspapers, magazines, books, anecdotes, etc. The selection of materials is generally initiated by the teacher; however, this need not continue to be the case. As classroom discussions progress, the students could and should help select their own materials.

Definition is not a specific phase of the model. Definition is, rather, a process by which the student and the teacher make a conscious effort to make clear to each other the language which they use to describe values, feelings, ideas, or simply things in general.

It cannot be assumed logically that what one person means by one term is what another person means when he uses the same term. For example, one student might state emphatically that he believes that criminals should be treated equally under the law. Another student states that equality under the law is unjust in many cases. The teacher might give the following simple example:

Two men are arrested for stealing. One man laughs at the police and says he didn't need the money, he just got a kick out of stealing. The other man, it is discovered, was only stealing because his family was starving and he needed the money to buy food. Both people have taken something that wasn't theirs. Is there a difference?

The first student states that this was not what he meant. He was only speaking about really hardcore criminals and crimes. Anyone can see that there is a difference between a person who commits a crime out of desperation and a person who is a hardcore criminal. The second student agrees that this is what he had been trying to say all the time.

In this case there was actually no controversy between the two students. The controversy which seemed to be apparent was a result of the way that each student spoke about his values.

It may be that one student does think that both men who have been arrested for stealing should get equally harsh punishment. But, it may be that the word *criminal* meant different things to each of the students and, when the terms were operationalized, the students saw that no controversy existed between them. Teachers must be aware that people— both students and teachers—use "loaded" or highly inferential terms in their everyday language. Making these highly inferential terms clear to others is at the heart of the definition process.

### Social Issues Model Phase I—Selection and Presentation

The selection and presentation of materials is normally the first phase in the Social Issues Model. The curriculum materials to be used in the classroom can be selected by either the teacher or students, or by a combination of input from both parties. The teacher might carry the major responsibility for material selection especially at the beginning of the class year, since students often have the idea that they do not have the ability to help with curriculum content.

The vast majority of textbooks do not deal systematically with social issues; consequently, the classroom teacher often has the responsibility to search for materials which would be appropriate for classroom use. The very nature of social issues materials also demands that materials be updated and contain relevant current data as well as historical content. Although the teacher needs to spend extra time and effort in the material selection process, increased student interest and learning should prove to be rewarding feedback.

There are many types of materials available, and the teacher should attempt to utilize a variety of materials when they are appropriate. Research has indicated that in many cases teachers fail to consider sources which can be used in the classroom. Songs and poetry offer a medium of expression which students can often respond to in a positive manner. Literature and especially novels offer a fruitful choice of materials which can be used effectively. The teacher can take portions of dialogue from a novel that contain the issue to be discussed and present them to the class. Role-playing exercises involving social issues content, as well as games and simulations, can and should be used in the social issues classroom. Paintings often deal with social issues content and can be analyzed productively by students.

Obviously newspapers, periodicals, and quotations provide another rich area for materials acquisition. Sometimes a seemingly small piece of material can lead into a spirited and productive lesson. For example, a photograph of a Mexican restaurant which appears to be in a *barrio* section of a town is shown with a police car parked in front. The students are asked to analyze what they think is going on in the photograph. The analysis of this single photograph leads into a discussion involving aspects of discrimination, stereotyping, etc.

What is suggested is that classroom materials are not just the printed word nor necessarily just in textbooks. After classes have been involved in social issues discussion, students will often begin to bring materials to class which they feel might contribute to a discussion already under way or on a topic they would like to consider in the future. The teacher, in this situation, might begin the lesson with only one or two selections of materials and then add materials as the topic is pursued. The teacher beginning social issues discussion may well experience frustration when attempting to assemble materials, but once a core of materials has been established on a particular issue, the task is easier. The teacher can then discard and add to the materials for use with future classes.

## EXAMPLES OF MATERIALS

Four examples of printed materials which could be used in a population control lesson are included to help make the first phase of the model more understandable. The selections in this sample lesson were purposely kept simple. Obviously, they do not contain all points of view and differ in their degree of objectivity. They are limited to written excerpts, but could also include other types of materials added by the teacher or students. The teacher who would like to try using the model with the sample material could write to the publishers for permission to have the four documents reproduced so each of the students would have a copy.

*Document I: Statement from a Social Scientist*

DOCUMENT SOURCE: Carl Pope, "Family Planning Is Inherently Genocidal, True-False," *Environmental Action* (May 15, 1971)

Black suspicions of the population movement run very deep; they are not confined to a few militants, and they are not to be allayed by statements by major population organizations that genocide is not intended. . . . The more serious source of Black fear is a strong suspicion that the actual policies to be followed on the path to zero population growth are anti-Black, and that much of the support for this idea is disguised racism. This argument receives strong impetus from at least three undeniable, deeply disturbing historical facts. The first is that the American public has traditionally attributed population growth to large families among the poor. And, in fact, recent surveys indicate that about three-fourths of the population believes that the poor contribute the largest share to population growth. Worse, three-fourths of the poor believe this. Now the fact is that less than one-third of U.S. births are accounted for by the poor and the near-poor combined, and a very small change in the fertility patterns of the middle and upper classes would have a much greater effect on population growth than a large change in the fertility of the poor. But so long as the public believes that the poor are responsible, it is likely to push for policies designed to influence the poor. And as long as the poor believe that they are responsible, it is quite understandable that they see in the talk of population control talk of controlling their population.

The second fact is that population policy in the United States has always been approached mainly as a matter of family planning, particularly of family planning for the poor. When families in the ghetto see elaborate family planning services provided for communities which lack even basic public health facilities for other medical problems, the assumption has to be that something other than their own welfare is being advanced. So the traditional concentration of the family planning movement on the poor, even though it may have been intended to serve poor women, and even though the poor women did in fact want and do in fact use these services, lends weight to suspicion of the population groups.

The third fact is that there have traditionally been attempts to force sterilization upon various minority groups; most recently three state legislatures have considered proposals to compel the sterilization of welfare mothers. Even where legislative sanction is lacking, it is clear that some welfare departments have attempted to force family planning or sterilization upon poor women in an attempt to keep down welfare rolls. That ZPG and Planned Parenthood have opposed these efforts is less significant to those involved than the fact that they have not always opposed them successfully.

*Document II: A Quotation from a Public Figure*

STATEMENT SOURCE: Dick Gregory, "My Answer to Genocide," *Ebony* (October, 1971)

My answer to genocide, quite simply, is eight Black kids—and another on the way. . . . There is ample evidence that government programs designed for poor Black folks emphasize birth control and abortion availability, both measures obviously designed to limit the Black population.

*Document III: This document is teacher designed but is based on factual data. Short stories and case studies written by the teacher can often be used to raise certain important value questions surrounding a controversial issue.*

DOCUMENT SOURCE: Teacher Designed

I am a medical missionary in the African country of Nigeria. I am concerned with saving lives. When I came to Nigeria in 1969, the country had a population of almost 60 million people. Nigeria has a very high death rate—about 25 people per 1000 per year—including a high infant mortality rate. I am one of many medical missionaries in Nigeria trying to alleviate pain and suffering.

The Nigerian birth rate is about 50 per 1000 per year. If my fellow medical missionaries and I are as successful as some of our colleagues in Singapore or Hong Kong, the death rate in Nigeria can be dropped to 5 per 1000 per year. However, there are problems. For one, Nigeria at present does not have the food to feed its population of 60 million. If we can stop the high infant mortality rate and lower the death rate in general to 5 per 1000, the population of Nigeria will double within 15 years. People are starving now and there is little hope that Nigeria could expand to feed 60 million people in the next 15 years—let alone 120 million.

*Document IV: A Quotation from Material by a Group Concerned with the Issue Being Presented.*

DOCUMENT SOURCE: Wayne H. Davis, "Thoughts on Feeding the Hungry." Reprinted by permission from *The Arizona Republic*, Hugh Moore Fund Campaign to check the population explosion.

Hungry people can outbreed the ability of this nation (United States) or any other to supply their food. We learned this once before with Public Law 480 with which we provided $15 billion worth of food to the hungry nations. The result was a dramatic increase in the number of hungry people, lowering of the per capita food consumption and general living conditions, and a decline in the efforts of these nations to feed themselves.

Recognizing this fact, an editorial in the February, 1969, *BioScience* said, "Because it creates a vicious cycle that compounds human suffering at a high rate, the provision of food to the undernourished populations of the world that cannot or will not take very substantial measures to control their own reproduction rates is inhuman, immoral, and irresponsible."

### Social Issues Model Phase II—Analysis

In the analysis phase students are asked to interpret the content of the materials presented. General questions are asked to focus on the content of the material. The goal for the students is to separate the specific material they are analyzing into its discrete parts. These parts might include: (a) what the material says; (b) what the intention is; (c) how the student thinks the material wants him or her to feel; (d) the action (what's happening) of the material; and (e) why it happened. (No order should be implied.)

For example, in the Carl Pope excerpt, Document I, the teacher might ask the students these questions.

(1) What is this excerpt generally about?
(2) What misconceptions does Pope say the general public holds about population growth?
(3) Why, does Pope say, are Blacks suspicious of efforts to control the population?
(4) What do you think was Pope's intent when he wrote the article?
(5) Does Pope recognize a controversy that he thinks exists? If so, what does he feel the controversy is?

These are sample teacher questions. For other materials (either the other documents suggested or other materials the teacher decides to add to the lesson) which are presented concerning population control, different—though related—questions should be asked. The basic teacher intent in the analysis phase is limited by design to what the material contains. However, questions of "why" and "what does this have to do with me" should not be ignored if asked by the students. This model is not intended as a step-by-step recipe. A teacher's statement "We'll talk about that later" might give the student the impression that the model is more important than actual student concerns. After the teacher has taken great pains to establish a classroom feeling that students' ideas and statements are an important part of the learning experience, a response like this could cost the teacher his or her credibility.

## SAMPLE DIALOGUE OF A CLASSROOM IN THE ANALYSIS PHASE*

Sample classroom dialogue of an actual presentation of Documents I and II is included to give the teacher a clearer idea of the type of teacher questions asked and the content of student responses in a secondary classroom.

*Teacher:* What does Carl Pope say are the Black fears?
*Student:* That they will all be wiped out by the White man.
*Student:* That their number will be cut by the plans of others for population control.

*Teacher:* How does he say the lower classes feel?
*Student:* The lower classes somehow feel that they are responsible, he says, for overpopulation even though this is not the truth.

*Teacher:* Looking at not only what Dick Gregory says but the words he uses, what does his statement say?
*Student:* Like, feel sorry for the Blacks. Well, not feel sorry for them—but don't look down on them. He feels that the programs are made just for the Blacks only—abortion, birth control—they are all made for the Blacks. Black people aren't the only people I know that need birth control information and other kinds of stuff.
*Student:* I think that Gregory is saying that he wants to keep having more children so that one of these days they can take over.
*Teacher:* Who's they?
*Student:* Well, Blacks. He's just tired of White rules.

*Teacher:* Do you think Dick Gregory's article agrees with Pope's article?
*Student:* What I get out of this is that Dick Gregory is against all population control measures. He must be. He says, "My answer to racial genocide," he says, "Eight kids and another one on the way." I think that he kind of overdoes it. He comes out kinda strong, I think. I don't think that we know enough about Pope from his article to know where he stands.

---

* Dialogue recorded in Mr. Nort Seaver's social studies class, Round Rock High School, Round Rock, Texas.

*Teacher:* What evidence do Pope and Gregory give concerning the population problem? Do they think that there is a problem?

*Student:* Somebody in the ghetto complains.

*Student:* Well, take a look at the highways. When you try to get somewhere there are thousands of cars. If you go to a movie, there are tons of people.

*Student:* I really don't think that there is a problem. He [the other student] was talking about overcrowded. When you drive, it's packed. All that this means is that there are not enough roads or movie houses. The world's big enough; it's just that we haven't built enough stuff for the people. I'm sure that there is a population problem somewhere—like the ghettos or India. But I don't think that there's one in the United States. Not like people say anyway.

## Social Issues Model Phase III—Clarification

The goal of the clarification phase in this model is to help each student understand where he or she stands on values that are relevant to the controversy being discussed. The student is asked to identify, examine, and make conscious decisions concerning what he or she values.

The teacher might want to use a variety of techniques to help the students clarify their own values. An example of such a device which could be used for the continuing population lesson is presented. The teacher might want to add some questions and eliminate others depending on his class. The purpose of the Student Clarification Questionnaire is to help individual students think about how they respond to some of the values inherent in the controversy being discussed.

### STUDENT CLARIFICATION QUESTIONNAIRE

*Directions:* Take a stand on the following statements. If you agree with the statement, write "agree"; if you disagree with the statement, write "disagree." As you are thinking about your response, weigh the following statements as they stand. Try not to get hung-up with conditional responses.* If this is impossible, and in some cases it may be, note the condition. These notes will be helpful in our discussion later.

_____   (1) The United States should give needy countries food.

_____   (2) Medical missionaries should not go to foreign countries.

* The term "conditional responses" might be confusing to the students. The teacher should explain what conditional responses are as, or directly after, the questionnaire is handed to the students. The teacher might say, "Try not to concentrate on all the varied circumstances in which a statement might occur. If you can, treat the statement in a general way. For example, in most instances how would you respond to the statement?"

(3) The United States should work through the United Nations or other institutions to provide birth control devices to other countries.

(4) The United States should provide birth control information and devices when they are requested by other countries.

(5) The United States should give aid to only those countries which first control their population.

(6) The United States should not concern itself with other countries.

(7) The population "explosion" is the result of poor, Third World countries unable to control their birth rate.

(8) People should be allowed to have as many children as they want, if they can afford them.

(9) A minimum wage limit should be set up for those people who wish to have children.

(10) Welfare mothers should be sterilized.

(11) If people, no matter how poor, want children, they should be allowed to have them.

(12) The United States should draw together experts to study the population problem. These experts should decide the optimum population figure and should have the power to enforce needed laws to insure this optimum population.

(13) The United States should work through the United Nations or other world organizations to draw together experts to decide an optimum population figure. These experts should have the power to enforce needed laws to insure this optimum population.

(14) The United States government should control and dispense all birth control devices and materials.

(15) A zero population growth can be achieved by the elimination of unwanted pregnancies.

(16) A married woman should be able to have an abortion without her husband's consent.

(17) Population control would cause the genocide of Blacks and other minorities.

(18) Women should have complete freedom with what happens to their bodies.

(19) Abortion should be permitted for married women but not for single women.

(20) No one dies from overpopulation.

Again, these are only sample statements that can be used. In our taped lesson, the students dealt with a single statement for an entire class period.

The clarification and the classification and comparison phases are in a sense parallel, as indicated on the paradigm on page 51, and should be interwoven if the students wish to discuss particular statements as they are asked. The class may respond more naturally if the flow of the discussion is allowed to move back and forth between the clarification and classification and comparison phases.

### Social Issues Model Phase IV— Classification and Comparison

In the classification and comparison phase of the model, students are asked to probe the underlying values in the material presented. This phase might contain a variety of activities. Normally the students are first asked to consider the basic values contained in the material. They are also asked to compare their own value statements with the value statements raised in the materials. The teacher also needs to ask students to consider other historical examples of social problems which contain some of the same underlying value questions. For example, during the first task—that of identifying the underlying values contained in the material—the class discussion with the population materials asks the students to probe the stated value positions and explore the implications of such positions. Some sample questions the teacher might ask include:

(1) What are some of the value conflicts which seem to be involved in the population control issue?

(2) How many sides are there to the controversy concerning population control? Are there more than two?

The discussion should ask students to speak specifically about the values inherent in the issue of population control. The teacher's goal is that the students extract the independent value questions that underlie the particular controversy that is being examined—in this case the particular values are those inherent to the discussion of population control.

Some values that could come from a class probing of the population control lesson are:

(1) Human freedom vs. the importance of social planning.

(2) Authority of society vs. the rights of the individual.

(3) Human survival vs. racial genocide.

(4) The question of raising children: money vs. choice.

During the second part of this phase, where the students are asked to compare their values with those contained in the material, the teacher might ask the students to refer back to their clarification questionnaire and see which of the values they have extracted from the materials are part of a position with which they agreed or disagreed.

During the last part of the classification and comparison phase, the teacher might ask questions which deal with other examples of similar value conflicts. For example, the student might be asked to list or discuss other conflicts of individual freedom and the authority of society. An example might be the banned Mormon practice of plural marriage.

The teacher might ask the following questions:

(1) What are some other examples of the stated value controversy?
(2) How do they compare or contrast with our example?
(3) Have similar questions been raised and resolved in the past? If so, how?

At this point in the model the students may decide they need additional material or resources to help them understand and possibly resolve the issues being discussed. The teacher might help the process by asking questions such as:

(1) Can our questions be supported or rejected by collecting factual evidence? Which ones? What evidence?
(2) What relevant data can be used to support, reject, or modify the stated position?

There is nothing sacred about this particular order of responding to the material. However, this breakdown of the classification and comparison phase should help the teacher understand some of the areas in which questions may need to be asked.

### Classification and Comparison Phase

Step One:    Probe the underlying values in the materials presented.

Step Two:    Compare the underlying values in the materials with student values.

Step Three: Discuss other examples of similar value conflicts.

### SAMPLE DIALOGUE OF A CLASSROOM
### IN THE CLASSIFICATION AND COMPARISON PHASE

*Teacher* (in response to a student's statement): So you think that sterilization is too permanent?

*Student:* I do not think that you are getting to the root of the problem when you sterilize people. Why not work on the incentives like the welfare loopholes? Let's get rid of those dumb incentives. There is something about the more illegitimate kids you have before getting married the more money you get. I know it is the truth because I have been studying case workers who visit, once a year, the mothers with illegitimate kids and they are getting welfare benefits.

*Teacher:* Do you think this is a question that we know enough factual information about or do we need to find more?*

*Student:* I think that we need to find more.

*Teacher:* How would we find this information?

*Student:* They all have case workers but I do not think this solution is working too well because the case workers are all overloaded. They cannot get around to as many people as they would like to.

*Student* (in response to another student): Isn't what you are saying is that because these people have more children than the number you think is right that they are now criminals in your book and do not have rights?

*Student:* No. You have to look at the reasons why these people are having more children. One, they do not know anything about contraceptives. However, I don't think that this is too common. Two, there are incentives in welfare checks. Three, they do not know how important it is to keep the number of children down. I think that you should work on the reasons these people are having these kids and not just plain sterilize them all.

*Student:* Look at all the magazines that totally deal with sex. Just get rid of these and that will help get rid of some of the problems.

*Student:* Oh, will it? Why don't we just get rid of everything and bring back the chastity belt. That should get rid of all the problems.

*Student:* If you tell someone that they cannot have kids that is just like taking away some of their unalienable rights first given to them by the Constitution. You just cannot tell people that they cannot have kids. You can offer them advice and show them having more kids would just bring more problems, but you just cannot pass a law and say people can only have this minimum amount. Having kids is a basic human right.

*Student:* He believes that human rights come before the rights of society; but, there is another side to the question. What about persons' responsibility to the rest of the world? If people show that they are not responsible, we have to take care of that problem too.

---

* The class may decide that it needs more detailed information concerning welfare payments. (The class in which this dialogue was recorded decided that it needed more than just hearsay evidence before the students could make an intelligent decision concerning this controversy.) If the class does not suggest the need for additional material, the teacher might make that suggestion. The teacher could bring in a chart indicating the amounts of payments to mothers, per child, on welfare. The teacher could remind the students of the previous discussion and ask questions such as:

"Yesterday in class we mentioned whether or not it pays to have more children when a mother is on welfare. Using the information on this chart, can we answer our question with more certainty?" The teacher could then proceed to use the chart as an additional piece of evidence to be analyzed by the class. Students should also be invited to submit other evidence.

*Teacher:* How can they tell if someone is handling the responsibility? Is it a question of money?*

*Student* (changes the subject): Greg says that he believes in human rights above all else. But, people have an obligation to society and to other people. Like having ten or fifteen kids is totally irresponsible all around. You're cheating yourself, you're cheating your children, and you're cheating the other people that you are crowding out of places. People have to be educated and told that certain things will happen if there is overpopulation and what they can do about these things.

*Student:* Is the point that you make them quit having children, or just give them the opportunity to stop having them?

*Student:* You can't force people to stop having children. They just need to be educated. I am not disagreeing with Greg; I am just saying that there is another side to the coin. We have to value human rights and their obligation to society.

*Teacher:* How do you get people to have responsibility to society?

*Student:* One way is to make laws.

*Teacher:* Are there other ways?

*Student:* A campaign like the Heart Fund or commercials on television. There have been campaigns that have worked in other countries. Bill told us about one that worked in Japan.

*Student:* I don't think that it is good at all to make laws. Sterilization and making laws are just too big a step. Look at who makes the laws in this country anyway. It is not the welfare mothers. It is generally the rich people. No wonder the minorities that we read about in the first article feel that people are out to get them.

*Teacher:* How do we enlighten people about birth control measures if they have some cultural or religious stigma against them?

*Student:* Look at religious sects like Christian Scientists. No matter what kind of logic you use they have already made this commitment to their religion. It would be very difficult to get them to take any sort of birth control devices.

*Teacher:* Would you say that Roman Catholics are in the same group?

*Student:* Possibly.

*Student:* Most Spanish families I know have lots of kids because they always have had. I know these migrant families who want more kids so they can get more money when they go North to work. The more people they have in the family, the better off they are.

*Teacher:* How do you appeal to people to have fewer children?

*Student:* Appeal to their emotions. A person has moral emotions, religious ties, and nationalistic emotions. If their religion says they should have lots of children and morally they feel like they can have children, then

---

* Other related questions which might be pursued by the teacher include: (1) Are all people fit to have children? (2) What does it mean to be a good parent?

you must appeal to their nationalistic emotions. You could say, "Look, the United States is too big as it is." You have to appeal to things that will move them. Appeal to the things that are not blocked by other various emotions.

*Student:* We have to show them that they are doing wrong.

*Teacher:* What does "wrong" mean? How do you decide if someone is doing "wrong" in this case?

*Student:* Well, I did not mean wrong. I just meant better in this case.

*Teacher:* Are we talking about a social question or a moral and ethical question? Should it be a social choice or an individual choice?

*Student:* At this point in time, it should be a social choice. Look, if you can't do it you can't do it. If you have all these people you can't feed, you can't support, and you can't do anything for, then you are just hurting them more to have more people. You have got to quit having people!

*Teacher:* Do you feel pressure, if you should marry, to limit the size of your family?

*Student:* I think that the pressure is reasonably strong. We have been educated to know that limiting the size of your family will be beneficial to everyone in the long run. It has sort of become an accepted policy in the United States. Education and not law is the best way to get people to limit their family size.

*Teacher:* Looking back over our class discussion, can we list some of the basic value conflicts that we have discussed?

As the class discussion continues, the teacher would help the students extract from the previous discussion the basic conflicts that they have talked about.

### Social Issues Model Phase V—Reflection

The reflection process underlies rational decision-making. After observing conflicts of values, discussing implications and effects, and identifying and examining values and how they affect the decision-making process, students need time to reflect upon how they have changed, if they have, their thinking and valuing.

Some questions that the students should be concerned with are:

(1) Have I changed my values? In what ways? Why?

(2) Have my values remained as they were? If so, why?

(3) Have I modified my values? In what ways? Why?

(4) Having made a decision about the issues involved, what are the implications of the decision? How do they affect me as an individual?

(5) What can I do about my decision?

(6) If I do act, what are the alternatives of my action?

The process of reflection might take several different forms. The students might be asked to respond to a written assignment dealing with some of the questions listed above, or the students might discuss some of the results of their thinking with the whole class or possibly in small groups.

### Social Issues Model Phase VI—Application

Making applications of knowledge gained from working through the Social Issues Model can move in a variety of directions. For example, a student might decide that having analyzed, clarified, classified and compared, and reflected upon his values he does not wish to apply his decisions concerning the controversy he has examined. He may have decided that there is no practical way in which he can apply his decisions. If the student has reached this decision after thoughtful reflection on the controversy, and he has decided that, in this case, he values non-involvement, this value decision should be respected by the teacher. The student should not be forced to adopt one of the teacher's values, if that teacher favored action.

Some questions a teacher might ask to help students in the reflective process are:

(1) Assume that you are in a position to solve most of the problems that we have discussed. Do you think that action should be undertaken? If so, by whom?
(2) In which of the cases would you say youth would have the hardest time affecting the social order? In which case would they have the least difficulty?

If the student decides that, concerning the particular controversy he has examined, he values involvement, the teacher can logically serve as a resource person to help the student decide the most fruitful way to apply his value decision. It is important to note, however, that the application process is not always essential to the student's working of the model.

### Evaluation

Evaluation is not an explicit phase of the Social Issues Model. However, no classroom dealing with controversial social issues should skip an evaluative process. When working with controversial social issues, it is important for teachers to think of evaluation from an expanded viewpoint.

If the teacher evaluates students by testing them on the content of their values after implying an open inquiry process, students will quickly, and correctly, assume that it is the same old game of looking for "right" answers only in a new way. If close-ended evaluation procedures are used after the first controversial social issues discussion, the teacher can feel reasonably sure that future discussions will not succeed.

If traditional evaluation tools are not effective, then what type of evaluation can and should be used? Since thoughtful decision-making is one of the goals of the Social Issues Model, student progress might be concerned with student ability to analyze, take a position, and logically evidence his or her position. The Michigan Social Issues Category System [1] provides a classroom observation scheme which allows the teacher to tape-record his or her class and then analyze types of evidence which are often offered to defend positions.

At the beginning of the semester, a student might offer reasons such as, "Just because that is what I believe," when questioned concerning his position. The same student may later begin to defend his position with an example of the consequences of taking a particular position. For example, when a student states that he believes in sterilization, he might say that the reason he believes it is "If we don't adopt sterilization practices, some people will continue to have children they cannot support." This doesn't mean that either the teacher or the other students accept the stated value position; however, it does mean that the individual students offer and accept reasons based upon their perceptions of the implications of their position. The teacher can then question the logic of the stated implications. Students may offer numerous "no public grounds" when controversial social issues are first discussed, but they should eventually gain more skill using other types of evidence.

The teacher can evaluate his own questioning skills as well as evaluate increased student ability to offer carefully considered evidence for value choices by using class recordings. If written evaluations are to be utilized, they need to be on the Evaluation Level of Bloom's Taxonomy.[2] The questions need to call for student judgment and defense. They should not contain single predetermined solutions. The clear emphasis should be on process, both during the lessons and during the evaluation, not on the acquisition of a specific product.


The Social Issues Model outlined in this section of the chapter does not provide all of the answers; however, it does provide a guide for teacher performance. Individual teachers should also remember that no model can substitute for their judgment. Adaptations and modifications can and should be used based on different types of students and classrooms.

### Social Issues Model
### An Elementary Example Phase I—
### Selection and Presentation

The selection and presentation of materials is not essentially different in the secondary and the elementary classrooms. Songs, poetry, literature, paintings, newspapers, periodicals, and quotations should be materials' sources in elementary as well as secondary classrooms. Care should be taken, as mentioned previously, that materials are fitted to the levels and the needs of the students.

Elementary pupils also need to be involved in the selection of materials to be studied in the school classroom. And, if ample opportunity is given by the teacher, the results of elementary students' selection of materials may be pleasantly surprising.

The following material can be given to elementary students with these instructions: *

*Directions:* Look at the three diagrams which show different types of societies. Check the one that you would like to live in. For the society you choose, circle an X or O showing that you would like to be a leader or a follower in that society.

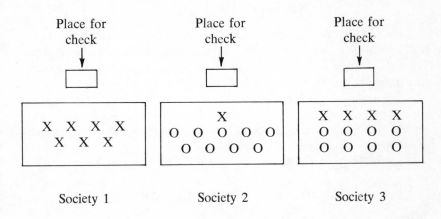

Key for all diagrams:  O = the people; X = the leader or leaders

---

\* These instructions should be read out loud, especially for younger students. This material has been used successfully from second grade through graduate school. Depending upon the class, the teacher might make use of the blackboard, overhead projector, or other devices to present this material. The teacher might also ask the students how they would react if forced to be either a leader or a follower in each of the societies.

## Phase II—Analysis

The following questions can be asked by the teacher to help the students interpret the content of the material presented. Like the Analysis Phase in the secondary classroom, the goal of the teacher is to separate the materials into discrete parts. The teacher, using this material, wants the student to discuss the similarities and the differences in the societies shown in the diagrams.

(1)  a. What is the first society like?
     b. How might people in this society live?
     c. How might the leaders in this society live?
     d. Is there a society or social organization in the world, that you know of, like the one in the diagram?

(Repeat the same set of questions for the second and third societies.)

These are sample teacher questions limited in design to analyze the content of the material. Again, however, if students choose to speak about their personal value judgments during the analysis phase, these questions and statements should not be dismissed or "put off" by the teacher.

## Phase III—Clarification

Like the Clarification Phase in the secondary classroom, the Clarification Phase in the elementary classroom is used to help the students understand their values about the issue being discussed. This exercise could also be conducted orally for younger groups who do not have the reading skills necessary to complete the questionnaire. The teacher should select the number of items which are appropriate for the needs of his or her classroom. Four or five of the statements might be sufficient for an early elementary classroom.

The following questions might be asked on a student questionnaire:

### STUDENT CLARIFICATION QUESTIONNAIRE

*Directions:* Write whether you agree or disagree with the following statements. If you agree with the statement, write "agree"; if you disagree with the statement, write "disagree."

_____  (1) Sometimes people should take orders from other people.

_____  (2) The main job of a leader is to give orders.

_____  (3) Some people are naturally leaders and some people are naturally followers.

_____  (4) Children should be seen and not heard.

_____  (5) All people should want to be leaders.

_____  (6) If a person is a leader, that means that he or she is smarter than a person who is not a leader.

_____  (7) A person who takes orders is not as smart as a person who gives orders.

_____  (8) People who are very poor would not make good leaders.

_____  (9) If an adult tells a young person what to do, that young person should do it.

_____  (10) When two people lead the same group, there will be trouble.

_____  (11) It is easier to be a leader than a follower.

_____  (12) Men are better leaders than women.

_____  (13) Women are better leaders than men.

_____  (14) White people make better leaders than Blacks.

_____  (15) Black people make better leaders than Whites.

_____  (16) A teacher should always be the leader in the classroom.

_____  (17) Leaders are better if they make strong rules and stick to them.

_____  (18) Leaders are better if they listen to the people whom they lead.

_____  (19) There are some definite rules that all people should follow no matter who they are.

## Phase IV—Classification and Comparison

The use of the classification and comparison phase in the elementary classroom is similar to the use of this phase in the secondary classroom. The goal of the teacher is to have the learners probe the underlying values in the materials presented. In this material, the students assess values inherent in the nature of leadership and authority. These values include the students' personal feelings about age, race, sex, etc. as these criteria pertain to the question of leadership.

In the discussion of the items on the *Student Clarification Questionnaire,* the students are asked to take a stand on the value statements, explain that posture in terms of their own experience, and compare that stand with the positions of other pupils and with outside sources.

During this discussion, the teacher should make a conscious effort to have learners examine how they arrive at their value decisions. Some possible questions include:

(1) How did you arrive at your decision(s)?

(2) Do you know whether your family would agree with you on your

answers to all of the statements? Some of the statements? Which ones? Why, or why not?

(3) Who do you think influences your decisions? Can you trace some influences to another person? Why do you think it is *that* person?

### Phases V and VI

The remainder of the phases of the model is essentially the same in both the elementary and the secondary classrooms. Examples of the uses of these phases can be found on pages 64 and 65 of this chapter.

## Some Models and Materials for Controversial Social Issues Education

This section of the chapter presents some of the models and materials commercially available to help the teacher who wants to include social issues in the classroom. Almost all of the models suggested can be used across grade levels; however, some of the actual lesson materials are designed for either secondary or elementary school classrooms. The elementary teacher could adapt the ideas behind some of the lessons to the skill level of his or her class. The secondary teacher might use the elementary strategies and think of alternative materials which could examine the same area of societal conflict at a more complex level. It is probably more helpful to think in terms of how one might use commercially prepared materials and adapt them to the needs and interests of one's class rather than whether they are labeled secondary or elementary. Of necessity, the teacher may not present material in exactly the same manner even to classes on the same academic level.

### Raths, Harmin, and Simon Approach

A value examination approach which can be utilized in social issues is outlined in the book *Values and Teaching* by Louis E. Raths, Merrill Harmin, and Sidney B. Simon. Raths, Harmin, and Simon start by asking how we have arrived at our values. They state that there has been no formal, procedural, or systematic method used by either the school or the family to help us arrive at a set of values. Values are not chosen through thoughtful examination of alternatives, they state. In their opinion, it is a false assumption that students will naturally arrive at a set of traditional values which they are conscious of and can use to make rational decisions.

The authors state that the schools, in the past, could hardly stand for a single set of traditional values. There were a number of "traditional" values and these "traditional" values were in controversy. Someone was for something, someone else was against it; and, to avoid controversy, schools chose to take no stand on any issue that might evoke controversy or conflict. Values were quietly abandoned as integral parts of the curriculum, and teachers concentrated on "teaching the facts." The implicit assumption was that the more facts students knew the more able they were to make "correct" decisions.

The authors state that many students are not aware of their values. The school is a place, they contend, where students should use a systematic procedure to discover what their values are and how strongly they hold them. The task of the teacher is essentially to help the student identify those things that he considers important and help him reflect on the reasons he values what he values. Ways to do this are to watch for everyday classroom clues to guide a meaningful values discussion and introduce special devices into the curriculum. They do not offer an instructional model for classroom use.

One such overt method they suggest is the "clarifying response." The clarifying response is made by a teacher to something a student says that encourages the student to think about the values involved in his actions. For example, if a student said to the teacher, "My older brother is coming for a visit," rather than responding by saying "Oh, that's nice," or "When will he be here?" the teacher wants to stimulate the clarifying thought of the student. He might say, "So your brother is coming, huh? Are you glad?" In responding, the student must consider what he values in this particular situation.

This type of procedure fits the sample lesson contained earlier in this chapter. The teacher might ask students to clarify responses they made to the population materials.

For example, students are discussing ways to lower the birth rate. One student argues that the problem is not only that there are too many children being born but also that there are too many children being born into families that can not financially afford them. One method to prevent overpopulation among the poor, he states, is by sterilization of welfare mothers.

Another student violently objects. This student points to several "what ifs." For example, "what if the family won a lottery or something and got rich?" or "what if a woman remarried a rich man?"

The teacher could say, "OK. Good point." This reaction would show that the answer has merit and has been accepted by the teacher. However, the response leaves the discussion stagnant.

Using a clarifying response, "So you think that sterilization is too permanent?" asked as a question, pushes the student to explore more deeply the reasons behind his statement. "What if" statements only have value in particular instances. The student may have stronger motives for making his statements. Using clarifying responses is a tactic to draw these deeper motives out into the open.

The teacher is not the only participant who can use clarifying responses. Students should learn to use this tactic to facilitate understanding of another student's statements. Often, the conflict of a controversy lies in the language used to explain it. Clarifying responses can uncover these language problems. Teachers should be sure, however, that they are willing to put their own responses to the test before they begin using clarifying responses as a tactic.

Another method suggested by Raths, Harmin, and Simon is called a "value sheet." A value sheet is a thought-provoking statement, account, or set of questions containing value implications for the student to consider and write about. For example:

## FRIENDSHIP

(1) What does friendship mean to you?
(2) If you have friends, did you choose them or did they get to be your friends by accident?
(3) In what ways do you show your friendship?
(4) How important do you think it is to develop and maintain friendships?
(5) If you plan to make any changes in your ways, please say what changes you will make. If you do not intend to make changes in your ways, write "No Changes." [3]

The teacher, using this method, must show the students that he or she is interested in what they believe and value. It is not the teacher's job to either praise or condemn the student for expressing particular beliefs. The teacher is to show, by his or her actions, that he or she wants the students to believe in something and to express their opinions about that belief.

The teacher adopts a non-judgmental position. It consists of (1) making the child aware that he or she is expressing values when he or she makes a value judgment, (2) reflecting that judgment back to the student so that the student can consider the meanings—both in thoughts and actions—of his or her statements, and (3) helping the student find ways to put his or her values into action.

The task of the teacher is not to direct the students to a predetermined conclusion by asking leading questions. Questions are asked to help the student see alternatives and arguments to his or her position. Clarifying questions are open-ended so the child can respond to the questions with a variety of alternatives.

### The California Social Sciences Education Framework

A second approach dealing with values and decision-making policies is the approach of the Social Sciences Education Framework for California Public Schools. In the California Framework, students are provided with a problem concerning what they should do in some specific case. They are led by the teacher, in a heuristic manner, to define the problem and list the values involved in the controversy. The teacher may help the student to clarify his values; but, the importance and priorities of the values must come from the students. In this approach, like the Raths, Harmin, and Simon approach, the students must be free to decide what values are of most importance. Never should the student be forced to accept one of the teacher's values.

The California Framework, more closely than some of the other approaches, offers a definite model for students to follow in making and evaluating a decision and the values involved. However, the steps are not discrete, and it may be difficult for students to decide when they have satisfactorily completed one of the steps.

The steps of the California Framework include:

(1) Define the problem.
(2) Identify the values involved.
    What values are going to be affected?
(3) Examine and define values.
    What, in clear terms, does each value mean? What are the priorities of the values?
(4) Identify relevant information.
    What are the facts in the controversy? What information do we need to know before we can give a solution?
(5) Generate trial solutions.
    What are the possible courses of action?
(6) Test solutions.
    Experiment, simulate the effects, or predict on the basis of known information what goods or harms each policy will do.
(7) Decide.
    Choose the solution which, according to the values priorities, seems most desirable.

For example, students decide that a controversial issue they should discuss is an incident where a White apartment owner refuses to rent to Blacks. First, according to the California Framework, the students should gather all possible information concerning that incident so that they can discover exactly what is happening.

Second, the students should reflect on those values that are going to be affected. For example, they might state that the person refusing to rent his apartment maintains that open occupancy violates his basic right to dispose of his private property as he sees fit. The person denied the apartment, the students might state, would maintain that he is being denied the basic rights of equal opportunity given by the American Creed.

Third, the students should decide in very clear and mutually understood terms what each of the values means to the participants in the controversy. Does it mean that the Black's health will be impaired? Or, does it mean that he will be harmed psychologically? Does it mean that the property or income of the White will be jeopardized? Whose rights are more important? For what reasons? Generally, the third step in the model is involved in looking at the particular conflict between the apartment owner and the person he refused to rent to.

Fourth, the students should synthesize the facts they gained analyzing this controversy and apply their decisions to general controversies of this nature. For example, what are some of the values which relate not just to this particular controversy but to all similar controversies? How, in general, are all apartment owners affected by this controversy? How are minorities affected by being denied equal opportunity? Are we sure that the information in the one controversy we analyzed is really representative of the general nature of the controversy? How do we know? If we don't know, how do we find out?

Fifth, the students should decide what possible solutions could be applied to the controversy on a local or national level. The students may decide that they have reservations about applying solutions or that there are implications of the problem that apply to some cases but not to all.

Sixth, the students test the solutions that they have generated against the knowledge that they have gained in the analysis of the controversy. What will the effects of the solutions be? Will they hurt one group of people more than another? Is this justified in the long run? Do the goods outweigh the harms? Can any harms be tolerated? Is it possible to give our solutions a realistic test? How? Do we need to test them?

Last, the students choose the solution to the controversy that, according to their values, seems to be the most desirable.

## Fraenkel Adapted Model

Another approach that offers a more structured model for student behavior is given by Jack R. Fraenkel in his book *Helping Students Think and Value*. Like the California Framework, Fraenkel accepts the basic Raths, Harmin, and Simon philosophy. Fraenkel believes that one of the most neglected areas of social studies education is value analysis and development. He states that it is extremely important and badly needed in the social studies curriculum.

As a result of this lack of value education, it is believed by Fraenkel that the American people are apathetic, unable or unwilling to speak out on issues of social concern. Young people are "bombarded" by a variety of conflicting value-claims leaving them uncertain about which ones to endorse. Since values underlie most human behavior and teachers cannot avoid implicitly teaching values anyway, the schools should consciously strive to help students learn to deal with value conflicts.

Fraenkel offers suggestions and models to identify values and explore value conflicts. One suggestion is a questioning technique in which the teacher asks the students to recall from a previous story, film, or real-life incident the behavior of an individual or group to explain why that behavior occurred as it did. Next, the students are asked to make inferences about the values of the individual(s) involved. They are then asked to hypothesize about their own behavior and values, and to make comparisons among the various values which have been identified and discussed.

The models offered by Fraenkel are adaptations of models developed as part of the Taba Curriculum Development Project at San Francisco State College.

Fraenkel suggests a procedure similar to the following for exploring value conflicts:

The student is given a reading or watches a movie in which individuals are faced with a choice between two or more conflicting alternatives. When this is completed, the teacher asks the class the following set of questions:

(1) What is this story about?
(2) What different things might the key individuals involved do (what alternatives are open to them)?
(3) What might happen to them if they do each of these things?
(4) What might happen to other people?
(5) What do you think each of them should do?
(6) Why?

After a sufficient amount of discussion about the values and the consequences involved in the story, the teacher helps the students consider their own behavior in similar situations. This is accomplished by asking the following set of questions:

(7) Has anything like that ever happened to you?
(8) What did you do?
(9) As you think back now, was it a good or a bad thing to do? Why?
(10) What else could you have done? [4]

The intent of the strategy is to show the student that there are a number of alternatives he or she can choose among rather than giving him or her the right "solution" to the problem. Fraenkel's assumption is that through realizing, discussing, and evaluating alternatives, students will become more aware of their own values, become more sensitive to the idea that all people hold values that at times conflict, realize that there are many different ways to deal with the same problem, and in the future be more willing to search for a variety of solutions rather than insisting on the first one that crosses their minds.

### Oliver and Shaver Jurisprudential Approach

The Oliver and Shaver Jurisprudential Approach is responsible for the Harvard Social Studies Project. In the Harvard Social Studies Project, Oliver and Shaver state that America is a pluralistic and diverse society in which there is a broad consensus on a number of basic values they call "The American Creed." Human dignity, freedom of speech, sanctity of private property, majority rule, the rights of the minority, etc., are examples of such basic values. They state that much of our history is a record of either conflicts between one of these general values and the specific value of a segment of our society or of conflicts between the priorities of the same value.

According to Oliver and Shaver, a controversial issue originates from the clash of two groups with divergent values or divergent value priorities. It is in the social studies curriculum where these controversies should be properly and systematically investigated. For example, in the American Education Publications' booklet *Science and Public Policy: Uses and Controls of Knowledge,* Oliver and Newmann use two short sections to discuss under what conditions, if any, certain scientific investigations and scientists should be censored in the public interest.

One section describes the trial of Galileo after he had alarmed the Church with his theories of the universe. Another section discusses an eccentric scientist with a bizarre theory. The students are asked to compare the two "stories." Questions concerning the stories are asked: "Would you support or oppose the action of the Church in prohibiting the publication of Galileo's book and force him to recant his beliefs?" "Would you support or oppose confining Hiram Lansing (the eccentric scientist) to a mental hospital?" "Justify your opinions."

Next, Oliver and Newmann give analogies and ask the students to relate these analogies to the issues being discussed. One such analogy is an article by Arthur Jensen in the *Harvard Educational Review* which presents evidence that Negroes on the average scored fifteen points lower than Whites on intelligence tests and that this difference is primarily hereditary or caused by a person's genetic makeup. The students are asked, "Do you think that Arthur Jensen should be discouraged from speaking out about his theory? If he insists upon making his views widely known, should a public agency be given the power to censor or penalize him?"

Oliver and Newmann then ask the students to discuss possible differences in the cases with similarities and differences of other situations in which a person's freedom is restricted to protect the welfare of society. Some other analogies they suggest are the sentencing of a convicted murderer to imprisonment for life, requiring youth to attend schools, disciplining a student for cheating, laws that prohibit the sale of obscene books, and quarantine rules that isolate diseased people.

By looking at such different situations in conflict throughout history, by viewing these situations in terms of concepts and theories, and by examining and evaluating various methods for reaching and justifying positions, students will gain certain powers of analysis that will aid them in discussing the value dilemmas on which public controversy thrives.

Primary to the strategies of the project is the jurisprudential approach to the conflict of equally tenable values. The authors disregard a traditional notion that controversy can be resolved by getting more and more factual information on the controversial topic. No matter how many facts one gets, they state, there are always basic value questions to be answered.

The method includes basically three steps: (1) the analysis of public controversy in terms of prescriptive, descriptive, and analytic issues; (2) the use of distinct strategies for justification and clarification of one's views of such issues; (3) systematic attention to discussion process as one deals with a controversial issue.

The authors ascribe to rational dialogue or collective inquiry on a variety of questions dealing with particular public issues. The process involves evaluating (matching facts or action against a given criterion) and making value judgments (deciding the criteria).

In this model the teacher uses a heuristic approach. He or she acts as catalyst, motivator, and discussion leader. He or she asks for clarification and substantiation of particular points; and, in general, he or she acts as a sort of analytical moderator for the discussion of the different points of view.

Oliver and Newmann state that one opinion or value is often as good as another. The criterion for evaluation rests on whether that opinion or value is based on sound and rational inquiry.

The material results of the Harvard Social Studies Project are the book *Teaching Public Issues in the High School* by Donald W. Oliver and James P. Shaver (Boston: Houghton Mifflin Company, 1966) and later 28 unit books by Fred M. Newmann and Donald W. Oliver.

The material content is designed for secondary classroom use; however, the model is applicable across grade levels. The 28 paper-covered unit books are on topics considered both public and controversial. Each booklet has a teachers' guide, specific strategies, and two objective tests. An overall guide to the materials, *Cases and Controversy,* is also available.

### Utah State—Analysis of Public Issues

Another approach that incorporates the philosophy that decisions should be made from consciously examined and freely held values is the Utah State University Project entitled *Analysis of Public Issues.* This project was co-directed by James P. Shaver and A. Guy Larkins. The Utah State University Project was influenced by the Harvard Social Studies Project and has many of the same methodologies. This material, like the Harvard Social Studies Project, is designed for the secondary classroom, but the model and teacher role are appropriate for all grade levels.

*Analysis of Public Issues* is based on the assumption that public issues are basically issues that involve questions of ethics—questions about rights and wrongs. The laws, policies, and social mores give indications to us of what we should support, but our response depends upon the values that we hold. The job of social studies curricula, the authors state, should be to help us clarify and analyze those values we hold as they relate to public issues.

Like the Harvard Social Studies Project, this program relies extensively on a Socratic dialogue between teacher/students or student/students. To utilize these materials successfully, Shaver and Larkins state, the teacher does not need extensive background in the disciplines. However, he or she does need practice in working with a heuristic approach in the classroom. Also included in the strategies are planned recitations, students' writing, seminar discussions of case studies, films, sound filmstrips, and simulation activities.

The program is focused on those enduring controversial issues rather than traditional topics. The materials create deliberate real-life situations of controversy and often purposely evoke strong feelings among the students. The students are then given the task of using concepts and critical thinking and applying them to the controversy. Some of the issues include the nature of decisions about public issues, inconsistency among beliefs, semantic problems, and ways to deal with value conflicts.

The student's progress is evaluated by his or her ability to apply the critical thinking concepts contained in the material to given situations. Case studies are full of incidents taken from daily societal events. Student involvement is mandatory. Cognitive information is used as supporting evidence of the concepts involved in the analysis of the controversy itself.

The materials include 32 bundles made up of audio tapes, filmstrips, transparencies, student booklets, and a text, *Decision-Making in a Democracy*. Each bundle has interludes in which case studies or suggested discussion topics can be included. The program is available from Houghton Mifflin Company, 110 Tremont Street, Boston, Massachusetts, 02107.

### Arnspiger, Brill, and Rucker Approach

This approach outlined by Arnspiger, Brill, and Rucker in *The Human Values Series* of textbooks is designed for elementary students. The philosophy of the series is based upon the goals of a democratic society and the school's needs in the shaping and sharing of human values. The authors list five basic points:

(1) The objective of school is realization of human worth in both theory and fact.
(2) The school which is oriented toward human dignity is one in which human values are widely shaped and shared.
(3) In such a school the formation of mature personalities whose value demands and capabilities are compatible with this ideal is essential.
(4) The long-range goal of the school is to provide opportunities for as many human beings as possible to achieve their highest potentials.
(5) The school must provide an environment in which the individual can seek human values for himself, with minimum damage to the freedom of choice and value assets of others.[5]

Arnspiger, Brill, and Rucker divide human values into eight categories of needs or wants which, they say, are of vital importance in all human activities. The eight categories are (1) respect, (2) power, (3) wealth, (4) enlightenment, (5) skill, (6) well-being, (7) rectitude, and (8) affection. (The authors give clear definitions of values and give some verbal equivalents.)

For example, in *Values To Live By,* Arnspiger, Brill, and Rucker have compiled several stories. Each story has (1) a synopsis and suggestions for introduction, (2) a word list for skill development and vocabulary enrichment, and (3) a coding of values inherent in each of the story's situations.

In one story a young boy, Dan, makes the mistake of teaming up with a group of delinquents who have committed serious offenses. One night the group assaults a young boy. Dan is picked up by the police and spends the weekend in Youth Hall, even though he protests that he hasn't done anything. Dan's father shows Dan the choices that he has and Dan thinks seriously about his predicament. In the end, Dan chooses to change his ways.

The authors state that *rectitude* is the value emphasized in the story. Dan, at first, values *respect* among his peers. This leads him to commit delinquent acts. The authors point out that the teacher can begin the discussion by telling the students that various choices are open to them when they face decisions about choosing their social companions. The teacher may then wish, the authors state, to guide the discussion toward the concept of being "popular."

In the value analysis at the end of the story, the authors discuss the alternative choices open to Dan and the values underlying each alternative. For example, the authors state "Dan gained new respect for the *power* of law enforcement officers for having been detained. . . . Dan finds that freedom to do what is anti-social in seeking *respect, affection, power,* and other values is temporary when the police place him in jail. Temporary freedom is replaced by a very severe deprivation of *power.* He also experiences very low statuses in *respect* and *well-being.* Time to reflect in the detention hall leads to increased *enlightenment.*" [6]

Using this approach, the teacher might assume a more heuristic approach than that suggested by the authors. By listing alternatives in the stories or having the students list alternatives in the story, the teacher could allow the students to draw their own conclusions based on the importance they give the respective values.

### Brandwein Value Examination

A second approach for elementary children is presented in the work of Paul F. Branwein, et al. in the textbook series *The Social Sciences: Concepts and Values.* Brandwein contends that the social studies curriculum is the place where decision-making concerning controversial social issues should be investigated. "Many of our adult citizens cannot read easily, but they do act, react, go to war, make peace, enter into contracts, vote, protest, communicate, and contribute to the man-made facts of the world." [7]

Material commonly taught in the social studies as cognitive information is in actuality often more concerned with the affective domain. The authors say that the statement "We hold these *truths* to be self-evident" really is stating "We hold these *values* to be self-evident." The overriding question that the social studies must concern itself with, the authors state, is basically "Where do I stand?" If the schools avoid teaching about values, they run the risk of leading students to believe that no values are worthwhile. Questions of public significance are questions concerning values, and, the authors state, the social studies is concerned first with questions of public significance.

In the strategy of this approach, the lessons are directed to concepts and concept formation. The activities of the students are given to value-seeking, value-defining, value-classifying, and value-application. The teacher's actions are involved in developing and setting the correct environment for the students' actions.

Brandwein's approach is essentially like some of the other approaches discussed. The student will:

(1) collect data;
(2) classify data;
(3) make inferences based upon the data;
(4) apply these inferences in situations where the student has to use his or her own judgment.

However, Brandwein states, once we have reached a value decision we are not at the end of our road. According to his model, clarifying or defining values is a circular path. As soon as a value is tested, we should apply it to a different situation and test it again. The student begins with a concept which is already part of his knowledge. The student isolates a problem or new situation that does not fit his concept. The student forms a working hypothesis to solve the problem by reading, discussion, speculation, observation, or seminar meetings. The student designs or redesigns an investigation to test the hypothesis. Then, the student begins with a new concept. He finds another situation or new problem that does not fit the concept. The student forms a new working hypothesis.

For example, in unit two in *The Social Sciences: Concepts and Values,* Brandwein deals with the concept of social behavior. The materials are included to help the student understand the main concept-statements:

(1) "Social systems are shaped by the values of interacting groups";
(2) "Social systems are made up of interacting groups"; and (3) "Socialization is carried out by interacting groups."

In looking at these concept-statements, Brandwein states that the student will extend his or her ability in:

- *Observing:* The child observes factors contributing to the development of cities; he also observes norms, roles, and values in the life of city-dwellers in Athens, Sparta, Rome, Koumbi, medieval towns, and modern industrial cities.

- *Comparing:* The child compares and contrasts different roles and levels of social class in cities of different periods.
- *Hypothesizing:* The child hypothesizes the need for social classes as a result of division of labor in cities.
- *Applying:* The child applies the idea of chronology to the history of early cities.
- *Inferring:* The child infers values from the development of roles and norms within society.
- *Generalizing:* The child generalizes about the interdependence of social classes and about the relationship of values to changes in work roles and social class in urban settings.
- *Analyzing:* The child analyzes the effect of city life on people of the middle class.
- *Predicting:* The child predicts the effects of world power on the people of Rome, predicts the need for urban centers in highly specialized economic systems, and predicts the effects of poverty and slum areas on the life of city-dwellers.
- *Classifying:* The child classifies behaviors as answering to the roles and norms of a social system.[8]

Evaluation of the student's progress is done by testing for evidence that a student either reinforced his original value or discarded his original value and adopted a sounder one. In the Unit Evaluation for the concept "social behavior," the authors ask the students to establish a new city on another planet or another place on Earth and then ask the students questions about this city. Questions include: "What sort of a location would you choose?" "Why?" "Whom would you want there?" "Why?" "Would there be any population limits?" "Why?" "What form of city government would you have?" "Why?"

All of the models and approaches discussed offer some guidance and direction for the classroom teacher searching for the skills and materials to present controversial social issues in the classroom.

### Summary

Research indicates that relatively few classroom teachers are currently involved in the systematic classroom discussion of controversial issues.[9] The demand for relevance is hardly debatable. The challenge is imperative. How can we afford not to provide the opportunity for our students to be actively involved in the examination of social controversy in the classroom when they will clearly be faced with such conflicts in real life? The preparation for tomorrow is today.

## FOOTNOTES

[1] Byron G. Massialas, Nancy Sprague, and Jo A. Sweeney, "Identification of Social Issues Teachers," conducted as part of a research study pursuant to contract OEC 3-7-061678-2942 with the United States Department of Health, Education, and Welfare, Office of Education. "Structure and Process of Inquiry into Social Issues in the Secondary Classrooms," p. 101.

[2] Benjamin S. Bloom, ed., *Taxonomy of Educational Objectives: The Classification of Educational Goals, Handbook I: Cognitive Domain* (New York: Longman, Green and Co., 1956).

[3] Louis E. Raths, Merrill Harmin, and Sidney B. Simon, *Values and Teaching* (Columbus: Charles E. Merrill Publishing Co., 1966), p. 95. For information about current Values Clarification materials or nationwide training workshops, write AMHEC (Adirondack Mt. Humanistic Education Center), Upper Jay, New York 12987.

[4] Jack R. Fraenkel, *Helping Students Think and Value: Strategies for Teaching the Social Studies* (Englewood Cliffs: Prentice-Hall, Inc., 1973), p. 244.

[5] V. Clyde Arnspiger, James A. Brill, and W. Rucker, *Thinking with Values* [Teacher's Edition] (Austin: Steck-Vaughn Company, 1973), p. 1.

[6] Arnspiger, Brill, and Rucker, *op. cit.,* pp. 87-88.

[7] Paul F. Brandwein, et al., *Principles and Practices in the Teaching of the Social Sciences: Concepts and Values* (New York: Harcourt Brace Jovanovich, Inc., 1970), p. T-36.

[8] Brandwein, et al., *op. cit.,* p. 54.

[9] Massialas, Sprague, and Sweeney, *op. cit.,* pp. 30, 33.

# PART TWO

*Examples*

*of*

*Specific Areas*

*of*

*Controversy*

# 3

# Should Traditional Sex Modes and Values Be Changed?

John F. Cuber, Martha Tyler John, and
Kenrick S. Thompson

## Introduction

THE SEGMENT of human experience with which this chapter is concerned embraces a variety of controversial issues in contemporary society which relate to sex, sexism, and differential intimate life cycles. There is a pronounced tendency to approach this diversity piecemeal, as if, say, women's liberation, consensual unions, and the push for abortion reform were totally separate. To be sure, they surface separately; a legislature can hardly consider abortion reform, consensual unions, and equal rights for women simultaneously. Viewing the matter more analytically, however, it is not difficult to comprehend a number of commonalities among them. It will be part of the thrust of this chapter to point out the interconnectedness of seemingly separate issues and the historical convergence of the thoughtways which support them and the thoughtways which challenge them.

There is probably no more ultra-controversial segment of American society than the one which we are undertaking to analyze here. Many if not most other controversial issues are of such a nature that the time-

*JOHN F. CUBER is Professor Emeritus, Department of Sociology, The Ohio State University, Columbus, Ohio.*
*MARTHA TYLER JOHN is Associate Professor, Bowie State College, Bowie, Maryland.*
*KENRICK S. THOMPSON is Assistant Professor, Department of Sociology, Northern Michigan University, Marquette, Michigan.*

honored expedient of compromise can bring the adversaries, if not to a final resolution of the issue, at least to the point of rational dialogue. But in this domain we tend to be dealing, at least for the traditionalists, with what are called "eternal verities." Not only are "principles" couched mostly in absolute terms, but the assumption, if not the outright assertion, is made that in addition to being absolute, they are inherent in the nature of things—that is, proper things. Thus, for example, if abortion is construed as "murder," then it cannot be condoned for anyone or for any conditions.

There is a peculiar trans-rationality which enters into the dialogue at almost every turn, despite the fact that in a number of instances the issues have been thoroughly investigated by sophisticated methods and respected researchers. The results are often cavalierly dismissed because the findings are offensive to precious prejudices. Numerous careful studies have accumulated, for example, to demonstrate that the presumed deleterious effects of divorce on children do not as a rule exist,[1] that women's employment outside the home does not have harmful effects upon the personalities of children,[2] and probably, even more shocking to many, that the effects of children upon the relationships between husband and wife are essentially negative.[3] It does little good to point out that the research findings in these respects are conclusive—it is almost as if the studies are too threatful to be trusted. This is the intellectual-emotional climate within which most "thinking" and reasoning in this area are couched.

## A Model for Understanding Controversy

A very useful model for analyzing controversial issues was formulated about thirty-five years ago by Richard C. Fuller, a sociologist at the University of Michigan.[4] It is noteworthy that the model was fashioned not as an academic model for analyzing social problems but was formulated as a *pedagogical device* for *teaching* about social problems at the college level. The model has proved, however, to be almost equally useful for societal *analysis*[5] as for the instruction of students concerning the processes by which problems emerge and are either resolved, ameliorated, or remain untouched.

*Values.* The key concept in the Fuller model is "values," fundamental beliefs concerning right and wrong, and especially the relative worth, of things. Some things are more important than others, therefore they will be pursued more vigorously, or even riskfully, if necessary. Many, if not most, of these values are *extra-rational*. We can usually verbalize them, but not always, and the verbalizations are heavily overhung, or perhaps undergirded, by deep emotional feelings.

*Diversity of Values.* No one needs to be told, moreover, that at least in societies like ours, there is a *diversity* of value positions. Thus, almost every concern becomes controversial, because the values of the interested parties clash at fundamental points. Sometimes we know what our values are and we can articulate them freely; at other times they are so unconscious that we are disturbed when our real values are exposed. This is notably true and frequently demonstrated in the cases of racism and sexism. Many a latter-day liberal who has conscientiously worked to "help blacks" and to "free" women from traditional bondage is drawn up short when it is pointed out to him, or when he realizes himself, that in his very attention to the problem, he has manifested a double standard, his versus that of the less fortunate who "needs" him. At the nub of almost every legislative hassle, professional confrontation, parent-child encounter, or man-woman issue are these value conflicts. The clash may be violent as in some interpersonal violence in a family or at the other extreme may be rather genteel, calm, and characterized by good will and an honest groping for solutions. It is obvious, of course, that the more deeply values are held and the less conscious the individual is of what his values are, the more inevitable it is that the tendency for encounter will escalate into confrontation or worse.

*Levels of Value Clash.* Fuller pointed out that the clash of values occurs on at least three separable levels: (1) At the first level, the clash of values centers around whether or not a problem exists. If the poor we shall always have with us, then poverty may not be a problem—just a fact of life. Since, however, people have other values too, the controversy at the first level really amounts to a determination of whether a condition is a "problem." The problem is not inherent in the condition; it springs from an effort to challenge the condition. (2) Assuming that the result of the controversy is a recognition that a problem exists, the attention then shifts to whether or not anything can be done about it. Thus, for example, if there has always been a "generation gap" but present adults have somehow outgrown it, then there is little reason to be concerned about current difficulties in communication and control between parents and children, schools and students, churches and their "young people." But if, as many people think, there is something new or different in contemporary society, then perhaps new approaches, new programs are called for. In a post-industrial society, even five years may bring a "generation gap," because of the sweeping nature and number of important changes. (3) If the problem is considered by consensus to be remediable, or even only ameliorable, we then move to the third step in the process. Almost inevitably a variety of proposals for the solution of the problem is put forth. For example, we currently have a frighteningly and devastatingly high incidence of venereal disease among teenagers—around 300,000 new cases each year in the United States,[6] and the rate appears to be accelerating. Few will deny that this is a problem or that "something should be done about it." But what? Should the schools and other agencies of society expose young people to horror movies on the subject? Or should efforts be made to reduce the sexual expression of young people? Or should they be induced to use medical services? Others insist that it is still the parents' responsibility to educate and, when necessary, to secure medical attention. Another position, however, is that teenagers are old enough to handle this matter themselves and should have free access not only to honest information but should be free to present themselves for medical treatment on their own volition, possibly without their parents' knowledge. But is this an invasion of the "rights" of parents? Are we more concerned with perpetuating "rights" (which many parents don't use) at the risk of seriously jeopardizing the health of thousands of young people? And so the controversy rages.

At the college level of instruction at least, many teachers have found the Fuller model to be pedagogically exceedingly useful, for one important reason at least: the student is able to combine his classroom experience with the real world outside. Any newspaper, newscast, or for that matter private conversation among his associates is almost inevitably a prototype of the Fuller model. The issues center around (a) whether or not there is a problem, (b) whether anything can be done about it, and (c) if so, what among the alternatives is to be preferred. Students are quick to distinguish these levels and in so doing clarify their own thinking as to what is going on in the controversial process and come to see the underlying dynamics of social change in a systematic way.

## Origins of the Issues

A necessary enlightenment for comprehending any controversial area is derived from giving attention to history. This means an honest, that is, not sentimentalized, look at the earlier order. This look must be at one and the same time sympathetic but not nostalgic, objective but yet empathic. Such a view reveals that, unlike the controversies of today, there was, say 75 years ago, a very high degree of consensus about the proper modes of conduct for men and women. The agreements weren't quite unanimous; hence we use the word *consensus*. The proscriptions for proper conduct were found in the teachings and pronouncements of the Church, the laws of the land, and perhaps most importantly in the informal opinions, enforcements, and assumptions of a "public opinion" on the subject. There was a remarkable convergence among these with the result that enforcement was relatively uniform and quite effective in molding a uniform character type.

## The Monolithic Code [7]

The tenets of the preceding order have been referred to as a *monolithic code* for men and women, parents and children. "Monolithic" is used advisedly. The code was universalistic. It did not maintain that marriage might be good for some people, consensual unions for others, and so forth. Marriage was *for all* adults, and while it was recognized that there might be a few spinsters and bachelors, every effort was made to admonish, coerce, or otherwise get them into the marriage mold. There were several basic tenets of this monolithic code:

(1) The correct adult mode of life was marriage.
(2) Marriages were "for keeps." (While divorce was theoretically possible, it was rare and severely disapproved.)
(3) Sexual conduct was to be limited to the married state. While it was recognized that "the flesh was weak," especially among the young, the weakness could readily be atoned for by getting married at the earliest possible time.
(4) Marriages should be fruitful. Children were not so much a privilege as an obligation, and the more of them the better.
(5) Parents should be responsible to their children at whatever cost and children should be obedient to their parents with a minimum of questioning and certainly no open challenge.
(6) Women's place was in the home. Again, it was reluctantly granted that under certain circumstances, such as the husband's illness or death, a woman might have to work, but the idea that she worked for self-expression or to embellish the family standard of living was almost unthinkable.
(7) There was a sharp division of labor between men and women in the home and out, and the power to make and enforce decisions rested primarily, if not exclusively, with the husband.

Here, then, was a totally sexist ideology. The lines between male and female were sharp and there was no equivocation. It was also, as we have said, universal, no recognition being made in the law or anywhere else that alternatives might be appropriate; in fact, they were most likely to be considered *in*appropriate, subject to much pressure to conform, and punishment and ridicule directed toward transgressors.

As everyone knows, the monolithic code, nestled in history, is in the eyes of many contemporaries archaic—or worse. Among rank and file Americans many of the tenets of the code are still held, at least for public consumption, but there are large and growing numbers who speak out against one or another aspect of the code, sometimes challenging it openly and at other times working vigorously for its reform or even abolition.

### Process of Challenge to the Monolithic Order

Why the reversal? The answer is complicated, but the process of change has, in a theoretical sense, really been quite orderly. Regardless of what particular aspect of change is under consideration, there appear to be at least three separable stages in the emancipation of persons in our society from the monolithic code.

(1) Stage one was probably there all along. Violations of the monolithic code have always occurred and were well documented in literature. Hestor wore her scarlet letter; Jane Eyre found her fulfillment with Mr. Rochester; and the long line of more explicit deviations occurred in the lives of ordinary people from hamlet to metro city. But these were *violations* of a code which was not seriously challenged as such. The code itself was, and still for many remains, essentially accepted, and even the deviants taught and still teach it to their children. As Kinsey reported 25 years ago, half of the married men and one fourth of the married women had been unfaithful to their spouses.[8] Yet practically no one, except perhaps a Bertrand Russell here and there, seriously and openly challenged the all-sufficiency of the fidelity aspect of the code.

(2) As deviations increased and became more widely known, a second stage set in. This is the stage which Robin Williams aptly called "the norms of evasion." [9] As violators of the code became more numerous and more or less openly acknowledged what they were doing and felt less and less guilty about it, a new, tacit code emerged: "We are not alone; there are many like us" became common rationalization. There is no longer the feeling of isolation from society, only a kind of cautious discretion about concealment, except for compatriots, of what one really thinks and does.

(3) Ultimately stage three took shape, a stage where American society now finds itself. This is the stage where the code itself is challenged, where in some cases open defiance occurs and where there are organized efforts to challenge one or another aspect of the code, by seeking legislative reform, Church reform, or direct appeal to a more tolerant public opinion. We see this in efforts in most states to secure liberalization of abortion laws, pressures by students upon college administrators to permit coeducational housing, and, of course, the women's liberation movement. Stage three really consists of two somewhat different mentalities, however; one is revolutionary; its main thrust is defiance of law and formal regulations, like the Catholic parents of a teenage daughter who "put her on the pill" because they realize that the code of premarital chastity is now essentially passé. They want to protect her from pregnancy, even though they know that both they and she are violating an inviolate code of the Church and also, for that matter, of the law in many states. The other thrust in stage three is also revolutionary but less

belligerent. It is manifest by people in various walks of life who openly work for change in the system, to the end that forcible adherence to the monolithic code may be terminated or at least modified. This is illustrated, for example, by prominent clergymen who appear before legislative committees considering abortion reform and call openly before television cameras for a virtual abolition of abortion controls. They do this, as anyone must know, at personal and professional risk, because there is a large and powerful segment of society which is not in tune with efforts of this sort. Another case in point involves university administrations, of which there are now many, which adopt a co-ed dormitory code permitting students who are not married complete freedom in living arrangements. Such decisions, being public, are fraught with risks, because there are substantial and sometimes powerful segments of the community definitely opposed to such alterations of the monolithic code.

## An Overview of the Crumbling Code

No aspect of the monolithic code as we have described it above is free of this kind of challenge:

(1) Growing numbers of responsible people at almost all ages now openly challenge the tenet that the appropriate life style for all adults is marriage.[10] From the consensual unions of students in the campus dormitories to the senior citizens' communities there is well known, widespread, and open rejection of the traditional admonition.

(2) Divorce, moreover, is neither rare, nor any longer a serious threat to one's social position when it occurs. Study after study has documented the fact that, despite a legacy of horror stories, divorcées typically quickly adjust to their new status, usually remarrying but suffering very little if any disprivilege, and making their way on the whole about as well as anyone else.[11]

(3) It is no longer possible to overlook the fact that both before and after marriage there is widespread sexual expression outside of matrimony.[12] Some forms of innovation, such as, for example, the "swinging scene," are widely known, given publicity in mass media and seemingly producing little shock in most circles. Careful studies show that premarital chastity is honored more in the breach than in the observance [13] and these facts appear to be little affected by class, religion, or region of residence.

(4) With good contraceptive technology now widely available, substantial numbers, particularly of young couples, are openly taking the position that they intend to produce no children.[14] Many of them virtually reverse the traditional axiom. Not only do they not accept the obligation to have children; they speak openly of a higher morality,

namely not to contribute to overpopulation. Others simply acknowledge that being the kind of people they are and following the kinds of life styles they prefer, children are simply contraindicated.

(5) The older forms of unquestioned authority of parents are challenged to the point of being scoffed at, not only by most children themselves but also by an articulate and forceful professional phalanx. Permissiveness in varying degree and for varying reasons has become the order of the day. Parents are admonished to allow and even to encourage children to participate in family decisions; schools set up mechanisms for the participation of children in more and more important decisions; and in various and sundry other ways there is tacit recognition that adults are no longer totally powerful or omniscient in their judgments.

(6) An ever-growing proportion of married women are now in the labor force,[15] even while their children are very young, using various kinds of parent surrogates to provide for the physical and psychological care of their children. What is particularly significant here is that these are not "hardship cases" for the most part, but rather are simple recognitions of the legitimacy of out-of-the-home employment for married women with children.

(7) The whole thrust of unisex has for many millions of Americans virtually eliminated, or at least severely compromised, the division of labor and differential power between the sexes. Increasingly, men and women not only dress more nearly alike, follow life styles more nearly alike, but also share more nearly equally in the decision-making processes which are essential to family living.

## A Bifurcated Sexual World

Enumerating innovations in the way we just have may lead to a serious misunderstanding. Each of these changes affects differing proportions of the population and in differing degree. Certainly not everyone lives or has lived in a consensual union; not all children challenge or are encouraged to challenge parental authority; not all women are employed outside the home; and not all persons at any age are seriously affected by the unisex trend. Statistics in these matters, while revealing, do not tell the whole story either. What is needed is some kind of a theoretical systematization of what is taking place, for whom, and to what extent.

### The "Straight World"

Despite the ubiquity of deviance from the monolithic code, a large proportion, probably a majority, of American people of all ages are not much affected either in ideology or in practice by most of the innovations with which we are here concerned, and which receive so great a play in academic and public discussions. This is the "straight world," not deviating very much from the older monolithic code as spelled out above. The good life for adults is marriage; children are taken for granted; parents are responsible to them; wives stay home and rear children; if a marriage is not totally satisfying, it is maintained anyway "for the sake of the children" and various and sundry other conventional reasons. A relatively clear division of labor between the sexes is observed and rationalized. And so on.

It would probably not be accurate to say that the straight world has not been at least somewhat affected by changes in the last half century, but at the same time, as one observes or speaks with the essentially silent majority, its men and women say about the same things and enact about the same drama as their grandparents did. To be sure, they have their difficulties, notably with a less than acquiescent child population. And women, even though they "stay at home," seem less and less sure that this is really the good life. Even though divorce is still a minority experience, it is not as unthinkable as it once was. And even though a clear sexual division of labor is still observed, there is a pervasive uneasiness among both sexes who more and more question whether it is the right way to get the family's business done. Nevertheless, the straight world is still conspicuously with us not only in actuality but even more strongly in ideology, and it is well to remember that the legal structure regulating sex and marriage has changed very, very little in the last fifty years. A few variations have occurred on the fringes such as somewhat liberalized grounds for divorce, and, should the equal rights amendment become a part of the Constitution, a changed legal substructure regarding the two sexes. Even if, however, the equal rights amendment should pass, it is the hard lesson of history that it takes a long, long time for the legal change to alter the ideology and life style of many if not most members of a society. (It is, for example, over 100 years since Blacks have been given "equal rights" by the Constitution and the struggle to get them is only just beginning.) Thus it appears likely that the ideological turmoil centering around sex and sexism in our time will not dramatically affect the millions in the straight world for a considerable time to come.

## The "Dropout Worlds"

The other branch of the bifurcation is, of course, more conspicuous and more dramatic. Parts of the counter thrust are well organized, highly visible and aggressive. Women's liberation is a case in point. In one way or another the society is daily reminded of the inequities between men and women in almost every respect; litigation to rectify these inequities goes on everywhere, and no reasonably intelligent person can escape the hard facts of surging redefinition.

Gay liberation, while not so well organized and certainly involving fewer people, has many of the same characteristics,[16] however—oppressed people refusing to accept inferior status and demanding not special privilege but equal rights in a society which prides itself, even if more self-righteously than accurately, upon its egalitarianism.

If we may speak of the straight world, then, we can also speak, we think, of "dropout worlds." The word "dropout" is used advisedly and in much the same sense as we refer to school dropouts. These are people who either do not accept the conventional way of organizing their lives or, having tried it, are unable to so continue. They drop out of the mainstream of society. Like the school dropout these are numerous, often well publicized forms of rejection of the straight world. None of these patterns involves a majority of people. The essence of the dropout mentality is a rejection of the rationale which justifies the straight world. Sometimes the rejection grows out of the recognition that the promise of reward for proper living simply is not realized. Couples who lead exemplary lives as models to guide their children have on average about as much difficulty as those who put forth less effort. Men and women who conduct themselves honorably according to societal codes are far from immune to the risk of divorce. Love is not enough to protect a spouse from "growing away" from a mate or from being "grown away from." Family discord, unconscious as well as conscious resentments, and vague discontents accumulate and drive wedges between mates and between parents and children which take an enormous toll of mental and even physical ill health and often result in outbreaks of tragic violence.[17] Far more murders occur among family members than on the streets!

In other instances, people drop out more or less deliberately because they are unable to meet the requirements of the straight world. The package of chastity-monogamy-fidelity in a hedonistic and sex conscious society is simply beyond the capacities of substantial numbers of people. They are faced with the hard choice of cheating on the system with consequent psychological problems of guilt and fear of exposure, or with a more forthright rejection of the tradition which amounts really to an acceptance of a non-monogamous and possibly even non-married morality. These, too, have dropped out of the straight world.

A catalog of dropout patterns or, as some interpreters prefer to call it, "alternative life styles" [18] has familiar components: consensual unions whether among college students, people in their middle years, or senior citizens, communal life styles whether or not one wishes to use the word "family" with respect to them, extramarital innovations such as swinging as well as other less formally organized escapes from traditional monogamous expectations, intentionally childless marriages, "open marriages"—all these are conspicuous as well as dramatic reminders of how far we have come in a relatively short time.

## Value Premises of Alternative Life Styles

It may be instructive, even if somewhat obvious, to consider the value premises of some of the alternate life styles which are now becoming prominent on the American scene.

### Consensual Unions

Consensual unions are justified by participants in them by several pragmatic as well as ideological considerations. With the high incidence of divorce and an even higher incidence of psychologically unfulfilled marriages which endure anyway, the logic for the consensual union is impelling to many. Sometimes a consensual union is simply a trial period to test whether or not a particular pairing has enough viability to warrant marriage. In other instances no marriage is anticipated, at least not with the current partner. Rationales vary but one way or another they come down to a rejection of lifelong monogamy as a desirable or as a practicable life style. There is, of course, the divorce way out, but even at best, it is embarrassing, expensive, and sometimes exceedingly humiliating. If a consensual union doesn't work out, there may, of course, also be psychological hurt, financial problems, and various awkwardnesses, but it is still a far less demoralizing form of disengagement.

### "Open Marriages" [19]

The rationale for "open marriage" is quite similar to that for the consensual union. Growing numbers of people find monogamous lifelong marriage with clear sex role differentiations simply too repressive. The insidious tendency in conventional marriage to regard and treat spouses as if one owns them is to many contemporaries simply an intolerable indignity and not workable anyway. Substantial numbers of people, especially among the young, moreover, are ill-adjusted to monogamy, yet they do form and wish to maintain a relatively permanent and primary relationship with one person but not to the exclusion of other intimate relationships over long-term or short-term periods. The openness is not entirely a narrowly sexual focus. It may involve any degree of intimacy from a more or less platonic friendship to actual co-habitation.

### *"Swinging"* [20]

The "swinging scene" is perhaps the most formally organized modification of monogamy. While customs vary from one part of the country to another and even within a given city, the common elements seem to be these: at stipulated times married couples meet for what is superficially like any other party, except that it is understood that each spouse has sexual access during the party to others than his or her spouse. Precautions are typically taken to keep the relationships fluid, that is, to change partners frequently and particularly to discourage the development of intense emotional ties, since these could easily be disruptive of the marriages, which swingers try to maintain on an enduring basis. One leading student of the swinging scene [21] has advanced the ingenious interpretation that swingers are really conservatives where marriage is concerned. They typically have children and relatively prominent social positions and out of a sense of responsibility to children and society they seek to maintain their marriages and at the same time enjoy the satisfactions of sexual variety. Since the swingers' sexual activity is by mutual consent and takes place chiefly within the direct view of the spouse, it is reasoned that it is not really infidelity. Not only is there mutual consent, but no deception is involved, and precautions are taken to minimize the possibility of emotional involvements which might jeopardize the marriage.

### *Communes* [22]

The communal life style also challenges the conventional exclusivity of traditional marriage. The living unit consists of several males and females often of considerable age spread, and the expectation, although there is no necessary obligation to this effect, is that sexual access is free. Children are considered to be members of the entire commune, are fed and guided by the collective effort. They are not regarded as the responsibility solely of their biological parents. Even identification of paternity is avoided. Property tends to be held communally; membership in the commune is somewhat fluid; members leave and are added from time to time. Although there are considerable variations from commune to commune, the clear tendency is to reject sharp sex role differentiation.

### *Co-Marital Sex* [23]

While this philosophy and practice overlaps in some ways with both consensual unions and open marriage, it is a somewhat distinct phenomenon. It refers to the legitimacy of extramarital relationships, from the platonic to the predominantly sexual, for married people who are essentially satisfied with their marriages, do not intend to terminate them, but who wish at the same time to have additional intimate relationships. The incidence of co-marital sex is far higher than casual observers realize, partly because of the large amount of anonymity which urban living permits and partly because there is direct concealment, because public knowledge of such relationships can in various ways be embarrassing. Sometimes co-marital sex is clandestine, but increasingly it is by mutual consent of the spouses, whether one or both actually participates. There is a popular supposition that relationships of this type are destructive of marriages, and sometimes they are, but there is mounting popular and professional opinion which supports their practicality and moral legitimacy. Again, it is another form of the widespread disenchantment with the enduring monogamous tenet of the monolithic code, and while manifestly different from swinging, or communes, or consensual unions, it has in common with them an effort to cope with the unwillingness and inability to live with the code.

### Childless Marriage [24]

Intentionally childless marriages constitute another growing life style. Motivations vary. One thread is ecological. There are simply too many people; why add to everyone's woes by producing more? Prominent also in the rationale for childless marriage is the candid recognition on the part of many people that they are not good parent material for any of a number of personality reasons. In other instances children are considered inimical to the occupational and recreational life styles which many urban people opt to follow.

### Subcontracting Parenthood

There is a growing reliance, even among couples in the straight world, upon parent surrogates of numerous kinds. Practically every community has child care centers available. In most communities these provide child care from 6 A.M. to 6 P.M. or even longer. The usual rationale is, of course, that this enables the mother to work outside the home, but not all women who utilize such services are employed and rarely do they work a twelve hour day! To put the matter bluntly, for substantial numbers of people who can afford it, there is a growing tendency to subcontract as much parental activity and responsibility as they can. There is a pronounced and growing public opinion to the general effect that child care centers are better in some respects than home care, since they are operated by persons of at least some professional status. Moreover, the only-child or two-child family thus gets exposed to other children, which is judged to be a positive factor in personality development.

### Abortion Reform

There is a strong thrust in the direction of radical revision of laws against abortion. Pressures are brought upon almost every session of every legislature to move in the direction of making abortion available at least in the early months to any woman who wants it. Few states have gone the whole way in meeting these pressures but here again is a clear tendency in the direction of liberalization of the older laws. The supporting rationales are more or less familiar—unwanted children are disruptive of families and tend to inherit influences which are psychologically harmful to themselves. Abortion is, after all, essentially an extension of the contraceptive idea, being made necessary only because of a contraceptive failure. Then, too, there are the "special cases," such as abortions after rape, serious health problems of the woman, non-compatible blood types of the potential parents, to mention only a few. The opposing rationale is well known too. Abortion is considered by many to be murder. Since a pre-natal organism has come into being, to terminate its life amounts to pre-natal euthanasia. Very general among our thoughtways is a sort of middle position; abortion is justified in the early stages of pregnancy, before "quickening," but in the latter stages is denied. This appears to be rather generally held by the medical profession, most doctors simply refusing to perform an abortion after the third or fourth month of pregnancy. There is probably no aspect of liberal sexuality more controversial than the abortion question. The very concept breaks not merely with law but with very deep emotional commitments to the sanctity of human life, even in the pre-natal stage. The intrusion of practical considerations into a decision whether or not to terminate the life of a fetus is, to many, simply incomprehensible and never justified.

### Unisex

Less easy to pinpoint may be the most revolutionary trend of all—the clear trend toward elimination of sex role differences. This is manifest in innumerable ways—the effort to eliminate employment differentials, the complete sharing of household and child care duties between the sexes, sharing of all recreational activities and, of course, the unisex trend in dress, speech habits, and etiquette. These changes have come unequally by region, class, and probably personal idiosyncracy, but there is no denying that this "liberation," as it tends to be called, is a growing characteristic of American life. The rationale for unisex is omnipresent. Since historically women have been more restricted than men, most of the pressures for change tend to be associated with the women's liberation movement. There is a clear tendency to think of tradition as oppressive and to rationalize change as liberating women from traditional oppressions. The more sophisticated exponents and students of the process, however, also point out that eliminating sexist thinking and practices is also liberating for men. The older sexist differentiation of male and female roles, duties, and privileges brought heavy burdens for men such as sole support of wife and children and legal responsibilities for all family members. A more equalitarian set of expectations shares duties as well as privileges.

### Gay Liberation [25]

Perhaps the sharpest break with tradition is "gay liberation." In essence the legitimation of homosexuality entitles an individual, consciously or otherwise, to choose his or her sexual identification and corresponding sexual outlets. He or she is not expected and/or forced to live his or her life on the basis of biological sex. There have always been homosexuals, of course, and in some societies homosexuality had a recognized position, but in our own traditions that was not the case. We do not know whether the present tendency to legitimate the life style of the homosexual has resulted in an increased incidence of homosexuality; there are simply no data. But it is clear that growing numbers of homosexuals of both sexes have ceased to hide their identity and are at least somewhat better tolerated than previously. The society probably has not quite come to the point of neutrality about homosexuality, although certainly tolerance has improved. Agitation for homosexual marriages between consenting adults continues, but the legal difficulties involved seem to preclude an early acceptance of the desire to legitimate homosexual unions by marriage.

### Bi-Sexuality

Bi-sexuality is even harder to measure. It is obvious, however, that a substantial minority of both men and women are in some overt degree bi-sexual. In the vernacular, the bi-sexual person is often referred to as one who can "go either way," that is, he or she can express his or her sexuality with either sex. He or she may have a clear preference for one or the other biologically defined sex, but as opportunity arises or as mood varies, he or she can and does receive and give sexual satisfaction either way. There is a substantial professional opinion to the effect that bi-sexuality has greatly increased in the last decade or two, but there is no clear proof. It is easy to assume a great increase simply because of greater visibility. With more open acknowledgment there may be only an apparent increase now that the need for concealment has partially diminished.

## Women's Liberation [26]

Women's Liberation seems not so much a distinct process as an integration of many of the value threads discussed in the preceding paragraphs: abolition of sexist thinking and policy with regard to employment, morality, life style and etiquette, abortion reform, expansion of day care center facilities, and so on. The movement appears to be most prominent among the more educated women (and men) and those of better than average social position. No one knows what proportion of American women supports Women's Liberation or even the various sub-types of their creed. But the influence of Women's Liberation should not be underestimated, nor the logic of their thrust be unappreciated, particularly where young people are concerned.

## Hypotheses Generated by the Issues

(1) Under current (especially urban) conditions, the nuclear family molded by the monolithic code is for many people no longer functional.[27] The most obvious evidence, although there is a studied reluctance by many to acknowledge it, is outlined in the preceding pages. Alternative life styles are the manifest evidence on the affirmative side of the proposition. While there is a clear tendency to evaluate these changes in moral terms, the causes and the consequences are largely pragmatic matters in the minds of their practitioners and/or advocates.

(2) When a conventional order of things becomes unworkable (or unbearable), experimentation with new (previously unthinkable) modes is inevitable. One cannot reject a life style and remain in a vacuum. Tacitly, the rejection expresses itself in a new mode, a new ideology, a new life style. A strong sanction system and a strong indoctrination system can sometimes delay the appearance of new modes, but if a social system is clearly dysfunctional, change cannot be contained for long.

(3) A pluralistic order seems likely to continue. Because all parts of the monolithic code do not present problems to all people, different kinds of life styles will emerge and tend to perpetuate themselves. Not

everyone is disenchanted with the same aspects of the code, at least not at the same time; not all are disenchanted to the same degree, and not all have had the same experiences or developed the emotional equipment to find fulfillment in the same new modes. This is a difficult concept for many to grasp. Since our traditions are universalistic, we tend to think, even when assessing change, that if some practice is better, it should be better for everybody. Efforts to enforce any innovation upon everyone are doomed to failure, because, as we have said, all do not have the same needs. Those, for example, who find monogamy too restricting may secure release by divorce, by swinging, by forming a commune, or by establishing an open marriage, and perhaps also by other ways. Yet these are exceedingly different modes; they serve people differently, because the people are different. A change which a person with one set of intellectual and emotional equipment can find fulfilling may be unthinkable for the next, with his set of intellectual and emotional equipment. And, it is well always to remind ourselves that for the majority of Americans, so far as we can now determine, the nuclear family and the monolithic code are still more or less adequate.

(4) Not all of the alternative life styles will be found to be equally workable or lasting. Some will prove to be more *viable* than others, because they are better adapted to the total conditions within which a life style must function. This is quite plausible on the face of it, but one is hard put to it to answer the next question; namely, which life styles *are* more viable, and how do we know it? There is really no objective test which can be applied and yield any credible results. All that one can do is make some imaginative projections, but when this is done, it must be with the full knowledge that someone else, equally objective, equally imaginative, equally intelligent, may come up with different judgments about the viability of this or that life style. At the risk of being tedious about the point made so many times already, viability is not a universal; it is a variable which is highly dependent upon particular persons or couples in particular milieus at particular times.

## Implications for the Classroom

The nuclear family is still more or less adequate for the majority of Americans, but a number of variations on the family living theme exists. The process of challenge to the monolithic code proceeds in a rather uneven, broken line. Furthermore, the outcome of much of the ongoing sex mode experimentation is uncertain. That a pluralistic approach to human sexuality will remain with us seems to be the only certainty one can glean from the present state of changing values.

Add to this ambiguity the fact that the school has had a century-long argument with itself as to whether it should be primarily the preserver and purveyor of societal ideal or the initiator of societal innovation and renewal. This debate has never been resolved, and thus the school has tried with varying degrees of success to do both of these things. The sum total of this combined dilemma oversimply stated is in effect, "We don't know for sure where we are going, and we don't know whether the school should lead or follow."

Given this double conundrum, the implications for the school in dealing with sex modes and values might be thought of in almost "Your guess is as good as mine" terms. Fortunately, the case is not entirely without a glimmer of hope and possible resolution. For one thing, the school will most certainly continue to deal with children and young people who are just beginning to identify themselves as unique human beings. If they are going to come to terms with plurality and change in society, students will need a strong, positive image of themselves as individuals.

"As one grows he identifies himself according to sex, race, physical appearance, achievement and the like. He also evaluates himself. His self-description and evaluation comprise his self-concept." [28] The school can provide information on any or all of these variables and in so doing may help the individual build a positive self-concept.

It would seem wise to begin by having teachers who will deal with this task directly in the classroom participate in workshops or take a minicourse in which they explore the dimensions of self-concept. This is recommended for two reasons. First, many teachers have poor self-concepts and such exploration might prove beneficial to them personally. Secondly, going through the process will point up many of the slight variations within the procedure, and will also provide a comfortable, assured experiential base from which to try a similar sequence with children.

### Self-Concept Exploration

The sequence that follows is designed with teacher materials, but will require only minor adaptations to be used with any age or grade level.

| INSTRUCTIONAL TASKS | INSTRUCTIONAL ACTIVITIES |
|---|---|
| I. Clearly identify the session objectives. | Do all three: |
| *(Initial activity should motivate, provide mind set, and provide an operational definition.)* | 1. Film: *To Sir With Love* (Guidance Assoc.) Discuss briefly with group. |

2. Have three or four people give case histories of well-known persons who believed in themselves in spite of odds. (Prepare these in advance.)

3. Use an overhead projector to look at several tentative definitions of self-concept and examine how "significant others" affect one's self-image. Examine some "killer" statements. ("Killer" statements do harm to, or "put down," another person.)

II. Provide information input and an opportunity for cognitive re-organization of the information.

*(Data may help the individual begin to examine his or her attitudes.)*

Select either A or B:

A. Break into small groups and examine resources from Teacher's Bibliography that deal with self-concept. Develop a list of the important topics dealt with by the authors. Be prepared to discuss one sub-topic with the entire class.

B. Define some of the sub-categories of society to which you belong (e.g., female, Chicano, college graduate). Look at statistics about career opportunities, income, or problems about one or more of your categories. Chart some of the information to share with others.

III. Provide for exploration of the affective component.

*(Attitudes have a feelings component which needs to be explored.)*

Again follow through on either A or B

A. With one other person from Step II, Group A, discuss the project you were just engaged in and explain why you chose to develop the particular component you did choose.

B. Provide teams from Step II, Group B, for role-playing in which the individual presents his/her feelings about the category career opportunities, income, and problems to a "Devil's Advocate."

IV. Use group interaction to define and explore possible improvement.

Do both of these activities:

1. Divide the class into two large groups based on their choice in Step

*(The group provides a testing ground for validity of ideas.)*

II. Have a leader work with each group using felt-tip pen and large first-grade "Experience Chart" newsprint. (Group A) Record the list of important topics. Discuss preferences and feelings about them. (Group B)

List the sub-categories and some of the problems associated with them. Discuss feelings about these categories.

2. Now hand out single sheets of paper. Have each person quietly and thoughtfully choose one self-concept component in which he/she is most interested and relate it to a sub-category that applies to him/her. Let the individual describe the present level of achievement and the goal for the future self. (Keep the descriptions to a reasonable time limit—perhaps, "One year from now I'd like to be. . . .")

V. Arrange for specific action component.

*(Providing practice helps stabilize the attitude.)*

Provide felt-tip pens and overhead transparencies at each table. Instruct the group in drawing flow charts and then have people in informal atmosphere draw a sequence of steps that will lead to the final goal they have just described. Have each one select a first step that is a small increment where the individual will surely succeed. Positive reinforcement is important. For example:

Toward a More Physically Attractive *Me*

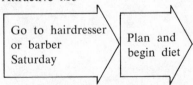

Suggest a teammate for each person to help him/her carry out his/her initial steps and to serve in a "buddy" check system later.

VI. Provide for analysis of the change process. Suggest other areas where the participants may apply the strategy on an individual, independent basis.

*(The individual may be able to utilize the process in modifying other attitudes that he/she wishes to change.)*

Develop a cycle of change, drawing suggestions from the group. Use board or overhead. List specific areas like women's rights for their future consideration.

## The Need for Open Strategies

Many people still do not acknowledge sex education as a legitimate part of the school curriculum. Furthermore, the concepts contained in the broader category of sexuality frequently evoke *extra-rational* responses and are therefore difficult to deal with in a highly structured learning environment. How then shall young people be prepared to deal with a society in which individual sex identification, the relationship of one individual to another as sexual beings, and the broadening of behaviors appropriate to a given sex role are all undergoing scrutiny and change? It seems clear that strategies must be provided that allow the student to select, develop, and process a topic in the manner that the individual student deems most appropriate. Procedures and activities need to be provided that will help the students raise questions and develop tentative answers.

Within the proposed approach, the teacher can serve as a resource person and as such can provide media and books, can raise or answer questions, and can even take sample questionnaires. Since recognition of more than one answer is one of the primary needs in a pluralistic society, a sharing of responses to a particular activity will be most beneficial. The teacher can aid in arranging such sharing situations.

The activities that follow are divided into categories and can be placed on 3″ x 5″ cards so that the student can select the topic and can pace himself/herself. A minimum of teacher assistance will be needed.

### INFORMATION PROCESSING ACTIVITIES

The classroom can provide activities that stimulate the students' curiosity and give direction for information processing. Gathering information and organizing data on controversial issues is an important skill.

1. Go to an employment agency. Ask for a list of jobs and talk to the agency about the possibilities for women or men in jobs that are dominated by the opposite sex.

2. Talk with a priest, rabbi, or minister about "woman's role in society." Then inquire specifically about woman's role in the religious organization which this individual leads. Speak to more than one such person so that you may compare opinions.

3. Interview two or more members of "rights" organizations regarding their perceptions of "The area of this movement that needs the most work is. . . ." Organize your notes and share them with the class.

4. Make a list of the organizations that are active in liberation campaigns in your community. Go to the headquarters of one of these organizations and volunteer to donate at least *one* day of work to the group. Write a "Dear Diary" report of the things that took place at headquarters while you were there.

5. Prepare an "opinionnaire" about family organization and distribute it throughout your school. Raise questions about "what is" and "what you feel is best" so that you do get the opinions of the students. Try the opinionnaire out on your own classmates and the teacher before you try to distribute it to a large number of people. Get your teacher's advice on stating questions in such a way that they can be easily and briefly answered, and easily tallied when you get them back.

   *"What is" example:* Who handles the monthly bills in your family?

   *"What you feel is best" example:* What is the best way for a family to make decisions that affect the group?

6. Read the Declaration of Independence or Bill of Rights. Place yourself in the role of a woman who feels enslaved and rewrite parts of the Declaration to safeguard your rights.

7. Have each child in the classroom bring in information about the work done by his/her parents. Note *after* the assignment how many students mention mother's work. Chart the information in the following manner. Give each child a sticky, colorful, square tab which he/she can place on the graph. The graph will resemble the following:

Factory worker   ☐ ☐ ☐ ☐ ☐

Doctor   ☐ ☐

Teacher   ☐ ☐ ☐ ☐

Grocery clerk   ☐ ☐

Postal worker   ☐

8. Make a retrieval chart of the following information:

WOMEN AT WORK

| | Average income | Fields of work | % in admin. | % of work force | % of work force 100 years ago |
|---|---|---|---|---|---|
| White Women | | | | | |
| White Men | | | | | |
| Black Women | | | | | |
| Black Men | | | | | |
| All groups | | | | | |

It is clear that one could use the same retrieval chart system to accumulate information about family structure, divorce rate, number of children per family, or numbers of co-educational dormitories on college campuses in this country.

9. Locate a commune. Interview or write for information about the work done and the people who do it. Also investigate the role of parents and children. Find out as much as possible about the life style of the people who live there. It might be wise to prepare a sequence of questions to which the individual could respond.

10. Go to the library and obtain copies of old newspapers (60 to 100 or 150 years old). If no actual copies are available, get photographs of old pages with information about situations or positions available. List the number that specify male or female wanted. Compare this with the job descriptions from the current *New York Times* or local paper that specify sex of the employee that is sought.

## SOCIAL INTERACTION ACTIVITIES

Students can learn much from their peers. They can learn to deal with the unexpected response. In role-playing with another individual a student will frequently say, "He wasn't supposed to say that." Real life is full of situations just like this, and students need practice in dealing with unpredictable situations.

In a pluralistic society it is essential that people recognize that there is more than one solution to a specific problem. When young people interact with each other, multiple solutions emerge rather naturally.

1. With a friend, develop a series of advertisements about makeup that would appeal to women. Now do the same for advertisements that would appeal to men. How did your advertisements differ? Make a list of the differences that you note.

2. There is a dress code in your school that requires girls to wear skirts. Boys cannot wear jeans. Many students think this is unfair. How might you get this changed?

3. "Man works from sun to sun, but woman's work is never done."
   "Telephone, telegraph, tell a woman."

   These are two examples of statements that have come down through the years. Discuss these with other students and think of other similar statements that could be added. In your discussion respond to these questions about each statement:

   (a) What does the statement mean?
   (b) In what cultures might this statement be used?
   (c) Why have the statements persisted?
   (d) How does the statement affect you when you hear it used?

4. Role-play in teams any of the following vignettes:

   *Mother:* You are the mother of three children and you are a lawyer and work from 9-5 every day. You are working on a very exciting case right now. Your husband has just come in the door from work. His boss has arranged a three-week business trip over Christmas for him. The children want the whole family to go.
   Act out what you will do now.

   *Father:* Your boss has just arranged a really great business trip for you. The children would be on school vacation. Your wife works in a law office. You have just come in to tell her about your big chance.
   Act out what will happen now.

5. *Person I:* You are an eighth-grade girl and you are trying to decide on the courses you should take in high school. You have always enjoyed the out-of-doors and you would like above all things to prepare to be a forest ranger. You are discussing this with your counselor. You say. . . .

   *Person II:* You are a junior high counselor and help advise students on high school programs. The young girl you are just meeting is very bright and is small and pretty—a nice youngster. She wants to be a forest ranger. There are very few female forest rangers, and the work can be physically demanding. You say. . . .

6. *Person I:* You are a sixteen-year-old boy and have been dating Jean for several months. She is really a fun person to be with and you like her a lot. Recently you have gotten carried away with loving her. Last night when you came home from a roller skating party she told you that she is pregnant. She has told her mother, and her mother has called your mother. Your mother has just told you she wants to talk with you as you come in the door from school. You say. . . .

*Person II:* You are the mother of a sixteen-year-old son. He is a great kid—bright, athletic, and affectionate. He has just become interested in girls. Jean is his first real girl friend. Jean's mother has just called and says that Jean is pregnant and that your son is the father of the child. He has just walked in the door. You say. . . .

7. You are a teen-ager and the kind of life style you would like to pursue does not really exist at the present time. Your notion is to have a small community of compatible people live on a large amount of land. They would help each other with work and share some things, but would not be a commune in the sense of sharing all wealth, work, etc. You are not really clear on all the details yet, but you are convinced that this is the way people should live. You are trying to convince your younger brother to join you in this venture. He is a skeptic, and you will need some carefully thought-out plans to convince him.

Discuss your idea with him and listen carefully to his point of view so that you can handle his arguments skillfully.

You are a teen-ager with an older brother who is a charming, convincing person and he is interested in having you take part in a "Community of the Future" venture. You are very unsure of the idea and not at all clear as to what it involves for you if you decide to join his group. You want to have some possessions of your own also. You are a very private person. You raise questions about the venture as you discuss this together.

## EXPRESSIVE ACTIVITIES

It is important that students learn to express their feelings, especially when they are dealing with sexuality—a topic that is value-laden. The activities that are provided here are designed to encourage students to explore how they feel about themselves and others.

1. Define "rights" as a strong feminist might define them in relation to the following topics (1) woman washing dishes, (2) fashion show, (3) female student in a mathematics class, (4) woman nurse.

2. Get a picture of a busy city street that shows many businesses, banks, etc. Look at it and try to imagine the jobs that one would do in the area. Which one would you choose for yourself? Why would you choose this one?

## EXPRESSIVE ACTIVITIES THAT EMPHASIZE SELF-CONCEPT

1. Act out a person who has been free to move about and is suddenly confined to a small area.

2. Close your eyes and imagine that you are a bird. You glide high above a river. You can see for miles. Become the bird. Think about its free-

dom and yours. How is the bird's freedom limited? How is your freedom restricted?

3. Make a "Map of Me." Note your natural attributes—what are your ocean depths like, your desert areas, your strengths that tower against the sky? What are your natural resources, your products, your recreational facilities? Collect pictures that will give information about these and other characteristics of yours. Make a collage of the pictures you have gathered.

4. What would a "perfect day" be like for a happy woman? A happy man? Be specific. What would she/he do? Where would she/he go?

5. Dance out a person who is gradually freed from boring work.

6. You are a "Nation of Number I." Draw a picture of a flag that will be a symbol of what you value most. Write a verse of your national anthem in which you indicate an interesting event that influenced you, or a symbol that represents you. Answer these questions:

How will you protect your nation from difficulties?

How will you govern and deal with those who are a part of your existence?

7. Make a divided collage of the You that exists at the present time and the ideal You. This might then represent problems and reality of the present and the rose-colored glow of the future.

### DYNAMIC—HYPOTHETICAL SITUATIONS

Toffler has told us that we must teach students to think about the future. If young people really wish to bring about change, then experimentation with ideas and applications before the fact would seem in order. Some extremely open situations are proposed in which students can propose solutions with "no holds barred." The criterion for dealing with the adequacy of the proposals would be the ability of the student or groups to identify interdependence and interrelationships among proposed possibilities.

1. Several students in a small group observe people in another culture. It is an ideal community because of the way people treat each other. Report on what you saw to the class or another small group of students.

2. Four teen-age girls and two boys are washed ashore on a remote, uninhabited South Sea island. How will the work get done? Will you seek help? If no one finds you for a number of years, how will you live? Will you marry? How will this be decided? Discuss this with a small group of classmates.

3. You favor a "community of the future" life style. Make a list of the important values you would want to see develop in your community. How would you convince community members that these values are crucial to the group?

## *Assessment*

The objectives for the school have been (1) to aid the student in developing a positive self-concept and (2) to provide strategies that will allow the student to develop skill in processing information and ideas related to sexuality in a more open manner. The assessment of these objectives is complex and long term. It would seem that an immediate assessment might help the student examine carefully his/her own position and his/her values regarding a certain concept. Grades in the traditional sense would not be advisable.

### SELF-CONCEPT

It is possible for a very young child to provide feedback on his/her feelings about himself/herself. A "smiling faces" can be administered in which the child marks the face that best shows how he/she feels about himself/herself. Here are some examples; other elements of self-concept would be included in an actual test.

**How I do things.**

**How other people like me.**

The same self-examination might be carried out with more mature students by using a more definitive scale. For example:

|  | Do not need to improve |  |  |  | Need much improvement |
|---|---|---|---|---|---|
| School achievement | \| \| | \| \| | \| \| | \| \| | \| \| |
| Health care | \| \| | \| \| | \| \| | \| \| | \| \| |
| The way I treat others | \| \| | \| \| | \| \| | \| \| | \| \| |

## OPENNESS—MULTIPLE SOLUTIONS TO PROBLEMS

There are several strategies for helping students clarify their thinking about issues. The activities used have suggested a receptivity to a variety of students' ideas. The assessment procedures should reemphasize this point, but at the same time underscore the notion that each student, at this point in time, does have an opinion about the topic of his choice.

There are no right or wrong answers to any of the examples given. They simply encourage the student to explore and choose.

## SEMANTIC DIFFERENTIAL

A broad topic can be presented and a number of descriptive terms. placed on a continuum or at ends of the continuum that will give an indication of how the individual feels about the topic when the scale has been filled in by the student. Example:

*Women are:*

| | |
|---|---|
| smart | stupid |
| ambitious | lazy |
| emotional | unemotional |

*People who live in a commune are:*

| | |
|---|---|
| normal | abnormal |
| happy | sad |
| good | bad |

Other stimuli can be used with any number of comparable terms.

## SENTENCE ITEMS

Another strategy for reinforcing openness but forcing some specificity is sentence stem completion. Open-ended sentence stems can be used to evoke a variety of responses. Example:

1. Women ought to ...............................................................................
2. Homosexuals are ............................................................................
3. I think the kind of clothes a man wears is .....................................
4. When I select a career I will ..........................................................

## MINI ROLE-PLAYING

Multiple solutions to a problem can be examined by using a mini role-playing situation, and eliciting responses either in writing or verbally that will show different ways this problem might be solved. Example:

You are a high school senior and are in love with a boy who is a sopho-more at the state college fifty miles from home. Your parents wish to send you to a private college that is halfway across the country. You could only see Rick twice a year if you go there. This is not what you want at all. You decide to . . . .

What are all the ways you can think of that this situation might be dealt with? List as many alternatives as you can.

Since all students will not be selecting the same topic, assessment might well be provided following a series of activities on a particular sub-topic such as "Liberation." The assessment scales may be pro-vided on 3″ x 5″ cards directly following the collection of activities cards on this topic. The cards can provide self-administering and self-scoring instructions. Answers may be provided on the back of each card or on a separate card that is held by the teacher until the student requests it to correct the past test. Comments for follow-up work can also be provided on a card for students who need or want more infor-mation on a particular sub-topic.

## Summary and Conclusion

It is probably apparent that the question which serves as the title for this chapter carries an implication which is to be seriously ques-tioned. Whether or not alternative life styles "should" be accepted, the facts of the matter are that they already are accepted and are viable for substantial minorities in American society, chiefly, but not exclu-sively, among the relatively young. To be sure, the issue remains as to whether legislative and bureaucratic regulation should encourage, ignore, or attempt to thwart these innovations. Here is where the collision of value systems is sharp and, in the minds of many, uncompromising as well. It is doubtful, for example, whether a referendum on college co-educational dormitories would pass, if the total population could express its approval or disapproval. There is no doubt, however, that among the population affected, the college students, permissiveness is highly endorsed. A reverse circumstance concerns abortion reform. Reliable polls show that the overwhelming majority of women approve of a liberal abortion policy, but so far legislators have been extremely re-luctant to modify laws in accord with majority women's opinion. It is noteworthy that almost all of the alternative life styles which we have discussed have come into being, either by circumvention or by defiance of existing legislation. In the case of women's liberation, however, reform appears to be coming about, or is at least being facilitated, by legal changes. In addition, informal pressure against discriminators appears to be effective also. Thus, it is difficult, objectively, to assess the relative effectiveness of formal legal changes and informal problem-solving. At the very least, it should be appreciated that changing values have almost invariably preceded legislative change or have been implemented in defiance of established law.

Not all constraints on behavior are those flowing from legislation, however. Church doctrines, informal public opinion, the mass media, formal education are also presumably influential, although it is not known in what ways or in what degree the influence flows. It is widely asserted that the present permissive portrayal of sex practices in television and the movies is "weakening the moral fibre" of Americans, especially the young. But there is no clear *evidence* that such a connection exists. Nor is it known, except in general terms, how effective church and public school teaching are in controlling behavior. It is obvious, however, that the emergence and growth of alternate life styles are tacit evidence of the ineffectiveness of such instruction, since the precepts and preachments of these ubiquitous institutions have long been contrary to such practices.

It is as easy to overestimate as it is to underestimate the impact of new values on what we like to call the "general society." As we have repeatedly pointed out, the traditional monolithic code, or minor modifications of it, appears still to be adequate for a majority of American people, but not necessarily for the young. It is as much an error to conclude that the nuclear family is rapidly collapsing as it is to assert that it is adequate. It is both—but for different people. Even this formulation can be an oversimplification, however. It is a normal condition of social change that for a considerable period of time, a marked ambivalence occurs for large numbers of people. One may, for example, accept abortion under certain conditions for the unmarried, but not for the married. Or one might approve consensual unions among the unmarried, but completely disapprove of co-marital unions among the married. And so on. Moreover, at different points in the life cycle, a person or a couple may hold different values. Further, this can come in almost any sequence. There is a popular myth that young people almost invariably tend to accept radical ideas and then become more conservative as they mature, but the reverse can and does occur too. And again, a person or a couple can hold to traditional values in one aspect of their lives but hold highly innovative values in other phases of their lives. This is why great caution should be observed in the use of such sweeping terms as a "liberal" or a "radical" or a "conservative" person. A couple may be fiercely monogamous for themselves but approve of co-educational dormitories and a completely permissive abortion *policy,* even though they would never even consider having an abortion themselves. Is such a couple "liberal" or "conservative"?

About all that can be reliably stated is that (1) new life styles exist; (2) they are viable for certain minorities, especially but not exclusively the young; (3) the majority is still essentially traditional; (4) most of the innovations are not buttressed by legal sanctions and many are clearly illegal, but enforcement appears to be weakening if not in some instances totally absent. The overriding conclusion is that while we have had monolithic antecedents, the present society is highly *pluralistic* and no clear and certain guidelines for the future can be foreseen.

Schools can hardly escape involvement, one way or another, in the current value confusion and controversy. On the one hand schools are admonished to "hold the line," i.e., to teach the "eternal verities," and on the other hand to "lead the way" to a better future. Given the current pluralistic environment, they can probably succeed at neither. What, realistically, they can do is to introduce students to the reality and possible viability of alternate life styles and to contravene the clichés on both sides. In short, through the medium of open discussion and open reading, students may be encouraged to examine themselves and to examine their environments and (hopefully) to appreciate the needs and limitations of both, to the end that they may find that delicate balance between personal need and desire and social acceptance in this vital life area of man-woman living.

## SUBJECT BIBLIOGRAPHY

1. Burchinal, Lee G., "Characteristics of Adolescents from Unbroken, Broken, and Reconstituted Families," *Journal of Marriage and the Family* 26 (February 1964): 44-51.

   Landis, Judson T., "A Comparison of Children from Divorced and Non-divorced Unhappy Marriages," *Family Life Coordinator* 11 (July 1962): 61-5.

   Nye, Ivan F., "Child Adjustment in Broken and in Unhappy Unbroken Homes," *Marriage and Family Living* 19 (1957): 356-61.

2. Burchinal, Lee G., *Maternal Employment, Family Relations and Selected Personality, School-Related and Social-Development Characteristics of Children*, Bulletin 497. (Ames, Iowa: Agricultural and Home Economics Experiment Station, October 1961).

   Hand, Horace G., "Working Mothers and Maladjusted Children," *Journal of Educational Sociology* 30 (January 1957): 245-46.

   Nye, Ivan F., "Employment Status of Mothers and Adjustment of Adolescent Children," *Marriage and Family Living* 21 (August 1959): 240-44.

   Nye, Ivan F. and Hoffman, Lois W., *The Employed Mother in America* (Chicago: Rand McNally and Company, 1963), pp. 118-120.

3. LeMasters, E. E., "Parenthood as Crisis," *Marriage and Family Living* 19 (1957): 352-55.

   Feldman, H., *The Development of Husband-Wife Relationships* (Ithaca, N.Y.: Cornell University, n.d. mimeographed).

   Hill, Reuben and Rodgers, Roy H., "The Developmental Approach," in H. T. Christensen, ed., *Handbook of Marriage and the Family* (Chicago: Rand McNally and Company, 1964), pp. 201-02.

4. Fuller, Richard C., "The Problem of Teaching Social Problems," *American Journal of Sociology* 44 (1939): 415-35.

5. See, e.g., John F. Cuber, Kenkel, William F., and Harper, Robert A., *Problems of American Society: Values in Conflict* (New York, Holt, Rinehart and Winston, 1964), pp. 26-59.

6. The National Commission on Venereal Disease (1972). *Say It So It Makes Sense,* "A Newsletter for Professionals" (Syracuse University, College for Human Development) I, no. 1, p. 1.

7. Cuber, John F. and Harroff, Peggy B., *The Significant Americans: A Study of Sexual Behavior Among the Affluent* (New York: Appleton Century, 1965), pp. 19-22.

8. Kinsey, Alfred C., et al., *Sexual Behavior in the Human Male* (Philadelphia: W. B. Saunders Co., 1948), p. 437.

9. Williams, Robin M., Jr., *American Society: A Sociological Interpretation* (New York: Knopf, 1970), pp. 420-31.

10. Roy, Rustum and Roy, Della, "Is Monogamy Outdated?," in Roger W. Libby and Robert N. Whitehurst, eds., *Renovating Marriage* (Danville, California: Consensus Publishers, Inc., 1973), pp. 59-73.

    Whitehurst, Robert N., "The Monogamous Ideal and Sexual Realities," *op. cit.,* pp. 38-47.

    Whitehurst, Robert N., "Changing Ground Rules and Emergent Life-Styles," *op. cit.,* pp. 309-20.

11. Bernard, Jessie, *Remarriage: A Study of Marriage* (New York: Russell and Russell, 1956), pp. 269-300 and 330-46.

    Bohannan, Paul, ed., *Divorce and After: An Analysis of the Emotional and Social Problems of Divorce* (New York: Doubleday, 1970). Selected articles.

    Hunt, Morton M., *The World of the Formerly Married* (New York: McGraw Hill, 1966), pp. 275-93.

12. Bartell, Gilbert, *Group Sex* (New York: Peter H. Wyden, Inc., 1971).

    Ellis, Albert, *The Civilized Couples' Guide to Extramarital Adventure* (New York: Peter H. Wyden, Inc., 1972), pp. 1-16.

    Libby, Robert W., "Extramarital and Co-Marital Sex: A Review of the Literature," in Roger W. Libby and Robert N. Whitehurst, eds., *op. cit.,* pp. 116-45.

    Neubeck, Gerhard, ed., *Extramarital Relations* (Englewood Cliffs, N.J.: Prentice-Hall, Inc., 1969). Selected articles.

13. Bell, Robert R., *Premarital Sex in a Changing Society* (Englewood Cliffs, N.J.: Prentice-Hall, Inc., 1966), pp. 159-72.

    Bell, Robert R. and Chaskes, J. B., "Premarital Sexual Experience Among Coeds, 1958 and 1968," *Journal of Marriage and the Family* 32 (February 1970): 81-84.

    Kinsey, Alfred C., et al., *Sexual Behavior in the Human Female* (Philadelphia: W. S. Saunders Co., 1953), pp. 248-93.

    Reiss, Ira L., *Premarital Sexual Standards in America* (New York: The Free Press of Glencoe, 1960), pp. 29, 80.

14. Rollin, Betty, "Motherhood: Who Needs It?," in Arlene S. and Jerome H. Skolnick, eds., *Family in Transition* (Boston: Little, Brown and Co., 1971), pp. 346-56.
15. Blood, Robert O., "Long-Range Causes and Consequences of the Employment of Married Women," in Joann L. and Jack R. Delora, eds., *Intimate Life Styles* (Pacific Palisades, California: Goodyear, 1972), pp. 227-34.
   Scanzoni, John, *Sexual Bargaining: Power Politics in the American Marriage* (Englewood Cliffs, N.J., Prentice-Hall, Inc., 1972), pp. 129-30.
16. Fisher, Peter, *The Gay Mystique: The Myth and Reality of Male Homosexuality* (New York: Stein and Day, 1972).
   Martin, Del, and Lyon, Phyllis, *Lesbian Woman* (San Francisco: Glide, 1972).
17. Steinmetz, Suzanne K. and Straus, Murray A., eds., *Violence in the Family* (New York: Dodd, Mead, 1974). Selected articles.
   Wolfgang, Marvin E., "Victim-Precipitated Criminal Homicide," *Journal of Criminal Law, Criminology and Police Science* 48 (1957): 1-11.
18. Cuber, John F., "Alternate Models from the Perspective of Sociology," in Herbert A. Otto, ed., *The Family in Search of a Future* (New York: Appleton-Century-Crofts, 1970), pp. 11-23.
   Delora, Joann S. and Delora, Jack R., eds, *Intimate Life Styles* (Pacific Palisades, California: Goodyear, 1972). Selected articles.
19. O'Neill, Nena and O'Neill, George, *Open Marriage: A New Life Style for Couples* (New York: M. Evans & Co., 1972), pp. 67-77.
   Rogers, Carl R., *Becoming Partners: Marriage and Its Alternatives* (New York: Delacorte Press, 1972).
20. Bartell, Gilbert, *Group Sex, op. cit.*
   Denfield, Duane and Gordon, Michael, "The Sociology of Mate Swapping: Or the Family That Swings Together Clings Together," in Joann S. Delora and Jack R. Delora, *op. cit.,* pp. 304-316.
   For an alternative view to "swinging," see Larry L. Constantine and Joan M. Constantine, *Group Marriage: A Study of Contemporary Multilateral Marriage* (New York: Macmillan, 1973).
21. Bartell, Gilbert, *op. cit.*
22. Fairfield, Richard, *Communes U.S.A.: A Personal Tour* (Baltimore, Md.: Penguin, 1972).
   Roberts, Ron E., *The New Communes: Coming Together in America* (Englewood Cliffs, N.J.: Prentice-Hall, 1971).
23. Libby, Roger W., "Extramarital and Co-Marital Sex: A Review of the Literature," *op. cit.*
   Smith, James R. and Smith, Lynn, "Co-Marital Sex and the Sexual Freedom Movement," *Journal of Sex Research* 5 (1970): 131-43.
24. Rollin, Betty, *op. cit.*
   Peck, Ellen, *The Baby Trap* (New York: Pinnacle, 1972).
25. Greene, Johnny, "Decadence By Invitation Only," *New Times* 2, 8 (April 19, 1974): 37-41.
26. Epstein, Cynthia Fuchs, *Woman's Place: Options and Limits in Professional Careers* (Los Angeles: University of California Press, 1971).
   Millett, Kate, *Sexual Politics* (New York: Avon, 1971).
27. Cuber, John F. and Harroff, Peggy B., *op. cit.*
   Skolnick, Jerome H. and Skolnick, Arlene S., "Rethinking the Family," in Arlene S. and Jerome H. Skolnick, *op. cit.,* pp. 1-32.
28. Klausmeier, Herbert J., and Ripple, Richard E., *Learning and Human Abilities* (New York: Harper and Row, Publishers, 1971), p. 219.

## STUDENTS' BIBLIOGRAPHY

An Annotated Bibliography by Diane Stavu in *School Library Journal* (January 1972). A selection of non-sexist children's books.

*Career Opportunities for Women, Why Not Be an Engineer?* (Washington, D. C.: Women's Bureau of U.S. Dept. of Labor, 1972).

*Dimensions of Personality* (Dayton, Ohio: Pflaum Company, 1972). Elementary grades book series dealing with self-concept.

"The Joy of Being You" (New York: Inside Out Publications, Inc., a subsidiary of Scholastic Magazines Inc., 1970). Primary grades—filmstrip.

"The Labels and Reinforcement of Sex Role Stereotyping" (National Education Association. Customer Service Section 148, 1201 Sixteenth Street, N.W. Washington, D. C., 1974). Filmstrip.

Lichtenberg, Margaret Klee, "In Pursuit of the Rare and Role-Free Children's Book," *Ms. Magazine* (October 1973).

*Little Miss Muffet Fights Back* (Children's Media Project, P. O. Box 4315, Grand Central Station, New York, 1972). A list of readings for children.

McCuen, Gary E. and Bender, David L., eds., *The Sexual Revolution,* Opposing Viewpoints Series (Anoka, Minnesota: Greenhaven Press, 1972).

Thomas, Marlo, "Free To Be You and Me" (New York: McGraw-Hill Book Company, 1974). Records, 1776 Broadway, New York. Ms. Records 1972 under Bell, primary grades.

*The Triple I Series* (New York: American Book Company, 1970). Grades 1-6 (self-identity). Includes emphasis on minority groups.

"The Work My Mother Does," *The New Open Highway* (Glen View, Illinois: Scott, Foresman and Co., 1972). Intermediate grades.

Women's Action Alliance, Non-Sexist Child Development Project, 370 Lexington Avenue, New York, N. Y., 1973. Packet outlining early childhood curricular materials.

## ADULTS'—TEACHERS' BIBLIOGRAPHY

Anderson, Scarvia, ed., *Sex Differences and Discrimination in Education* (Worthington, Ohio. Charles A. Jones Publishing Company, 1972).

Cooper, James L. and Cooper, Sheila, M., *The Roots of American Feminist Thought* (Boston: Allyn and Bacon, Inc., 1973).

Cott, Nancy F., ed., *Root of Bitterness* (New York: E. P. Dutton and Co., 1972).

Feldman, David and Sears, Pauline, "Teacher Interaction with Boys and Girls," *National Elementary Journal* (November 1966).

Frazer, Nancy and Sadker, Myra, *Sexism in School and Society* (New York: Harper and Row Publishers, 1973).

Friedman, Jean E. and Shade, William G., *Our American Sisters: Women in American Life and Thought* (Boston: Allyn and Bacon, Inc., 1973).

Greenleaf, Phyllis Taube, *Liberating Young Children from Sex Roles: Experience in Day Care Centers, Play Groups and Free Schools* (Somerville, Maine: New England Free Press, 1973).

Hamacher, Don E., *Encounters with the Self* (New York: Holt, Rinehart and Winston, Inc., 1971).

McCuen, Gary E. and Bender, David L., eds., *The Sexual Revolution,* Opposing Viewpoints Series (Anoka, Minnesota: Greenhaven Press, 1972).

Mead, Margaret, *Blackberry Winter: My Earlier Years,* Touchstone Books (New York: Simon and Schuster, 1972).

Minuchin, Patricia, "Sex Differences in Children," *National Elementary Journal* (November 1966).

*Ms. Magazine* (New York: Ms. Magazine Corporation).

Scott, Ann Firor, "Women in American Life," in *The Reinterpretation of American History and Culture* edited by William H. Cartwright and Richard L. Watson (Washington, D.C.: National Council for the Social Studies, 1973).

*Sex Role Stereotyping in the Schools,* edited by National Education Association. (Customer Service Section 148, 1201 Sixteenth Street, N.W. Washington, D.C., 1974).

Shaftel, Fannie and Shaftel, George, *Role Playing for Social Values* (Englewood Cliffs, N. J.: Prentice-Hall, Inc., 1967).

Stanford, Gene and Roark, Albert E., *Human Interaction in Education* (Boston: Allyn and Bacon, Inc., 1974).

Trecker, Janice Law, "Women in U.S. History and Textbooks," *Social Education* Volume 35, No. 3 (March 1971).

# 4

# Should the Study of Death Be a Necessary Preparation for Living?

## David D. Stafford

### Introduction

WORD meanings accompanying tattoos such as "Death Before Dishonor," "Born To Die," and "Death Has No Friend" were less well remembered than their design, color, or location. And how appalled I was upon perceiving the cross design peering from beautiful red roses with the word "Mom" etched in blue across its face. But my aversion to death began long before the military years. As a child I somehow knew old people died *first*. "Grandfather, is there a heaven?" "If there is," he answered, "I don't see how it can be better than that which we have here." But later, after watching life slowly ebb from a cancer patient sharing my room, sensing his suffering, listening to his comatose hallucinations, "Let me up; it's time to pick peaches!," and seeing the arms struggle to overcome the straps as they sought his genitals made me realize that life, for some, was different.

"Jake, you mean they pay two dollars for every one we bring?"
"Ya, but it must be in good condition—no cuts."
"How many pop bottles will we need?"
"About fifty little ones for the cheapest trap."
"Wanna run the line now?"
"We only set them yesterday."
"Time enough for that marsh."

*DAVID D. STAFFORD is Chairperson and Teacher, Secondary Social Studies Department, Northland High School, Columbus, Ohio.*

"Listen! What's that noise?"

"Sounds like a rabbit eating a carrot."

"Come on, let's see."

Into the clearing we ran and there, feverishly chewing the foot from the trap, was a large muskrat. Seeing us, it frantically circled and jerked against the trap. The blood made a palsy-like pattern on the clean snow. We killed the muskrat quickly, and then we had popcorn at the Saturday matinee. It's all right to fish, shoot rabbits, and slaughter cattle, for they were put here by God for man.

"That's where Carpenter was after he drowned." How well that river was remembered. I swam it probably ten times last summer and nothing happened to me. 'Course, I was a better swimmer than Roy.

"You mean that old house over there? Why in there?"

" 'Cuz that's where dead people go, stupid."

"Dead people?"

"Ya, come on. Let's go see one."

"You mean there's some there now?"

"I'll show you. Come on."

With the shutting door, the hot, dry radiator heat cancelled the winter air. I saw him lying there, that old man, and bolted from the room with the director's question, "Are you friends of the family?," ringing in my ears. But, of course, he was dead; he was old.

I was swallowed by euphemisms. Everyone had "passed away," "departed this life," was "laid to rest," gone on a "long journey," was "sick" or "old," or had "been called by God for a mission." Funeral parlor flowers also were "beautiful," and everyone looked "natural." The old were put in nursing homes, the sick in hospitals, and the others died on highways or in far-off lands. I was part of the "Pepsi-generation." I could always dye that gray away and never get old. Death became impersonal. It was simply un-American to die. Then my brother died. He was not "old," nor "sick," nor planning any "mission for God." No longer could the concept of death be denied.

My experiences are not unique. Everyone has or will experience similar ones. Save cryogenics, where humans are frozen awaiting the cure where thawing and restoration follow, death is one of life's certainties. All that lives must die; for without one, the other can't be. It is a common denominator which we all share. Compare the sounds a baby makes struggling for that first breath with those from a dying man's last gasp. Is one not to be found in the other? From the day we begin living, we become engaged in the process of dying. To come to a full understanding of death is to prepare for living.

## The Nature and Importance of This Issue

Time, progressing along the birth-death continuum, simply lends sophistication to the knowledge of terminality. Are there not expressions of wonderment on infant's faces prior to leaving wakefulness and entering sleep? And upon waking, watch them gather their consciousness as if to ponder where they have been. Do they know they were, and then suddenly not? Does the infant equate separation with loss? Why are experiences of moving, perceiving new faces, or observing parents disappearing behind closing doors so traumatic? Why do infants so intently observe passing clouds and automobiles, falling leaves, and snowflakes which disappear upon the window? What happens when things do not return like objects in flushing toilets, the closing curtains which drive the light from the room, the dispersing white steam from the vaporizer, or the empty applesauce dish? Is the infant not learning to conceive being-nonbeing? In the following is Tim experiencing separation and loss?

Tim was a twenty-eight-month-old Catholic child who developed a neuro-blastoma and was hospitalized seven times over a period of five months prior to his death. He was an only child and conceived prior to the marriage of his nineteen-year-old mother and twenty-one-year-old father. During the course of his illness, Tim developed bone pain, massive liver enlargement, and exophthalmos. He was treated with surgery, irradiation, and chemotherapy. The parents' grief was accentuated by their old shame concerning Tim's untimely conception and by their feelings of guilt triggered by their inability to conceal from themselves or others the irritation they felt toward the child for causing them an impossible financial burden. As a consequence of these emotional factors the parents rarely visited the child while he was in the hospital and only mechanically cared for him at home.

During the initial hospitalization for diagnostic tests, Tim responded with anger and negativism toward the staff, but by the end of the first week he became increasingly apathetic. The same empathetic and energetic nurse was assigned to Tim each time he was admitted, and she often visited him during his interim outpatient appointments. Prior to each discharge, Tim's parents were reluctant to take him home, and with subsequent hospitalizations he would return to the ward detached and withdrawn. It was recognized that this was not entirely due to his physical debilitation because following two or three days on the ward, regardless of whether or not the treatment regimen was altered, his interest and vigor would substantially increase. It was also clear that when his nurse-mother-substitute was off-duty for more than one day, Tim's anger-followed-by-apathy pattern would quickly return. During his last days when Tim needed additional care, it was arranged for this mother surrogate to "special" him. His parents were notified that he was terminal but were not present at his death. Tim remained relatively alert and died peacefully, holding onto the nurse's hand.[1]

When, exactly, does the child distinguish between animate and inanimate objects? For the three-year-old, death is equated with the ability to return from a temporary absence. Coffins only serve as restraining devices. If people were not buried they could move about. Can the child ever comprehend the finality of death when the "Coyote" dies numerous times only to reappear physically unharmed, when the Queen in *Cinderella* dies because she was cruel, and when the little, sweet grandmother emerges unharmed from the stomach of a wolf in *Little Red Riding Hood* because she was good?[2] Is our concept of death distorted by cartoons, fairy tales, and fables? Everything which moves is alive.[3,4] A person can even be "very badly killed."[5] According to Piaget, anything which moves [clouds] or is of use to the child is alive. In the fourth year, the child is approaching the fact that death is personal and inevitable. But still, "things" cause death such as hospitals, misbehaving, sickness, or age.

**Case B:**

A girl, 4 years 4 months old. On this occasion the action takes place around the doll's house. There is a mother, a father, a little girl, and a baby boy.

*B:* The lights are out. It's dark.

*Dr.:* If the lights are out?

*B:* The kids get scared.

*Dr.:* What is there to be scared about?

*B:* They would get lost.

*Dr.:* Anything else?

*B:* They could get killed.

*Dr.:* In the dark?

*B:* They might have an accident. They couldn't see where to go. Not know where they're walking.

*Dr.:* They might get killed if they couldn't see where they're going?

*B:* Well. They might walk into the woods by mistake. I'm pretending they're in the woods.

*Dr.:* And if they get killed?

*B:* They die.

*Dr.:* Then?

*B:* They go in the graveyard.

*Dr.:* Have you seen a graveyard?

*B:* I once saw someone get buried.

*Dr.:* Did you really see it?

*B:* Well—No.

*Dr.:* What happens when people are buried?

*B:* I don't know. I saw my great-grandma killed?
*Dr.:* You saw your great-grandma killed?
*B:* She got too big and too old.
*Dr.:* When they get too old they die?
*B:* Yes. My mother told me people die. They get buried. Before they get buried they just get in a box and they put them in a truck.
*Dr.:* Then?
*B:* (Silence) I wish you would say the words. What I was trying to think of.
*Dr.:* What words?
*B:* They have all kinds of boxes.
*Dr.:* For different people?
*B:* Big sizes.
*Dr.:* Then after the people are in the boxes and buried?
*B:* They come out. Somebody digs the dirt off them.
*Dr.:* They can't do it themselves?
*B:* No. They take the box out. I'm thinking where they go.
*Dr.:* Where dead people go?
*B:* In the woods.
*Dr.:* They go in the woods? Do they do anything?
*B:* How can they do anything when they're dead? In the box.[6]

In the five-to-nine-year-old stage, death is accepted, but the self is usually exempted. "Why do we die?" is being questioned, followed by "It isn't fair" comments.[7] That which causes death has a personality of its own, and whoever can escape the "death-man" does not die.[8] From this age onward the child knows bodily functions cease upon death. What is the purpose of growing up if it is to end in death? For most of us from age eleven to that "experience of experiences," death is denied by an elaborate system of euphemisms. What should we tell a child who questions the death of his father?[9] Should the child be told the father is "with the angels," is "sleeping," has lived a good life and is "now in heaven"? If mother has "gone on a long journey," will the child feel that he may not have been loved, and that he was thus abandoned? Will he want to go on that two-week vacation? Is the penalty for being good to die, even if we may go to heaven? How can we get to heaven if we are put into the ground? If I become ill, I may die, even if that illness is a common cold. If Daddy is "sleeping" will the child show fear at bedtime?[10] Granted this questioning stage by children is difficult to answer by adults, but will it later become easier if we continue to say flowers "wilt" or "fade," and that pets are "put to sleep" and do not die?

The questions *will* be asked, and there are ample opportunities in which to embark upon an answer. Dead insects on windshields, dead leaves, the death of a pet, etc. are occasions which present themselves for discussion. Should euphemisms be tossed aside? There are a host of questions thought of, seldom asked, and usually never studied. Let's pause momentarily and delve into a few of these questions.

Why do we die? According to Anaximander (c. 610-547 B.C.) our death is a penalty for breaking away from that which we were before we were.[11] If we were born to die then we never should have existed in the first place. Because we do exist, we must have violated that to which we were originally ordained, and thus the penalty for being is nonbeing or death. If the Lord gives and if the Lord "hath taken away," perhaps Epictetus (c. 60-117) was correct in thinking life was simply a loan. If life is a loan, should then death be the only way to repay the debt?

What is death? Is death simply a journey to another world or dreamless sleep as Socrates (469-399 B.C.) thought, or is it the belief held by Seneca (c. 4 B.C.-65 A.D.) that death is simply being that which we were before we were?[12] If at one time we were not, why become disturbed at once again being not? Is death the accumulation of all past injuries?[13] If the heart can be revived by massage, stimulants, pacemakers, electric shock, or transplants should the cessation of a heart beat define death? Should death be regarded as that point when the electroencephalogram (EEG) measures the brain's activity as zero? Langone[14] reported an EEG taken on a cat whose brain was then removed and frozen for 200 days. The brain was revived by circulating warm blood through it, another EEG was taken, and upon comparison identical patterns were recorded! Is death the cessation of cell division? Harry Foster[15] reports the criteria established by Dr. Christian Barnard to define death: [The heart must display] "no electrical activity for five minutes," [the absence of] "spontaneous respiration," and when the brain does not respond to stimuli (a flat EEG). Should death be that which is necessary for organ transplantation?

Should every man have the same claim to life? With the advent of life-saving or "death-postponing" devices such as respirators, organ transplantations, pace-setters, kidney machines, etc., the question is not easily answered. Langone[16] estimates that there are between thirty- to fifty-thousand deaths per year in America of individuals who cannot get treatment for kidney diseases. If the machines cost on the average of $37,000 per year to maintain, who should be saved?[17] The criteria, according to Fulton,[18] as to who has priority for the machines' use are the married under 45 years of age with young children who have a post-high school educational background, and who have displayed a potential to contribute. Should men be selected over women and whites over non-whites? Should a younger person with future potential, or an older skilled individual be saved? Should anyone be saved in light of the population explosion? If one is an organ donor, should his or her life be prematurely shortened in order to secure a needed part? [19]

Mitford [20] estimates that there are between 1,500 and 2,842 "plantings" per tax-exempted cemetery acre. If the average cost of a grave is $150 and the acre was purchased for, say, $3,000, is dying the ultimate money-maker? A local cemetery caretaker told me that if all the people in America died, they could be fit, quite easily and with room to spare, in the State of Rhode Island. Due to religious connotations regarding cremation, and fear of the worms from below, many seek shelter in mausoleums. They are "in" for economic and status considerations as well. "Going up, please" could conceivably increase the "slots/acre" by a fivefold factor, and the crypt with the "view from the top" is more expensive. Mitford further reports that "the average mausoleum sale, nationally, is $720 for a single crypt."

At the funeral home, besides carefully arranged flowers (Mitford states that between "65-70 percent of the flower industry's revenue, or 414 million per year, derives from the sale of funeral flowers."), temperature controlled rooms, register books, soft music, an impressive show room, cremation clothes for sale, and good company, what else may we expect?

On a recent classroom field trip to a funeral home, we were not shown the embalming or "preparation" room. The reason, according to the director, was that "We lack the proper facilities necessary to maintain our professional standards, so our other Chapel handles that part while our room is currently being used for storage." Perhaps in that room we may have witnessed that which Mitford so aptly describes.

To return to Mr. Jones, the blood is drained out through the veins and replaced by embalming fluid pumped in through the arteries. As noted in *The Principles and Practices of Embalming,* "every operator has a favorite injection and drainage point—a fact which becomes a handicap only if he fails or refuses to forsake his favorites when conditions demand it." Typical favorites are the carotid artery, femoral artery, jugular vein, subclavian vein. There are various choices of embalming fluid. If Flextone is used, it will produce a "mild, flexible rigidity. The skin retains a velvety softness, the tissues are rubbery and pliable. Ideal for women and children." It may be blended with B. and G. Products Company's Lyf-Lyk tint, which is guaranteed to reproduce "nature's own skin texture . . . the velvety appearance of living tissue." Suntone comes in three separate tints: Suntan; Special Cosmetic Tint, a pink shade "especially indicated for young female subjects"; and Regular Cosmetic Tint, moderately pink.

About three to six gallons of a dyed and perfumed solution of formaldehyde, glycerin, borax, phenol, alcohol, and water is soon circulating through Mr. Jones, whose mouth has been sewn together with a "needle directed upward between the upper lip and gum and brought out through the left nostril," with the corners raised slightly "for a more pleasant expression." If he should be bucktoothed, his teeth are cleaned with Bon Ami and coated with colorless nail polish. His eyes, meanwhile, are closed with flesh-tinted eye caps and eye cement.

The next step is to have at Mr. Jones with a thing called a trocar. This is a long, hollow needle attached to a tube. It is jabbed into the abdomen, poked around the entrails and chest cavity, the contents of which are pumped out and replaced with "cavity fluid." This done, and the hole in the abdomen sewn up, Mr. Jones's face is heavily creamed (to protect the skin from burns which may be caused by leakage of the chemicals), and he is covered with a sheet and left unmolested for a while. But not for long—there is more, much more, in store for him. He has been embalmed, but not yet restored, and the best time to start the restorative work is eight to ten hours after embalming, when the tissues have become firm and dry.

The object of all this attention to the corpse, it must be remembered, is to make it presentable for viewing in an attitude of healthy repose. "Our customs require the presentation of our dead in the semblance of normality . . . unmarred by the ravages of illness, disease or mutilation," says Mr. J. Sheridan Mayer in his *Restorative Art*. This is rather a large order since few people die in the full bloom of health, unravaged by illness and unmarked by some disfigurement. The funeral industry is equal to the challenge: "In some cases the gruesome appearance of a mutilated or disease-ridden subject may be quite discouraging. The task of restoration may seem impossible and shake the confidence of the embalmer. This is the time for intestinal fortitude and determination. Once the formative work is begun and affected tissues are cleaned or removed, all doubts of success vanish. It is surprising and gratifying to discover the results which may be obtained."

The embalmer, having allowed an appropriate interval to elapse, returns to the attack, but now he brings into play the skill and equipment of sculptor and cosmetician. Is a hand missing? Casting one in plaster of Paris is a simple matter. "For replacement purposes, only a cast of the back of the hand is necessary; this is within the ability of the average operator and is quite adequate." If a lip or two, a nose or an ear should be missing, the embalmer has at hand a variety of restorative waxes with which to model replacements. Pores and skin texture are simulated by stippling with a little brush, and over this cosmetics are laid on. Head off? Decapitation cases are rather routinely handled. Ragged edges are trimmed, and head joined to torso with a series of splints, wires and sutures. It is a good idea to have a little something at the neck—a scarf or high collar—when time for viewing comes. Swollen mouth? Cut out tissue as needed from inside the lips. If too much is removed, the surface contour can easily be restored by padding with cotton. Swollen necks and cheeks are reduced by removing tissue through vertical incisions made down each side of the neck. "When the deceased is casketed, the pillow will hide the suture incisions . . . as an extra precaution against leakage, the suture may be painted with liquid sealer."

The opposite condition is more likely to present itself—that of emaciation. His hypodermic syringe now loaded with massage cream, the embalmer seeks out and fills the hollowed and sunken areas by injection. In this procedure the backs of the hands and fingers and the under-chin area should not be neglected.

Positioning the lips is a problem that recurrently challenges the ingenuity of the embalmer. Closed too tightly, they tend to give a stern, even disapproving expression. Ideally, embalmers feel, the lips should give the impression of being ever so slightly parted, the upper lip protruding slightly for a more youthful appearance. This takes some engineering, however, as the lips tend to drift apart. Lip drift can sometimes be remedied by pushing one or two straight pins through the inner margin of the lower lip and then inserting them between the two front upper teeth. If Mr. Jones happens to have no teeth, the pins can just as easily be anchored in his Armstrong Face Former and Denture Replacer. Another method to maintain lip closure is to dislocate the lower jaw, which is then held in its new position by a wire run through holes which have been drilled through the upper and lower jaws at the midline. As the French are fond of saying, *il faut souffrir pour être belle*.

If Mr. Jones has died of jaundice, the embalming fluid will very likely turn him green. Does this deter the embalmer? Not if he has intestinal fortitude. Masking pastes and cosmetics are heavily laid on, burial garments and casket interiors are color-correlated with particular care, and Jones is displayed beneath rose-colored lights. Friends will say, "How *well* he looks." Death by carbon monoxide, on the other hand, can be rather a good thing from the embalmer's viewpoint: "One advantage is the fact that this type of discoloration is an exaggerated form of a natural pink coloration." This is nice because the healthy glow is already present and needs but little attention.

The patching and filling completed, Mr. Jones is now shaved, washed and dressed. Cream-based cosmetic, available in pink, flesh, suntan, brunette and blond, is applied to his hands and face, his hair is shampooed and combed (and, in the case of Mrs. Jones, set), his hands manicured. For the horny-handed son of toil special care must be taken; cream should be applied to remove ingrained grime, and the nails cleaned. "If he were not in the habit of having them manicured in life, trimming and shaping is advised for better appearance—never questioned by kin."

Jones is now ready for casketing (this is the present participle of the verb "to casket"). In this operation his right shoulder should be depressed slightly "to turn the body a bit to the right and soften the appearance of lying flat on the back." Positioning the hands is a matter of importance, and special rubber positioning blocks may be used. The hands should be cupped slightly for a more lifelike, relaxed appearance. Proper placement of the body requires a delicate sense of balance. It should lie as high as possible in the casket, yet not so high that the lid, when lowered, will hit the nose. On the other hand, we are cautioned, placing the body too low "creates the impression that the body is in a box."

Jones is next wheeled into the appointed slumber room where a few last touches may be added—his favorite pipe placed in his hand or, if he was a great reader, a book propped into position. (In the case of little Master Jones a Teddy bear may be clutched.) Here he will hold open house for a few days, visiting hours 10 A.M. to 9 P.M.[21]

And then there is that proverbial question: What happens to us after we die? A must for anyone teaching the ideas of mortality vs. immortality is the book *Death and Western Thought* by Jacques Choron from which the following is heavily drawn. After death is there total annihilation? Does the soul survive while the body decays? Does the personality disintegrate, the body, or both? After death do we become something else, thus making the life-death progression circular; or is the progression linear? If we dream of the dead are they really dead?

For Aristotle (384-322 B.C.) our offspring are the only part of us surviving after death. Is this why we procreate? Do men write or do memorable deeds in order to "live on" after death? What about offspring who precede parents in death? Do we, after death, enter the body of a woman to be reborn in the child? Is our immortality to be found only in the continuation of the species? For Thales (c. 640-546 B.C.) all is water and if all is one then change (death) is acceptable, for we live on in water which is all. The body decays and the soul dissolves for Epicurus (341-270 B.C.), for death is the termination of all sensation both physically and spiritually. Plato speaks of universals (forms) which we (particulars) mirror. Because the soul can comprehend these forms (*thee* wisest of the wise, *thee* most beautiful, etc.), it in itself must be eternal. Schopenhauer (1788-1860) agrees with Plato, for how can organisms occupying a scale lower than man continue to live while man cannot?

David Hume (1711-1776) asks why our knowledge is confined to this life if there is another life. For Hume we are lacking in perceptions in infancy, we then develop and mature, and finally, in old age we begin to decay or lose our perceptions. So eventually we become that which we were—nothing. However, Bruno (1548-1600) would disagree. Space is infinite and because of that fact, nothing can end. Death merely transforms us from one state into another. This other state cannot be nothingness, for there is no end to infinity. Klages (1872-1955), however, sees everything as having a limited existence. Scientists tell us earth at once was not. Therefore, how can individual existence be always? Leibnitz (1646-1716) takes the position that all that is at one time was something else. Compressed humus eventually becomes coal; therefore, we are imperishable. We are simply developed or transformed into something else. The debate is endless, but perhaps we may only find the "true" outcome as described by Jaspers (1883-1969). For

Jaspers, we are constantly in situations with death being the ultimate situation. In the ultimate situation, we become aware that there is nothing or we become aware of our continued existence. Should such questions be brought to the fore and examined?

Finally, we enter the five stages of dying as outlined by Kubler-Ross.[22] In the *Denial* stage, statements such as, "No, not me, it can't be true" are frequently heard. As in the earlier years, death always happens to others. Next comes the *Anger,* or "Why me?" stage with the anger being displaced toward religious concepts. As the child cannot understand how Daddy got to heaven after watching the father placed into the ground, so the adult cannot understand why God gave us life only to take it away. Someone is to blame for my dying, and that someone is much like the "death-man." Then we begin to *Bargain.* Rules are obeyed and smiles are given in exchange for favors. "If I don't misbehave, I won't die." The fourth stage is that of *Depression.* "Why grow up at all if it is to end like this?" Finally, but not always, we *Accept* the fact of our terminality.

Miss T was a young woman in her thirties, black, single, and had been self-supporting. She had lost one hand in an accident, but, with the encouragement of her employer, had done a masterful job of overcoming this handicap; for example, she could type and knit. She was sent to our hospital for evaluation of a kidney condition that was found to be much more serious than anticipated.

The patient was eventually told that she needed to be signed up on the "kidney machine program" in order to live. Only two local hospitals had such programs for the indigent and both turned her down. When she was returned to our hospital, the staff had a hard time facing her. They had grown attached to this kind, soft-spoken woman and they could not comprehend that she was "condemned to death" as they referred to it. Nurses and the social worker felt the impact very deeply as they had the most contact with her. They felt both guilty and angry, raising questions about who has the right to choose who shall live and who shall die. They continued to visit her, but felt increasingly awkward and finally asked us to present her in our seminar—not so much for the patient's need as for themselves.

I interviewed Miss T a few days later. The hospital chaplain took part. Her trouble had begun, she said, with a shortness of breath about six months earlier. Doctors agreed that she had hypertension and malfunctioning kidneys. Medicine had not helped. Renal dialysis was recommended. She could not pay for treatment—it is costly—and she could not obtain it free. She felt rejected. At one of the three hospitals that she was in, the doctors were mainly of foreign extraction and she could not understand them. The food was not what she was used to. Toileting was a problem. The bathroom was down the hall. The bedpan service was poor.

She became mentally confused at this hospital, and often felt consciousness slipping away—"A little pile of smoke would come over, and I'd just fall asleep." She had repeated dreams of an operation and cure. When her sister called from California, Miss T told her she did not need to be on a kidney machine: "Everything is going to be all right."

By the time she came back to our hospital, she recognized that she was having difficulty distinguishing between her dream and reality. But she did come to face reality and it hurt her: "I was not accepted for the dialysis machine."

As her disease progressed, despite strict control of her fluid intake, her eyes began to fail. She could not crochet, knit, or read the Bible someone brought her—"So now I've taken up sleeping." Now, however, she had ordinary dreams. She did not lack for visits from friends and nephews, but her mother and sisters lived too far away to come.

She was a Methodist and had gone to church. She had some questions about God and the hereafter: 'You go to church, you hear people confess of seeing God, of God coming to them and cleansing their minds out. That has never happened to me; and I was wondering, does it really happen to people, or did it . . . just never happen to me?"

She had been a generous, giving person, and had helped persons in greater need than herself. So she was not concerned about God's judgment on that score. But she had not, as the chaplain phrased it, had a "bright religious experience," a sense of discovering God and being transformed. Was this what worried her?

"I feel that I am not getting any better, and will not get any better," she said. "I might ask now, why should I have to suffer so long? Why can't God come and get me now and take me out of misery? . . . Of course, doctors can do everything—that's their job, to try to save lives. But I just wonder, are they doing too much to save my life, since they know they cannot?"

At this point, Miss T began to tire. Within a few minutes, we drew the interview to a close. Her last comment was: "I don't know—I have a setup in my mind like there are two gardens, a garden here on earth and a garden in heaven; and I'm just waiting on God to say which of the gardens He wants me to work in."

At the end of the week following the interview I suddenly wanted to see this patient once more. There was an unraised question still hanging in the air and I thought it would be better to attempt to bring it out in the open. The weekend was coming up and with it perhaps increased loneliness. She might feel better to discuss the "unfinished business" once more. When I headed toward her room I was not sure what to say or how to start. It was just a sense of urgency to "do it now." I invited both a priest and a social worker to attend, but neither showed up. Thus I sat by her side and shared with her the feeling that we had to talk about it once more, not knowing exactly what "it" was.

Miss T looked at me with relief and acknowledged that she too had a sense of urgency. She too felt that there was a big and important question which she wanted to ask and which needed an answer. And so we sat—

almost like two children—digging in the dark and searching for something lost, not quite knowing what we had lost.

Miss T kept saying, "I know I am bad, bad, bad . . ." and though I did not share this feeling with her, we attempted to find out what she was bad about. Was it because she was black, or single and had no children, or because she had lived with a man and was not married? We went through the whole range of things that society could condemn but nothing "felt right." Finally I was ready to give up and said something to the effect that "only God knows what you should be bad about." She looked at me with a sigh of relief and almost cried: "That's it. God! I have been calling Him for help for the last few days. God help me! And I hear Him say in the back of my mind: "Why are you calling for help now and have never called when things were well? What do you say to that, Doctor Ross?"

She looked at me like a frightened child now, asking, demanding, an answer. For a glimpse of a moment I wished the priest was there. He would have had an answer, I thought. She looked at me and after what seemed like an eternity, she said again, this time very quietly, "What is your answer to that?" Now I heard myself talk quietly, naturally, without struggling for words. It suddenly seemed to be a very simple question. I asked her to share with me a picture of children playing in the playground. Mother is in the house minding her own work. Suddenly a little boy falls and hurts his knees. What do you think happens?

She looked at me surprised and answered: "The little boy cries and calls for Mother."

"What happens next?" I said.

"Mother helps him back on his feet and consoles him until he is all right."

"What happens next?" I insisted.

The same surprised look came over her face, as if she wondered why I would ask such a simple, almost silly question. "The boys go back to play and Mother continues her housework."

"The children have no use for her right now, isn't that right?"

She confirmed it and I continued: "Do you think Mother resents that?"

"A mother," she said almost angrily, "wouldn't resent that!"

I looked at her very seriously and replied, "A mother wouldn't resent it, and Father would?" pointing up into the sky. . . .

She looked with the happiest face I had seen in a long time, holding my hand lightly and smiled. She repeated almost inaudibly: "If a mother can accept that, Father will, too. How could I ever doubt that?" After a few moments of the most peaceful silence, she continued, "My time comes very close now, but everything is all right. I shared with you my concept of death, passing from this garden into the next. What is your concept?"

I thought for a while, and still looking at her face, I said, "Peace." Her last words were "I will pass into my garden very peacefully now." Miss T died a few hours later in her sleep.[23]

We have finally come to the end of the continuum with the questions being more sophisticated and more difficult to answer. However, when the questions asked are correlated with the age group from which they arise, the significance of the questions becomes equally important. Should we cast aside the euphemisms prior to entering the dying stages and attempt to examine and resolve our questions, or should we continue the masquerade in our death-denying culture?

## Some Sub-Issues Related to the Major Problem

For quite some time we have entered "Nature's Scheme" to examine, modify, alter, develop, and propose how we *ought to* progress in the early years along the birth-death continuum. We have terminated "life" by abortion. We have prohibited life by the use of birth control pills, vasectomies, and sterilization. We have induced and controlled the quality of life (by artificial insemination, hormone treatments, test-tube babies, selective breeding, and genetic manipulation. Erikson, Spock, Freud, and Piaget (to mention a few) propose how we ought to or do progress. At the other pole, we have dealt with capital punishment and murder. Should we not take a fresh look at the termination of life? If an individual has no say in his conception and has conducted his life through various crisis situations for forty years, should he, barring accidents, have the right to "peg-out" by his own choice?

### Should Cryogenics Be Incorporated in the Prolongation of Life?

If a person is frozen and held in a state of suspended animation for twenty-five years awaiting the discovery of the cure, what might be the quality of his life once restoration had occurred? Will magazine companies assemble a twenty-five page booklet pointing out our societal changes as was done for returning Vietnam prisoners of war? Will the adjustments be difficult for a World War II Japanese soldier who recently "surrendered"? How valid will this person's skills be in this new world? Should it be mandatory for these people to return to school? What would a dyed-in-the-wool Republican do if his party had become defunct? If our belief were that our immortality existed only in our offspring how would we react, if, upon returning, we discovered our children had died? Would such a person be able to function if our society had returned to the Hammurabi Code of an "eye for an eye"? Suggested classroom resources might be *The Prospects of Immortality* by Robert Ettinger, dealing with the medical, social, and legal implications of cryogenics and *The Second Genesis* by Albert Rosenfeld, concerned with resuscitation from clinical death, prenatal tampering, and control of behavior.

## Should the Practice of Infanticide Be Legalized?

If a mother dies in childbirth and there are no other family members to care for a surviving baby, should the child be killed, or should tax-supported foster homes, day care centers, or massive nurseries be formed? Should weak or deformed children be killed or allowed to die as was practiced in ancient Sparta? In societies where incest is not prohibited, as described in *Hawaii* by James Michener, should a genetically mutated child be submerged in the ocean? Should female infanticide be practiced for population control? Should a cancer-stricken single parent who feared her imbecile son would be left unattended be convicted for killing him? [24] "I sent my wife to the garden . . . and placed Jessie in the corner by the gas copper. She closed her eyes and went limp." [25] So testified Gorden Long after gassing his seven-year-old deformed daughter. Were the attempts to abandon Hansel and Gretel because there was not enough food to go around tending toward infanticide? If there are 30,000 babies born each year in America whose condition, if they survive, will be that of a vegetable, should doctors terminate their lives? [26] Should the courts have the right to overrule parents who refuse to sign surgical authorization forms because they deem their child is better off dead? [27] Suggested classroom resources could be *Oil of Dog* by Ambrose Bierce where oil is made from unwanted babies, *The Unconquered* by Somerset Maugham where a French woman drowns her child who was conceived in rape by a German soldier, *Mila 18* by Leon Uris where a crying child is strangled in order for the group to avoid detection by the Nazis, *Wonderland* [28] by Joyce Carol Oates where a father with a pregnant wife and suffering severe economic strain kills his children, and *Rosalie Prudent* by Guy de Maupassant where a lonely girl becomes pregnant and kills the child to avoid becoming ostracized.

## Should Genocide Be Prohibited?

Article II [29] from the United Nations General Assembly defines genocide to mean any of the following acts committed with intent to destroy in whole or in part a national, ethnic, racial, or religious group, as such: "killing members of the group, causing serious bodily or mental harm to members of the group, creating conditions calculated to bring about physical destruction of the group, imposing measures intended to prevent births within the group, or forcibly transferring children of the group to another group." Should a nation, in time of war, have the right to eliminate members of any of the above mentioned groups if those groups are the ones being fought? If any group displays adverse or detrimental characteristics harmful to the general populous should the group be eliminated? As of March, 1970, the United States had refused to ratify the 1948 U.N. Resolution. Why? [30] Why does a raven never aim at the eye of another raven, and a wolf not kill another wolf who has bared its throat, while man kills his own species? [31] Was the My Lai massacre of March, 1968 an example of genocide? Was the dropping of the atomic bomb on Hiroshima an example of genocide? [32,33] Suggested classroom resources could be *Bury My Heart at Wounded Knee* by Dee Brown where at the Sandy Creek Massacre, tobacco pouches were made from breasts and scrotums, *The Kimono* by Don Gorden found in *The Writing on the Wall* by Walter Lowenfels which deals with the effects of radiation from the atom bomb, *Andersonville* by John McElroy where 13,000 Union prisoners died, *The War—A Concise History 1939-1945* by Louis Snyder which deals with Nazi sadism, or the *National Lampoon, November, 1973 Encyclopedia of Humor* which shows beheading in India, Jews in concentration camps, and Indians in America.

## Should Suicide Be Legalized?

The Department of Health, Education, and Welfare reports that there were 21,372 suicides in America in 1968. Another 200,000 tried it,[34] and it is the tenth leading cause of death. Deaths due to accidents total 114,864. Dublin [35] reports that 25-33 per cent of suicides are reported as accidents. Also, approximately 15 per cent of all single car accidents resulting in death were suicides. The actual number of suicides is twice those reported. If the choice is either death now or death later, should those who wish to leave when they choose be prohibited from doing so?

If suicide violates the self-preservation instinct, then do celibates violate the sexual fulfillment need? [36] If we are God's property, then should He decide our life? Williams states that poison is also God's property, so why did He leave it here? If God makes us suffer for our own salvation, then is suicide against the will of God? Do we all have a "cross to bear"? If "Thou Shalt Not Kill" includes suicide, then should we not become vegetarians, abolish capital punishment, and prohibit war? Does cruel and unusual punishment found in the Constitution conflict with "Thou Shalt Not Kill"? If there is an instinct in animals to die by refusing food or crawling under the porch, do not humans have the right to decide when they should die? [37] If Christ was the Son of God and if he possessed God-like qualities, could he have, had he wished, refused to be crucified? If so, then did he not consent to his death, which is suicide? If heaven is that eternal bliss described,

then why prolong our stay here on earth? Who controls our body—
the State, ourselves, or God? [38] If we control our body, is suicide then
homicide of the self? If we have self-determination, should we then
have certain inalienable rights—the right to die? [39] Are we not slowly
committing suicide by using drugs, alcohol, or tobacco?

If the Purañas permit persons who "suffer from incurable diseases"
to commit suicide by drowning, starvation, or falling from cliffs, should
the same right be given us? [40] Dublin [41] lists five reasons recognized by
the Marias as justifying suicide. He further reports that the most dominant motive for suicide among the Mohave Indians is "a desire to
achieve reunion with the dead." In India, a common practice was for
the widow to throw herself upon her husband's funereal pyre. Alvarez [42]
reports that suicide for the Vikings was second only to death in battle
for entry into Valhalla, that violent death was a "passport to paradise"
among the Marquesas Islanders, and that the Tasmanian aborigines
committed "suicide as a race by refusing to breed" because they were
hunted for sport. He also mentions people offering themselves for
execution to amuse the public. Tickets would be sold with the money
going to the heirs.

Should we be offended when a citizen protests the policies of his
nation by committing hara-kiri, by burning himself to death as did
Buddhist monks during the Vietnam war, or by shooting himself as
did Paul Cabell [43] because of racism in the high schools? Should we
respect the captain who goes down with his ship? If a soldier falls
upon a hand grenade to protect his comrades and dies, should he be
given a medal? Is the fighting of duels a form of suicide? Should one
commit suicide to escape from torture at the hands of an enemy?
Should people with fatal diseases be permitted to commit suicide? Should
children be allowed to commit suicide upon suffering from the loss of
a parent?

A 6½-year-old boy was admitted to a psychiatric service after a serious
suicide attempt. He stated clearly that he wanted to kill himself so that
he could join his dead father in heaven. The father had died suddenly of
a myocardial infarct a year prior to the boy's admission. The boy presented
a graphic description of his fantasied life with his father in heaven. In
essence, it was a fun-filled life, an endless picnic in an eternal park. He
kept asking, "How do you know it isn't so?" In spite of thorough discussion,
he persisted in his belief—encouraged by his mother who believed the
same thing. The conflict was resolved by the child when he announced one
day that he had decided that he would wait for God to send him to heaven
since that was His work. Follow-up evaluation four and six years later
revealed that he was making an excellent adaptation. He still believed that
it would be God's decision but, "The whole thing is in the back of my
mind." [44]

Suggested classroom resources could be suicide notes found in Lester and Lester,[45] a quote by Kirillov in Dostoyevsky's *The Possessed* which says man invented God so as not to kill himself and one in *La Nouvelle Héloïse* by Rousseau which says that we have a right to cut life short if it is a burden, the songs *Think I'm Gonna Kill Myself* by Elton John, *Richard Cory,* and *Most Peculiar Man* by Simon and Garfunkel, a letter from Dorothy found in *Harper's* of February, 1973, a suicide test published in *Science Digest* of November, 1972, and the books *Suicide* by Jacques Choron, *In a Darkness* by James A. Wechsler,[46] and *The Savage God: A Study of Suicide* by A. Alvarez.

### Should Voluntary Euthanasia Be Legalized?

"I am a broken piece of machinery. I am ready." [47]
(Last words of Woodrow Wilson, January 31, 1924.)

Eight-hundred-sixty people per day (more than one individual every two minutes) die of cancer in America. Thirty-three out of every one-hundred die from cardiovascular diseases, and respiratory ailments claim another thirteen per cent.[48,49] If we are, or do become, one of the twenty-million Americans aged sixty-five or over,[50] will we also become a "broken piece of machinery"? Ninety per cent of us desire death from natural causes,[51] but for few of us is the wish realized. Should we begin now to question the quality of our life before we become terminal, bedridden, paralyzed, diapered, or tube-fed, or should we play the odds, hoping to escape such an end? Is it better to live a meaningful existence, or better merely to survive? Should the quantity of human life be emphasized over its quality. Levine and Scotch [52] state that the "median length of time between onset of illness and death is 29 months," of which 6 weeks of special care are required among terminal patients.[53] Will we become a "vegetable" with complete dependency upon others? Will we physically decay to the point of disgust?

Should a patient be told that he is suffering from an irreversible, terminal disease? Depending on the survey, between 70-90 per cent of the doctors interviewed favor telling the patient, while between 77-89 per cent of the patients said they wanted to be told.[54,55] The exact number who *are* told falls far short of these figures, and the patients must discover for themselves by acting out their final role as Glaser and Strauss [56] so aptly describe. The patient enters the *Closed Awareness* stage where the terminality is kept secret by the staff and family. His terminality is shrouded by "medical jargon" and coded progress reports kept "out of reach." Conversations center around "non-harmful symptoms" and "medical procedures used during the operation." Suddenly, when the patient senses further "bodily deterioration," when conversations center around "present and not future events," when the staff becomes paternalistic, when "further tests become necessary," or "facial expressions to direct questions break down," the dying person enters the *Suspicious Awareness* stage. The word *cancer* in conversations is quickly registered. The reason is sought for the move to the new floor. Reactions to loaded questions such as, "It's not cancer is it, Doctor?," "Will I get better?," "I'm going to die, aren't I?," [57] are carefully observed. Special favors granted without explanation, the doctor's optimism or lack of it, and the amount of time staff personnel spend with him serve as further clues. If the charade is not halted, the players enter the *Mutual Pretense* stage where the patient knows he is terminal, but the game is continued. The patient pretends by "dressing for the part of the not-dying patient," "grooming," "applying make up," "going to the toilet by himself," or by "fixing up the room so it looks like home." Nurses counter by commenting on "how lovely your hair looks this morning," serving meals on time, changing sheets frequently, and ignoring any slips the patient might make. Finally, but not always, the *Open Awareness* stage is reached where the pretense is dropped. The questions we have and the answers we seek must come fast; for pain and sedation have increased, while time is running out. Should the patient be told?

If we can choose where to die—on a battleground, in nursing homes, centers for the aged, housing developments for Senior Citizens—should we have the right to determine how to die, or should others decide for us? Will we receive the same treatment if we are "hoboes," "derelicts," those with "criminal records," histories of "drug addiction" or "alcoholism" who have contributed little to society [58] as compared with presidents, generals, astronauts, etc.?

## Stages in Considering This Controversial Issue

The remaining part of this chapter will deal with the fifth sub-issue: Euthanasia. In 1950, Dr. Herman Sander was charged "with the murder of a cancer-stricken patient. Dr. Sander had given the patient ten cc's of air intravenously four times and she died within ten minutes." [59,60,61] Mrs. Waskins, suffering from leukemia and in extreme pain, begged her twenty-three-year-old son to kill her. The jury found the son not guilty by reason of insanity.[62] On June 20, 1973, Lester Zygmaniak, using a shotgun, killed his brother, George, who was paralyzed from the neck down as the result of a motorcycle accident.[63,64] In December, 1973, Dr. Montemarano was charged with injecting an overdose of potassium chloride into Eugene Bauer's veins, as Bauer was suffering from cancer of the throat.[65,66]

Do we have a right to die in dignity? Surely "a society that condones death in war of young men who want to live, should be willing to permit the death of an aged person who wants to die." [67] Should this right be confined to only aged people, or also to those of age, in sound mind, who previously choose how they wish to die if particular circumstances arise? Are there certain cases in which it is really indecent to continue living? [68]

## The Origin of the Issue

Who decides who shall live and who shall die? In Sparta, defective children were hurled from the cliffs or left to die from exposure. Both Plato and Aristotle favored the death of deformed children. Strabo, the geographer, tells of the Island Cos where custom ruled that the very aged who, "having outlived their usefulness to society, would gather annually as for a banquet and quit the world in unison by drinking together a lethal poison." [69] In America, the Omaha and Hopi Indians left the aged behind on the trail [70] while the Comanches preferred death in battle before old age.[71] Hinton reports that the old were buried alive in Samoa. If a parent showed signs of senility, it was the duty of the son to kill him in Fiji. The aged and insane were shot by the Montagnais of Labrador while in Sudan the deaf and dumb were buried alive.[72] An Eskimo family would set an aged member adrift on ice to die.[73] But those are examples where the family or society has decided how we die. Should we have a right to decide for ourselves? In 1967, a notice was placed on the bulletin board at the direction of Dr. McMath at Neasden Hospital in London, England, which stated who were not to be resuscitated. "The very elderly, over 65, those with malignant diseases, chronic chest disease, or chronic renal disease" were not to be saved.[74] Have we no control over our lives?

Putting to death such a person in Italy is a crime if the person is under eighteen years of age. Russia has an eight-year prison term for the same offense [75] while in Switzerland a doctor may put poison in the hands of a patient, but not administer it himself.[76] Although the usual procedure in the United States is to try a person for murder, the jury generally returns a verdict of innocent by reason of insanity. In America, if one is dying from a terminal illness and refuses to sign hospital surgical authorization forms (depending on the state wherein he resides), the court may overrule his objections. Even if the husband is comatose, the court may overrule the wife's objections.[77] Because the courts have refused to meet the issue head-on, we are placed in the position of trying to decide which course to follow as each occasion arises. Should society decide, and, if so, who should be included? Should one's relative decide—as in the Zygmaniak case—or should one's doctor decide—as in the Sander and Montemarano cases? Should one decide for himself before the occasion arises?

## Definition of the Issue

The two forms of euthanasia encountered in the readings are active or direct, and passive or indirect. The former is a deliberate, intentional act to *shorten* or end life. The injection of air into the veins is one such example. The latter is deciding not to do anything which may *prolong* life. This could take the form of patients themselves electing not to take medicine, ceasing treatments which may prolong life, or withholding treatments altogether.[78,79,80] The problem is really drawing the line between prolonging a patient's life and prolonging his dying. Depending on the viewpoint held, teachers might use both definitions when discussing the hypothesis.

Although not appearing in the writings of antiquity, the word *euthanasia* is Greek in origin.[81] Eu = well and Thanatos = death; thus, we arrive at an easy or good death. And if it is voluntary, we choose our own death.

## Some Hypotheses Generated by the Controversial Issue

If voluntary euthanasia is legalized, then those participants might be in violation of the Sixth Commandment.

If voluntary euthanasia is legalized, then resources, space, and time would be released for the proper care of others.

If voluntary euthanasia is legalized, then doctors would be in violation of the Hippocratic Oath.

If voluntary euthanasia is legalized, then attempts to find cures become meaningless and there is an admission to defeat.

If voluntary euthanasia is legalized, then the law might become a protective device for those who wish to include dissenters, low academic achievers, racial or religious groups, or college professors.

If voluntary euthanasia is not legalized, then the Eighth Amendment to the Constitution is violated, for we would not be doing all we could to relieve pain.

If voluntary euthanasia is legalized, then a mistake found in diagnosis could not reverse the process.

If voluntary euthanasia is not legalized, then we are refusing to face the moral dilemma the issue generates.

If voluntary euthanasia is legalized, then so must suicide.

If voluntary euthanasia is legalized, then the legal process to safeguard the act would be too cumbersome to be effective.

### Some Data Related to the Hypotheses

*Mark:* Let's face it, James, speaking strictly from a Judeo-Christian framework, the legalization of euthanasia, be it voluntary or not, violates God's commandment—Thou Shall Not Kill.

*James:* Mark, I agree. However, can we be positive that the translation from the Hebrew is accurate? I mean, suppose the commandment had some qualifiers such as Thou Shall Not Kill unless . . . or Thou Shall Not Kill, but thou may allow to die if . . .

*Mark:* Okay, but suppose the interpretation of Thou Shall Not Kill means thou shall not commit murder. It is murder if we assist in euthanasia, and self-murder, or suicide, if the patient assists himself. And don't hit me with the argument that if we allow for no exceptions, then we must outlaw war, become vegetarians, and prohibit capital punishment.

*James:* I don't know. There just seem to be inconsistencies in singing "Onward Christian Soldiers Marching Off to War" with "Thou Shall Not Kill." Are you sure your opposition to euthanasia does not stem from the horrors of the gladiatorial shows? Is dying for martyrdom justified while voluntary euthanasia is not?

*Mark:* You don't understand. Suffering paves the way to salvation. It is the atonement for our sins, and a means of obtaining grace.

*James:* Ya, but if suffering is a "blessing in disguise" then why try to relieve any suffering? Why even set a broken leg?

*Mark:* Now you're tending toward the absurd. The question is "Do we or do we not have the right to play God?" [82]

*James:* I think the question is "Is God a personal or a group God?" If a person chooses to avoid suffering by consenting to euthanasia, it is the person and not the group who must answer to God. Even Pope Pius XII agreed that we are under no obligation to use extraordinary means to keep people alive.

*Mark:* Using extraordinary means to keep people alive is different from using direct means to kill them.

*James:* Let me tell you about Delores Heston, a 22-year-old Jehovah's Witness. She was severely injured in an automobile accident and scheduled for surgery in which blood transfusions would be part of the operation but her mother said no, and signed a form freeing the hospital from liability. The hospital persuaded the court to appoint a guardian who signed the surgical form, the operation was successful, and the patient lived.[83] Had she been allowed to follow her religious beliefs, she would have died.

*Mark:* That doesn't violate what I've been asserting all along. She should have been saved.

*James:* You missed the point. According to *your* religious ideas she should have been saved. Her religious convictions do not hold with blood transfusions.

*Mark:* Death is natural and is controlled by God. By man injecting death, God's scheme is violated.

*James:* But artificial insemination, sterilization, and abortion also interfere with God's scheme. If we control life, shouldn't we also control death?

*Mark:* I'm simply saying we should not kill people. When God wants us, He will call.

*James:* Let's leave God out of it and consider the economic factor. Dr. Sackett, a physician and a member of the Florida Legislature testifying before the Senate Committee on aging, has estimated in Florida alone, it would cost five billion dollars to allow "1500 individuals retarded to the point that they are bedridden, diapered, tube-fed, and completely unaware to live out artificial lives prolonged by the marvels of science." He goes on to say that the money "could better be used on persons with illnesses that could be cured, such as those that need kidney transplants." [84] What can you say to that?

*Mark:* It costs $37,000 per year to operate a kidney machine. [85] Do you think the money saved would really be used to help those who are less fortunate? Seems like I heard that argument used during Vietnam. If we pulled out of Vietnam, the money could be channelled to other areas. Health and education haven't received any economic boost. And if we stick strictly with transplants and forget the machines, where and how do we get the needed parts, and who should the recipients be? This time you really talked yourself into a quagmire. Are you suggesting others ought to be included rather than only the terminally ill?

*James:* No. I think some guidelines are necessary, but we must consider the additional space gained in our hospitals and the doctors who could be released to care for those who can be cured. Let me read you this quote from the *Times:* "Sometimes these living 'corpses' have 'survived' for years, draining the financial and emotional resources of families or of society before the last physical simulation of life was lost." [86] Besides, doctors like to send patients home to die so needed space can be put to better use.

*Mark:* You're too much! Earlier you mentioned a personal God instead of a group God, and now you bring in how society can benefit.

*James:* Okay. Consider it in another aspect. In youth, consumption exceeds production and society makes the investment in hope of a future payoff. In the adult years, production exceeds consumption, and the surplus goes to support individuals and groups. But with the elderly, their consumption greatly exceeds production and there is no future expectation of contribution.[87]

*Mark:* Can't the richest nation in the world afford to decently care for the elderly? Don't they have a right to dignity in their remaining years?

*James:* That's what I've been trying to tell you. They *do* have a right to "peg-out" upon their own choosing.

*Mark:* But let's not forget one more thing.

*James:* Such as?

*Mark:* Such as the fact that many do not and would not choose to die because they themselves feel useless, but because they sense they are a burden to their families. Often familial members themselves convey feelings of contempt to the patient.[88,89]

*James:* What do you think about the Hippocratic Oath?

*Mark:* I'm glad you brought that up because if doctors participated in euthanasia, they would violate their ethical standards.

*James:* Sounds like the confidentiality-of-this-office argument to me.

*Mark:* Be serious, James. It clearly states that "to please no one will I prescribe a deadly drug nor give advice which may cause his death." [90]

*James:* Aren't you leaving part of it out?

*Mark:* What do you mean?

*James:* Well, here's another interpretation: "I will use treatments to help the sick according to my ability and judgment, but never with a view to injury and wrongdoing. I will not give anyone a lethal dose if asked to do so, nor will I suggest such a course." [91] What do we do if the help the sick themselves want is a lethal dose? Oh, wait a minute. Let me read you another addition to the Oath. "Into whatever houses I enter I will go into them for the benefit of the sick and will abstain from every voluntary act of mischief and corruption and, further, from the seduction of females or males, bond or free." [92] Don't you think it is time to write a new code of ethics rather than following one which is 2300 years old? Really now, talking of seducing females.

*Mark:* It may not be as outdated as you think.

*James:* Why not?

*Mark:* Suppose the intent was to keep the doctor from killing the patient in order to prohibit the doctor and the spouse from receiving the property of the deceased? A modern example would be to euthanize a patient thus cutting out one beneficiary of a will and installing another.

*James:* Okay, but suppose you have a life insurance policy that pays

off at age 70 and are terminally ill. Perhaps the spouse would persuade the doctors to embark on life prolongation techniques in
order to receive the insurance.

*Mark:* Would that really do any good? Think about your economic
arguments. And another thing. As long as you so freely use
quotes, let me give you one. Dr. Christian Barnard wrote that he
was close to committing euthanasia on a woman suffering from
cancer when suddenly he decided that he was "violating not only
the laws of social man, but also my own most personal ethic."
He went on to say that the next day the woman rallied and lived
for several years.[93]

*James:* Might doctors engaged in the transplantation business prematurely shorten the life of a patient in order to secure the needed
part? If the patient had voluntarily consented to euthanasia, it
would not make a difference, but if he had not (which is your
position) then euthanasia may be performed anyhow.

*Mark:* That really is a dilemma. Let me complicate it by saying that
the Nightingale Pledge for Nurses also prohibits the administration
of any harmful drug.[94] Doctors are trained to deal with life and
you suggest they must now cope with death?

*James:* Mark, physicians are not only bound to heal, but also to relieve pain. I think the dilemma from a doctor's view is—should
they do all that is possible to keep the patient alive if that course
prolongs pain and suffering? The mere preservation of life must
not be the sole objective of treatment.[95]

*Mark:* Hey, I just thought of another one. Suppose euthanasia is performed and then a cure was discovered. You can't deny modern
medicine has done wonders in this area. We have insulin for
diabetics and vaccines for smallpox, typhus, polio, and cholera. All
have been defeated.

*James:* I suppose this tends toward an economic argument, but some
diseases can't be truly diagnosed without considerable expense and
suffering on the patient's part. Now I can use your old argument—
aren't there some overzealous relatives who want all possibilities
explored? Haven't we heard, "Do all you can, Doctor"?

*Mark:* If but a few lives are saved, does that not justify the attempt?
Perhaps we will never find a cure unless drugs are tested in humans.

*James:* Do you suggest keeping people alive simply to gain medical
knowledge?

*Mark:* I suppose I do. How else can the cures be tested? Would you
favor treating pneumonia that a terminal patient had contracted?

*James:* No.

*Mark:* Well, I do.  We do have effective cures for pneumonia, and once
that is arrested, we can experiment on the patient to find a cure
for the cancer.  We must take the attitude that there is no such
thing as an incurable disease.  If attitudes like this aren't taken,
we would still be chained to the earth by gravity.  Can you say
with certainty a condition is hopeless?

*James:* What happens if the cure turns out to be a half-cure?  Perhaps
even if a cure is found, rehabilitation would be improbable.  I
admit cures could stop the further spread of, say, cancer, but they
can't repair the damage already done.

*Mark:* Perhaps the temporary cure would be long enough for that person to do something he has always wanted to do, such as travel
or write a book.

*James:* That's a good point.  Maybe a time limit to find a cure before
euthanasia is performed could be set up.  How do you react to this
story?

One day a middle-aged woman became suddenly blind in one eye.  The
terror of this unheralded experience was rapidly offset by recovery of
vision in subsequent weeks.  Attacks of giddiness and shaking of the legs
and head followed, again to improve but again to reappear.  This was the
onset of multiple sclerosis, a disorder where disseminated foci of damage
occur throughout the brain and spinal cord.  Slowly but inexorably the
patient was forced to bed and was ultimately unable to leave it because of
paralysis of the lower limbs.  Soon, control of the bladder and anal muscles
led to incontinence of urine and faeces.  Bed sores developed and were so
large and deep that the underlying bones of the pelvis were eroded as well.
This abject image of misery and pain was kept going by the frequent administration of antibiotic and pain-relieving drugs.  Is it justifiable to prolong such a life, if life it be?  In this question we are faced with the fundamental problem of the meaning of man's existence.[96]

*Mark:* It's a very powerful story.  Now let's hear your reactions to this
one.

When a middle-aged man became giddy a cerebellar tumour was diagnosed and removed.  The pathologist's report was surprising: he said that
this tumour was derived not from brain tissue but rather from cancer of
the bronchus.  Careful examination of the man's chest revealed a small
tumour in his lung.  Despite the likelihood that he had widespread cancerous
disease the lung tumour was removed.  The patient survived, and there was
no recurrence of neoplastic disease.  This is an example of an unlikely but
occasionally possible event that is not unappreciated in medicine.  Such
cases support the views of those who fear the indiscriminate application of
the principles of euthanasia.  If the surgeon had not tried to save this life,
as indeed he might well have been justified in not doing in view of the

heavy odds against success, the man would have surely died of lung cancer.[97]

*James:* You really balance out the sides, don't you?

*Mark:* Say, James, I would like to regress a bit to a point you cleverly avoided answering. Remember when we were discussing the economic argument and I asked if you favored including others for euthanasia than only the terminally ill?

*James:* Yes.

*Mark:* If the law is passed to euthanize the terminally ill will it be extended to include those on welfare, noncontributors, those of another race, the deformed, the idiot, or the senile? The Nazis used euthanasia as a catchall, and I heard somewhere that blankets infected with smallpox were distributed among American Indians for the benefit of the settlers.

*James:* Undoubtedly, this is one area where stringent guidelines would have to be drawn and enforced. Can we even be positive that any law will not be violated? Suppose the health department, upon immunizing school children, decided at the same time to sterilize a select group. We would never know for at least ten years, and once the act was performed, the damage could not be repaired.

*Mark:* It's still a great concern to me. Once the inhibitions are removed, it seems more likely the law would be violated by stretching the technical terms the law contained.

*James:* Yes, but the inhibitions are removed for soldiers in war time, and they don't return home to carry on with a disregard for the law. Furthermore, we execute prisoners, and that practice did not extend itself to those serving terms for a lesser crime.

*Mark:* I'm still not convinced. Let's see if Mr. Wolff and Mr. Hilson can help clear this up in History class tomorrow.

*Mr. Wolff:* You two have displayed behavioral patterns like this all year.

*Mark:* Ah, come on Mr. Wolff. It isn't that James and I don't enjoy the class, it's just. . .

*Mr. Hilson:* It's just that we couldn't get a sound out of you two when we covered the crime-criminal unit last six weeks.

*Mark:* No, not really. It's just that we have had that prison reform stuff since the ninth grade. But we got to thinking that if controversy is generated over putting to death a convicted murderer, then think of the flak over putting to death a person who has done nothing wrong. Can you help us?

*Mr. Hilson:* Well, we can try. Are you ready, Mr. Wolff?

*Mr. Wolff:* Ready, Mr. Hilson.

*Mr. Hilson:* Okay, first I think I have to side with Mark and agree that euthanasia should not be legalized. Take pain, for instance. There are few cases where pain can't be alleviated. If you consider radiation or X-ray therapy, morphine or heroin for drugs, or surgery where nerves between the brain and pain are severed or neurosurgical operations, it becomes readily apparent that most of the terminally ill do not suffer.

*Mr. Wolff:* Even if that were true, the quality of life would have to be considered. My wife is a nurse and told me that in some cases, pain is only alleviated by injecting so many drugs that the patients are constantly in a comatose condition. We also have to look at psychological pain. How about the person who is not in pain but can't walk, swallow, or urinate?

*Mr. Hilson:* We will have to do some research to see how many are aware when they enter the dying stage. Most are probably comatose toward the last anyway. And as for the quality of life, if the body had quality, it would not be in the dying state.

*Mr. Wolff:* They are in the comatose state because they become addicted to the drugs, and the injections to relieve pain must come more frequently. Sooner or later the doctor will have to administer a dosage large enough to relieve the pain which will be fatal, or he will have to leave the patient without relief. Should a person whose pain is relieved, but whose mind is in the twilight zone be allowed to live?

*Mr. Hilson:* But we are accustomed to pain throughout our lives and take various drugs for relief. Often the drugs have a psychological effect by deluding us to think the pain has subsided.

*Mr. Wolff:* Let me read you this little tidbit from *The Guardian*:[98] "The stark truth is that all patients dying of old age must now expect, as a matter of routine, to be forced through an additional period, sometimes a long period of pain and/or acute discomfort before death finally comes." If that characterizes old age imagine if the old also had cancer.

*Mr. Hilson:* Why did the article say they can now expect? At one time could they have not expected to be forced through that period? I think I'll tell your wife that that part—in sickness and in health till death do us part—has no meaning to you.

*Mr. Wolff:* Ah, yes, but tell her also we have a right to life, liberty, and the pursuit of happiness. If pain is happiness or life, I would just as soon have neither.

*Mr. Hilson:* How about the 8th Amendment to the Constitution which forbids cruel and unusual punishment? You took that position when you opposed capital punishment by saying we ought to punish the cause of the crime, and not the person who committed it.

*Mr. Wolff:* There goes the bell, fellows. We'll have to continue this later.

*Mark:* Well, James, what did you think?

*James:* Those two teachers simply confused me more than I was before. How about you?

*Mark:* Same here. Let's go get some lunch.

*James:* I made some real simple mistakes on my math test and I want you to go over the problems with me.

*Mark:* You say you made some mistakes? That's really a scream.

*James:* What's so funny about it?

*Mark:* Suppose a doctor made a mistake in diagnosis and the patient was euthanized. This is one mistake which can't be corrected.

*James:* We are all fallible. There are no 100 per cent safeguards in anything.

*Mark:* What happens if a patient wishes to fight on, but is in such a state he can't convey his thoughts? Would he be a candidate for euthanasia?

*James:* By it being a voluntary act, we can avoid that situation.

*Mark:* But suppose he agreed to it one day while in pain, and the next day changed his mind. How can we be sure what his true intent is?

*James:* That's a difficult one to answer. If it's possible to make a mistake by completing some action, it is also possible to make a mistake by not doing it. There are always words left unsaid or missed opportunities by not acting.

*Mark:* I think the whole idea of having the patient concur that he is better off dead raises more problems.

*James:* How is that?

*Mark:* Well, if he is in pain, how can a reflective decision be made? Should we stop administering drugs so a decision is made while his mind is not hazed?

*James:* Why not have provisions drawn up before the disease arrives?

*Mark:* Could you bind yourself by contract to be killed in the future?

*James:* Seems like we're kind of running around in circles. Let's check with some other teachers for ideas and meet at my house tonight.

*Mark:* Okay. See you tonight.

*James:* Hi, Mark. Come on in. Did you find out any goodies to help clear up the controversy?

*Mark:* I sure did. I checked first with Mrs. Plummer, the Humanities teacher, and she brought out some interesting questions.

*James:* Come on, tell me.

*Mark:* Okay. She first asked who would decide to turn off life-saving machines and, secondly, at which point should the "plug be pulled." She asked if it is a question of killing people or one of letting people die, one of causing harm or permitting harm to occur. She wanted to know if I thought it would be degrading to allow my body to decompose. And then she hit me with one which really staggered me. Are you ready for this?

*James:* Get on with it.

*Mark:* She wanted to know that if euthanasia were legalized if a system of rites would follow.

*James:* What do you mean by that?

*Mark:* Well, we have formalities and phrases set up for everything else, so maybe we would have the last shot instead of the last dinner. Instead of the religious leader with his Bible, we would have the euthanizer with his needle. We would also have to invite certain people to observe the termination, maybe even high school field trips could be included. Of course, a special room at the end of the hall would be where the euthanizer would "operate," and instead of the last walk, we would have the last carting.

*James:* Wow. That's powerful.

*Mark:* Yea, what did you learn?

*James:* First, we are going to have to study the laws regarding suicide and murder. Mr. Wolff's wife said the staff becomes angry with patients who attempt suicide.

*Mark:* Why?

*James:* Because they like to have control, and a person who attempts suicide shows he is in control of his faculties.

*Mark:* What else?

*James:* Mr. Evans suggested we deal with the legal aspects of the controversy. He said it has taken three years so far for a judge to rule on whether students belong in our school district or in another district. Once a person consented to be euthanized, would parents, courts, siblings, etc., appeal the decision? Safeguards would have to be established and enforced. A panel of people representing various fields would have to be selected to decide which of the candidates qualify.

*Mark:* Let's see if we can do an Independent Study with Mrs. Hutchins to set up the legal machinery.

*James:* Okay.

*Mark:* This summer why don't we research homicide and suicide and try to put it all together in the fall?

*James:* That sounds great. Listen, I'm going to have to split.

*Mark:* Okay, catch you later.

## Some Tentative Conclusions

Have you ever seen the bumper sticker which reads: *Kidneys—Donate Them; Don't Bury Them*? An ever-increasing number of Americans donate blood, eyes, kidneys, and even bodies to foundations or medical schools. Let's face it, most of us like life, and if we can't live then at least our benevolence aids those who can. This emphasis we show toward longevity poses some problems. If you are an organ donor, your life may be prematurely shortened in order to secure the needed part—especially if you show signs of being terminal. Perhaps insurance companies would invoke their suicide clause and refuse to pay organ donor policyholders. Should organ transplants be made available to everyone, or should restrictive criteria for use be outlined? Should the elite and/or contributors have priority?

If artificial hearts increase life expectancy to say age 200, would mandatory birth control be incorporated? Think of the prospect of retiring at age 120 instead of 65. Of course, some of us could flood the colleges and get dual doctoral degrees. Dr. Pickering of Oxford thinks his profession will be able to replace every part except the brain and thus the time will come when "those with senile brains and senile behavior will form an ever-increasing fraction of the inhabitants of the earth." [99] As life expectancy increases, society will have to determine the allocation of resources based on age. We have already seen that the elderly consume more than they produce.

Our entire society as we know it today would be radically different. Think of what fewer births and longer lives would do to the funeral industry. Educators would be forced to deal with leisure as a classroom topic. Massive shuffleboard parks with checker and chess tables ringing their perimeters would be built. Americans would have to be taught how to relax!

In the future, man will die when someone has determined that he should, or when he himself decides. Who will be the death allocator? Will society echo the voice of O'Brien, the Party functionary of Ingsoc, in *1984* who said, "In the future, there will be no wives and no friends. Children will be taken from their mothers at birth, as one takes eggs from a hen. Procreation will be an annual formality like the renewal of a ration card. Our neurologists are at work upon it now." [100]

## Suggested Methods for Dealing with This Issue

The teacher might wish to begin with the early years on the birth-death continuum. Topics to discuss could be the control of conception,[101] sterilization, and abortion found in William's work, and prenatal

tampering found in *The Second Genesis* by Alfred Rosenfeld. Working
our way along the scale, *Flowers for Algernon* by Daniel Keyes dealing
with operating to increase IQ, and *One Flew Over the Cuckoo's Nest*
by Ken Kesey dealing with mental patients might be used. In the later
years, *After Many a Summer Dies the Swan* by Aldous Huxley, where
a millionaire searches for eternal life, or *I Will Fear No Evil* by Robert
Heinlein, where an old man's brain is transplanted into a new body,
might be used. *Old Age in a Changing Society* by Zena Blau could be
incorporated toward the end of the continuum. *The Prospects of Immortality* by Robert Ettinger, dealing with cryogenics, is another. And
then a slow lead into the problems of euthanasia could begin by handing
out a story on mongoloid babies,[102] or perhaps the following response
by a mother to a judge who suggested having an institution care for her
child suffering as a result of thalidomide:[103] "That was a solution for *my*
problem, but not for my child's." Another effective handout is when
Moses is telling the Lord that the commandment "Thou Shalt Not Kill"
should be revised to read "Thou shalt not kill any person between the
ages of minus four months and 18 years at a distance of less than 500
yards with any of the following. . . ."[104] The stage is now set for the
case of Mrs. B who is dying of cancer.[105]

A subtle approach would be to pass out the poem *Dog's Death,*[106]
and then begin to have students react to that loss. Students may be
asked to list occasions when animals ought to be "put to sleep." Humans
might be added, and the responses would determine if the direction
taken would tend toward infanticide, genocide, or matricide. Eventually, euthanasia could be incorporated. Perhaps the Gallup Poll
showing that 67 per cent of young people favor euthanasia could
be used.[107]

A field trip to a decrepit nursing home, or a series of photographs
taken on the terminal floor are other methods by which to begin the
unit.

The methods employed often depend upon the available materials
and community resources. A must for anyone favoring the direct shocking approach is to pass out and discuss the poem *A Flat One.*[108]


A FLAT ONE

> Old Fritz, on this rotating bed
> For seven wasted months you lay
> Unfit to move, shrunken, gray,
> No good to yourself or anyone
> But to be babied—changed and bathed and fed.
> At long last, that's all done.

Before each meal, twice every night,
We set pads on your bedsores, shut
Your catheter tube off, then brought
The second canvas-and-black-iron
Bedframe and clamped you in between them, tight,
Scared, so we could turn

You over. We washed you, covered you,
Cut up each bite of meat you ate;
We watched your lean jaws masticate
As ravenously your useless food.
As thieves at hard labor in their chains chew
Or insects in the wood.

Such pious sacrifice to give
You all you could demand of pain:
Receive this haddock's body, slain
For you, old tyrant; take this blood
Of a tomato, shed that you might live.
You had that costly food.

You seem to be all finished, so
We'll plug your old recalcitrant anus
And tie up your discouraged penis
In a great, snow-white bow of gauze
We wrap you, pin you, and cart you down below,
Below, below, because

Your credit has finally run out.
On our steel table, trussed and carved,
You'll find this world's hardworking, starved
Teeth working in your precious skin.
The earth turns, in the end, by turn about
And opens to take you in.

Seven months gone down the drain; thank God
That's through. Throw out the four-by-fours,
Swabsticks, the thick salve for bedsores,
Throw out the diaper pads and drug
Containers, pile the bedclothes in a wad,
And rinse the cider jug

Half-filled with the last urine. Then
Empty out the cotton cans,
Autoclave the bowls and spit pans,
Unhook the pumps and all the red
Tubes—catheter, suction, oxygen;
Next, wash the empty bed.

—All this Dark Age machinery
On which we had tormented you
To Life. Last, we collect the few
Belongings: snapshots, some odd bills,
Your mail, and half a pack of Luckies we
Won't light you after meals.

Old man, these seven months you've lain
Determined—not that you would live—
Just to not die. No one would give
You one chance you could ever wake
From that first night, much less go well again,
Much less go home and make

Your living; how could you hope to find
A place for yourself in all creation?—
Pain was your only occupation.
And pain that should content and will
A man to give it up, nerved you to grind
Your clenched teeth, breathing, till

Your skin broke down, your calves went flat
And your legs lost all sensation. Still,
You took enough morphine to kill
A strong man. Finally, nitrogen
Mustard: you could last two months after that;
It would kill you then.

Even then you wouldn't quit.
Old soldier, yet you must have known
Inside the animal had grown
Sick of the world, made up its mind
To stop. Your mind ground on its separate
Way, merciless and blind,

Into these last weeks when the breath
Would only come in fits and starts
That puffed out your sections like the parts
Of some enormous, damaged bug.
You waited, not for life, not for your death,
Just for the deadening drug

That made your life seem bearable.
You still whispered you would not die.
Yet in the nights I heard you cry
Like a whipped child; in fierce old age
You whimpered, tears stood on your gun-metal
Blue cheeks shaking with rage

And terror. So much pain would fill
Your room that when I left I'd pray
That if I came back the next day
I'd find you gone. You stayed for me—
Nailed to your own rapacious, still self-will
You've shook loose, finally.

They'd say this was a worthwhile job
Unless they tried it. It is mad
To throw our good lives after bad;
Waste time, drugs, and our minds, while strong
Men starve. How many young men did we rob
To keep you hanging on?

I can't think we did you much good.
Well, when you died, none of us wept.
You killed for us, and so we kept
You, because we need to earn our pay.
No. We'd still have to help you try. We would
Have killed for you today.

## Recommended Materials for Classroom Use

I. *Quotes from To Come Full Circle* [109]
   A. "To live in the presence of death makes us brave and strong.
   That is why our people never fear death. We love life and
   we live in danger. We do not fear life because we understand
   that life and death are necessary to each other." [110]
   B. "When you were born nobody set an exact date. . . . Some
   preparations were made. . . . When your body was ready, it
   came. . . . It will know when it is ready to leave. . . . We'll help
   it. My hand will know, it will reach for the pills." [111]

II. *Case Histories*
   A. "Dwight D. Eisenhower was not permitted to die so easily. A
   pacemaker, a defibrillator, and modern drugs helped prolong
   the former President's life through an amazing series of crises—
   seven heart attacks, intestinal blockage, and pneumonia." [112]
   B. The Case of Mrs. B. [113]
   C. Alsop, Stewart. *Stay of Execution.* Pleasantville, New York:
   Reader's Digest Condensed Books, Vol. I, 1974. A writer for
   *Newsweek* suffering from leukemia.

III. *Books*
   A. Ross, Eulalie. *Children's Books Relating to Death: A Discussion.* [114] Ross deals with literally hundreds of books. There are
   picture books for the younger child discussed centering around

family relationships, abstract ideas, and God. Discussions on books for older children include folk and fairy tales, fantasy, myths, hero tales and legends, family stories, animal tales, etc. Cancer killing Tom Dooley, a brain tumor killing John Gunther's son, and the life-death struggle of Anne Frank are a few mentioned under *Heroes of Today*.

B. *The Dead* by James Joyce, *Billy Budd* by Herman Melville, *Noon Wine* by Katherine Porter, *The Pilgrim Hawk* by Glenway Wescott, *The Overcoat* by Nikolay Gogol, and *The Bear* by William Faulkner are six excellent books for secondary students available for 95¢ (for all six) from Dell Paperbacks #7996-35. Marya Mannes in *Waiting for the End* says that if accident or disease left her unable to read, see, or hear, death would be preferred. An annotated bibliography on euthanasia is available from The Euthanasia Educational Fund, 250 West 57th Street, New York, N. Y. 10019. You may wish to write to Betty Schwartz at Cleveland Heights High School, Cleveland, Ohio for a comprehensive guide on *Man and Death* prepared for high school English.

IV. *Photographs*
A photograph of an empty picture frame, an empty rocker on a wooden porch, or a funeral procession in rush-hour traffic serves to generate discussions.

V. *Films and Filmstrips*
An excellent thirty-minute film from a religious viewpoint is *Though I Walk Through the Valley,* which captures the adjustments Mr. Brouwer and his family make regarding his terminal cancer. It is available for a rental fee of $25 from MEA, Finksburg, Maryland 21048. *Brian's Song* is a must for any unit on death and dying. The color sound filmstrip *Living with Dying* is available for $40 from Sunburst Communications, Pound Ridge, New York 10576.

VI. *Tapes*
Available for $15 each on 18 different areas of death are tapes from the Center for Death Education and Research, 1167 Social Sciences Building, Minneapolis, Minnesota 55455. Included are such topics as crib death, adolescent suicide, children and death, the role of schools, a study of the older widow, stages of dying, etc.

## Evaluating Student Growth

The teacher may wish to have his or her students assume that they have just been informed of the death of someone very close to them and have class members write about what they feel, see, hear, or sense from the moment the event is known to the ride home after the funeral service. Students may write again after the unit is completed. The teacher may check to see if the students have redefined death, if euphemisms are still being used, if funeral expenses are still the same, etc.

The teacher could have students write their own epitaphs and obituaries, select the music they would desire, or describe what they would do if they only had one year of life left. Again, after the unit, revisions could be encouraged and the "whys" for the changes discussed.

The teacher may wish to administer a questionnaire on the order of the following selected items taken from a psychology book.[115] Who died in your first personal involvement with death? Possible answers here were family, friend, stranger, public figure, or animal. As to how death was talked about in your family, the possible answers range from openly to never recall any discussion. The extent of the belief of a life after death, the frequency your own death is thought about, the age at which you would choose to die, the causes of death, the personal preference of how you wish to die, and questions on suicide are a few representative samples from the 74 items. Depending on the dominant responses from the class, the teacher may wish to deal with one particular aspect of death, such as immortality. Changes in beliefs could then be evaluated.

### Possible Ways Learners Might Implement Their Beliefs

In this author's opinion, there is no substitute for student involvement. The student must first gather resources, and this may be done by writing to any of the following places:

American Association of Suicidology
Department of Health
2151 Berkeley Way
Berkeley, California 94704

American Cemetery Association
250 East Broad Street
Columbus, Ohio 43215

American Monument Association
P. O. Box 523
Olean, New York 14760

Associated Funeral Directors Service
7405 Manchester Blvd.
St. Louis, Missouri 63143

Casket Manufacturers Association of America
708 Church Street
Evanston, Illinois 60601

Center for Death Education and Research
1167 Social Science Building
University of Minnesota
Minneapolis, Minnesota 55455

National Association of Cemeteries
1911 North Fort Meyer Drive, Suite 409
Arlington, Virginia 22209

National Foundation of Funeral Services
1600-1628 Central Street
Evanston, Illinois 60201

National Funeral Directors Association
135 West Wells Street
Milwaukee, Wisconsin 53203

National Funeral Directors and Morticians Association
734 West 79th Street
Chicago, Illinois 60620

Continental Association of Funeral and Memorial Societies
1828 L Street N.W.
Washington, D. C. 20036

Cremation Association of America
1620 West Belmont Avenue
Fresno, California 93701

Euthanasia Educational Council
250 West 57th Street
New York, New York 10019

Foundation of Thanatology
630 West 168th Street
New York, New York 10038

Guild of American Funeral Directors
30112 Silver Spur Blvd.
San Juan Capistrano, California 92675

Jewish Funeral Directors of America
4217 Ninth Street, N.W.
Washington, D. C. 20011

International Association for Suicide Prevention
2521 West Pico Blvd.
Los Angeles, California 90006

Memorial Society Association of Canada
5326 Ada Blvd.
Edmonton, Alberta T5W 4N7

Monument Builders of North America
1612 Central Street
Evanston, Illinois 60201

If the teacher has assigned *The American Way of Death* by Mitford,[116] which the author feels is necessary, then a host of opposing viewpoints are brought to the fore. For example, students could do an economic cost analysis of the average cost of a funeral in their class. These prices are obtained by field trip experiences to vault manufacturers, casket manufacturers, monument companies, cemeteries, and funeral homes. If Mitford is correct in saying the average cost of an American adult funeral is $1450, then students ought to compare their cost sheet with not only that figure, but with the figures given by the Continental Association as well. The Columbus (Ohio) Memorial Society has an agreement with Cook and Son Funeral directors where four plans with four price ranges are offered. Plan One is immediate cremation without embalming for $185, Plan Two, burial without embalming for $325, Plan Three is cremation after embalming for $440, and Plan Four is burial after embalming for $400. The variance between various figures will stimulate interest.

Also, according to Mitford, florists have pressured funeral directors to persuade survivors to purchase flowers. As funeral directors write, and send (you pay) obituary notices to the newspapers, a student might want to make a phone call in which an imaginary funeral is being arranged for an out-of-state relative whose last wish was to omit flowers to determine if "please omit flowers" would actually be placed in the newspaper. The number of omissions of flowers in local obituary columns might be noted.

A host of religious speakers might be invited to share their concepts of death and after-life with the class. Of course, the class ought to be prepared to ask questions based on the arguments against immortality so a balanced discussion may take place.

Students may wish to compare and contrast attitudes, values, customs, and mores of two different cultures. The American way of death may be as unique as American politics.

What would some economic implications be if the majority of Americans began to favor cremation?

Students may wish to write to the Kidney Foundation for literature or see how much a medical school would pay for their bodies.[117] Ohio students can obtain a copy of *Human Organ Transplantation, Staff Research Report #109,* June, 1973, by writing to the Ohio Legislative Service Commission, Director, David A. Johnston, Columbus, Ohio.

Students could compare the literature from the Cremation Association of America with that from the American Cemetery Association. What does each have to say about the other?

The class as a whole may wish to subscribe to a morticians' magazine, and perhaps look for reasons why we ought to be embalmed. Information from the state laws regarding embalming, and data from the health department on disease surrounding death could be analyzed.

A Living Will [118] and the Patient's Bill of Rights [119] obtained from the Euthanasia Educational Council along with the Confidential Statements from the Continental Association of Funeral and Memorial Societies could aid the student to plan his own death.

The class may wish to examine the theme of death so prevalent in our popular music, or study the expressions of death in art or literature. Perhaps a comparative analysis between the local television stations regarding programs dealing with violence could be made.

Students may wish to discover how much Social Security and Veterans' Benefits pay toward funeral costs, and possibly decide "death insurance" is not necessary.

### Summary

Many questions have been posited along the birth-death continuum. The final question is, "Should these questions have been raised in the first place?" It is for you, the reader, to decide.

## FOOTNOTES

[1] Bernard Schoenberg, Arthur C. Carr, David Peretz, and Austin H. Kutscher, editors, *Loss and Grief: Psychological Management in Medical Practice* (New York: Columbia University Press, 1970), pp. 54-55.

[2] Earl A. Grollman, editor, *Explaining Death to Children* (Boston: Beacon Press, 1967).

[3] John Hinton, *Dying* (Baltimore: Penguin Books, Inc., 1967).

[4] Herman Feifel, *The Meaning of Death* (New York: McGraw-Hill, 1965).

[5] Edgar N. Jackson, *Telling a Child About Death* (New York: Hawthorn Books, 1965).

[6] Gregory Rochlin, *Griefs and Discontents* (Boston: Little, Brown and Company, 1965).

[7] Schoenberg, Carr, Peretz, and Kutscher, *op. cit.*

[8] Feifel, *op. cit.*

[9] Jackson, *op. cit.*

[10] Grollman, *op. cit.*

[11] Jacques Choron, *Death and Western Thought* (New York: Collier Books, 1963).

[12] *Ibid.*

[13] Hinton, *op. cit.*

[14] John Langone, *Death Is a Noun* (Boston: Little, Brown and Company, 1972).

[15] Harry Foster, *The Right To Die with Dignity* (New York: The Euthanasia Educational Fund, Inc., 1971), p. 8.

[16] Langone, *op. cit.*

[17] Alexander Shana, "They Decide Who Lives, Who Dies," *Life Magazine* 53 (November 9, 1962).

[18] Grollman, *op. cit.*

[19] "The Telltale Heart," *Newsweek* 82 (October 29, 1973): 69.

[20] Jessica Mitford, *The American Way of Death* (New York: Simon and Schuster, 1963).

[21] *Ibid.*, pp. 70-74.

[22] Elisabeth Kubler-Ross, *On Death and Dying* (New York: The Macmillan Company, 1969).

[23] Orville Brim, Jr., Howard Freeman, Sol Levine, and Norman Scotch, editors, *The Dying Patient* (New York: Russell Sage Foundation, 1970), pp. 161-165.

[24] "Mrs. Brownshill," *The Times*, London (December 3, 1934): p. 11, col. 4; (December 4, 1934): p. 14, col. 2; (March 4, 1935); p. 11, col. 3; and *The New York Times*, New York (December 2, 1934): p. 25, col. 1; (March 3, 1935): p. 3, col. 2; and *Time*, (March 11, 1935): 21.

[25] "Goodby," *The Times*, London (November 23, 1946), p. 2, col. 7; (November 29, 1946): p. 2, col. 7.

[26] "Shall This Child Die?," *Newsweek* 82 (November 12, 1973): 70.

[27] "Infant Dies; Court Rapped," *Columbus Dispatch*, Columbus, Ohio (January 18, 1974): 34 and (February 25, 1974): 10B.

[28] Joyce Carol Oates, *Wonderland* (New York: Vanguard Press, 1971), pp. 50-51.

[29] United Nations General Assembly, *Text of Universal Declaration of Human Rights*, adopted December 10, 1948.

[30] Arthur D. Morse, "Why Doesn't the U.S. Outlaw Genocide?," *Look Magazine* 34 (March 10, 1970): 40.

[31] Konrad Lorenz, "On Killing Members of One's Own Species," *Bulletin of Atomic Scientists* 26 (October 1970): 3.

[32] Michihike Hachiya, *Hiroshima Diary* (Chapel Hill: University of North Carolina, 1955), pp. 170-174.

[33] Betty Jean Lifton, *Return to Hiroshima* (New York: Atheneum, 1970).

[34] Langone, *op. cit.*

[35] Louis L. Dublin, *Suicide—A Sociological and Statistical Study* (New York: Ronald Press, 1963).

[36] Granville Williams, *The Sanctity of Life and the Criminal Law* (New York: Alfred A. Knopf, 1972).

[37] A. B. Downing, editor, *Euthanasia and the Right to Death* (Los Angeles: Nash Publishing, 1969).

[38] Richard Boeth, "Now, A Right To Suicide?," *Newsweek* 18 (October 29, 1973): 78.

[39] Thomas S. Azasz, "The Ethics of Suicide," *Intellectual Digest* (October 1971): 53-55.

[40] Upendra Thakur, *The History of Suicide in India* (Delhi: Jain Publishers, 1963).

[41] Dublin, *op. cit.*

[42] A. Alvarez, *The Savage God: A Study of Suicide* (New York: Bantam Books, Inc., 1973).

[43] Loundon Wainright, "The Man in the Middle," *Life Magazine* 73 (July 21, 1972): 55.

[44] Schoenberg, Carr, Peretz, and Kutscher, *op. cit.*, pp. 358-359.

[45] Gene Lester and David Lester, *Suicide* (Englewood Cliffs: Prentice-Hall, Inc., 1971).

46 James A. Wechsler, *In a Darkness* (New York: W. W. Norton and Company, Inc., 1972).

47 *Time* 102 (July 16, 1973): 36.

48 Hinton, *op. cit.*

49 *Department of Health, Education and Welfare:* Vol. II (Rockville: The Department, 1971).

50 Ruth O. Russell, "The Right To Choose Death," *The New York Times* (February 14, 1972).

51 Hinton, *op. cit.*

52 Brim, Freeman, Levine, and Scotch, *op. cit.*

53 Hinton, *op. cit.*

54 *Ibid.*

55 Foster, *op. cit.*

56 Barney Glaser and Anselm Strauss, *Awareness of Dying* (Chicago: Aldine Publishing, 1965).

57 Hinton, *op. cit.*

58 Brim, Freeman, Levine, and Scotch, *op. cit.*

59 Daniel Maguire, "Death, Legal and Illegal," *The Atlantic Monthly* 233 (February 1974): 72-85.

60 "The Case of Dr. Sander," *The New York Times* (February 24, 1950): p. 15, col. 5; (February 28, 1950): p. 1, col. 2; (March 7, 1950): p. 1, col. 1; (March 10, 1950): p. 1, col. 6; (June 29, 1950): p. 31, col. 6; and (December 2, 1954): p. 25, col. 6.

61 *Time* (January 9, 1950): 13 and (March 13, 1950): 23.

62 Maguire, *op. cit.*

63 *Ibid.*

64 "Jury Frees Brother As Mercy Killer," *Cleveland Plain Dealer* (November 6, 1973).

65 "Mercy Killing Trial Told of Fatal Needle," *Cleveland Plain Dealer* (January 4, 1974).

66 "The Case of Dr. Montemarano," *Columbus Dispatch* (January 14, 15, 16, 22, 24, and 25, 1974) and (February 6, 1974).

67 Russell, *op. cit.*

68 Joseph Fletcher, "The Patient's Right To Die," *Harper's Magazine* 221 (October 1960): 139-143.

69 Morris H. Saffron, *Attitudes Toward Euthanasia* (New York: The Euthanasia Educational Fund, Inc., 1970), pp. 3-4.

70 Hinton, *op. cit.*

71 Langone, *op. cit.*

72 *Ibid.*

73 Alan Lockwood, *Moral Reasoning* (Columbus: Xerox Corporation, 1972), pp. 19-23.

74 Brim, Freeman, Levine, and Scotch, *op. cit.*

75 Langone, *op. cit.*

76 David Hendin, *Death as a Fact of Life* (New York: W. W. Norton and Company, 1973), pp. 66-96.

77 *Ibid.*

78 Langone, *op. cit.*

79 Downing, *op. cit.*

80 Hendin, *op. cit.*

81 Saffron, *op. cit.*

82 Gilbert Cant, "Deciding When Death Is Better Than Life," *Time* 102 (July 16, 1973): 36-37.

83 Hendin, *op. cit.*

84 "Doctors Divided Over Euthanasia," *The New York Times* (August 8, 1972).

[85] Shana, *op. cit.*
[86] Grace Elliott, *To Come Full Circle* (Hackensack: Industrial Media Services, 1972).
[87] Brim, Freeman, Levine, and Scotch, *op. cit.*
[88] Langone, *op. cit.*
[89] Brim, Freeman, Levine, and Scotch, *op. cit.*
[90] Langone, *op. cit.*
[91] Downing, *op. cit.*
[92] Brim, Freeman, Levine, and Scotch, *op. cit.*
[93] Hendin, *op. cit.*
[94] Barbara Allen Davis, in *Dilemmas of Euthanasia* (New York: The Euthanasia Educational Fund, Inc., 1971), p. 17.
[95] "Measures Employed To Prolong Life in Terminal Cases," *New York Academy of Medicine* 49 (April, 1973): 349-351.
[96] Downing, *op. cit.*, p. 148.
[97] *Ibid.*, p. 149.
[98] *The Guardian* (April 25, 1967).
[99] Helen Shaffer, "Prolongation of Life," *Congressional Quarterly, Inc.: Editorial Research on Health Topics* (July 13, 1966): 143-160.
[100] Russell Kirk, "The Politics of Death," *American Politics* (March 23, 1971): 315.
[101] Williams, *op. cit.*
[102] Elaine Freeman, "The God Committee," *The New York Times Magazine* (May 21, 1972).
[103] Downing, *op. cit.*
[104] John Dedek, *Human Life: Some Moral Issues* (New York: Sheed and Ward, Inc., 1972).
[105] Thomas Powers, "Learning To Die," *Harper's Magazine* 242 (June 1971).
[106] John Updike, "Dog's Death," in Hannah Haupp, Joy Littell, Lilla Heston, and Sarah Solotaroff, compilers, *The Family—The Concepts of Man* (Evanston: McDougal, Littell, and Company, 1972), p. 51.
[107] "Euthanasia Poll," *Reader's Digest* 104 (February 1974): 113.
[108] W. D. Snodgrass, *After Experience* (New York: Harper and Row, Publishers, 1968).
[109] Elliott, *op. cit.*
[110] Pearl Buck, *The Big Wave* (New York: Scholastic Book Service, 1949).
[111] Jessamyn West, *A Matter of Time* (New York: Harcourt, Brace, and World, 1966).
[112] Hendin, *op. cit.*
[113] Powers, *op. cit.*
[114] Grollman, *op. cit.*
[115] *Involvement in Developmental Psychology Today* (Del Mar: Communications Research Machines, 1971), pp. 138-147.
[116] Mitford, *op. cit.*
[117] *Suggested Form for Making Anatomical Gifts* (New York: The Euthanasia Educational Fund, Inc., n.d.).
[118] *A Living Will* (New York: The Euthanasia Educational Fund, Inc., 1973).
[119] *Patient's Bill of Rights* (New York: The Euthanasia Educational Fund, Inc., n.d.).

# 5

# Should the Majority Rule?

Anne R. Peterson

## Introduction

WHEN people consider a controversial issue, they "choose up sides." Not only will some people take a particular stand with regard to an issue that is either "for" or "against," but "most" people, a *majority* (i.e., 50% + 1), will take one stand over another; while only "some" people, a *minority* (i.e., less than half), will take the other side.

It can be argued with some persuasiveness that every widely held point of view begins as an outlook held by only a minority of people. In fact, until a majority of people come to hold a particular outlook, that point of view remains an issue of controversy.

When an idea is first introduced, it is given a period of time to be tested in order to determine how it will fare with "the people." All of us are familiar with the process whereby a majority point of view is constructed and sustained. Whether we have focused on a political candidate, support for a community project, neighborhood or school policy, or have been asked to reconsider some of our most deeply held values or religious outlooks, we have all been part of the process whereby would-be leaders compete with one another for our support of their point of view. Sometimes we have stood with "most" of the people, with the majority; at times we have been in the minority position. Probably most of us have been on both sides. Whatever the outcome, however, the process of "choosing up sides" in the light of evidence available to confirm or deny a particular point of view is the very essence of thinking about controversial issues in a reflective manner.

Since this Yearbook is devoted to a consideration of controversial issues, it seems appropriate to begin in this chapter by examining the circumstances under which value should reside in the majority point

*ANNE R. PETERSON is Instructor, Department of Education, Colgate University, Hamilton, New York.*

of view. Thus, this chapter will inquire into the process of decision-making that is based on the commonly held rule of procedure in our society: the majority should rule.

Discussion will focus on a series of case studies that can serve as a means for introducing the various issues related to the problems of rule by a majority. Some cases will be more appropriate for younger children; others for older students. At the end of the chapter will be a list of suggested supplementary readings and other materials suitable for extending reflection into the issues raised by the chapter as a whole.

A number of the authors of this Yearbook are dedicated to the notion that students should be encouraged to complete the process of reflective thinking by making a commitment to action regarding a particular controversial issue of importance to them. This chapter, however, is not designed to promote action so much as it is to heighten *awareness* of some of the general considerations that a person faces when he/she prepares to take and defend a stand on a controversial issue.

### The Nature and Importance of This Issue

Rule by the majority is a procedure of democratic decision-making. In our own country, reliance on majority rule reflects the value Americans place on (1) seeking to do what most people want to do, and (2) trying to provide the greatest good for the greatest number of people. Only in a society which holds such views and attempts to respond to the "will of the people" will efforts be made to poll the citizenry in order to gauge how they feel about something. What is true on the national and state political levels also has become a procedure for small-group decision-making. As Americans, we are used to the idea that groups of people should act according to what most of their members believe is the best plan.

When a majority of people agree to something, the implication is that enough people agree so that a decision *can* be made. If more than half the members of a group reach a particular decision, then that decision will be abided by. Further, a majority point of view is essential if a decision is to be implemented. Those in the majority can with confidence proceed along a particular course of action, compelling, if need be, the members of the minority to go along.

Commitment to democratic government assumes a trust in the ability of the people to govern justly and well. When people have faith in the reasonableness of men, they tend to agree with Abraham Lincoln's optimistic statement: "You can fool some of the people all of the time; you can even fool all of the people some of the time; but, you can't fool all of the people all of the time." Contrast this with the remark said to have been made to Thomas Jefferson by Alexander Hamilton: "Your people, sir, is a great beast." As an apologist for an aristocratic view of government, Hamilton had little faith in the ability of the masses to make wise decisions. He saw the common people as little more than a herd of animals easily swayed by appeals to their emotions and led astray by gifted orators and other charismatic leaders.

If men and women as individuals are assumed in our society to be thoughtful and reasonable, it follows that groups of individuals can likewise be trusted to come to mutually acceptable decisions that are sound and fair. We tend to feel that when most people in a group or society come to share a particular outlook, that outlook should be implemented. This belief in the innate reasonableness of men and women is fundamental to our system of government, and it has an interesting implication for issues of majority/minority rule. If the view of the majority can be assumed reasonable, then that of the minority must be assumed reasonable as well.

Thus, this chapter will not be concerned if the majority should *ever* rule; since, obviously, rule by the majority is an accepted procedure of group decision-making in our society and one that has proven to be successful, expedient, and time-saving. Rather, it will explore the circumstances under which a part of a group, the larger part, the majority, can legitimately claim to speak for the group as a whole. It is hoped that by virtue of some of the issues raised in this chapter, when students are asked to evaluate a particular group decision which they have participated in formulating, they will ask themselves: "Should the majority rule in this particular case?" While usually it is a member of the minority who first raises this question, it would seem to be the responsibility of all thoughtful group members to attend to it as well.

Three basic questions can be asked to determine if a majority has been accurately and justly derived:

(1) Was the support given to the majority point of view strong enough to enable the group to abide by that point of view?
(2) Did most of the members of the group participate in the process of arriving at the majority point of view?
(3) Was the issue under discussion handled according to appropriate democratic and reflective procedures?

(1) *Was the support given to the majority point of view strong enough to enable the group to abide by that point of view?*

*The need for consensus.* When faced with an important decision, a group must come to a consensus (i.e., agreement) about what it will do. When a group agrees to abide by the will of the majority, it has, in fact, agreed that all members will act as if they are one person. Obviously, then, a decision-making group must be made up of people who *can* agree with one another. Individuals within the group who have strong feelings must be able to *compromise*. Different points of view must be reconciled. The group must be able to act as a whole, or it will flounder, lose direction, and, finally, cease to function as a group at all. If a potential for consensus is not evident, then no real group may exist. Instead, there will only be a random collection of individuals, each doing "his/her own thing." Obviously, if no group exists, no majority can exist either.

Smaller groups are likely to be homogeneous ones, making a consensus easier to reach. As groups grow larger and people have less and less in common, consensus can become more difficult. In large groups, while members may come from quite different backgrounds, agreement around *issues* can be the basis for common action. Thus, members of a neighborhood can meet to discuss building codes; voters in a city can decide whether or not to install bicycle paths; and citizens across the United States can go to the polls to elect a president.

If a group is to function at all, a potential for consensus must exist.

*The need for a significant majority.* The number of people who constitute the majority is another crucial factor related to its legitimate right to speak for a group. While what "most" people (i.e., at least 50% + 1 within a group) want may be a sufficient basis on which to make some decisions, it may not be adequate for others. The more controversial or important an issue is, the more desirable it becomes that the majority be a large one.

If the majority is only slightly larger than the minority, then members of the minority may resent the group decision reached. Under such circumstances, the minority may feel that the group decision is such a tenuous one that it might easily have been different. There may be "hard feelings" among members of the minority, and group dissension and wrangling may result. The minority can become obstructionist as the individuals within the minority persist in their opposition to the group decision, because they feel there is still a strong possibility that it can be reversed.

*The need to limit alternatives.* While a group can consider more than two alternatives to a decision, the more voting possibilities there are, the more difficult it will be for one possibility to claim a clear majority. Group opinion can fragment in the face of numerous alternatives, and, even when one point of view prevails, it may only represent the views of a small part of the group. This is not to say that a premium should be placed on narrowmindedness when a group considers a problem, but it does suggest that before a group attempts to make a final decision, it is wise to allow discussion to continue until thinking coalesces around two or three positions. When the issue comes to a vote under such circumstances, it is more likely that there will be strong support for one alternative, and this in turn will help to make the decision reached more effective.

In state and national elections there is a tacit recognition of the need to limit alternatives. Almost from the first, there have been only two major political parties in the United States. Third parties have been formed, but few have lasted for more than one or two elections. The views they have represented have usually been incorporated into one of the two major political parties—if those views have survived at all.

(2) *Did most of the members of the group participate in the process of arriving at the majority point of view?*

When a decision is made by a majority vote, it must be asked if the people who participated in the decision-making process were all who could or should have done so. Because access to the group is limited, some decisions are the result of a "biased sample"—to borrow a term from social science research. If only a portion of a group participates in formulating a decision, the majority polled will not represent the "true group."

*The need for inclusiveness.* In order for the rule of the majority to stand, ideally, all people who will be affected by a particular group decision should be included in the process of decision-making.

With regard to national political decision-making, in recent years certain groups, formerly excluded from the process of decision-making, have gained access to it. Blacks and young people ages eighteen to twenty years old are good examples of groups which, for different reasons, had not been active in political decision-making. Certain inequities in voting district boundaries in some states tended to bias voting samples in favor of rural—rather than urban—interests, until this was changed as a result of a Supreme Court ruling. Women did not vote in national elections prior to 1920, nor did they vote in local political contests until after the turn of the twentieth century. Obviously, as new groups gain access to the decision-making process, the "majority" view will change.

If key people are excluded from participation in the process of decision-making, a majority view may not in fact exist at all. Instead, an influential, *vocal minority* will conduct the business of the group. This can happen particularly when members of a group are actively excluded from participation or are apathetic, uninformed, or unorganized. Some critics have argued that the American governmental system has, for most of its history, been a government by just such a vocal minority: namely, white males over twenty-one with property! Certain lobbies to Congress, such as the American Medical Association and the National Rifle Association, function as vocal minorities. It is known that these groups are well organized and financed and that they are very successful in presenting their special points of view to members of Congress. A majority of Americans in the decision-making public may favor tough gun control laws, but Congressional representatives are more likely to hear the "views of the people" from the better organized National Rifle Association, which is opposed to such legislation. Unless those who favor strong gun control measures can become organized, their views may lose out and go unheard. Certainly, we have ample evidence of this phenomenon in the history of the United States.

*The need for an accurate gauge of group sentiment.* If a society is to respond to the "will of the people," there must be some way of gauging the views of the people in a manner that accurately reflects them. Usually, a poll or a formal vote in a referendum or election provides such an index of group feeling about an issue.

In small groups, such as clubs or associations, the majority point of view is easily determined by verbal agreement or other signs of assent. Since people are in face-to-face contact and usually know one another, they can readily determine what each one thinks about a particular matter. When a group decision must be made in a small group, everyone usually has the opportunity to express himself/herself personally on the issue at hand. When a decision is reached under such circumstances, everyone usually has had a fair opportunity to hear and be heard before a final vote is taken. As groups grow larger and individuals within them have less and less personal contact, gauging majority opinions with any accuracy becomes more and more difficult.

Public opinion polls are becoming rather reliable gauges of popular feeling about issues, particularly at the national level. Professional politicians now make it a practice to use such polls to determine their potential success with voters and to see how voters are reacting to the policies put forward and supported. Advertisers also use polling techniques to determine the impact their products are making on a particular market. Many independent news gathering organizations cite the results of spot polling to highlight their reporting on certain issues. It must be remembered, however, that a public opinion poll is not a vote and does not represent an occasion for deliberate choice on the part of the electorate. There is no guarantee that polls accurately reflect public opinion, and there is always the possibility that pollsters can be in error to the extent that they were in the famous misprediction of Harry Truman's defeat for election in 1948. More ominously, unscrupulous use can be made of the results of polls by showing apparent support for a politician or a point of view that may not actually exist. Those who are eager to stand with the majority, regardless of the consequences, could be misled by deliberately altered public opinion poll results.

Voting thus remains the best "democratic" method of gauging concerned public opinion, despite the fact that many fail to exercise their option to do so. While election results can be falsified or inflated, this has become a rare occurrence. In fact, Buckminster Fuller and others have suggested that the technological means are now at hand for all members of the electorate to vote on every issue of national concern merely by using a telephone signal or a voting mechanism installed in each home, perhaps connected to the television set. If these technological improvements were instituted, the problem of gauging the majority view accurately would be nearly solved. Yet, might there be any difficulties with such devices?

*The need for full group participation.* Even if all who should participate in a group are able to do so and even if an accurate method of gauging group opinion is available, it will have little effect unless each individual participates in the process of decision-making. It is estimated that only about one-half of all eligible voters have participated in Presidential elections since 1960. Since the popular vote in both 1960 and 1968 was very evenly divided between the two Presidential candidates, it can be said that in those years only about one-quarter of the voting public elected the President! This voter apathy is evident at all levels of government in the United States and is particularly discouraging when only a handful of voters is permitted to decide whether a school levy will carry or whether a municipal program is adopted, and so on. When decisions are made by a minority of those directly involved, there is always some question as to their legitimacy—except when it can be shown that a majority of people chose not to vote! However, if people fail to exercise their right to vote and to participate in a group decision, they must also take responsibility for what the group decides in their absence.

(3) *Was the issue under discussion handled according to appropriate democratic and reflective procedures?*

*The need for reasonable discussion.* We have already noted that this society places great faith in the reasonableness of men and women. A "reasonable" discussion is difficult to define with any precision, however. For the purposes of this chapter, we might say that a reasonable discussion is conducted when a group engages in the process of reflective thought. This implies the careful consideration of alternatives in light of the data to support each possibility. A reasonable person remains fairly open-minded. He/she suspends judgment until "all the facts are in." In a reasonable discussion, people are asked to make primarily *cognitive* decisions, rather than ones based on appeals to their emotions.

*The need for ample time to discuss the issue.* Democratic decision-making is a time-consuming process. An individual ruler or a small ruling clique can make decisions rapidly and implement them with relative speed. Not so a democratic group or society. Time must be allowed for sufficient discussion. Those who are in disagreement must be allowed to persuade others of their points of view or must be won over to another point of view altogether. In order that a group not be misled in a decision, it must have time to acquire all the evidence necessary to make that decision an informed one.

Even though considerable time is spent making a decision under democratic circumstances, resort to a group vote to determine a majority is actually a time-saving measure. Imagine, for example, how long it would take to reach national decisions if everyone had to agree! The process of persuasion and rational discussion under such circumstances would conceivably be so time-consuming that decisions would never be made. Rule by majority permits a group to make decisions crucial to its welfare without insisting that everyone agree with every decision at every time.

*The need to hear the minority view.* Closely related to the above criteria for democratic and reflective procedures is the requirement that the minority point of view in a group discussion be given a full and fair hearing.

The Bill of Rights to the United States Constitution provides a succinct statement of the rights of the minority. Incidentally, the Bill of Rights attests to the fact that while our Founding Fathers may have feared the consequences of mob rule, they were equally concerned about the dangers of an unrestrained ruling group. The first ten Amendments to the Constitution suggest that a legitimate protest movement cannot be summarily dismissed as a mob without a fair hearing.

The First Amendment insures the freedom of speech, the freedom of the press, and the right of people to assemble *peaceably* in order to "petition the Government for a redress of grievances." The Fourth Amendment insures citizens against unreasonable searches and seizures. It also prescribes the conditions under which search warrants can be obtained. The Fifth Amendment provides protection for citizens against unwarranted arrest and against any actions that would deprive a person of life, liberty, or property, "without due process of law." From the point of view of a person holding a minority view on any issue, this amendment insures that no one will be menaced or threatened without legitimate cause for the beliefs he/she holds. The Sixth Amendment enlarges on the Fifth by providing for a "speedy and public trial." This implies that people who might be viewed as political threats to a government cannot be tried in secret, nor can they be kept in jail to await trial for an unreasonable period of time. The Seventh Amendment provides for trial by jury, a hearing before one's peers. The Eighth Amendment provides for the equitable treatment of all who have been accused of breaking the law. It provides that there shall be "no cruel and unusual punishment inflicted" against any person for any reason—even someone who espouses an unpopular point of view. The Ninth and Tenth Amendments reaffirm that the source of power within the United States is in the people or their representatives at the local, state, and national levels.

Although the Bill of Rights is familiar to us all, there is always the temptation, particularly where a group is under pressure to make a decision, to cut short the points of view of those who seem "on the fringe" of the group's emergent outlook, the majority view. The provisions of the Bill of Rights remind us in every group situation to avoid the pitfalls of the "tyranny of the majority." As we have noted, a dissatisfied minority, while it may be temporarily forced to comply with a majority-derived decision, cannot be silenced forever. The minority can rise up with a vengeance that can ultimately destroy the group which attempted to silence it. Much as the "bad fairy" in several popular children's stories who appears to lay a curse on the group which excluded her, the minority cannot be ignored. When William Lloyd Garrison founded his anti-slavery newspaper, the *Liberator,* in 1831, his statement of editorial policy included a classic warning to all who would dismiss the minority view of an issue: "I will be as harsh as truth," he wrote, "and as uncompromising as justice. . . . I am in earnest —I will not equivocate—I will not excuse—I will not retreat a single inch—and I will be heard!"

It seems appropriate in this connection to mention an aspect of majority/minority relations which can act to justify dismissing the minority point of view; namely, the fact that because the majority is the "winning" side of an issue, its view is assumed correct and final.

It has been remarked upon more than once that Americans as a society are preoccupied with winning, with being victorious in some way or another. Many Americans accept fully Coach Vince Lombardi's statement that "Winning isn't everything. It's the *only* thing." A "winner" will not only bet on the Number One football team, back the victorious political candidate, but buy the sort of products that "most" other people buy, from soap to cereal.

Being in the minority has profoundly negative connotations in our society. What are we to make of the people who support the team that always loses; who back political candidates who espouse "lost" causes; who watch television programs that are eventually forced off the air because of poor viewer ratings; who buy products that only one person out of four or eight bothers with? Unless the minority is a select and privileged group, such as the so-called "Beautiful People," it seems only a collection of "losers." There is something deemed inherently good about the majority view precisely because it is the majority view, the winning side, the side that "makes it." If a point of view loses out, the assumption is made that something is wrong with it.

One of the reasons for the prevalence of this point of view may lie in the study and practice of history. Being in the majority—and hence "winning"—means being remembered and recorded. The losing side on various issues is often lost in obscurity unless some tireless historian or doctoral candidate unearths it. Children often play a game called "Historical Trivia" which, among other things, can involve naming the person defeated for the Presidency or Vice Presidency in each election year. The reader might try this game himself and see how he does for the elections held just since 1920!

Sometimes the minority view not only loses out historically, but is labeled villainous and evil in its defeat. How many of us, for example, can now understand the thinking of Loyalists during the American Revolution or of the Southern slave owners prior to the Civil War? Gore Vidal, in his novel *Burr*, a fictionalized biography of Aaron Burr, a New York politician who was accused of treason during the administration of Thomas Jefferson for attempting to establish an "empire" for himself in the Louisiana Territory, reminds us that the "loser" often has his side of a story. The activities for which Burr was labeled a traitor were very similar, indeed, to the land speculation that such authentic American heroes as Andrew Jackson and Henry Clay engaged in.

While the minority view and those who hold it may not triumph in their own lifetimes, it has often been the case that those viewed as "cranks" and malcontents come to be honored for the courage of the stands they took or for the especially gifted vision they held. All such inventors, social theorists, explorers, crusaders, and other men and women of strong conviction and personal integrity remind us that "winning" or "losing" should not be the reason for taking a personal stand.

Rule by majority is merely a procedure for group decision-making, not a means of verifying ideas. This is why the rights of minorities are so important to maintain. "Correctness" may in fact reside in the minority view; and unless it is given a hearing, the group may be misled into a hasty and ignorant decision. Recall the story of "The Emperor's New Clothes." Although the children who "saw through" the clever scheme to defraud (and defrock!) the Emperor were initially punished for their insight, their willingness to voice the minority point of view saved a good deal of embarrassment in the long run!

In the next section, we will consider some of the issues that are raised when groups agree to abide by a rule of the majority.

## Issues Related to the Major Problem

### Should a Simple or a Concurrent Majority Rule?

A simple majority represents just 50% + 1 of any group. It is the slimmest majority possible and, as such, has several defects when a group must decide highly controversial or important issues. Among the defects of a simple majority are the following:

*1. A simple majority is unstable.* If the majority is a narrow one, as has been mentioned, the possibility always exists that a decision based upon it could easily be reversed.

*2. A simple majority can result from appeals to emotion.* Individuals in a group find it hard to be in unanimous agreement unless they are considering an issue that they no longer consider controversial. Usually, thinking about a matter of importance will divide a group—or a society—into a number of different "camps." Occasionally, efforts will be made by individual leaders to "stampede" a group decision by eloquent appeals to emotion. If a simple majority is all that is required to settle an issue, it is obvious that a would-be leader needs to persuade fewer people to achieve such a majority than would be the case if two-thirds or more people had to agree to something. While the use of a simple majority does not imply that decisions reached using that procedure are inherently emotional, it is easier to mislead some of the people than most or all of the people within a group.

*3. A simple majority may not represent the true group majority.* We have already noted the problems of including everyone in the decision-making process. Often, chance alone can determine who can or will vote on an issue. If there is a snow storm on election day, for example, many who might otherwise have voted will tend to stay home. If members of a group are unable to attend a decision-making session, a measure may be adopted that might have failed if they had been present. The majority view in such cases obviously does not represent a majority at all and the slimmer that majority is, the less reliable it can seem.

**Case #1:**  The Brown family includes Mr. and Mrs. Brown and four children: Helen, 15; Michael, 10; Mitchell, 8; and Vicki, 6. They have only one television set and this means that time is frequently spent deciding which television program the entire family will watch. As we peek in on the Brown family some of the dynamics of rule by majority will be revealed.*

*Setting: Brown family dinner table.*

*Mrs. Brown:* Guess what? Tonight the movie "Eternal Love Story" is going to be on Channel 5. Remember that, Bob? We saw it on our first date together.

*Mr. Brown:* How could I forget that! You cried your way through the whole thing and ran out of Kleenex. I had to get up and get you some napkins from the candy counter and you cried your way through those, too. I made sure that our next date was for bowling!

*Helen:* That really sounds romantic.

*Mr. Brown:* It does?

*(Younger children giggle among themselves.)*

*Helen:* Not your date, silly! The movie. It must really be good.

*Mr. Brown:* Well, then . . . why not pop some corn and we'll all see it again—just for old time's sake? You kids can see the movie that brought your Mom and Dad together.

*(Younger children groan.)*

*Vicki:* Tonight the cartoon version of Grimm's Fairy Tales is on and me and Mitchell were going to watch that.

*Mitchell:* Yeah! I don't want to watch some old movie.

*Michael:* Me either. The Grimm Fairy Tale thing sounds *much* better!

*Mr. Brown:* Let's take a vote. How many for Grimm's Fairy Tales? (Michael, Mitchell, and Vicki raise their hands.) How many for "Eternal Love Story"? (Mr. Brown, Mrs. Brown, and Helen vote for this.) It looks like a tie.

**How should this dilemma be solved?**

**Case #2:** Mrs. Marks' fifth-grade class is trying to decide where to go for its class outing at the end of the year. Several suggestions have been made, and Mrs. Marks has listed them on the board. They are:

Picnic at Pinehurst Woods
Picnic at Tru-Fun Amusement Park
Field Trip to the Science Museum

---

* This case and others involving the Brown family are designed for younger children to illustrate some of the arguments which follow. Children can use these skits as the basis for brief class playlets or puppet shows. The teacher might encourage children to embellish the situations given, adding their own words wherever possible. The teacher could ask learners to think of similar situations which have occurred in their own families, at school, and elsewhere. If children are too young for these activities, perhaps they can listen to the skits and then draw a picture illustrating each situation. Older students may simply read through the skits for background to some of the case studies to be presented later on.

When the vote is taken, the totals stand as follows:

| | |
|---|---|
| Picnic at Pinehurst Woods | 12 |
| Picnic at Tru-Fun Park | 17 |
| Science Museum | 4 |

Mrs. Marks said, "I guess that most of you want to go for a picnic at the Amusement Park. This trip will cost extra for the rides and refreshments, but I think we can easily arrange for a bus to take us there."

Just then, Billy raised his hand and said. "I won't be able to go to the Amusement Park. (He had voted for the Science Museum.) My parents can't afford to give me the extra money for rides. I'll have to go and sit all day and that won't be *any* fun for me. Why can't we go to Pinehurst Woods for a picnic, since many of us want to go on a picnic anyway? Let's take a revote on the best place to go for a picnic."

Mrs. Marks turned to the class and said, "Shall we take another vote as Billy has suggested?"

Peggy raised her hand and said: "I don't think we should. The majority rules and most of us kids want to go to the Amusement Park. Let's leave it at that."

***What should the class do? What is likely to happen if the class follows Billy's suggestion? What will happen if they follow Peggy's suggestion?***

The above case illustrates the difficulty deciding where a "true" majority resides when voting is split among more than two alternatives. In such a case, the true majority may be more philosophical than numerical. A voting tally can thus "mask" subtle differences among those who appear to be in the minority when in fact they are not. Quite often, members of the minority share a great deal in common with those of the majority, but disagree on one or two important points. If issues are reworked and solutions reframed, a new majority coalition can emerge.

This situation existed nationally in our country prior to the Civil War. At that time, the States of the Union were divided into sections. For some years, even though the population of the Northern states increased rapidly, the North and South were evenly balanced in the Senate. Each time a new state petitioned to be admitted to the Union, demands were made that it indicate whether it would stand with the North or with the South. States favoring slavery were grouped with the South, although the differences between the two sections went beyond differences in attitudes towards slavery. Thus, when a State favoring slavery was admitted to the Union, a non-slave state had to be admitted as well.

As the United States gained population and settlement moved westward, a new section of the country emerged, the West, and competition between the North and the South for influence with the West was heated, beginning in the 1840s. Defenders of the "Southern way" soon realized that they would be overwhelmed by an alliance of the North and West. It was at this point that John C. Calhoun, a South Carolina Senator, came forward with a unique suggestion. Rather than depending on votes in Congress to settle major issues, Calhoun suggested that the entire government be reorganized such that each section had the power to veto a piece of legislation that it felt would threaten its own particular interests. Each section would be represented in a three-part Chief Executive, rather than by just one President. If one section vetoed a piece of legislation and the other two favored it, the two sections that agreed would have to vote that legislation with a large majority (at least two-thirds of all Congressional representatives) in order to see it pass. Calhoun thus invented the notion of a *concurrent majority* which he suggested as an alternative to a simple majority for national decision-making. Calhoun's scheme of government placed a premium on a high degree of agreement among all the sections of the country. Each section could either join with the other two or veto actions that the other two might take. This way, no one section or even an alliance of two sections could dominate the third.*

Supporters of Calhoun's ideas pointed out the virtues of having a strong majority rule, rather than rule by a simple and often hastily assembled majority. Those who opposed the measure noted that decision-making would drag on for much longer than it already did in Senate debates. If a concurrent majority idea were established, they argued, nothing would ever get done. Decisions would not be made and the country would flounder dangerously.

The United Nations Security Council is organized along lines reminiscent of Calhoun's concurrent majority model. For some years, the United States and its allies stood in opposition to the Soviet Union and its allies. Measures favored by one group were often vetoed by the other. Cold War politics often made the veto power more significant than the ability to agree on common action. The breakdown of older power blocs and the emergence of an independent "Third World" faction in the United Nations have altered the decision-making process within the Security Council, making it more able to function along the lines of a concurrent majority than had been the case.

Sectional differences (i.e., North vs. South) are no longer so signifi-

---

* Calhoun's political philosophy is contained in his *Disquisition on Government*, published after his death in 1850. Students may want to read for themselves Calhoun's design for a new government and decide if it could have prevented the Civil War. Many regard Calhoun as America's preëminent political philosopher during the nineteenth century by virtue of his unique proposals for governmental reorganization.

cant in our country as are differences in the population between rich and poor, young and old, and the "establishment" and emergent racial and ethnic minorities. How could each of these groups be better represented at all levels of government? Should any groups be given special consideration, more representation than other groups?

### Should the Majority Have the Right To Compel the Minority To Adopt Its Point of View?

We have already noted the circumstances under which a majority— simple or otherwise—can be said to speak for the group. Once a decision has been made, however, the problem arises as to how far the majority will be willing to go in order to see to it that all members of a group comply with the decision reached.

The person who stands with the minority, especially when the minority is a small one relative to the group, stands little chance of reversing the group's decision. Under these circumstances, the minority person can decide to do one of the following: (1) abide by the decision of the group and remain silent; (2) abide by the decision of the group, but protest that decision (again, the Bill of Rights provides for the means of orderly protest); (3) refuse to abide by the decision of the group, while remaining within it to protest; or (4) refuse to abide by the decision of the group by leaving the group altogether. (Many Americans are descended from individuals who emigrated, rather than remain within groups or societies that they disagreed with. This is a familiar option, but one that is less commonly accepted today.)

Groups differ with regard to how completely they provide the above options. In some groups, protest is possible; in others it is not. Certain groups can afford to allow their members to refuse to do something; others cannot. Finally, there are groups that are difficult, if not impossible, to leave. What then is to be done with the minority individual who refuses to abide by a group decision while remaining within the group itself?

Case #3: Mrs. Brown has had a long day and does not have the energy to cook a full meal for her family of six.

Mrs. Brown: I'm just worn out from all the cleaning and waxing and other work I've done today. Why don't we all go out to a fast food place and get some dinner?

Mr. Brown: That sounds okay to me. Where shall we go?

Mitchell: Let's get a bucket of chicken and have a picnic.

Michael: Yeah!

Helen: I would rather have a pizza. We haven't had one for a long time.

*Vicki:* I want a cheeseburger.

*Mr. Brown:* Well, everyone seems to want something different. Can we decide on one place so I don't have to drive all over town to get dinner?

*Mrs. Brown:* Chicken sounds good to me.

*Helen:* I'd settle for chicken.

*Mr. Brown:* Well, Vicki, it looks like everyone wants chicken tonight.

*Vicki:* Well, *I* don't want chicken. I want a cheeseburger with pickles.

*Mr. Brown:* Sorry, Honey. You'll have to settle for chicken.

*Vicki:* (Bursts into tears.) I *never* get to do anything I want.

***Should Vicki be forced to eat chicken for dinner? If she doesn't have chicken, what can she do?***

**Case #4:** It is after lunch on Thursday. Miss Howard says to her class, "How many want to work on their arithmetic?"

A show of hands confirms what she had suspected. The class enjoys arithmetic. They have just learned how to work with fractions and most of the children are eager to continue solving some of the problems they started yesterday—all, that is, except Keith Harmon.

Since the time after lunch on Thursdays is usually spent drawing, Keith had been counting on drawing a picture of the racing car (in metallic purple) that he had been designing in his imagination for the past two days. Arithmetic was no fun as far as Keith was concerned and, in fact, he *hated* it.

So, he raised his hand and said, "I don't feel like doing arithmetic. Can I draw instead?"

Becky Morris (who also didn't like arithmetic) cut in before Miss Howard could answer. "It wouldn't be fair if Keith got to draw while the rest of us have to work on arithmetic."

***Should Keith be required to do what the rest of the class is doing?***

**Case #5:** The Amish, a religious group which has settled in Pennsylvania, Ohio, Indiana, and parts of Illinois, place great emphasis on maintaining a simple life style. Members of this religious group dress in clothing that was worn in the nineteenth century. They wear no bright colors. Certain members of the group do not use mechanical devices of any kind, and, on Sundays, these members ride to church in buggies pulled by horses.

Most states in the union have some form of compulsory school attendance law which requires that children between the ages of six and sixteen attend some form of public or approved private school. The Amish feel that an eighth-grade education is sufficient preparation for the sort of life they want their children to lead. Thus, Amish children leave public school after the eighth grade and return home where they are trained to be housewives and farmers, in accordance with the traditional Amish life style.

***Should this religious group be allowed to continue to defy state school laws?***

**Case #6:** Constance Moore is a noted home designer and artist. Many of her designs for household items have won artistic recognition and have been widely copied. When Constance and her husband, who is an architect, moved into the new city of Middlegrove, they promised themselves that they would design a home that would fulfill the dreams of both.

After much careful shopping around, they located a site overlooking a ravine that they felt would be the ideal place for their dream home. They purchased more than an acre of land and held it until they could afford to build. Meanwhile, the undeveloped land on either side of the Moores' was sold to a building contractor who planned to build a series of American colonial homes in the area. He offered the Moores a considerable sum for their property, but they refused to sell.

By the time the development of Colonial Acres—as it was called—was well underway, Constance and her husband finalized their plans for their home. Both of them had spent many hours perfecting these plans for what can only be described as a completely original house. It would make use of unusual building materials in unique color combinations. When finished, it would represent a large piece of modern sculpture at the same time that its design would capitalize fully on the beauties of the wooded ravine. While the house did not fit in with the colonial theme of the rest of the development, Constance and her husband were hopeful that the woods surrounding their property would shield them from having to view the hastily built pseudo-Williamsburg-style homes that were being completed.

By the time the Moores got around to filing their building plans with the city, several families had already settled in Colonial Acres and a neighborhood spirit was beginning to form. When it was learned that the Moores planned to build a "far-out" house in the neighborhood, many of the new residents became concerned. They met together and signed a petition protesting the building of the home and indicated their willingness to take the Moores to court in order to stop them from ruining the architectural integrity of their neighborhood.

*What should the Moores do? Should they give in to community pressure? Does the neighborhood community have the right to demand that they conform to the architecture in the development?*

**Case #7:** Joe Allessandro is married and has four children. His wife is pregnant with their fifth child. While Joe works hard, the Allessandros have no savings. All the money that Joe earns is quickly used for food, rent, and other expenses. By the end of every month, the family is often so short of money that it must make do with canned soup and vegetables until the next paycheck arrives.

Understandably, then, when Joe was hired by the Sidewall Construction Company and given a raise in pay of $35.00 per week, he was elated and convinced that now he could keep up with the bills that had been accumulating.

On the first day at work, Joe was met by the union organizer. He welcomed Joe to the job and then asked, "Are you a member of the Builders' Union, Local 63?" Joe replied, "No, I'm not. I don't believe in unions. They take your money, but all you get is a few benefits in return. When the higher-ups decide to strike, even if things are tough at home, you have to walk off the job. Believe me, I need every dollar I earn just to keep my head above water."

The union organizer looked at Joe hard as he said, "We all got problems, fella, but we run a closed shop here at Sidewall Construction Company and if you want to work here you'll have to join the union. The initiation fee is $150.00. Dues are $25.00 a month. Let me know when you can pay up."

*Joe has thirty days to join the union or lose his job. What should he do under these circumstances? Does the union have the right to force him to join?*

The above cases provide a cross-section of instances when the views of the majority are challenged by a minority individual or group of individuals. Each one is open to a good deal of speculation, since in each case the rights of the majority to compel the minority are not clear-cut.

There is a special group of circumstances, however, during which many people feel that the majority is fully within its rights to compel the minority to comply with its decisions. Usually such situations occur during a national emergency such as a declared war. During wartime, the national government must be certain of the cooperation of its citizens, and measures are often taken which would be hotly protested in more normal times.

During the Civil War, for example, Abraham Lincoln suspended the right of *habeas corpus* which provides that no one can be arrested unless he/she is charged with a specific violation of the law. Lincoln hoped thus to detain a number of suspected Confederate spies. During World War I, a series of laws was passed aimed at limiting "seditious" speech and the activities of would-be spies. A number of convictions were made under these laws and several were argued and appealed until they were settled by the Supreme Court. In the decision of *Schenck* vs. *the United States* (1919), Justice Oliver Wendell Holmes, Jr., wrote the majority opinion of the court and articulated some of the special privileges of a government during time of war. Schenck was accused of interfering with attempts to draft soldiers for the war by mailing out circulars which spoke against the war and by delivering speeches near draft boards encouraging young men not to enlist. Holmes wrote:

The most stringent protection of free speech would not protect a man in falsely shouting fire in a theater and causing a panic. It does not even protect a man from an injunction against uttering words that may have all the effect of force. . . . The question in every case is whether the words used are used in such circumstances and are of such a nature as to create a clear and present danger that they will bring about the substantive evils that Congress has a right to prevent. It is a question of proximity and degree. When a nation is at war many things that might be said in time of peace are such a hindrance to its effort that their utterances will not be endured so long as men fight and that no court could regard them as protected by any constitutional right.

The doctrine of "clear and present danger" has remained a standard for evaluating governmental action against individuals in times of national emergency. It is thus generally accepted that the majority has the right to compel the minority when national survival is at stake.

**Case #8:** It is the year 1985. Mark Rogers is twenty years old and the United States is at war. The Dynamic World Alliance has declared war on the United States as a result of efforts made by American soldiers to seize oil in several Middle Eastern cities. The shortage of oil has created a severe depression in the United States and members of the Dynamic World Alliance have been withholding oil deliberately from American buyers in order to blackmail the national leadership into a policy aimed at a take-over of Pakistan, where vast uranium deposits were discovered a few years ago.

The President has gone to Congress with his demand for war and it was voted immediately. The draft was reinstituted, and thousands of young men and women rushed to enlist in the war effort.

Mark, however, does not plan to enlist. He is unalterably opposed to wars of any kind. When he was three years old, his father was killed in the war in Vietnam. Mark remembers his classmates in school asking him whether his father had "wasted" villages and killed civilians in "Nam," and he was ashamed to admit at the time that he honestly did not know. He had not known his father at all.

While awaiting his draft notice, Mark and a group of his friends gathered together to form a war protest group. They pooled their savings and printed a leaflet showing some of the casualties of former wars involving the United States, including the burned and maimed children of Vietnam. The leaflet warned potential enlistees that they were contracting to commit murder against their fellow men. Standjng in front of the major enlistment office in the city, Mark and his friends passed out their literature. They were soon reported, and the police arrived to arrest them. As the police approached Mark said:

"Our right to protest yet another unjust American war is protected by the First Amendment."

The police were not deterred by this warning, and the officer in charge said, "This is no ordinary war, young man. We're fighting for our very survival as a nation. If you can't see that, that's your problem, but you and your friends aren't going to poison the minds of loyal young citizens with this illegal written material. This country has given everyone a better life than most people in the world only dream of. You and your friends are under arrest."

*Which side of this argument is the correct one? Does a war effort always justify restrictions on the rights of citizens?*

Sometimes, even when the majority is within its rights to compel the minority to abide by its decisions, it is unable to do so because the minority has adopted a posture of threat or blackmail of some kind. A *coercive minority* can be particularly successful in gaining its ends, largely because of its willingness to engage in violence. In a society that values human life, as does our own, threats against even a small segment of the population cannot be taken lightly.

Coercive minorities of several kinds have been prevalent in recent years. Hijackers, kidnappers, and guerilla terrorists committed to a variety of causes are examples of coercive minorities. Terrorist politics can be devastatingly effective, as we have seen in our own time. The best way to counteract such groups remains a mystery.

**Case #9:** Vicki is playing with a pack of playing cards in the living room of the Brown home just as Michael and Mitchell enter.

*Michael:* So you've got the cards! Hand them over, Vicki. We're going over to Eddie's house to play poker.
*Vicki:* No! I'm playing my own game. Go get another pack.
*Mitchell:* There aren't any more. We only have one deck. (*At this point, both boys approach Vicki and begin to grab the cards from her. She bursts into tears, lying back on the floor and kicking to show her displeasure.*)
*Mr. Brown* (entering from the kitchen): What's going on in here? What are you guys doing to your sister?
*Michael:* We need the cards to take over to Eddie's, and Vicki won't give them to us.
*Vicki:* I was playing with them first. They tried to grab them.
*Mr. Brown:* I don't like it when you two boys gang up on your sister. If she was playing with the cards first, then you'll have to find something else to do.
    (*Vicki returns happily to her game.*)

*Should Vicki have been allowed to win her way in the manner she did? Did the boys have the right to take the cards from her? Should the situation have been handled differently?*

**Case #10:** The Independent Truckers' Association has met to protest a new federal regulation that would require all truckers to pay a standard fee/toll in order to use the Interstate Highway system. Ordinarily, and since it was constructed, this system has been freely available to all motorists. The regulation was passed because Congressmen were convinced that the cost of repairing this highway system should fall on those who use— and abuse it—most often. Estimates are that eighty per cent of all the repairs on this highway system are the result of truck use. Ordinary automobile traffic does not subject the highway system to the overloading and stress that trucking does.

The ITA is already angered about the cost of diesel fuel. Members of the association feel that it is becoming impossible for the independent trucker to make a living. Most of them have invested considerable capital in their trucking rigs and find that each trip they make earns them less and less money. The new Interstate Highway tax seems the last straw.

The husband and wife team of Jack and Paula Lewis are particularly enraged at this new development. Their entire life is lived on the road and with each month, it seems, they earn less and less money. On their past two runs they didn't even break even. The Lewises hold a meeting in their home for the twenty-seven most radical members of the ITA.

"It's time for some decisive action," says Paula. "I'm tired of the way that we small business people get dumped on while the big corporations go right on pulling in money hand over fist. The government doesn't care what happens to us. Those crooks are in it for the money, too."

"I agree," says Bill Hoffman. "Let's really show how we feel. Let's block all the Interstate Highways leading into the Black Hills National Park. If people don't meet our demands to repeal this new tax, we'll blow up that rock with the four Presidents on it! I know where we can get all the dynamite we need for that. If we take this kind of protest action we'll get national publicity and people will see that they can't keep pushing us around!"

A moment of silence followed Bill's bold suggestion, but after the group considered the plan, it agreed to it wholeheartedly. Preparations took several weeks and included locating a ballistics expert who could blow up the monument if it had to be done. Then, during the height of the tourist season, the radical ITA put its plan into operation. Immediately news reporters poured into the area. The group was featured on TV. Several members gave exclusive press interviews to specially selected reporters.

*If you were the President of the United States, how would you deal with this crisis situation? What will be the consequences if the demands of the radical ITA are met?*

### Should Representatives of the People Respond to a Silent Majority?

The concept of a "silent majority" has been used frequently in recent years by several politicians who have hoped to stress that their actions, while on the surface unpopular or questionable, were undertaken in response to a special series of communications from people who are either too proud or too timid to express themselves openly on a particular issue. Presidents such as Woodrow Wilson and Franklin D.

Roosevelt appealed to a sort of silent majority when they spoke for the "forgotten man" in American society.

The implications of rule by a silent majority are rather interesting. How is a silent majority polled? How does it express itself to the person who responds to its demands? Why does it choose to remain silent, when, evidently, its point of view is widely respected and eagerly followed?

**Case #11:** The students at Mapleshade Senior High School have been circulating a petition calling for the establishment of a smoking area for those students whose parents have given them permission to smoke. This has long been an issue of concern to students. The smokers are eager for the right to smoke in the open, unharassed. They basically resent having to "sneak" cigarettes in washrooms or in cars out in the parking lot. Several people have been suspended for smoking, even when they are allowed to smoke at home. Another part of the student body does not particularly care to smoke but is tired of entering stalls in the school toilets only to be choked by the smoke left behind from a hastily puffed cigarette. Also, periodic "shakedowns" involving locker and pocket searches for cigarettes have seemed demeaning and childish.

When the petition was ready to be presented to the principal, it contained the names of 879 of the school's 1100 students. When the Smoker's Rights Committee presented the petition to Mr. Bell, the principal, he said, "I am impressed that you students would take it upon yourselves to try to change school policy in this manner. However, a petition alone won't be sufficient to insure smoking rights in the school. I have a responsibility to the parents of this district, and I know that they don't want their children smoking on school property. Therefore, I'm afraid that I will have to turn down your petition."

Mary Murphy, a leader of the SRC, then said: "Why don't you suggest that the voters vote on this issue at the next referendum? One is scheduled in three months, and that way we would know for sure what the people want and don't want for students in the school."

Mr. Bell replied, "I'm afraid that's out of the question. This next referendum is a particularly sensitive one. We need a budget increase for some of our special programs, particularly in the athletics department. How would it look to be asking for money for a sports program and the right to smoke on school grounds at the same time? Take my word for it, the voters of this district want to keep this school in the best possible running order. Smoking is prohibited for minors, and most parents in this district support that regulation. As principal, I am merely acting on behalf of the parents when I say that there won't be any changes in smoking regulations in this school."

*Mr. Bell is responding to the outlook of a silent majority as he perceives it. What should the students do now that Mr. Bell has made the position of the school administration clear?*

### Should a Person Obey a Law He/She Doesn't Agree With or Thinks Is Wrong?

This final issue goes to the heart of the rights of members of a minority view. Law in our society is not a static phenomenon. Laws are continually being reviewed, reworked, and reevaluated within the court system. In every case, it can be said that laws embody the views of "most" people for the times in which they are passed. This is to say that law reflects the values of an era, rather than creating them. Sometimes, however, laws are passed that prove impossible to enforce, even when they have won strong support. As mentioned in Chapter 1, the 18th Amendment to the Constitution is an example of this. Although widely endorsed, the Prohibition Amendment was impossible to enforce in practice. The drinking minority who opposed the Amendment continued to purchase "bootleg" alcohol, and an organized criminal superstructure was fostered and sustained in the atmosphere of law-breaking that prevailed, particularly in urban areas, after the Amendment became law.

Sometimes laws are passed that are blatantly unjust or that discriminate against certain groups in the population. When this happens, the question arises as to how individuals should respond to such laws.

One school of thought suggests abiding by the law while protesting its contents. People who hold this view argue that laws are the "cement" which holds our society together. If one law is consistently violated, they feel, a general disregard of other laws will be encouraged. People will be tempted to move from "small" crimes to more and more significant ones. As a consequence, the orderly rule of law will give way to chaos and anarchy.

The signers of the Declaration of Independence—a law-breaking document, if ever there was one—gave evidence of sympathy with this view of the function of law. They were careful to emphasize in the Declaration that they did not take breaking the law lightly. As a result, the Declaration states, "Prudence, indeed, will dictate that Governments long established should not be changed for *light and transient* causes. . . ." (Emphasis added.) This inherently conservative view has remained a key value in American political and social outlook.

Another school of thought urges the outright violation and defiance of unjust laws in the hope that protest will dramatize their defects, particularly in court cases. Arguing that law is flexible and subject to reinterpretation, this group feels that citizen involvement in the process of law-making will not breed anarchy but a more democratic system of laws.

Currently, there is a widespread feeling that the use of marijuana should be legalized. Those who want the right to smoke marijuana freely point to the futility of legislating moral and personal actions. Many openly break the law (or say they do) by buying and smoking marijuana in their homes and in some public places. Those who oppose the legalization of this drug point out that the physical effects of marijuana are still not fully known. They also cite the evidence that more than ten million people in this country are alcoholics and argue that while laws cannot regulate personal moral behavior, a government can assume responsibility for regulating dangerous drugs which can be misused by members of the public in order to protect them from themselves. Legalizing a drug such as alcohol or marijuana does not automatically end the problems that a society can have with it and with those who use it.

Are there other current laws that are of questionable validity? Students may want to inquire into the laws they confess they violate regularly, such as traffic laws. They may also want to look into the many municipal and state laws which are archaic and eccentric in the context of our times with a view towards working to have them repealed or declared invalid.

**Case #12:** Brian Fogel and his family moved to Capital City just before the beginning of school. Before moving to Capital City, the family had lived in a suburban community outside of a major urban area. In that community, Brian and his friends had evolved a life-style that was considered acceptable by adults and young people alike. Students attended school in jeans and T-shirts, many of which were printed with slogans of one sort or another. Brian's hair, while not unkempt or disorderly, is shoulder-length.

Main High School—which Brian will attend—faced the issue of a student dress code two years ago. After much political activity, it was decided that while male students could wear jeans to class, they could not dress in T-shirts. Female students could wear slacks, but not jeans. While girls could wear their hair any length, boys were required to keep theirs cut a minimum of two inches from their shoulders. A schoolwide referendum confirmed this code, and it has been followed, without incident, ever since.

On the first day of class, Brian was ushered into the principal's office and informed that he could not enter school until his hair was trimmed in accordance with the school dress code. He was sent home and advised to return with his parents when he had complied with school policy. Already homesick for his old friends and old school, Brian vowed to his mother when he got home that he would not return to Main High School—ever.

Brian's mother pleaded with him to be reasonable and to comply with the regulations of his new school. She pointed out that he would only be compromising part of his old life-style and she noted, "When in Rome, do as the Romans do."

*Should Brian follow his mother's advice or should he protest the school regulations and remain at home?*

**Case #13:** The Bleecker family owns a summer cottage on Lake Wyonka in central Wisconsin. Their home is located several blocks from the public beach. A number of times the children, who are teen-agers and good swimmers, have walked to the beach only to find no lifeguard on duty. State law prohibits swimming on a public beach unless a lifeguard is present. Thus, each time this has happened, the two girls have had to walk back home.

On one particularly hot day in early August, the Bleecker girls walked to the beach and again found no lifeguard on hand. Too hot to return home without at least a "dip," and knowing that they were strong swimmers anyway, the two took a chance and waded into the water. Soon they were happily frolicking in the lake, oblivious to the patrol car which had pulled up. Suddenly they heard a sharp whistle blast. They turned to see a patrolman gesturing to them to swim ashore.

As they walked up on the beach, the officer said, "You kids know it's against the law to swim without a lifeguard. Get your things. You're coming into town with me and I'm going to slap a citation on your parents for permitting you to do this."

"Wait a minute, officer," said Carol Bleecker. "What are we supposed to do on a hot day like this when the lifeguard doesn't feel like putting in an appearance? We both can swim, and I think it's our right to make use of this beach. We shouldn't be at the mercy of an unreliable lifeguard."

*Were the Bleeckers justified in using the beach in the absence of the lifeguard?*

**Case #14:** Mr. Tunnard is in his study filling out his federal income tax form. He is in a dark mood as it seems that he'll be paying much more than he had planned to.

Mrs. Tunnard knocks lightly at the door to indicate that she has brought her husband a snack and some coffee. As she enters, Mr. Tunnard says:

"Every year I fill out this tax return form and wonder why I bother! What has this government done for me and people like me, but back me to the wall financially for programs and policies I disagree with and don't support? Millionaires pay less tax than I do, while big corporations find so many special loopholes that they hardly pay their way in this society. Even public officials tamper with their tax returns, claiming deductions that are questionable and often downright illegal! Meanwhile, people like me, members of the vast middle class in this country, shoulder the tax burden. We pay for everyone else and it just isn't fair!"

Mrs. Tunnard attempted to soothe her husband by pointing out that every country taxes its citizens, some even taking half of each person's personal income.

But Mr. Tunnard was ready for this line of argument. "Sure they tax heavily in other countries, particularly in Western Europe, but look what they get in return! Their medical care is paid for. Public housing and transportation are available for everyone. There are life insurance and unemployment compensation benefits. Education is state-supported and of uniform quality. Here you have to be poor or aged—or both—to qualify for such things. Those of us who work hard for our money and stay off the public dole and plan our children and our lives with care and social concern are penalized! It isn't worth it to be a hard-working American anymore. Every year I pay more and more in taxes and get less and less.

"Quite frankly, Erica, I've been doing some hard thinking about all of this and I've decided *not* to file a tax return this year. This will be my way of protesting the mess that taxpayers like myself have been forced into. The government can keep what they've already gouged me for, but that's it! Eventually, I'll be called in for an audit, but until then, I think I will get some of my friends together to protest this whole system. Until the government starts giving the middle class some tax breaks, I'm through paying out!"

*How would you react to Mr. Tunnard's plan? What will be the consequences of his proposed action? Can individual protest have an impact on the wider system of government?*

## Summary

This chapter has explored the process of democratic decision-making that is based on the assumption that the majority should rule. We have seen that rule by majority is a way that a group—or society— can make and implement decisions even when some people cannot agree with the decisions reached. While rule by majority takes more time than would rule by a small decision-making elite, it provides the best method available of responding to the will of the people at all levels of government. It was emphasized, however, that majority rule is only a procedure of group decision-making and not a means of verifying the "correctness" of ideas.

Before the larger part of a group (the majority) can legitimately claim to speak for that group as a whole, nine conditions were put forward which, ideally, should be met. A group should: (1) have the potential for consensus, (2) decide an issue by as large a majority as possible, (3) engage in sufficient discussion prior to making a decision so that it considers limited alternatives, (4) include each person who will be affected by the group decision in the discussion, (5) make use of an accurate method of gauging group sentiment, (6) include each person who will be affected by the group decision in the voting procedure, (7) commit itself to conducting a rational discussion, (8) allow ample time to discuss the issue under consideration, and (9) give a fair hearing to the minority point of view. If the above conditions are met, a decision arrived at according to the procedures of majority rule can be relied upon and enforced.

After the chapter explored the circumstances under which confidence could be placed in the majority point of view, a series of case studies was used to highlight some of the problems that are raised when a group agrees to abide by a rule of the majority. These were: (1) Should a simple or concurrent majority rule? (2) Should the majority have the right to compel the minority to adopt its point of view? (3) Should representatives of the people respond to a silent majority? and (4) Should a person obey a law he/she doesn't agree with or thinks is wrong?

In sum, this chapter was aimed at creating an awareness of the considerations that a person faces when he/she prepares to take and defend a stand on a controversial issue which may result in standing either with or against the majority view.

## SUGGESTIONS FOR FURTHER READING

For a wealth of ideas about readings, simulation games, and audio-visual materials appropriate to each individual teacher's needs which would be related to the topic of majority rule, consult the current *Social Studies School Service Catalog.* This contains descriptions of hundreds of teaching materials and aids. If you do not have a copy, write to the Social Studies School Service, 10,000 Culver Blvd., Culver City, California 90230.

The National Council for the Social Studies has published three books which could be of use to teachers interested in pursuing some of the issues related to majority rule.

Connery, Robert H., Leach, Richard, and Zikmund, Joseph, II., *Reading Guide in Politics and Government* (Washington, D.C.: NCSS, 1966).
Riddle, Donald H. and Cleary, Robert E., eds., *Political Science in the Social Studies,* 36th Yearbook (Washington, D.C.: NCSS, 1966).
Robinson, Donald W. et al., *Promising Practices in Civic Education* (Washington, D.C.: NCSS, 1967).

Other materials of value to the teacher interested in building his or her professional background to the topic of majority rule are the following:

### Books
Buchanan, James M. and Tullock, Gordon, *The Calculus of Consent: Logical Foundations of Constitutional Democracy* (Ann Arbor: University of Michigan Press, 1962).
Commager, Henry Steele, *Majority Rule and Minority Rights* (New York: Oxford University Press, 1943).
Dahl, Robert A., *Who Governs? Democracy and Power in an American City* (New Haven: Yale University Press, 1961).
Hunt, Maurice P. and Metcalf, Lawrence E., *Teaching High School Social Studies,* 2nd edition (New York: Harper and Row, 1968).

Kendall, Willmore, *John Locke and the Doctrine of Majority Rule* (Urbana: University of Illinois Press, 1965).

Key, Valdimer O., *Public Opinion and American Democracy* (New York: Alfred A. Knopf, 1961).

Lindblom, Charles E., *The Intelligence of Democracy: Decision-Making Through Mutual Adjustment* (New York: The Free Press, 1965).

Shaver, James P. and Larkins, A. Guy, *Decision-Making in a Democracy* (Boston: Houghton Mifflin Company, 1973).

Tocqueville, Alexis de, *Democracy in America,* 2 vols. (New York: Vintage Paperbacks, 1961; originally published in 1835).

## Articles

Griffith, E. S., Plamenatz, J., and Pennock, J. R., "Cultural Prerequisites to a Successfully Functioning Democracy: A Symposium," *American Political Science Review* 50 (1956): 101-137.

Heinberg, John G., "Theories of Majority Rule," *American Political Science Review* 26 (1932): 452-469.

Horowitz, Irving L., "Consensus, Conflict and Co-operation: A Sociological Inventory, *Social Forces* 41 (1962): 177-188.

McClosky, Herbert, "Consensus and Ideology in American Politics," *American Political Science Review* 58 (1964): 361-382.

Pennock, J. Roland, "Majority Rule," in the *International Encyclopedia of the Social Sciences* (New York: The Macmillan Company and the Free Press, 1968). Vol. 9, pp. 536-539.

Pennock, J. Roland, "Responsiveness, Responsibility, and Majority Rule," *American Political Science Review* 46 (1952): 790-807.

Prothro, James W. and Grigg, C. W., "Fundamental Principles of Democracy: Bases of Agreement and Disagreement," *Journal of Politics* 27 (1960): 276-294.

Ward, Benjamin, "Majority Rule and Allocation," *Journal of Conflict Resolution* 5 (1961): 379-389.

Willhoite, Fred H., "Political Order and Consensus," *Western Political Science Quarterly* 28 (1963): 695-705.

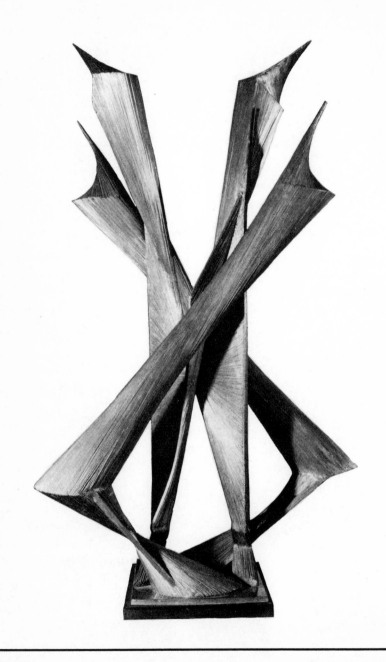

# 6

# Should Integration
# Be a Societal Goal
# in a Pluralistic Nation?

James A. Banks

## The Assimilation of European Immigrants

MOST people living in the United States, except for the American
Indians, are descendants of immigrants who came from many different
nations and represented a wide variety of ethnic and cultural groups.
The ethnic, cultural, and racial diversity of American society is unsur-
passed in the human experience and is one of the most amazing chapters in history. Most nationality groups came to North America hoping
to improve their economic conditions; some also sought better social
and political opportunities. African immigrants differed from all others
since they came to this country involuntarily.* As Redding has
poetically stated, they came in chains.[1]

While most immigrants who came to America were in search of a
Dream, many of their hopes were shattered when they confronted the
harsh realities of this land. By the late 1700s, the English immigrants
dominated most of the social, economic, and political institutions of

---

* While some criminals and other European social outcasts were forced to
immigrate to America, Africans were the only *nationality* group that came to
America involuntarily.

The author would like to thank the National Academy of Education for providing financial assistance in the form of a Spencer Fellowship which enabled him
to do the research on which this chapter is based.

---

*JAMES A. BANKS is Professor of Education, College of Education,
University of Washington, Seattle, Washington.*

the colonies. Anglo-Saxon culture was the ideal by which all other ethnic groups were judged. Thus, early in Colonial times, groups such as the French Huguenots, the Germans, the Irish, and the Scotch-Irish were discriminated against because of their ethnic and religious differences. Almost from the beginning of our national history, non-English ethnic groups were victimized because of their cultural differences. Despite the cherished mythical beliefs about American society that are taught in school, cultural and ethnic differences were neither accepted nor encouraged in early European America.[2] The English, who were the most powerful ethnic group, rejected groups which differed from themselves culturally and racially.[3] The more groups differed from the English the more they were rejected. Thus, the French Huguenots were disdained more than the Germans.

Southern and Eastern European immigrants, such as the Greeks, the Italians, and the Poles, who started immigrating to the United States in large numbers in the late 1800s, were strongly disliked by the "old" immigrants, such as the English and the Germans. By the end of the nineteenth century, groups like the English and the Germans were banding together to damn the "new" immigrants from Southern, Central, and Eastern Europe. Most of the early German immigrants were, by the late 1800s, *culturally* indistinguishable from the English. The "old" immigrants carefully distinguished themselves from the "new" immigrants, whom they considered culturally and racially inferior to Northern and Western Europeans. The nativistic feelings toward Southern and Eastern Europeans soared in the late nineteenth and early twentieth centuries, and culminated in the Immigration Act of 1924, which virtually stopped immigration from Southern and Eastern Europe and the non-Western world.[4] The Immigration Act of 1924 was one of the most blatantly racist documents in American history.

European immigrants, like the Germans, the French Huguenots, the Jews, the Poles, and the Italians, tried desperately to maintain their ethnic cultures and institutions in America. They banded together in their ethnic communities: the Germantowns, the Little Italys, and the Irish settlements. These immigrants tried to perpetuate ethnic institutions, like the ethnic church, school, and newspaper, and to assure their cultural survival in North America. Despite the vigorous efforts by European immigrants to establish and maintain their identities in America, their efforts were largely doomed because the goal of American society was *assimilation* and *integration*. Few ethnic differences were tolerated and almost none were encouraged.

Assimilation became synonymous with the attainment of Anglo-Saxon values, speech, and behavior. The European immigrants were forced to acquire Anglo-Saxon cultural characteristics. The penalties for remaining "ethnic" were severe. If immigrants remained markedly Italian, Polish, or Irish, they were denied full participation in American life. Thus, immigrants often changed their names from Polinski to Jones, moved out of their ethnic communities as soon as they could afford to, and prohibited their children from speaking European languages. They urged them to become "100% Americans." The school penalized and ostracized children who looked and talked "ethnic." Other institutions, such as the courts and industry, aggressively tried to assimilate and "Americanize" the European immigrants. After assimilation, integration into the dominant Anglo-Saxon society took place. When Poles and Italians became assimilated, they usually lived in the same neighborhoods, went to the same schools, and eventually intermarried. Except for religious groups like the Jews, Catholics, and Greek Orthodox, intermarriage rates among European Americans are extremely high.

## Assimilation and Non-European Ethnic Minorities

Non-European peoples have been in America longer than Europeans. The Indians were living on this continent when European explorers arrived here in the fifteenth century. The ancestors of Mexican-Americans had settled in what is now the United States Southwest in the 1500s. Africans came to the Americas with the earliest Spanish explorers in the sixteenth century. Despite their historic roots in America, non-White peoples were the victims of the most harsh conditions in America because their physical and cultural characteristics were most unlike those of the English and other White Americans. Consequently, non-European minorities were soon regarded as inferior savages who were non-human.

While the societal goal for European immigrants was *assimilation* and *integration,* the goal for non-White ethnics was *cultural assimilation* and *exclusion.* Ethnic minorities were encouraged, and often forced, to give up their unique values, languages, and other cultural traits, and to acquire those of White Anglo-Saxon Protestants. However, the non-European ethnic confronted a cruel impossibility: White skin was held out to him as an ideal, yet he could not become White. Consequently, no matter how Anglo-Saxon a Black or a Chinese became, he was still judged inferior by the larger society and denied full participation within it. Thus, he was a "marginal man," caught within and between two cultures. He was frequently rejected by his own culture because he had, in its view, rejected it. He could not enter the mainstream society because of his skin color.

Partly because ethnic minorities were unable to fully assimilate into the dominant society,* but also because of their ties of ethnic kinship, non-White ethnic institutions became salient parts of American society in the nineteenth century. Some of the most important ethnic institutions were organized within Black communities. These included Black schools such as Howard, Fisk, and Atlanta Universities, Black churches, insurance companies, and other businesses. Most of these institutions were organized by Blacks for Blacks. Ethnic organizations were also formed in other minority communities in later decades, including the League of United Latin American Citizens in 1928 and the Japanese American Citizenship League in 1930. Most of these organizations were formed to help particular ethnic groups to attain greater civil rights.

Segregation was practiced throughout the United States in the antebellum period. However, it did not become widely legalized until after the Civil War. In 1896 the Supreme Court ruled, in the *Plessy* vs. *Ferguson* case, that "separate but equal" facilities were constitutional. This decision sanctioned and encouraged the proliferation of Jim Crow laws that soon spread throughout the South and much of the North and Midwest. In most Southern states, Blacks were sent to segregated and inferior schools, were not allowed to eat at lunch counters, and were often prevented from voting with a series of ingenious devices such as the grandfather clause, the poll tax, and the literacy test. Other minority groups, such as Mexican-Americans and Asian-Americans, did not escape the forces which tried to segregate ethnic minorities into inferior institutions. In 1906 the San Francisco Board of Education ordered all Asian-American children to attend a segregated Oriental school. Because of diplomatic pressure exercised by Japan, this order was later rescinded.

### The Challenge to Racial Segregation

The first major Black civil rights organizations in the United States were organized around the turn of the century after Afro-Americans had experienced one of the most poignant periods in their history. Most of these organizations, such as the NAACP and the National Urban League, fought for racial integration because their leaders felt that Afro-Americans and other excluded ethnic minorities would attain equal rights only when they were allowed to fully participate in White American economic, political, and educational institutions. These organizations practiced what they preached. Their governing boards and staffs were integrated. In fact, liberal Whites played the key roles in shaping

---

* See Milton M. Gordon, *Assimilation in American Life: The Role of Race, Religion, and National Origins* (New York: Oxford University Press, 1964).

policy in the earliest days of American civil rights organizations such as the NAACP and the National Urban League.

Concentrating most of their efforts on the courts, and ably led by the NAACP Legal Defense Fund counsel, integration advocates won major victories in the courts in the 1930s, the 1940s, and the 1950s. In the 1930s and 1940s, segregation of Southern and border state universities suffered major blows. In a long series of cases, the Supreme Court, which had staunchly defended segregation in the 1890s, consistently ruled that Afro-American students had a right to attend graduate and professional schools in their native states. Consequently, segregation in state universities in such states as Texas, Oklahoma, and Missouri crumbled. The legal battle for integrated education culminated in 1954 when the Supreme Court ruled that segregation of children in the public schools was "inherently unequal," because it did irreparable harm to children's hearts and minds. Integration advocates hailed this historic decision. However, they did not know that there were rough days ahead for school integration.

### Frustration and Disillusionment with Integration

Passed largely in response to the historic "March on Washington" in 1963 and the ghetto rebellions of the Sixties, the Civil Rights Act of 1964 was another major victory for integration advocates. It was the most comprehensive civil rights bill in American history and prohibited discrimination in public accommodations and in employment. The bill also gave more teeth to other civil rights bills which had been enacted since 1957. However, even when this bill was enacted, many people who had been staunch advocates of integration had begun to seriously question its value for Afro-Americans and other oppressed Americans. Many opponents of integration had intensified their efforts to oppose it. School integration was proceeding at a snail's pace, and had resulted in violence in many places in the South. Also, Whites in many communities had established segregated "private" schools that were supported with public funds. In some communities, such as Prince Edward County, Virginia, all of the public schools were closed.

Many Black social activists, who had earlier advocated integration, began to see it as an illusory goal that was not directly related to the improvement of the Black people's condition. What Afro-Americans needed, they argued, was *power,* since they were politically alienated and at the bottom of the economic ladder. Once Blacks attained power, they would be able to attain full participation in American society. Thus, these activists maintained, focusing on integration as a major goal was counterproductive.[5]

These sentiments were steeped within the Black community when Stokely Carmichael coined the phrase "Black Power" during a civil rights march in 1966. "Black Power" became the slogan of a movement which advocated Black pride, Black ownership of property, Black voting for Black candidates, Black control of community schools, and Black self-determination. Advocates of this philosophy were dubbed Black "separatists" and "segregationists" by many Whites and some Black integrationists. Some student Black Power advocates demanded separate dorms on college campuses, Black Studies programs, often for Black students only, and symbolized their pride in Blackness by wearing African tikis and Afro hairstyles. While this movement is and was exceedingly important in the Black community, especially among the Black intelligentsia, surveys indicate that most Black Americans are still committed, in principle, to an integrated society.

Integration, especially in education, made new enemies when Northern school systems were ordered to desegregate in the 1960s and 1970s. Most Northern Whites were verbally committed to school integration during the 1950s when it was largely restricted to the Southern and border states. However, some of the most violent reactions to school integration, symbolized with the word "busing," were triggered when Northern, Western, and Midwestern school districts were ordered to desegregate. In 1971 several buses were bombed in Pontiac, Michigan the day before they were to be used to cross-bus Black and White students.[6] An anti-busing bill was supported by President Nixon and enacted by Congress in 1972.

In recent years colleges and universities have been under the gun to more fully integrate their faculties and student bodies because of federal affirmative action policies. Some universities, such as the University of Washington in 1974, have faced the possibility of losing federal funds because of their lack of compliance with federal regulations related to affirmative action. Affirmative action programs have created bitter controversy because many Whites argue and believe that members of minorities who are less qualified than they often are given preference for jobs in industry and for admission to professional schools and colleges. In 1973 Marco DeFunis, Jr. sued the University of Washington Law School for "reverse discrimination" when the school allegedly admitted minority applicants who were less qualified than DeFunis.

DeFunis was supported by several Jewish organizations, including the Anti-Defamation League of B'nai B'rith, the American Jewish Committee, and the Jewish Rights Council. The nation eagerly awaited the Supreme Court's ruling on the nationally debated case. However, both the supporters and opponents of DeFunis were extremely disappointed when the Court issued its ruling on the case April 23, 1974. The Court decided to evade the central issue in the case and ruled that the case was moot because DeFunis would soon graduate from the University of Washington Law School.

While many Whites argue that minorities are getting unfair advantages under affirmative action programs, many minorities believe that institutions are not committed to effective affirmative action, but hire only a few token minorities, often not the most qualified ones, to serve as "window dressing." It is further argued that these "token" minorities, most of whom are believed to be hired with federal "soft" money, are released as soon as the federal money dries up. Minorities noted that monies for manpower and educational programs were rapidly declining by 1974, and that few encouraging signs were in sight.

## Integration and Social Controversy

Controversy has always existed in America regarding the treatment of ethnic groups who were excluded from full participation in the mainstream society. Controversy has arisen over questions regarding whether these groups should be forced to assimilate or maintain their ethnic cultures, and the extent to which they should be encouraged or permitted to participate in the institutions of the dominant society.

Since the late 1800s, much controversy has surrounded federal policy toward the American Indian. Federal policy has shifted from an emphasis on extreme assimilation to the encouragement of some degree of ethnic identity. When Native Americans were conquered and placed on reservations in the late 1800s, White authorities began efforts to "civilize" them. The goal of federal policy was to quickly assimilate Indians into the dominant society.[7] In 1887 the Dawes Severality Act was passed to implement the new policy of assimilation. It was clear by the late 1920s that this policy had failed miserably. In 1934 Congress passed an act which sanctioned a new policy toward Indians that enabled and encouraged them to keep aspects of their cultures. Today, controversy still exists about the relationship which the federal government should have with American Indians.

In the last several decades, much controversy has arisen about the integration of ethnic minorities into mainstream American society. These controversies are likely to continue until racism and discrimination are eliminated from American life. While integration was the major goal of most civil rights advocates in the 1950s, many of them were emphasizing pride in ethnic heritage, ethnic political and economic power, and ethnic self-determination in the 1960s and 1970s.[8] Many saw integration, at best, as a secondary goal. Some leaders considered integration antithetical to ethnic self-determination and cultural survival. Integration, they argued, demanded cultural assimilation, "cultural genocide" in the language of some, and geographical dispersion of the group, which destroys ethnic communities and thus their strong base for political power. These spokesmen pointed out that Black schools were often closed when desegregation plans were implemented, and that Black teachers and administrators often lost their jobs or were given inferior jobs when school integration occurred.

Other groups were opposing integration in the 1970s for different reasons. Many Whites in the North strongly opposed school integration plans which required the use of buses. Politicians took up their cause and became staunchly "anti-busing." Legislation designed to greatly reduce busing for school integration was enacted in the 1970s. Many individuals and groups also opposed affirmative action programs designed to achieve integration in public and private institutions for the reasons noted above.

Despite the articulate and aggressive groups that were opposing integration, integration had its strong advocates.[9] These individuals and groups argued that within a pluralistic society racial and ethnic integration is the only viable way for minorities to gain full participation in American life and for White Americans to acquire the attitudes which they must have if we are ever going to have an open society. Traditional civil rights groups continued to fight segregation in the courts. Segregated Northern schools became one of their key targets. They experienced a number of successes as district courts ordered Northern school districts to desegregate.

Segregation in public accommodations, housing, and employment continued to be fought in the courts in the 1970s. The courts forced several major industrial firms to implement affirmative action programs to integrate their labor forces. By 1974 it was *illegal* to deliberately maintain segregation in most public and private institutions in the United States. *Yet, ironically, racial and ethnic segregation was a salient characteristic of American life in 1974.* Nearly 90 percent of the White students went to predominantly White schools; most Blacks attended Black schools. Blacks, as well as most other ethnic groups, were concentrated in segregated communities. Most Blacks, Whites, and other ethnic groups were married to members of their own groups. What was most ironic in 1974 was that many minority spokesmen as well as groups which they regarded as their oppressors were both advocating forms of segregation, but for different reasons.

Considering whether integration should be a major goal in a culturally pluralistic society will require students to seriously examine their values and racial attitudes, to gather data needed to state and test hypotheses, and to derive and formulate generalizations. They will also have the opportunity to make decisions which are consistent with their values and act on them within the school and the larger community.

## Some Sub-Issues Related to the Major Problem

There is a large range of questions related to integration in a pluralistic society that students can state and research. Open housing, ethnic separatism, interracial marriage, and affirmative action are some of the key issues and problems which the class can explore when studying about ethnicity and race in American life. Specific problems related to the major question posed in this chapter follow.

*Should minorities be judged by different criteria than Whites when applying for employment and admission to colleges and universities?*

Ethnic minority groups, such as Afro-Americans and Mexican-Americans, often perform poorly on I.Q. and other standardized tests used by firms and educational institutions to select and screen employees and students. Consequently, the use of these tests and selection devices is *one factor* which has limited the number of minorities in predominantly White colleges and universities and in certain occupations. Many minorities believe that they are often required to have higher qualifications than Whites to get the same types of jobs and to achieve greater than Whites to earn the same promotions and recognition.

Some authorities maintain that these tests are discriminatory and that minorities perform poorly on them because they are standardized on White middle-class subjects and do not reflect the cultures and experiences of ethnic minorities.[10] Others, such as Arthur S. Jensen and William Shockley, believe that some minorities perform poorly on I.Q. and other tests because they are genetically inferior to Whites.[11]

The key issue in this complex problem is how employers and educational institutions can select competent minorities without using tests and selection devices which discriminate against specific groups.

*Should institutions establish quotas for hiring and admitting ethnic minorities?*

To assure that a significant number of minorities will hold leadership roles within it, the National Education Association established minimum quotas for minority participation in 1974. The NEA constitution and by-laws require that there be a minimum of 20 percent ethnic minority representation on the board, executive committee, and on all other committees. The Anti-Defamation League of B'nai B'rith, a Jewish civil rights organization, hotly contested the NEA policies, calling them "unlawful, undemocratic and racist." [12] Jews were not included among the groups which the NEA specified as minorities. The ADL argued that setting quotas was "reverse discrimination," and that individuals should be given positions solely on the basis of their qualifications and not on the basis of their ethnic group membership. NEA officials argued that both ethnicity and competency must be considered to assure minority participation since past policies had resulted in the virtual exclusion of ethnic minorities from key roles in the organization. NEA officials also maintained that it was important that ethnic minorities have key leadership roles because they provided the organization with unique kinds of points of view.

There are other dimensions to the problem of quotas. Quotas make some ethnic minorities uneasy because they feel that once a firm or an organization has filled its quota for a particular minority group, such as American Indians, other highly qualified Indians will not be hired.

*Should minorities be permitted to establish separate facilities and organizations in publicly supported institutions?*

In the 1960s, Black students at some colleges and universities demanded that separate dormitory facilities be provided, that only Blacks be allowed to teach and enroll in Black Studies courses, and that Whites be prohibited from joining Black student organizations.[13] The students who made these demands were small minorities at predominantly White institutions that had, for a variety of reasons, historically admitted few or no Afro-American students. These students argued that they were alienated and frustrated on these campuses and experienced much discrimination. They felt that they needed separate dormitories and courses so that they could comfort each other and maintain a sense of ethnic identity. They maintained that Whites shouldn't teach or enroll in Black Studies courses because their racism made it impossible for them to understand the Black experience. Further, they argued, Whites were part of the problem and Black Studies should focus on ways in which Afro-Americans can liberate themselves from the oppressor.

Many integrationists, Black and White, argued that the students were segregationists who were trying to establish apartheid on the campuses of tax-supported institutions.[14] They felt that such demands were illegal and unconstitutional and that college and university officials should staunchly resist them. Some schools, however, did grant Black students some of their demands. Integrationists also argued that if these demands were met, many of the legal gains made by civil rights groups in the 1950s against segregation would be greatly threatened. They felt that White segregationists would use concessions made to Afro-American students as part of their argument to reestablish segregation in predominantly White institutions and in public accommodation facilities.

*Should busing be used to desegregate the public schools?*

When district courts ordered Northern school systems to desegregate, most of them had to bus Black and White children to integrated schools because most Americans live in tightly segregated communities. Strong resistance and violent reactions to busing designed to achieve racial integration erupted in many White communities when White students were bused to desegregated schools.[15] Most of the resisting White parents argued that they were not opposed to integrated schools, but wanted their children to go to school in their own neighborhoods and did not want them to take long bus rides across town to attend desegregated schools.

Integration advocates argued that such parents were opposed to racially integrated schools and not to busing since 43 per cent of all children are bused to school and only 3 per cent are bused to achieve racial integration. Integration spokesmen maintained that the parents who were objecting to the busing that was done to achieve desegregated schools were not objecting to the much greater busing done to take children to segregated schools. Busing, they argued, was only opposed when it was used to bus children to desegregated schools.

*Should interracial and interethnic marriage be encouraged and socially accepted?*

Although most ethnic minorities marry within their own ethnic groups, interracial marriage has increased greatly between some ethnic groups in recent years. In 1924 only 2 per cent of the Japanese-Americans in Los Angeles County married outside of their ethnic group. Forty-nine per cent of them married outside of their ethnic group in 1972.[16] Between 1966 and 1971, 31 per cent of the Jewish-Americans who married did not marry other Jews.[17] Although the number of Black-White marriages is still very low, there has probably been an increase in the number of Blacks dating Whites, especially on college and university campuses where the number of Black students increased substantially during the 1960s.

Some ethnic spokesmen are alarmed by the increase in the number of interracial marriages and the increase in interracial dating. Most Orthodox Jewish-Americans believe that interracial marriages will undermine the Jews' sense of ethnic kinship and cultural identity. Some Japanese-Americans also perceive interracial marriages as a threat to Japanese-American values and institutions. Many Blacks, especially those who are nationalistic in their views, are strongly opposed to Black-White dating and marriages.[18]

Other people who oppose interracial dating and marriage argue that life is too difficult for interracial couples in American society, and that until the larger society can accept interracial marriage, people of different races should not marry. Such individuals also argue that people of different races should not marry because life is very difficult for their children, who are not fully accepted by either race.

People who defend interracial dating and marriage maintain that America is a free nation, and that every person has a right to date, love, and marry whomever he or she wishes as long as the relationship involves two mutually consenting adults.

### Stages in Considering This Controversial Issue

#### Gathering Scientific Data

To make an intelligent decision on a social issue such as "Should integration be a societal goal in a pluralistic nation?" the students will need to acquire knowledge. However, decisions can be no better than the knowledge on which they are based. To make reflective decisions, students must study high level concepts and master key generalizations. Generalizations can be taught in a variety of ways. However, it is necessary for students to use the *scientific method* to derive generalizations needed for decision-making. When planning lessons to help students gain knowledge, the teacher should identify social science concepts and related generalizations which will help them to make intelligent decisions. Concepts should be selected from several disciplines, such as sociology, anthropology, history, and geography. *Discrimination, assimilation, ethnic group, culture, powerlessness,* and *separatism* are key concepts related to integration. After key concepts are identified, organizing (or key) generalizations related to the concepts are identified, and sub-ideas related to the organizing generalizations and to the content chosen for study are stated. A detailed example of this type of curriculum planning will not be presented here since the author has discussed it at considerable length in his other writings, including several NCSS publications.[19]

#### Value Clarification

After the students have had an opportunity to derive social science generalizations related to a social issue, they should undertake lessons that will enable them to *identify, analyze,* and *clarify* their values related to them. Value lessons should be conducted in an open classroom atmosphere so that the students will be willing to freely express their beliefs and to openly examine them. If the teacher is authoritarian, the students will not express their actual feelings and attitudes. Beliefs which are unexpressed cannot be examined. Because of the way in which the teacher is viewed by most students, it is a good idea for the teacher to withhold his or her views on controversial issues until the students have had an opportunity to express their beliefs. When a teacher reveals his or her position on a social issue, many students will make statements which they feel the teacher wants them to make rather than say things which they actually believe. The teacher who opens a discussion on interracial marriage or open housing by saying that everybody should have the right to marry whomever he or she pleases, or that open housing laws violate a seller's constitutional rights, cannot expect the students to state opposing beliefs. While some students will openly disagree with the teacher, most will not. The writer is not suggesting that the teacher should not state his or her positions on issues. However, experience suggests that when a teacher openly expresses his or her views early in class discussions the dialogue usually becomes stifled or slanted in one direction.

## Decision Making and Social Action

After the students have derived social science generalizations and clarified their values regarding the social issue, the teacher should ask them to list all the possible actions which they could take regarding integration in their school and community, and to predict the possible consequences of each alternative. It is imperative that the alternatives and consequences which the students identify and state are realistic and are based on the knowledge which they have mastered during the scientific phase of the unit. Alternatives and consequences should be intelligent predictive statements and not ignorant guesses or wishful thinking. After the students have discussed and weighed all of the alternative courses of action, they should decide on courses of action most consistent with their values and implement them within their school or community. For example, the students, or some of them, may decide that integration should be a major goal in a pluralistic society but that integration does not exist within their school. They might design a voluntary transfer plan with a local Black (or White, etc.) school and present it to the Board of Education for action. Figure 1 on page 210 summarizes the major steps we have discussed for studying a social issue.

FIGURE 1—THE DECISION-MAKING PROCESS*

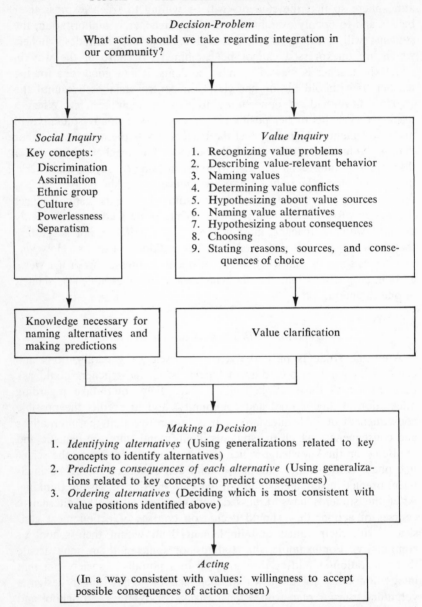

* Adapted from James A. Banks (with Ambrose A. Clegg, Jr.), *Teaching Strategies for the Social Studies* (Reading, Mass.: Addison-Wesley, 1973), p. 497. Reprinted with permission of the author. Copyright © 1973 by Addison-Wesley Publishing Company.

## The Origin of the Issue

The teacher can begin a study of the key issues discussed in this chapter by asking the students to cut out items in the newspaper which deal with such issues as busing, open housing, affirmative action programs, and discrimination in employment. Examples of such cases in recent years were the violent reactions to busing which erupted in Pontiac, Michigan in 1971, the school desegregation order issued in Detroit by Judge Stephen J. Roth in 1972, and the DeFunis case related to affirmative action at the University of Washington Law School in 1973.

## *The Definition of Key Concepts*

When studying problems related to cultural pluralism and racial integration, the class should clarify the definitions of key terms and reach general agreement about what they mean. Terms such as *integration, race, desegregation, separatism, racism, discrimination,* and *cultural pluralism* are some of the key concepts which should be defined when racial integration is studied. Several of these terms are discussed below.

Some writers make a distinction between *integration* and *desegregation.* They define *desegregation* as the mere physical mixing of different racial and ethnic groups. *Integration,* for these writers, means much more. It occurs only when mutual respect and toleration develops between different racial and ethnic groups who are members of the same institutions.

*Separatism* is sometimes said to exist when ethnic groups who are excluded from the dominant society establish ethnic organizations and institutions to meet their exclusive needs. Students can explore other definitions of separatism and identify instances of it within their communities. When discussing separatism, the class should try to distinguish *separatism* and *segregation.* These terms are highly related and are often confused. Separatist institutions are designed to help an ethnic group attain self-determination and political power and to enhance its ethnic culture. Segregated institutions in *minority communities* are usually created by the dominant society in order to keep minorities subjugated. These types of institutions are designed and controlled by the powerful groups in a society and not by the ethnic minority community. Thus, *separatist* and *segregated* institutions in minority communities are fundamentally different in structure and function.

Students will also need to define a *culturally pluralistic society.* We *can* define a culturally pluralistic society as an open society in which individuals are able to take full advantage of the social, economic, and educational advantages of a society, and yet are able to maintain their unique ethnic identities and allegiances. Individuals would not necessarily have to become assimilated into the dominant culture in order to satisfy their survival needs.

The examples above are given merely to suggest the kinds of working definitions which students can formulate for some of the key concepts in this chapter. Many other examples and definitions could be given. It is extremely important for students to know how the concepts which they are using are defined by themselves and others. Without a clear understanding of the key terms which they are using, their most diligent research efforts will be frustrated.

### Hypotheses

There are an infinite number of hypotheses related to racial integration and cultural pluralism which the students can formulate when studying about race relations in American society. What follows is a list of *possible* hypotheses which students can formulate and test.

*If minorities are required to meet the same qualifications as Whites, then most institutions and firms will remain predominantly White and segregated.*

This hypothesis is based on the assumption that most ethnic minorities, perhaps for a variety of reasons, will be unable to successfully compete with Whites for jobs and in educational institutions if present criteria and methods are used to screen and select employees and students. An opposing hypothesis might state that if minorities are required to have the same qualifications as Whites, they would eventually be able to satisfy them because minorities could and would obtain the experiences and knowledge needed to do so.

*If institutions and firms establish quotas for minorities, some qualified minorities and Whites will be discriminated against.*

This hypothesis assumes that there are more qualified minorities for positions and slots than quotas would provide for, that some nonqualified minorities may be hired in preference to qualified ones, and that if a White and a minority are equally qualified, firms with quotas would hire the minorities until their quotas had been attained. It also assumes that qualified minorities would not be hired once such quotas were reached. A different hypothesis might suggest that firms and schools will recruit and hire minorities only if they are required to fulfill quotas.

*If open housing laws are enacted and enforced, then Whites will be forced to sell their homes at a tremendous loss.*

This hypothesis assumes that property values are greatly reduced when ethnic minorities move into predominantly White neighborhoods. A related hypothesis might state that if open housing laws are not enacted and enforced, housing segregation will increase.

*If busing is not used to desegregate the public schools, most Blacks and Whites will continue to attend racially segregated schools.*

This hypothesis assumes that because of the housing patterns of Blacks and Whites, busing is necessary to desegregate the public schools. Another hypothesis might state that if open housing laws were enacted and enforced, neighborhood schools would become voluntarily integrated.

### Testing the Hypotheses

The students will need to gather data to test the hypotheses which they have formulated. Because of the nature of the hypotheses formulated above and the short history of most civil rights programs and legislation, little historical data are available about the effects of laws which prohibit segregation and discrimination. Also, like any other problems related to human behavior, problems in race relations are exceedingly complex. It is difficult to establish causal relationships with a large degree of certainty, such as if A then B, or if there is forced school integration (A), conflict (B) will develop between Blacks and Whites. There are too many other variables which may influence either A or B and thus affect the outcome of busing in a particular community. How forced integration affects the relationships between Blacks and Whites in a particular community may depend on who made the legal decision, whether a local or federal court, the extent of racial hostility within the community before the court order, the percentage of Blacks and Whites in the community that are involved in the busing program, the types of Black and White leaders in the community, and many other variables.

When students are gathering data to test hypotheses related to racial integration, they should be helped to see how difficult it is to establish relationships with a high degree of reliability. Another caveat is in order. Much of the information related to ethnic and racial problems is highly emotional and biased. It is often presented to support or invalidate a particular position. Examples of these types of studies abound in the literature on race relations. Rivlin has perceptively called this kind of research "forensic" social science.[20] Studies written in the forensic tradition include Jensen and Shockley's work on Black-

White intelligence, Jencks et al.'s study on equality of educational opportunity, Banfield's *The Unheavenly City,* and Moynihan's *The Negro Family: The Case for National Action.*[21] Pro-Black positions on issues are presented in most of the articles in the *Black Scholar.*[22] One way to partially solve this problem is to present the students with readings that support both sides of an issue, and which present data that support specific viewpoints.

Historical data on college admissions and employment of minorities will shed light on the first hypothesis stated above. Most minorities are poorly represented in the higher paying jobs in industry and government. However, even fewer held white-collar jobs before the civil rights legislation of the 1960s. The table below indicates that the percentage of Blacks in the labor force who are white-collar workers has increased greater than the percentage of Whites who are white-collar workers in recent years. When the Civil Rights Act of 1964 was enacted, many industries developed special incentive programs for the recruitment and hiring of ethnic minorities.

BLACK AND WHITE WHITE-COLLAR WORKERS*

|  | 1957 | 1970 | Per cent Increase |
|---|---|---|---|
| Per cent of Blacks in the labor force that were white-collar workers | 12.8 | 27.9 | 15.1 |
| Per cent of Whites in the labor force that were white-collar workers | 44.2 | 50.8 | 6.6 |

* Adapted from *Statistical Abstract of the United States* (Washington, D.C.: U.S. Government Printing Office, 1971), p. 133.

Since the 1800s, most Afro-American college students have attended predominantly Black colleges. In 1938, 97 per cent of Black college students were attending Black colleges. When affirmative action programs were implemented in response to federal legislation, predominantly White colleges and universities aggressively recruited minority students, created special programs for them, and modified their admission requirements so that more promising minority youths could be admitted. The number of Black students attending predominantly White universities increased substantially in the 1960s. In 1970, 56 per cent of all Black students were attending predominantly White colleges and universities.[23] However, the number of Blacks in these colleges was still only a very small percentage of their total populations.

In studying the kind of information presented above, the students might conclude that their data lend some support to the notion that if minorities are required to meet the same qualifications as Whites, firms and institutions may remain predominantly White. However, the severe limitations of their data and the possibility that many other factors besides the modification of qualifications influenced the number of minorities that entered institutions in the 1960s must be considered before they close their investigation. Such factors as more aggressive recruitment of minorities, more financial support for them, more extensive and improved counseling and supportive services, and the rising level of expectations among ethnic minorities, may have been the *major variables* which led to an increase of ethnic minorities within predominantly White universities and firms. Thus, the students would have to conclude that their hypothesis was at best only partially and feebly supported by their data.

### Some Tentative Conclusions

Below are some tentative conclusions which the students *might* reach after they have studied about racial integration and examined their values regarding racial mixing.

1. Ethnic minorities should be required to have the same qualifications for jobs and to enter college as any other persons. However, the ways in which these qualifications are determined should be modified so that they reflect ethnic diversity and so that minorities will not be victimized by discriminatory tests and other selective devices which are based exclusively on the dominant culture. Institutions and firms should aggressively recruit minorities to increase the pool from which they can select. This type of policy will, in the long run, result in the hiring of minorities who are as qualified as their White counterparts. In the short run, however, it might mean that industries and universities will not be able to increase the numbers of minorities in their populations at a very rapid rate.

2. Institutions should not establish quotas for minorities, but should implement affirmative action programs that will enable them to aggressively recruit minorities and give preference to them if minorities and Whites are equally qualified. The goal should be to have an integrated staff or student body which includes people who represent diverse ethnic and racial groups, and not to get a specific number from each ethnic group. This policy will result in the employment of minorities but will not restrict their number or encourage the hiring of minorities

who are less qualified than White employees, or the admission of minority students who cannot succeed in college.

3. Open housing laws should be enacted in all communities to assure that every American will have the opportunity to buy the house which he or she wants and can afford regardless of his or her race or ethnic group. If effectively enforced, open housing laws are not likely to result in many interracial communities since Whites usually move out of neighborhoods when minorities move into them. No legal actions should be taken to prevent freedom of movement by Whites. However, planned interracial communities should be established since people who grow up in interracial communities have more positive racial attitudes and are more likely to live in interracial neighborhoods and to send their children to interracial schools.

4. The establishment of interracial schools should be a major goal of American society. Any reasonable plans, including those which require busing, should be implemented if they are needed to establish and maintain desegregated schools. Parents who are opposed to interracial schools and/or busing should have the right to take their children out of the public schools. However, they should not be allowed to dictate or unduly influence school policy. Major societal goals should take precedence over the whims of special interest and pressure groups. If a school district takes a strong position vis-à-vis interracial schools and busing, hostile pressure groups, which are usually small but vocal minorities, will eventually accept the school's policy and lose both community support and wide public forums for their views.

### Suggested Methods for Teaching about
### Integration and Public Controversy

#### Initiating the Unit

The teacher can begin a study of integration and public controversy by reading the class a current *case study* taken from the newspaper or a news magazine that deals with a controversial policy and/or issue related to integration. An example of such a case study taken from a newspaper and questions which the class can discuss follow:

NEA CONSTITUTION, BY-LAWS ARE RACIST, ILLEGAL, ANTI-DEFAMATION LEAGUE SAYS

PALM BEACH, FLA. The Anti-Defamation League of B'nai B'rith has condemned as "unlawful, undemocratic and racist" the new constitution and by-laws of the National Education Association. . . ."

According to Peirez, the NEA Constitution specifically designates as ethnic minorities, Blacks, Mexican-Americans, other Spanish-speaking groups, Asian-Americans and Indians. The NEA authorizes those minorities alone to nominate minority candidates for its board of directors and executive committees.

It further requires that there be a minimum of 20 percent ethnic minority representation on the NEA board, executive committee and all other committees and that delegates to its national representative assembly from state and local affiliates be allocated on the basis of the ethnic minority percentage of the population or be denied credentials.

The NEA Constitution also provides that nominations for NEA President be restricted to certain ethnic minority groups if, after 11 years, no member of such a group has been elected.[24]

## Questions:

1. Do the quotas established by the NEA Constitution constitute reverse discrimination? Why, or why not?

2. Should institutions and organizations practice reverse discrimination when trying to compensate for past injustices? Why, or why not?

3. Does the NEA Constitution violate the civil rights of Whites? Why, or why not?

4. What effects do you think the NEA Constitution and by-laws will have on minorities in the organization? On Whites in the organization? Why?

### Social Science Inquiry

When the teacher has launched the study of integration with a case study such as the one above, the students should study historical information which will enable them to understand the forces that have shaped public policy regarding racial integration. Attention should be given to the legalization of segregation which took place in the decades after the Civil War. Individual students could be asked to prepare and present reports on the following topics:

> the Black codes
> the poll tax
> the grandfather clause
> the Dred Scott Decision
> Plessy vs. Ferguson

When these reports are presented to the class, the students should discuss these questions: Why did segregation become widespread in the post-Civil War period? Why was it legalized? How did these laws affect Black Americans? White Americans? Other Americans?

• Ask the students to pretend that they are the Supreme Court in 1896 and that they are hearing the case of Homer Plessy, a mulatto who complains that he has to sit in separate cars on trains that pass through his native state of Louisiana. Plessy argues that this type of segregation violates protection guaranteed to him by the Fourteenth Amendment to the Constitution. Ask individual students to role-play the roles of the Supreme Court justices, Homer Plessy, and the prosecuting and defense attorneys. After the arguments on both sides have been presented to the Court, the judges should deliberate and then rule on the case. After the role-play situation, the class should discuss:

a. ways in which their simulated court was similar to and different from the actual Supreme Court in 1896;
b. whether the role-players were able to successfully assume the attitudes and viewpoints of people who lived in 1896;
c. what the "separate but equal" doctrine meant in 1896 and what it means today.

• At the turn of the century, two major civil rights organizations were formed to fight for the rights of Afro-Americans: the National Association for the Advancement of Colored People and the National Urban League. It was also during this period that two major civil rights leaders became nationally eminent, Booker T. Washington and W. E. B. DuBois. Washington and DuBois became staunch opponents because they held opposing views about racial equality and the ways in which the Afro-American should be educated. Ask the class to read Washington's autobiography, *Up From Slavery,* and selections from W. E. B. DuBois's *The Souls of Black Folks.* The class should discuss the views of these two men and determine which of their ideas were valid and which were not. After the class has discussed the views of DuBois and Washington, ask two students to role-play a debate between the two men regarding steps which the Afro-American should take to achieve racial equality.

• Most of the national civil rights organizations in the early 1900s were interracial. Ask the students to do required readings on the history and development of the NAACP and the National Urban League. When they have completed the readings, they should compare and contrast these two organizations with the Niagara Movement and earlier Black protest movements, such as the Negro Convention Movement and the African Civilization Society. Particular attention should be paid to: (1) reasons why the organizations emerged, (2) who made policy and held key positions within them, (3) types of problems which arose within the organizations, (4) the major goals of the organizations, and (5) ways in which the organizations succeeded or failed and why.

• Black separatist movements developed early in American history. Some of the earliest were led by such Blacks as Martin R. Delany and

Paul Cuffee. Ask the students to research the lives of these men and to present dramatizations which show ways in which they were advocates of Black nationalism. Marcus Garvey, another Black separatist, attained eminence in the 1930s. Ask the class to read his biography, *Black Moses,* by E. D. Cronon, and to list ways in which Garvey was similar to and different from earlier Black nationalist leaders.

• In the 1930s, 1940s, 1950s, and 1960s racial segregation received a number of severe blows, which culminated in the Brown Decision of 1954 and the Civil Rights Act of 1964. Ask the students to develop a chronology which lists the major civil rights legislation which was enacted between 1930 and 1964. After the chronology is developed, the students should discuss these questions:

a. What were the major social and political factors which led to the passage of each of these bills?

b. Why has racial segregation actually increased in American society in recent years even though so many civil rights bills have been enacted?

• The major goal of the civil rights movement in the 1950s was to desegregate public accommodation facilities and other institutions. Action tactics and court battles achieved much desegregation. However, by 1965, many Afro-Americans, especially young Black activists, were disillusioned with the attainments of the movement and realized that integration alone would not eliminate the Afro-American's major social, economic, and political problems. These young activists felt that both the goals and tactics of the movement should be changed. They issued a call for "Black Power!" The students can gain an understanding of the concept of Black Power by reading *Black Power: The Politics of Liberation in America* by Stokely Carmichael and Charles V. Hamilton. Many Black integrationists rejected the views of Black Power advocates. Ask the class to thoroughly research the views of the men and women listed below and to simulate a national convention of Black civil rights leaders in which they discuss the problem, "What should be the future course of Black Americans: Integration or Separatism?"

| | |
|---|---|
| (a) Martin Luther King, Jr. | (i) Shirley Chisholm |
| (b) Roy Wilkins | (j) Bobby Seale |
| (c) Roy Innis | (k) Huey Newton |
| (d) Angela Davis | (l) Imamu Amiri Baraka |
| (e) Stokely Carmichael | (m) Richard G. Hatcher |
| (f) H. Rap Brown | (n) Julian Bond |
| (g) Vernon Jordan | (o) Ronald V. Dellums |
| (h) Rev. Jesse Jackson | (p) Barbara Jordan |

Individual students should be asked to research and play the roles of each leader in the convention. After the major question has been discussed, the convention participants should then develop an action agenda for Black Americans in the 1970s which they all can endorse.

## *Value Inquiry*

After the students have had an opportunity to gather factual data related to integration, they should examine their values, attitudes, and beliefs regarding racial mixing. A wide variety of strategies and materials can be used to help students to examine and clarify their values. Some valuing exercises appropriate for studying about integration are given below. These strategies are adapted from techniques developed by Simon, Howe and Kirschenbaum.[25]

### SPREAD OF OPINION

The teacher should divide the class into several small groups and give each of the groups a piece of paper with one of these issues written on it:

> forced busing
> interracial marriage
> open housing laws
> reverse discrimination
> separatism
> quotas
> interracial adoptions
> interracial dating
> segregated fraternities and sororities

Each of the groups should identify a number of positions which can be taken on the issue given to it. Each member of the group should write a statement defending one of these positions, whether he or she agrees with it or not. When the statements have been completed, the students should discuss each issue and state their own positions on it.

### UNFINISHED SENTENCES

The teacher should ditto the following list of statements and give a copy to each of the students. The students should be asked to complete the statements with the words and phrases which they first think of when they read each statement. After the students have completed the statements, the teacher should divide the class into small groups and ask the students to discuss, "What I learned about myself from this exercise."

1. If I were Black (or White, Mexican-American, etc.) I would. . .
2. People who riot are. . .
3. Most Blacks are. . .
4. If a Black (or a Mexican-American, etc.) family moved into my neighborhood, I would. . .
5. If I were forced to ride a bus to an integrated school each day, I would. . .
6. If my sister married a Black (or a White, etc.), I would. . .
7. People of other races make me feel. . .
8. A *racist* is a person who. . .
9. If I were called a *racist,* I would. . .
10. Most Whites are. . .
11. Special programs created for minorities are. . .
12. Minorities who participate in special programs are. . .
13. People who are opposed to interracial busing are. . .
14. Minorities who score poorly on I.Q. tests are. . .

## STRONGLY AGREE/STRONGLY DISAGREE

The teacher should duplicate the following list of statements and give a copy to each of the students. Ask the students to indicate the extent to which they agree or disagree with the statements by writing one of the following letter combinations in front of each statement:

SA = Strongly agree
AS = Agree somewhat
DS = Disagree somewhat
SD = Strongly disagree

After the students have responded to each of the statements, divide the class into small groups and ask the students to discuss their responses in their groups.

_____ 1. I am prejudiced toward some racial and ethnic groups.
_____ 2. I would not live in a predominantly Black (or White, etc.) neighborhood.
_____ 3. People who riot should be put in jail.
_____ 4. Most Mexican-Americans are poor because they are lazy.
_____ 5. Most Whites are racists.
_____ 6. I would encourage my sister to marry a Black (or a White, etc.) if she wanted to.
_____ 7. Minorities should meet the same college admission requirements as Whites.
_____ 8. I.Q. tests are unfair to minorities and should be abandoned.

_____ 9. Students should not be required to be bused to desegregate schools.

_____ 10. Only Blacks should teach Black Studies.

_____ 11. Universities and firms should establish quotas for minorities.

_____ 12. Black militants are racists.

_____ 13. White fraternities and sororities should be required to admit Blacks, Mexican-Americans, Asian-Americans, and other ethnic minorities.

VALUES GRID

An effective summary valuing activity for this unit is the valuing grid. Make copies of the following chart for each of the students.

| ISSUE | 1 | 2 | 3 | 4 | 5 | 6 | 7 |
|---|---|---|---|---|---|---|---|
| 1.  forced busing | | | | | | | |
| 2.  interracial housing | | | | | | | |
| 3.  interracial marriage | | | | | | | |
| 4.  interracial dating | | | | | | | |
| 5.  racial quotas | | | | | | | |
| 6.  segregated schools | | | | | | | |
| 7.  Black separatism | | | | | | | |
| 8.  racial riots | | | | | | | |
| 9.  White racism | | | | | | | |
| 10.  affirmative action programs | | | | | | | |
| 11.  Black English | | | | | | | |

Ask the students to make brief notes about how they feel about each of the eleven issues listed in the chart. Each of these issues will have been discussed during earlier parts of the unit. The following seven questions are taken from the valuing strategy developed by Simon et al.[26] List the following questions on the board and explain each of them to the students.

1. Are you *proud* of (do you prize or cherish) your position?
2. Have you *publicly affirmed* your position?
3. Have you chosen your position from *alternatives?*

4. Have you chosen your position after *thoughtful consideration* of the pros and cons and consequences?
5. Have you chosen your position *freely?*
6. Have you *acted* on or done anything about your beliefs?
7. Have you acted with *repetition,* pattern, or consistency on this issue?

Ask the students to write "Yes" or "No" in each of the squares in the chart to indicate their responses to each of the seven questions for each issue. When the students have individually completed the grid, they should break up into groups of threes and discuss as many of their responses as they would like to discuss.

### Decision Making and Social Action

When the students have gathered scientific data and clarified their values, they should identify *alternative courses of actions* which they can take regarding integration in a pluralistic society, and the *possible consequences* of each course of action. Individuals and/or groups should then formulate plans to implement courses of action which are most consistent with their values. Below are some possible action projects which some of the students may decide to implement.

ACTION PROJECTS

1. If the school is segregated: Developing and implementing a volunteer transfer plan with a local school whose population is predominantly of another race.
2. Conducting a survey to determine the kinds of jobs which most minorities have in local hotels, restaurants, and firms, and, if necessary, urging local businesses to hire more minorities in top level positions. Conducting boycotts of local businesses which refuse to hire minorities in top-level positions.
3. Conducting a survey to determine the treatment of ethnic groups in all of the courses and textbooks in the school and recommending ways in which the school curriculum can become more integrated; suggesting that a permanent review board be established to examine all teaching materials and determine how they treat ethnic groups. Presenting these recommendations to appropriate school officials and pressuring them to act on the recommendations.
4. Conducting a survey to determine what local ethnic organizations and leaders are within the community. Inviting some of them to participate in school programs and projects, such as assemblies and classes.

5. Conducting a survey to determine whether the school and public libraries have adequate collections of books and materials about American ethnic groups. If necessary, recommending books and materials which should be purchased and pressuring the libraries to buy them.

6. Conducting a survey to determine what local laws exist (and how they are enforced) regarding open housing, discrimination in public accommodations, etc., and, if necessary, developing recommendations regarding changes which should be made in the laws or in the ways in which they should be implemented. Presenting these recommendations to appropriate public officials and pressuring them to act on the recommendations.

7. If the school is racially segregated: Developing plans for exchange activities and programs with a school whose population is predominantly of another race.

8. Conducting a survey to determine the racial and ethnic composition of the school staff (including secretaries, teachers, janitors, etc.) and, if necessary, recommending appropriate action to take to make the school more integrated. Presenting these recommendations to appropriate school officials and pressuring them to act on the recommendations.

9. Conducting a survey to determine whether the posters, bulletin boards, photographs, and school holidays reflect the ethnic diversity of American life and, if necessary, implementing a plan to make the total school environment more integrated and multiethnic.

10. If the school is interracial: Conducting a survey to determine if there are examples of racial conflict and tension within the school. If there are, formulating and implementing plans to alleviate these problems.

### Summary

Students should have ample opportunities to discuss questions and problems related to integration and cultural pluralism because some of the most serious problems within our society result from ethnic conflict and misunderstanding. Each student should develop, within an open classroom atmosphere, commitments to courses of action which he or she has reflectively derived.

My own position on this complex issue is that our major societal goal should be to create an *open society:* one in which ethnic groups can freely participate and yet maintain their cultural characteristics and institutions. In such a society, individuals and groups could practice integration or separatism as long as these options were freely chosen and did not adversely affect other individuals and groups.[27] When integration becomes the major goal of a society, the dominant group usually defines the terms on which integration will take place. Ethnic institutions are destroyed, and ethnic cultures are eliminated. Many examples of these types of phenomena have occurred in the name of racial integration in our society in recent years.[28] When an ethnic group's sense of peoplehood is destroyed and its political power is dissipated in the name of integration, integration has become an oppressive weapon and a political tool of the dominant society.

# FOOTNOTES

[1] Saunders Redding, *They Came in Chains* (New York: J. B. Lippincott and Co., 1950).

[2] The term *European America* is used here to designate America after the settlement of European immigrants.

[3] Maldwyn Allen Jones, *American Immigration* (Chicago: University of Chicago Press, 1960), pp. 39-63.

[4] John Higham, *Strangers in the Land: Patterns of American Nativism 1860-1925* (New York: Atheneum, 1972), p. 324.

[5] These views are perceptively articulated by Barbara A. Sizemore, "Separatism: A Reality Approach to Inclusion," in Robert L. Green, ed., *Racial Crisis in American Education* (Chicago: Follett Educational Corporation, 1969), pp. 249-279; and by Harold Cruse, *The Crisis of the Negro Intellectual* (New York: William Morrow, 1967).

[6] Robert L. Green, "Racism in American Education," *Phi Delta Kappan* 53 (January 1972): 274.

[7] Alvin M. Josephy, Jr., *The Indian Heritage of America* (New York: Bantam Books, Inc., 1968), pp. 345-366.

[8] Stokely Carmichael and Charles V. Hamilton, *Black Power: The Politics of Liberation in America* (New York: Vintage Books, 1967). [Diverse views on integration are presented in "Which Way Black America? Separation? Integration? Liberation?," *Ebony* 25 (August 1970).]

[9] Whitney M. Young, Jr., *Beyond Racism: Building an Open Society* (New York: McGraw-Hill Book Co., 1969); and Roy Wilkins, "Whither 'Black Power'?," in Mortimer J. Adler, Charles Van Doren, and George Ducas, eds., *The Negro in American History Vol. 1* (Chicago: Encyclopaedia Britannica Educational Corporation, 1969), pp. 112-115.

[10] William H. Boyer and Paul A. Walsh, "Innate Intelligence: An Insidious Myth," reprinted in James A. Banks and William W. Joyce, eds., *Teaching Social Studies to Culturally Different Children* (Reading: Addison-Wesley Publishing Company, 1971), pp. 90-97.

[11] Arthur R. Jensen, "How Much Can We Boost IQ and Scholastic Achievement?," *Harvard Educational Review* 39 (Spring, 1969): 273-356; and William Shockley, "Dysgenics, Geneticity, Raceology: Challenges to the Intellectual Responsibility of Educators," *Phi Delta Kappan* 53 (January 1972): 297-307.

[12] "NEA Constitution, By-laws Are Racist, Illegal, Anti-Defamation League Says," *New York Teacher* (February 3, 1974).

[13] For an exploration of these issues see John W. Blassingame, ed., *New Perspectives on Black Studies* (Urbana: University of Illinois Press, 1971).

[14] See Kenneth B. Clark, "A Charade of Power: Black Students at White Colleges," in Blassingame, *ibid.,* pp. 116-122.

[15] Green, *op. cit.,* p. 274.

[16] Akemi Kikumura and Harry H. L. Kitano, "Interracial Marriage: A Picture of the Japanese Americans," *The Journal of Social Issues* 29 (No. 2, 1973): 69.

[17] Dorothy Rabinowitz, "The Trouble with Jewish-Gentile Marriages," *New York* 6 (August 20, 1973): 26.

[18] Ponchitta Pierce, "Marriage and the Educated Black Woman," *Ebony* 28 (August 1973): 160-166.

[19] See James A. Banks (with Ambrose A. Clegg, Jr.), *Teaching Strategies for the Social Studies: Inquiry, Valuing and Decision-Making* (Reading: Addison-Wesley Publishing Company, 1973); James A. Banks, "Liberating the Black Ghetto: Decision-Making and Social Action," in Richard Wisniewski, ed., *Teaching About Life in the City* (Washington, D.C.: National Council for the Social Studies, 1972), pp. 159-183; and James A. Banks, "Teaching for Ethnic Literacy," *Social Education* 37 (December 1973): 738-750.

[20] Alice M. Rivlin, "Forensic Social Science," *Harvard Educational Review* 43 (February 1973): 61-75; see also Joyce A. Ladner, ed., *The Death of White Sociology* (New York: Vintage Books, 1973).

[21] Jensen, *op. cit.;* Shockley, *op. cit.;* Christopher Jencks, et al., *Inequality: A Reassessment of the Effect of Family and Schooling in America* (New York: Basic Books, Inc., 1972); Edward C. Banfield, *The Unheavenly City* (Boston: Little, Brown and Co., Inc., 1970); and Daniel P. Moynihan, *The Negro Family: The Case for National Action* (Washington, D.C.: U.S. Government Printing Office, 1965).

[22] A collection of articles reprinted from the *Black Scholar* is in Robert Crisman and Nathan Hare, eds., *Contemporary Black Thought* (New York: The Bobbs-Merrill Co., 1973).

[23] Alan Pifer, *The Higher Education of Blacks in the United States* (New York: Carnegie Corporation of New York, 1973), p. 37.

[24] "NEA Constitution . . .," *op. cit.*

[25] Sidney B. Simon, Leland W. Howe, and Howard Kirschenbaum, *Values Clarification: A Handbook of Practical Strategies for Teachers and Students* (New York: Hart Publishing Company, Inc., 1972), pp. 35-37, 241-257, and 252-254.

[26] *Ibid.,* p. 36.

[27] James A. Banks, "Curricular Models for an Open Society," in Delmo Della-Dora and James E. House, eds., *Education for an Open Society* (Washington, D.C.: Association for Supervision and Curriculum Development, 1974), pp. 43-63.

[28] James A. Banks, "The Destruction of Black Schools: An American Tragedy," *Educational Leadership* 30 (December 1972): 269-271.

## TEACHING MATERIALS

### Books for the Students

Acuña, Rudy, *A Mexican American Chronicle* (New York: American Book Company, 1971).

An excellent and comprehensive textbook which treats both the historical and contemporary life of the Mexican-Americans.

Banks, James A., Banks, Cherry A., *March Toward Freedom: A History of Black Americans,* sec. ed. (Belmont, California: Fearon, 1974).

A comprehensive survey of Afro-Americans written especially for teenagers. Illustrated.

Cordasco, Francesco, and Bucchioni, Eugene, eds., *The Puerto Rican Experience* (Totowa, New Jersey: Littlefield, Adams, 1973).
An excellent collection of readings which deal with diverse aspects of Puerto Rican American life.

Finkelstein, Milton, Sandifer, Hon. Jawn A., and Wright, Elfreda S., *Minorities: USA* (New York: Globe Book Co., 1971).
This junior high school text contains excellent chapters on the major American ethnic groups.

Hsu, Francis L. K., *The Challenge of the American Dream: The Chinese in the United States* (Belmont, California: Wadsworth, 1971).
A good general treatment of the Chinese-American by an eminent social scientist.

Japanese American Curriculum Project, *Japanese Americans: The Untold Story* (New York: Holt, 1971).
Designed for use in the intermediate grades, this book treats selected aspects of Japanese-American history and contemporary life.

McLuhan, T. C., ed., *Touch the Earth: A Self-Portrait of Indian Existence* (New York: Pocket Books, 1972).
A collection of powerful and poignant statements by Native Americans on a variety of subjects.

Morales, Royal F., *Makibaka: The Pilipino American Struggle* (Los Angeles: Mountainview Publishers, 1974).
An interesting account of the Filipino's plight and struggles in the United States.

Pearson, Keith L., *The Indian in American History* (New York: Harcourt, 1973).
A useful general history of American Indians for junior high school students, although it contains some over-generalizations and misconceptions.

Shaver, James P., and Larkins, A. Guy, *Decision-Making in a Democracy* (Boston: Houghton Mifflin, 1973).
An excellent book which describes ways in which students can analyze and examine social issues.

## Films

*All the Way Home.* Producer/Distributor: Fellowship of Reconciliation, 1964.
A fictionalized drama about a Black couple's attempts to purchase a home in a White community.

*The American Indian Speaks.* Producer/Distributor: Encyclopaedia Britannica Educational Corporation, 1973.
Powerful questions about Indian survival are explored in this film. Case studies focus on the Muskogee, Creek, Rosebud Sioux, and the Nisqually.

*How the West Was Won . . . And Honor Lost.* Producer/Distributor: McGraw-Hill, 1969.
A powerful film presentation of the betrayal of the Indian through broken treaties and removal.

*Mexican-Americans: Invisible Minority.* Distributor: Indiana University Audio-Visual Center.
An excellent film in two parts which depicts the problems and aspirations of the Mexican-Americans.

*Mexican Americans: Quest for Equality.* Producer/Distributor: Anti-Defamation League of B'nai B'rith, New York.
Various aspects of Mexican-American communities are discussed by Dr. Ernesto Galarza.

*Of Black America: Black History: Lost, Stolen or Strayed.* Producer/Distributor: Columbia Broadcasting System, New York, 1968.
A revealing and powerful film about Black-White relations in America which is skillfully narrated by Bill Cosby.

*Of Black America: Portrait in Black and White.* Producer/Distributor: Columbia Broadcasting System, New York, 1968.

Based on a nationwide survey, this is an informative film about Whites' attitudes toward Blacks and how Blacks feel about Whites.

*Segregation Northern Style.* Distributor: Anti-Defamation League of B'nai B'rith, New York.

This CBS documentary film deals with problems encountered by Blacks when they try to buy homes in White communities.

*To Live Together.* Producer/Distributor: Anti-Defamation League of B'nai B'rith, New York.

The difficulties encountered by children at an interracial summer camp is the subject of this film.

## Books for the Teacher

Banks, James A., *Teaching Strategies for Ethnic Studies* (Boston: Allyn and Bacon, 1975).

A handbook for educators which includes historical information on American ethnic groups, key concepts for ethnic studies programs, exemplary teaching strategies, and annotated bibliographies for students and teachers.

Della-Dora, Delmo, and House, James E., eds., *Education for an Open Society* (Washington, D.C.: Association for Supervision and Curriculum Development, 1974).

A hard-hitting and refreshing collection of essays on key issues in cultural pluralism and education.

Henderson, George, *To Live in Freedom: Human Relations Today and Tomorrow* (Norman: University of Oklahoma Press, 1972).

A perceptive and lucid treatment of major concepts in human relations.

Steinfield, Melvin, ed., *Cracks in the Melting Pot: Racism and Discrimination in American History* (New York: Glencoe Press, 1973).

An excellent collection of readings on racism in American history. Many ethnic groups are discussed.

# 7

# Should We Believe
# That Our Planet Is in Peril?

## James L. Aldrich and Anne M. Blackburn

### Introduction

APPROACHING the study of the environment as a controversial issue
has distinct advantages. The greatest is that it assumes differences of
opinion exist about the subject—a comment that has to rank as one of
the major understatements of all time, for there is even disagreement
regarding what the word *environment* means:

> . . . Is it rolling hills and winding streams?

> . . . Is it a scientifically measurable finite conglomeration of varied
> physical resources?

> . . . Is it the cement-covered, plastic-wrapped Madison-Avenued
> modern city?

> . . . Is it the collective sensing of individuals in a community
> about that community?

> . . . Is it mood-tempered perceptions of single human beings?

It is each of these, and their every interaction.

JAMES L. ALDRICH is staff member and Treasurer, Threshold, Inc.,
Washington, D. C.; Member, IUCN Commission on Education; Vice-
Chairman, U.S. National Committee for Man and the Biosphere
(UNESCO); former Senior Associate, Conservation Foundation, Wash-
ington, D. C.
ANNE M. BLACKBURN is Public Education Specialist, Interstate
Commission on the Potomac River Basin, Bethesda, Maryland; Mem-
ber, Advisory Committee, Threshold, Inc., Washington, D. C.; former
Coordinator, Secondary School Curriculum Development Project, Con-
servation Foundation, Washington, D. C.

Such overlapping and sometimes conflicting definitions provide the glib-tongued with opportunities to cast doubt upon the question of whether the environment indeed has problems. But whether we listen to the extreme predictions of doom or merely take heed of the troubles that we can plainly see and smell in our skies and waters, there is at least some reason to question whether we can continue our present environmental practices for much longer. The ability of the earth's natural systems to recover from our blunders is seriously threatened by our increasing numbers, the extent of our ability to abuse our environment, and our individual and collective desires to have more and more of everything for more and more of all of us.

The issues are complex and subject to a variety of interpretations, but there are few people who would suggest that there are no environmental problems. What these problems are, who caused them, and how they can be resolved are the points where opinions diverge. Even the problems represent a widely varying range of concerns.

In recent years there has been increasing awareness that the world's resources are limited, that there are significant gaps between the world's known available natural resources and the demands of expanding populations for water, energy, food, and material goods. As larger numbers of these expanding populations seek to share in the affluent way of life that has previously been the privilege of a small percentage of the world's people, pressure on the limited resources is further aggravated.

Not only are the world's resources being used at an increasingly staggering rate, but through growing evidence about the interrelatedness of the natural systems of this planet, we have come to realize that extraction, use, or disposal after use of one resource—air, water, mineral, wildlife—for humans has impact on other natural resources and other humans. Sometimes these impacts are quite unpredictable and ultimately of more significance than the primary action.

**Item:**

When DDT began to be sold commercially in 1946, it was regarded as a major triumph for humankind. It controlled insect carriers of yellow fever, typhus, cholera, sleeping sickness, and dysentery. It was the farmer's answer to crop pests. But no one knew exactly what it would do in the environment. Factors that appeared later—and that we did not know when we started to use DDT—were such things as these:

1. It persisted in the soil for 15 years or longer.
2. It appeared in oceanic birds and in penguins of the Antarctic, and at first no one knew how it reached them.
3. It was discovered to pass off as a vapor from the soil or water into the air. It was carried about, then, by winds, all around the world.
4. It was stored and concentrated in natural food chains of many kinds.

5. It is now present in animal life and human beings almost everywhere. We have it in our body fats, the Eskimos have it, our children have it, fish, oysters, birds, mammals have it.
6. It works itself out of a job, so to speak. When it is used to kill flies, it kills almost the whole population of flies where it is used—all but a very few. These few flies are somehow resistant to it. These few breed up a new population resistant to DDT. On this new breed, we have to use some other chemical.
7. It apparently hasn't hurt human beings. The American Medical Association, for example, went on record last year that the theory that DDT causes cancer is unproved speculation.

With this variety of factors, (and there may be more yet to come) it is not a matter for surprise that the scientists have had quite a time dealing with this problem. The vast complex of interrelationships between this particular chemical, and the thousands of kinds of soil organisms, the cycles pursued by carbon, nitrogen, oxygen, hydrogen, water, and other substances or elements, the chemical reactions in the atmosphere, the photosynthetic activities of green plants that produce our food and our oxygen, the millions of interactions among plants and animals—all these involve an almost fantastic maze of relationships not only beyond the scientists, but beyond any computer or combination of computers so far devised.[1]

Examination of environmental dilemmas will also reveal that there are distinctions in environmental concerns between the affluent and the poverty-stricken. Whether we refer to people or to nations, the view of what constitutes an environmental problem can vary considerably. Environmental questions related to affluence are more likely to be the side-effects of wealth: poor land-use practices resulting from uncontrolled suburban sprawl; disposal of the wastes of excesses. For those less fortunate, the questions will be the more basic ones of health, sanitation, housing, adequate transportation and often contending with greater concentrations of air and water pollutants. For the poor, the issue is how to get a piece of the affluent environment.

With further analysis, it soon becomes evident that existing decision-making processes, whether they be industrial, governmental, or personal, are inadequate; for we frequently do not know, and sometimes do not seem to care to know, what we are doing when we alter our immediate environment. Those acts which in the past could be done with seeming immunity because of the amazing recuperative powers of nature are now overpowered by the weight of our numbers, the effects of uncontrolled technological tampering with natural systems, and a demand for material forms of comfort that in many cases goes far beyond reasonable needs.

When agreement is reached that environmental problems do exist, the range of possible attacks on the problems and the ramifications of the identified alternatives present another mind-boggling complexity. Of foremost importance is the economic impact of remedial measures proposed for environmental improvement and resource conservation. If hitherto cheap resources are limited, products will become more expensive, and the economic impact may be the greatest on those who can least afford it.

**Item:**

If the estimated cost of pollution-control devices on cars is $500, it will mean a 20% increase in the cost of a $2500 car, but only a 10% increase in the price of a $5,000 car, a regressive effect which hits even harder at the owners of older used cars.

In the broadest interpretation, the confrontation is between a way of life that millions are living (and many more aspire to) and the ultimate survival of humankind.

There may be no realistic hope for the present underdeveloped countries to reach the standard of living demonstrated by the present industrialized nations. The pollution and natural resource load placed on the world environmental systems by each person in an advanced country is probably 10 to 20 times greater than the load now generated by a person in an underdeveloped country. With four times as much population in underdeveloped countries as in the present developed countries, their rising to the economic level of the United States could mean an increase of 10 times in the demand for natural resources and pollution levels in the world environment. Noting the destruction that has already occurred on land, in the air, and especially in the oceans, no capability appears to exist for handling such a rise in the standard of living for the present total population of the world.[2]

Our society is foremost in its concern with the many issues about the environment that are raised, because our society's way of life is the most threatened by consideration of these issues. We are the world's greatest per capita consumers of resources and producers of waste. With only minor recognition on the part of a few stalwart conservationists, we have traded away many of our most valuable resources for short-term rewards. We have gouged the earth for what it could give us; we have used our streams and lakes and oceans as dumping grounds, showing no concern for the future; we have dammed our rivers, paved over the land, and made irreversible changes in the natural systems. Belatedly, we are coming to realize that some of our environmental manipulations boomerang, producing unanticipated consequences.

But when we confront and try to cope with these environmental issues, we find ourselves having to ask some very difficult questions of society and ourselves. If we cannot maintain our present level of consumption without even more serious impact on our environment, or our cost of living, what are the trade-offs that individually and collectively we are willing to negotiate? Is 20 per cent poorer air worth the second 300 horsepower chariot? What would you take—$10, $100, or $1000 a week—to drink water only 10 per cent poorer than you do now? How about a job versus no job? A local tax-producing industry versus a cleaner river? What is your "price" for unconscious tolerance of urban blight, suburban sprawl, a plastic world and throwaway resources?

Words are a cheap catharsis. Living as we do in a crisis-conditioned society, we are inclined to believe that if things are really bad that we need only to inform people, muster support, and get on with resolving difficulties. Unfortunately, it doesn't work that way for two related reasons: First, people have become (or maybe always were) relatively immune to crises situations until the impact is highly personalized. The last several years have seen more than a few environmental prophets spewing forth predictions of environmental hellfire and brimstone if we didn't mend our ways and give up hedonistic environmental excesses. But the audiences for these dire predictions are people who have lived through atomic bomb scares during the late 1940s, the fallout shelter binge, political assassinations, the continued butchering of humankind in "localized" wars, dirty politics, and even an occasional street corner prophet declaring the end of the world. People cannot effectively confront every crisis, every traumatic social re-evaluation that the media thrust before them. Each new warning, each new big scare, takes its toll of our sensibilities.

Only the young, perhaps the very young, are really affected, because it is their first BIG scare; their first encounter with their inheritance. The slightly older may become easily discouraged, and begin to shop around for a new cause or purpose in which they can discover personal and social relevance. If they become too jaded, then they look for ways to turn off or drop out of society. Slogans and "Madison Avenue" campaigns which are directed to the need for action and promise a test of our moral fiber become a ritual in which we seek to cleanse ourselves of our social sins. Most often the action and commitment called for become lost in the rhetoric of "tomorrow we must do something."

There is an emotional threshold which people are reluctant to cross when their very existence is threatened. When their normal routine is disrupted by crisis, then they work to resolve the crisis. Once it is resolved, they are prone to forget it. As Ralph Nader has said, "There is too much outrage and too little action."

The second reason that simply making people aware of environmental problems will not resolve these problems is even more critical. The real controversy surrounding environmental issues is that we are challenging our very way of life. If we really examine what the quest for environmental preservation means, if we assess the changes necessary in our daily lives, then we come back to a whole range of complex interrelated social issues. When environmental issues are pursued to the point of making decisions and taking action, we come face to face with the essential ambiguity of our personal existence; and we must deal with the fear of leaving what is familiar, what we know as a way of living, and proceed to the unknown with the realization that there may be no return.

In some respects we are already late in planning for the immediate future—it is already with us. There are more than 3.5 billion people in this world and projections indicate that there could be double that number by the year 2010. Environmental damage has been done, is being done, and will be done. We are not about to abandon our comforts completely to return to some form of primitive existence. Industry cannot overnight place environmental quality before profits. The issue is not either/or; it is not whether we should use natural resources or not. Rather it is whether we promote the rational, equitable use of all our resources, including human resources.

Perhaps most serious of all (the false issues) has been the tendency to equate conservation with low levels of consumption of natural resources and with a total rejection of technology. Such a view of conservation, while it may have an appeal to those who have always had high levels of consumption and an oversupply of technology, has no appeal whatsoever to the underprivileged majority of mankind. Furthermore, it has very little to do with the goals of conservation which are properly directed toward achieving a high material standard of living based on rational use of the Earth's resources. There is no necessary conflict between conservation and technology or conservation and international development. Only with the aid of the highest technology can the goals of conservation now be achieved. Only through adequate attention to ecological knowledge and conservation values can the goals of economic development be achieved without serious and unwanted environmental disruption. Only through development can most of the world's people gain sufficient necessities to begin to appreciate the meaning of "environmental quality." [3]

## The Nature and Importance of the Environmental Challenges

Observable, measurable adverse changes that have occurred with increasing frequency throughout the earth's environment support the view that our planet is indeed in peril.

This is not the place for a treatise on the physical environment, but it is useful to provide a little background on the arena for all environmental crises—the biosphere.

Ray Dasmann, in his excellent book *Planet in Peril,* wrote: "The biosphere has been defined as that layer of soil, water and air upon the surface of the earth within which all life exists and of which it forms a part. It is that combination of living things with their physical environment which is to be found from the depths of the oceans up to the lower limits of the atmosphere." [4] It is a dynamic, constantly interacting system in which death and decay as we know them are vital to maintaining the process. As Dasmann points out, ". . . nearly every atom or molecule to be found in the human body today has been used before by other men at other times or by animal and plant life." [5] People are only a small part of this system. As such, we are highly dependent on the other components and on the overall functioning of the system to support our continued existence.

The biosphere can be divided for descriptive purposes into three nested shells or spheres. The *atmosphere,* which extends hundreds of miles above the earth's surface, is a gaseous envelope in which our terrestrial system and the energy from the sun interact. It plays a major role in the earth's weather patterns which in turn affect the various climates. It is a protective blanket which supports, and in turn is modified by, life on earth. Despite the massive natural forces at work in the atmosphere, it is particularly susceptible to the by-products of technology in both gaseous and particulate forms.

The *hydrosphere,* or waters of the earth, covers almost 70% of the planet's surface. It was the seedbed for all the forms of life which now exist on earth, and all life is still dependent upon water. The major importance of the hydrosphere to life is in the dynamics of water movement known as the hydrologic cycle, and water is in constant movement. There is no overall shortage of water for human purposes; however, there is an unequal geographic distribution of water which causes shortages of useful water, particularly in agricultural areas.

The rocky crust of the earth, or rocks and the soils derived from it, constitutes the *lithosphere.* Most of the chemical components of life come from this part of the biosphere. Soil is the essential substance for terrestrial life on earth. It originates from weathering of rock and is further enriched by living things; the soil in turn serves to feed and sustain plant and animal life.

The atmosphere, hydrosphere and lithosphere are all interrelated through the actions of yet another component of the system: the various forms of life. Dasmann points out that some estimates suggest ". . . that at least three million species of plants, animals and micro-organisms have appeared on earth. . . ." [6] These various forms of life, as a part of the overall system, modify the world we live in and depend on. One of these life forms is the human being. The interaction of humans, their communities and institutions have been labeled the *sociosphere*. Each of the various living things fills a unique niche or "profession" in the web of life. Humankind and its technology have had an impact on the total system of the biosphere which recently has far exceeded its ability to restore itself through natural processes. Many of the environmental problems which in the past were relatively isolated by being restricted to particular regions or practices have now been expanded; some, such as the exploitation of energy resources, now encompass the entire planet.

Smoke from the Ruhr Valley darkens the air of Belgium and the Netherlands and even creates "brown snow" in Sweden. Finland's fisheries are damaged by outpourings of mercury from the factories of Britain and Europe. Oil spilled from American tankers stains the beaches of England. Mexican waters in the Gulf of California have been polluted by chemical-laden waters discharged by the Colorado River.[7]

The magnitude and complexity of these problems have frequently been compounded by the very measures we have devised to resolve them and by our inadequate understanding of the systems with which we were tampering.

**Item:**

Where DDT has been banned from use, poisonings increase among people who use other and frequently far more dangerous chemicals. In one country in Central America, upwards of a thousand people died this way within about a year after DDT was banned.

Extreme difficulty in raising some crops—such as cotton—is expected if DDT cannot be used, because we do not have other satisfactory sprays at the present time.

Several million people depend on cotton for a living in this country. Some of the chemicals used instead of DDT on cotton kill honeybees that pollinate the plants so that they produce seed. Very large losses to the beekeepers and to the people raising crops dependent on bees for pollination are on record where these substitute sprays have been used.

Other methods of insect control are being developed that may enable us to get along without DDT later on. I underscore later on, however, because the scientists say we are still quite a long way away from being able to depend entirely on these new methods.[8]

There are two assumptions that are key focal points in any environmental controversy:

> . . . there is a limit to the world's natural resources and we are
> rapidly exhausting the known supplies of these resources; there

is just so much here, the only significant thing coming in from outside the biosphere is energy from the sun. . . .

. . . our present use of many of these resources results in our fouling or destroying other resources including living systems which have been serving to maintain and restore the quality of the biosphere. . . .

Acceptance of these assumptions immediately triggers incredibly complex questions guaranteed to keep forensics alive for centuries, and "to provide largesse for consulting engineers, grants for academicians, and rhetoric for politicians without necessarily achieving the level of knowledge and (most important) the integrated *perspective* necessary to work our way back towards a healthier, more stable environment for life including Homo Sapiens." [9]

We are facing critical decisions the importance and severity of which are truly awesome.

• Should we accept that we are stewards for future generations?

• Should we assume that intelligent action will result if people are provided the information about the problems? Can we assume we know what should be taught?

• Should we provide massive support for research aimed at developing a better understanding of the interrelationships existing within our biosphere and sociosphere?

• Should highest priority be given to developing new technology aimed at solving pollution problems and utilizing recycled resources?

• Should everyone have an inalienable right to the same standard of living?

• Should industry be expected to place social responsibility before market profitability?

• Should wealth be distributed more evenly?

• Should there be an international government for resource allocation and/or pollution control?

We are finally realizing nature is going to hold us accountable for the effects of our activity upon the natural systems. The delicately balanced interrelationships which constitute the biological web of life are threatened by human actions. If we do not experience shortages of vital resources first, then we are likely to unleash ecological disasters of various magnitudes and consequences. Our belief in "new frontiers," whether they be overexploited or underexploited natural resources or new technologies, is suddenly being confronted by the subtle operations of our life-support systems. The complexity and variety of natural interactive relationships when further extended by human operations tend to confound analysis. Even the fantastic capabilities of our computers are limited by the human ability to identify the right problems and ask the right questions. As a result, we often resort to simplistic models in attempting to analyze our actions on these systems. When dealing with social systems we are prone to weigh our judgments in terms of quantitative analysis, because we are short on understanding the qualitative aspects of human endeavors. Assessing the impact of the environmental crisis upon human existence is a third focal point of environmental controversy. It is a major determining factor in whether we can achieve understanding and correction of environmental crises. "If mankind destroys itself it will not be because of the intrinsic wickedness of man's heart; it will be because of his inability to wake up to the realistic alternatives and their consequences," [10] warned Erich Fromm in 1964. We have generally thought of "alternatives and consequences" as they refer to our use of natural resources; the problem is even more complex.

The twentieth-century environmental dilemma has resulted from the application of a philosophy which regarded the earth and its resources as existing for the benefit of human beings; the function of these resources within the natural systems of the earth was virtually ignored. One invention after another increased the ability to control and manipulate segments of the natural systems, always backed by the assumption that to do so was "right," and the belief that the quality of human life would improve—if one chicken in every pot is "good," two have to be better.

The belief that following the orderly dictums of science and technology could cure all human unhappiness seemed well-founded. Science provided a systematic and logical means of sorting out and categorizing the infinitely intricate natural processes which took place in human surroundings. Technology was the applied science: reordering those natural processes to better fit human desires. Together science and technology formed the dynamic duo—tunneling through obstructing mountains, redirecting rivers, overcoming human inability to fly, changing deserts into irrigated farmlands, probing the inner core of the earth for resources, miraculously transforming crude oil into plastics and energy, mold into penicillin, and uranium into the ultimate ability to control. The power of science and technology to accomplish good seemed so unlimited that soon other facets of human existence were being managed according to successful scientific techniques. The health of the individual was measured in productivity; the egg-crate construction of schools reflected the egg-crate discipline-oriented approach to learning;

higher education began to specialize in the production of specialists. Soon much of the measurement of human activity was being expressed in terms of numbers, percentages of growth and expansion; and these terms became the accepted indicators of human progress. A subtle evolution had occurred: methods first adapted and supported to improve human life had become themselves the measurements by which the quality of human life was judged. No longer was the plight of the actual individual considered as long as the life of "the norm" or the "composite" was estimated to be improving.

But has the great glut of gimmicky products and the incessant growth for growth's sake provided personal fulfillment for people? Apathy, frustration, anger and dismay characterize the citizenry, young and old, affluent and indigent in urban and rural communities:

What had gone out of American life as one sees it in the city and suburb? Essentially . . . a sense of direction . . . we were all of us passengers on a great ocean liner. . . . The ocean, however, is unknown, and no one, not a single soul, knows whither the ship is bound.[11]

No longer do experts think government programs can remedy most of the defects in the way growth occurs. No longer do many authorities claim to know what to do, for example, about the drabness and lack of variety of much new residential and commercial development, the unwillingness of many suburban communities to provide housing (and, thus, access to jobs) for people of modest means, the dehumanization of even our prosperous downtown areas, which are increasingly given over at street level to bland, nine-to-five enterprises that contribute neither delight nor charm to our community life. It is as though the drive has gone out of our search for solutions, and a great weariness has set in.[12]

It is a sick society that can beat and murder black people in the streets, butcher thousands of people in Vietnam, spend billions of dollars on arms to destroy mankind, and then come to the conclusion that pollution is America's number one problem.[13]

Pollution is not America's number one problem, but environment is—environment as perceived by and an influence upon each human each hour of each day. We are suffering from a serious decline in the quality of the environment as it affects humans—singly and collectively. Individual potential, the very human characteristic that holds the greatest promise for solving our present environmental crises, is critically threatened by present conditions.

A meaningful study of any environmental problem must include the humans' perception of that problem; just as any plans for pollution abatement or resource management must be measured not only by how effectively they will preserve the vitality of the natural environment, but by whether the proposed action will in fact reach, support and better sustain the inner human environment. In our stress-filled pursuit of economic goals, human resources, as well as natural resources, have suffered and been badly abused. Human conservation and environmental restoration must be joint goals—reestablishing threatened human potential as well as the integrity of the natural world. We have identified and accepted the need to provide environmental protection to the hydrosphere, the atmosphere, the lithosphere, the sociosphere; before we can hope to remedy the ills that beset the biosphere, we must also face and fill the needs of the "psychesphere," the environment of the inner self.

If survival is the only thing that counts in nature, then why or how did any life higher than that of a bacterium ever come into being? [14]

## The Response of Education
## to the Environmental Controversy

Among both educators and environmentalists, environmental education has often been a password to confusion. As with many issues whose partial solution seems to lie within the realm of education, environmental issues have served as the rallying ground for many diverse groups, each with its special educational interests and needs. Educators have sought to understand the growing influence of environmental considerations developing in their fields of specialization. Thus, science teachers requested information on "Water Quality" and "Water Monitoring Techniques," and social studies teachers requested materials on "Population Pressures," key points as they sought to teach about changes that were occurring in the environment. Gradually the unique problems within the emerging area of environmental education have become recognizable—and there are several of them:

• Because of the transdisciplinary nature of environmental concerns, single discipline approaches are inadequate. A biology class monitoring a stream and discovering pollution caused by a local industry is ultimately faced with the economic, social and political aspects of the problem as well as the purely scientific.

• Educators are forced to deal with an approach radically different from their own educational experience, as value discussions once carefully skirted by classroom teachers are found to be inextricably wound into any really meaningful understanding of topics like water quality, land use, or growth.

• Available textbook material frequently discusses environmental concerns in such global terms and broad generalizations that it provides little tie-in with identifiable local realities and, thus, holds less relevance for students.

• And when the committed, dedicated teacher seeks in-depth related information or learning opportunities in the surrounding community, he or she has to be willing to embark on an uncharted, joint learning experience with the students, complete with all the shortcomings and frustrations such a situation can produce.

In an article entitled "Environmental Education as an Arena of Creative Conflict," which appeared in the April, 1972 issue of *International Understanding at School,* Peter Harper stated that:

The unresolved dilemmas of the subject will create great problems for teachers. Not only will they be confused by the conflicting views of the "experts," but the asking of even fairly obvious questions will lead to criticism of established institutions and vested interests. It can be expected that these interests will be quick to denounce "biased" educational practices that threaten their prerogatives. Further, any fundamental questioning of traditional values, attitudes or world-views may threaten psychological security among teachers and pupils themselves. There may be strong conflicts between home and school, and between teachers and educational authorities.[15]

These difficulties are not limited solely to education about environmental issues, but they are magnified when dealing with environmental concerns because of the complexity of the problems and the almost inevitable confrontation with conflicting values. This may lead to a temptation to be cautious and avoid topics which raise too many troublesome questions, or resort to the more subtle cop-out of discussing the issues from a philosophic position alone—intellectually curious, but personally uninvolved. But education (if it can be called that) of this sort is often irrelevant and boring to today's youth. It is not the open innovative adventure that stimulates the mind to explore new conceptions of the world we live in. When the more cautious approach is pursued, we opt for a substitution procedure or change of labels. We seek ways to supplement or replace one segment after another of existing curriculum materials and teaching styles. Instead of pressing for educational reforms, we settle for patching the model we have. We give it a patina of relevance which fosters a situation in which the more we change, the worse we get. If education takes this easy way out and does not respond to the needs at hand, then environmental quality and improvement, by any definition, are pushed further into the future. And just possibly out of reach.

The current public concern with the quality of the environment offers an exciting intellectual scheme for organizing and promoting educational experiences which provide the opportunities for exploring our individual and communal physical, social and psychological "environments." Environmental quality provides a common goal through which to transform education from a reflection of society as it has been to a vision of what society can be. What we have before us is an opportunity to make significant reforms in educational practice by providing experiences and materials which by their very form as well as content offer opportunities for each student, each individual, to explore and build relationships to the many environments he or she lives in.

The rash of materials development and educational writing that has occurred during recent years is strong evidence of the discontent with existing educational practice. All the education critics do not, of course, agree, but whether one reads Holt, Bruner, Drucker or Silberman, one will find two major themes: the irrelevance of subject matter as now taught and organized, and the failure to truly individualize learning. Rather than teaching about the interrelatedness and wholeness of life we have isolated and fragmented the educational fare. The simplistic distortions that we have taught have not satisfied either the educational or emotional needs of the individual student.

In the past, the public has equated going to school with education. The role of the school was to transmit information and instill traditional values. The society of today is one changing so rapidly that skills and information become outmoded, and traditional values are under challenge.[16]

**Item:**
The average child watching an average amount of television is exposed to 22,000 commercials a year.

Students form an audience whose ideals and commitments have not yet been mortgaged to the existing way of doing things. The process of education, which at best has been a faithful mirror of a society passed, is decreasingly relevant to the needs of today's and tomorrow's students.

Education must recognize itself for what it is: it may be the product of history and society, but it is not their passive plaything. It is an essential factor in shaping the future, particularly at the present moment, since in the last resort education has to prepare mankind to adapt to change, the predominant characteristic of our time.[17]

As Oregon Governor Tom McCall stated, "We need visionaries so that we do not produce a future that is just an extension of the past." For our country today is trapped in a crisis-reaction pattern, blundering from one isolated solution attempt to another. In "A Nation Seeks Its Goals," Daniel J. Moynihan pointed out, "Virtually all of the critical national problems of today could have been anticipated well in advance of their reaching critical proportions. Many were, but these anticipations did not enter into the decision-making processes of the United

States government." [18] Meanwhile, the great industrial-political power machine grinds on; and for each land area that is paved over, each resource that is consumed, each added pollutant, each new, demanding baby—our positive options lessen:

Each action we take alters the total system in ways we do not understand and makes the next crash program more immediately necessary and more ultimately hazardous.[19]

### Environmental Dilemmas in the Classroom

How does education face questions which challenge the economic basis, religious beliefs, social goals, political strategies, personal ethics, and personal aspirations which have guided our society—questions raised by statements such as:

World population is growing by 70,000,000 people every year. This is the fastest growth in man's history, and the rate is still accelerating. We will number four billion in 1975 and, if current trends continue, we can expect to reach eight billion well before the year 2000. This population is making more and more demands on its environment. We are taking fresh water out of the ground twice as fast as natural processes replace it. The demand for electric power in the U.S. is doubling every ten years, and most power comes from the heavily polluting combustion of coal. We are building 10,000,000 cars a year—twice as many as we made only 17 years ago, and cars burn gasoline, grind rubber tires to dust, wear asbestos brakes into an acrid powder.

The population explosion and pollution are direct descendants of old gods—industrialization and science. Without drastically changing its priorities, world population will collapse in less than a century from the effects of pollution, food shortage, disease and war. . . .

The conclusion is inescapable. If the world is to achieve equilibrium at a material standard of living at or close to the level now enjoyed by the developed nations, world populations and industrialization must be considerably lower than current averages.[20] (Excerpt from "An End To All This" by Richard M. Koff. Originally appeared in *Playboy* magazine; copyright © 1971 by Playboy.)

Education that confronts these matters is not an "easy" subject for the teacher or the student. It is fraught with ambiguity, disagreement, and controversy. It is also, however, limitless in its challenge.

**Item:**

Each of the energy supply options being promoted today to meet the nation's increased consumption of energy comes attached with an environmental price tag. For this reason, none of the means of increasing energy supply appears very attractive from the point-of-view of our environment. But the dilemma is that we live in a high-energy civilization. It will take time to become somewhat less plugged-in. Thus the unenviable task for us is to decide which energy source is least bad. At stake are valuable and very tangible goods: our air, oceans, plains and deserts, beaches, mountains and perhaps our very lives.[21]

There is no magic formula for introducing and using environmental studies in the classroom. The starting point may occur in any subject; it may be the result of discussion introduced by the students; or it may be generated by issues covered in the local news media. The environmental problems that we seek to explore are, by the virtue of their controversial nature, subject to a wide range of interpretations. All of these interpretations have validity in their proper frame of reference. There is no set of facts, no orderly, prescribed path to follow which will lead to unfettered understanding and resolution of the environmental crisis. What must be kept in mind are the goals of meaningful confrontation with environmental issues. The three key crisis points have been identified as:

• The resources upon which we depend for necessities and luxuries are limited.

• We face grave problems because of the pollution and wastes resulting from our use of resources.

• The quality of the human environment is under threat as well as the natural environment.

Effective study of environmental issues will interweave these vital considerations into all activities and discussions. It will approach the problems as human-caused and humanly-solvable, but probably not by solutions that now exist.

Our students are going to have to find better ways than we have of saving or inventing new sources of energy, and creative ways of designing homes, communities, schools, and cities which will support and enhance human existence, not just raise economic indexes. Learners' concepts about property and modes of transportation will have to change. Recycling and reuse of resources must expand, or else limited resources will be depleted sooner, as we bury ourselves in our own effluence.

**Item:**

Critical world problems exist for which there is no technical solution. These are problems of reaction, adaptation and values.[22]

**Item:**

Power company projections are that energy demands will double every ten years. In 70 years this will require generating plants 250 feet apart on the entire coastline of Florida.[23]

**Item:**

The urban freeway system has been a tool of both social injustice and environmental destruction; practically all major land-use changes and development in our cities and suburbs have come through the initial thrust of where the big roads will go . . . the urban freeway has devastated the inner city . . . cities now devote almost 50% of their land to the care, feeding, storing and moving of automobiles.[24]

**Item:**

U.S. citizens produce 360 million tons of solid waste a year; 82% lands in dumps and landfills. This is equivalent to covering 80,000 acres per year 6′ deep.[25]

Simplistic answers just are not possible anymore. Land and resource development actions in every nation, the poorest to the most rich, affect every other. Planning can never again be considered purely on a personal, local, regional, or even national basis.

Too often by default we have permitted our technological capabilities to shape our principles, as though what one is capable of doing provides adequate ethical justification for doing it.[26]

Now education must structure learning situations in which creativity and cooperation become the guidelines, not competition; fostering situations in which the implications and effects of alternative actions are examined *before* decisions are made. It will not be enough to show a film or to develop a unit on pollution. The materials and experiences available to the student need to relate to the world in which he or she lives, need to help him or her make sense out of conflicting evidence and goals.

### Teacher and Student: A Problem-Solving Team

The most effective approach to the study of environmental problems brings students and teachers together in a learning-teaching pattern as a problem-solving team. This method makes use of the widely varying strengths of the students, some of whom may well be more concerned, committed, and knowledgeable than their teachers. It encourages the full range of their perspectives and creativity to interact and to participate positively in the process of compromise, an inevitable factor in any environmental decision. However, even the most motivated groups will flounder without some means of analyzing an environmental problem.

## TOOLS FOR ANALYSIS OF THREE TYPES OF PROBLEMS

The first task of the Problem-Solving Team is to recognize the nature of the environmental dilemmas confronting it. Most will fall into one of three general categories:

(1) personal decisions with environmental implications;
(2) local community or regional problems—often a result of poor or inadequate planning;
(3) a problem whose nature is so complex that it has global significance.

Working on the third type of environmental problem is by far the most difficult, but can be made possible by breaking the interrelated factors into manageable thought units. Debating whether a certain resource should be developed will illustrate how the multiple factors and variables can be handled.

In the past, development of resources was considered almost exclusively on the basis of anticipated positive impacts:

Example: *Projected Positive Results of Resource Development:*

ECONOMIC: It will add a needed product or service to the market; it will provide jobs; it will strengthen the economy.

SOCIOLOGICAL: It will improve the standard of living.

POLITICAL: It will strengthen the power base of the political jurisdiction in which the activity is located.

**Item:**

A proposed $250 million dollar factory in Jacksonville, Florida would hire 10,000-12,000 people; it would generate $5 million in tax revenue; it has promised a 23% minority hiring.

A greater consciousness of the multiple and interacting effects of resource utilization led in 1969 to the enactment of federal legislation which requires Environmental Impact Statements (EIS) for those federally funded projects which will have significant impact on the natural and human environment. The broader perspective for decision-making supplied by EIS helps eliminate two weaknesses in previous planning processes: (1) the tendency for economic and political decisions to be made on the basis of short-term goals; and (2) the tendency to make decisions based on local conditions alone, for Environmental Impact Statements require consideration and evaluation of the role the resource plays in natural systems, and strive to promote compatible ways to use the resource so that human use will not come at the expense of some segments of our natural supporting systems.

**Item** *(continued)*:

The Jacksonville factory, which would assemble floating nuclear power plants, would be sited on 900 acres of marsh and bayou along the St. John's River. 1300 acres in all would be subject to dredge-and-fill activities. Two-thirds of all the fish and shellfish along the East Coast spend their early lives in marshes like the one which would be destroyed.

Environmental Impact Statements also require anticipation and evaluation of negatives that might be precipitated or accented by the proposed action.

## Possible Negative Effects of Resource Development

POSSIBLE ECONOMIC NEGATIVES: How much more energy will be used in production and utilization of products?

Will growth patterns in the producing area be drastically altered?

Are full costs being considered: the resource, energy, pollution, and disposal costs of the action?

POSSIBLE SOCIOLOGICAL NEGATIVES: Will claims of life quality improvement be broadly-based or touch only an élite group?

POSSIBLE POLITICAL NEGATIVES: Will politically palatable decisions outweigh important economic, social, or environmental considerations?

Does this local action fit the overall goals of the region?

Has legislative consideration been given to long-range resource allocation?

**Item** *(continued)*:

Proponents claim that Jacksonville would be growing itself and providing needed energy for other parts of Florida. (It would bring an expected 14,000 new residents to Jacksonville and an estimated 420 new businesses.) Opponents warn that a floating reactor accident could cause large-scale and long-lasting contamination of the world's oceans; they object to this massive action when the Atomic Energy Commission is not even expected to act on whether to use such floating plants until late in 1975.

Blacks are siding with industry in this confrontation; they feel they must because of the 23% hiring guarantee. Opponents argue that unplanned, sudden growth in Jacksonville's population will *cost* taxpayers because of the increased needs for services (schools, roads, sewers, police, firemen, etc.).

TRADEOFFS: Compromisers are trying to attract clean industry to the area to provide jobs without endangering the important ecological marsh area. However, every municipality is trying to do the same thing: attract the positives and avoid the negatives.

The confrontation between projected positives and possible negatives identifies conflicts such as, "Does the addition of these products or services to the economy offset increased use of energy and additional solid waste that will be generated by production and disposal?," and it will help assess the basic question: "Does depletion or use of this particular resource for this particular purpose represent rational use of the resource?" The intensive environmental impact process adjusts the parameters of resource development planning to include long-term economic goals and effects, full costs of product development and utilization, regional economic and environmental impact, and long-term allocation of the natural resource. Long-term sociological and environmental considerations balance more short-term political and economic aims. The resulting process for decision-making is complicated but achievable. We must realize, however, that no two different geographic locations may ever reach the same conclusions about the same environmental dilemma—because conclusions will vary depending upon the:

global location

political strength and philosophy of the jurisdiction

economic strength and philosophy of the jurisdiction

the overall population

the population density

the degree of industrialization

differing concepts of life quality

The day may come when such decisions as resource development, resource allocation, economic specialization, pollution control and pollution abatement are made by a supranational environmental agency. But regardless of whether some multi-national, globally-impacting environmental project is being contemplated, or one human individual is evaluating his or her own lifestyle, each critical decision made at each critical point is a value judgment. There is no escape from the reality that the responsibility for the future quality of all life lies in human hands.

At first, a teacher may find few individuals and fewer groups of students interested in/or capable of handling discussions of global environmental responsibilities. A student is more likely to respond to/and come to comprehend the complexities of environmental decision-making by delving into the second category of environmental concern, a local, identifiable environmental problem. Here, too, a simplified pattern for helping to sift out the overt and covert ingredients that are contributing to/and caused by the visible problem may be helpful.

*Analysis of an Identified Environmental Problem*

| PROCESSES | EXAMPLES |
| --- | --- |
| I. Problem sensing | "I couldn't breathe on Monday." |
| II. Problem identification | "The air was badly polluted." |
| III. Problem definition | "There was a severe air inversion." |
| A. Contributing problem | "A folk festival had brought many extra cars to the area. This increased the amount of pollution being 'held' over the city." |
| B. Problems caused by identified problem | "Many people had stomach upset. congestion, eye irritation, and fatigue." |
| IV. Causes of the problem | |
| A. Overt | "The air inversion was a 'natural' occurrence; but the lack of transportation alternatives added to the problem." |
| B. Covert | "Ads have convinced a lot of people that they ought to have cars—for status and things like that." |
| V. Sources of the pollution (listed by general category) | "Automobiles" "Airplanes" |
| VI. Elected officials' attitudes about the problem | "The people in public office are really concerned about the pollution problem." |
| VII. Proposed governmental solutions | "National legislation has been passed. The EPA has set goals. Local areas are working to meet the EPA standards." |
| VIII. Other solutions (action by citizens, industry, etc.) | "More car pools, parking taxes, people riding the bus, bike trails, etc. The auto industry is making more smaller cars, and even if it is because of the energy shortage, it still helps towards cleaner air, especially because the new cars also have cleaner emissions." |
| IX. Impact of proposed solutions on life-styles and/or life quality | |
| A. Positive | "If the air were cleaner some people would be more healthy and could live longer. People could save money and get more exercise by |

walking and riding bikes. A lot of things would be cleaner. Some foods could be safer."

B. Negative

"It won't be as easy to get to some places quickly. Cars with pollution devices cost more. It is not cheap to reduce or eliminate some pollution problems. Some industries might shut down and jobs could be lost if it costs a lot to meet EPA standards."

X. Tradeoff time (comparison of alternative solutions)

"Mass-transit systems could reduce pollution and conserve energy, but they would cost a lot and take some freedom away from people who like to drive their own cars—by themselves—to work. Smaller cars would cost less, take up less space, use less gas, produce less pollution, and require fewer raw materials; but they would not have as much 'zip,' or be as comfortable on long trips, or earn as high a profit for manufacturers and sellers, and small cars may not be as safe in a crash."

XI. Recommended action (legislative, punitive action against polluters, citizen education, etc.)

"If the new EPA regulations are strictly enforced there should be a big improvement in the amount of air pollution from industries. But, we need to spend more dollars on mass transit systems, and for bike trails and making bus commuting more comfortable and faster. Then maybe more people would leave their cars at home. We should really think before we build more roads, or add lanes to existing ones. It seems as though that, instead of easing traffic flow, new roads just stimulate growth and sooner or later the problem is as bad or worse. I wonder if you could give a Tax Incentive to encourage builders to locate high rise apartments and office buildings near existing or planned public transportation systems. Maybe people who carpool or use public transportation to work and shop could be given stubs or something like that to record the number of trips and miles—and that could be turned into a tax deduction, too. One of the biggest problems, though, is the person with a low income who can't afford to live close to his or her job. How do you keep such persons from being penalized for something they can't control?"

### *Understanding the Implications of Personal Decisions*

The first type of environmental problem—the personal decision—may be the easiest to analyze, because it is least complicated; but it may also be the hardest to deal with, because it requires each person to look at his or her own behavior and to consider his or her right to pursue certain actions.

A tool for studying this type of problem is an "environmentally-oriented radar scanner" with "blips" that will activate in the proper sphere, acknowledging the possible impacts of the alternatives being considered:

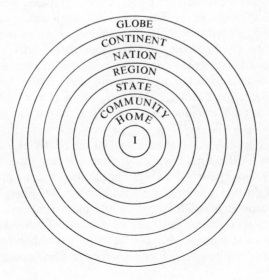

The "radar scanner" adapts itself to pondering questions which relate directly to the individual but have broader environmental implications.

Example: *Should I buy a mini-bike?*

POSITIVES: Fun, transportation, independence, good peer status symbol . . .

NEGATIVES: Noise pollution, harmful to natural environment if misused (destroys vegetation, starts erosion), uses gasoline, uses metals in production . . .

QUESTIONS: What would happen to the natural environment of the world if the same percentage of the population in all countries demanded, owned, and operated mini-bikes? How much expansion in recreational vehicles can global fuel resources stand? Should mini-bikes be limited to use at certain spots designed for them, and only on a rental basis?

If such limits were placed, whose jobs could it affect? Would those people have transferable skills?

## HOW THE PROBLEM-SOLVING TEAM CAN FUNCTION

A problem-solving team can be composed of one teacher and a few students, or involve a full interacting, interdisciplinary effort among issue-oriented students in different school systems. Activities which can become subjects for the problem-solving team approach are virtually limitless. In Pennsylvania, Project KARE (*K*nowledgeable *A*ction to *R*estore our *E*nvironment) involves K-12 students from a five-county area that reaches from center-city Philadelphia to rolling farmlands many miles away. Students pursue their own interests in widely varying activities near their respective schools. In addition, in a superior example of urban-rural cooperation, the students from these widely different environments meet, exchange information, and interact over their interests. The rural students participating in water quality testing visit with their inner-city counterparts and see the river, which is in excellent "health" when it leaves their communities, in its algae-choked, detergent-topped, citified form.

At another school, students have studied the effects of modern human beings on the local natural environment and are now restoring a 20-acre tract as it would have existed during Indian times—planting trees, berries, and shrubs. Elementary school children are brought to the site for living history lessons delivered by the older students.

At still another school, high school students are working with the Army Corps of Engineers, studying the impact of urbanization on their local watershed; while younger learners recycle Christmas trees by making wildlife shelters and check dams at an outdoor laboratory they are helping to develop.

In each situation, students are observing and learning about the physical environment that surrounds them and recording the positive and negative effects of human activity on that environment. The students are gaining greater understanding of environmental relatedness and of human responsibility; each is in an atmosphere in which he or she is free to react, perceive, interpret, and act to the fullest level of his or her creative ability.

In judging the human quality of an environment, it is essential to keep in mind that passive exposure to stimuli is not enough to elicit individual development. The stimulus becomes formative only if the organism is given a chance to respond to it actively and creatively. Amusement parks and zoological gardens, richly endowed as they may be, are no substitutes for situations in which the developing child can gain direct experience of the world through active participation. Juvenile delinquency is probably caused to a very large extent by the failure of the modern world to provide opportunities for the creative expression of physical and mental vigor during a human being's most active period of development.[27]

Catalysts for furthering environmental awareness and understanding are everywhere in the community. They can be action-oriented (as in the case of the students who are building their own outdoor lab); they may be classroom discussions aimed toward creative solutions to observed local problems (as with the sixth graders in Annandale, Virginia, who, when confronted with the problems of traffic jams and rising air pollution in their community, came up with suggestions for a series of canals for pedal-powered boats which could carry workers and freight . . . sheltered bicycle paths for all-weather use . . . and pedi-cars traveling on their own right-of-way). At first glance, the idea of "canals" seems silly; but what if a community were to solve its local flooding problems by creating just such a series of canals?

Sometimes classroom discussion of an environmental problem will precipitate an effective problem-solving technique. One elementary school was distressed about the visual pollution that confronted individuals every day, such as their own ugly, bare school ground. Students made a huge sky-ground paper mural and hung it on one wall of the cafeteria, and initiated a newspaper recycling project. Since it is estimated that each ton of recycled paper saves 17 trees, whenever a child brought in a stack of newspapers equivalent to 1/17th of a ton, he or she got to place a paper tree on the mural with his or her name on the tree. Money from the recycled paper was used to buy shrubs and trees for the school ground.

## AN ADDITIONAL GOAL: PRACTICE IN PROBLEM PREVENTION

After high school students have analyzed several specific environmental situations regarding resource development or pollution control, they may welcome the challenge of wrestling with future concepts. In such discussion, the teacher remains a learning facilitator, working among the broad differences between the students to encourage as in-depth an examination of alternatives as possible.

One topic which could stimulate lively discussion, or lend itself to research and subsequent role-playing, would be to debate whether it would be possible to establish a "Supranational Environmental Agency," to plan the "best use of all the land" on earth.

• What parameters would the decisions be based upon? Which "best use" of land, the one that suits our aesthetic, or our economic measurements?

• Could one decide upon land uses without first establishing what total population there would be; for adequate land would have to be preserved to assure an ample food supply? Population densities would have to be considered: concentrations of people have a much greater detrimental effect on natural systems than do scattered populations, for they make great demands on the land, water, and energy supply of an area, and discharge greater water and air pollutants.

• Perhaps this agency will have to regulate exploration, development, and use of *all* natural resources. Perhaps it will also have to regulate pollution abatement programs and monitoring programs after lower pollution levels have been reached.

Goals for the super-powerful agency will be the easiest aspect to reach agreement upon. The "nitty-gritty" will begin when the structure, the policies, and the financing are discussed:

• Who should run the agency, the industrialized countries which are most sophisticated in resource exploration and development? Or the underdeveloped nations which have many times over the combined populations of the industrialized ones? Would people in underdeveloped countries ever get a chance at an "improved" quality of life? Should population constraints be the same in each country?

The birth rate in the United States is 25 times more important than the birth rate in India in determining whether our world has any ecological future at all. An American baby born today will have this effect on the environment during his or her lifetime:

   use 26 million gallons of water;

   use 28 tons of iron and steel;

burn 1,200 barrels of petroleum;

waste 13,000 pounds of paper;

eat 50 tons of food;

consume $10,000 in public expenses;

throw out 10,000 bottles, 17,500 cans, 27,000 bottle caps;

destroy 2.3 automobiles (the manufacturers help a good bit);

use 35 rubber tires;

throw away 126 tons of garbage;

eject 10 tons of particulate air pollution.[28]

Paradoxically, a starving Indian child makes virtually no demand on the environment.

• In pollution control, who should foot the bill: the countries that have the great populations, or the big users of resources who cause pollution?

**Item:**

The average American uses more electrical power than 55 Asians or Africans; a single American accounts for more detergents, pesticides, radioactive substances, fertilizers, fungicides and defoliants in the rivers and oceans than are produced by a thousand people in Indonesia.[29]

• If America were taxed as a heavy resource consumer and polluter by this international agency, should all American citizens pay equally in a country where "¾ of the corporate wealth is controlled by approximately 1% of the people"? [30]

• Would such a tax be fair to the inner-city Black family which is "four times as likely to be overcrowded as a white family . . . four times as likely to fall victim of forcible rape and robbery" . . . where "three of every ten dwellings are dilapidated or without hot water, toilet, or bath . . . and many more are fire traps"? [31]

The questions go on and on and on, and the answers become more and more difficult.

## Summary

We are now on the threshold of a remarkable opportunity to engage in nothing less than the conscious participation in determining the future of our own species. Fantastic potential lies in a technology that can transplant organs in humans and explore outer space. But that technology must be humanized. In the future, technological capability must be tempered by an unprecedented awareness of ourselves and of the environment that nurtures and is nurtured by us.

In the conscious quest for environmental awareness—and thus for self-conscious evolution—we must rework our tradition-hallowed institutions to make them more viable and more responsive. Of these institutions, education, through its broad and continuous contact with the young, faces the greatest challenge, and has the greatest opportunity.

Here is the universal cause around which all can rally; here is the rationale for changing a stale, outmoded system; here is the moment to choose continuous existence, by adopting within our educational system such attitudes, perspectives, and goals as open-endedness, objectivity, flexibility, inventiveness, resourcefulness, and self-fulfillment.

A teacher affects eternity; he can never tell where his influence stops. If centuries from now the descendents of our present students are living lives more just and more humane than those of their forebears; if their days are less cluttered with trivia, if their values are sounder, their thinking straighter, and their creativity higher . . . we will have more than justified our existence. Our times may be bad, but among us are good people, young and old. . . . With them lies our faith in the efficacy of free choice, our trust that individuals, when provided with understandable options among values, will choose wisely within, or at times despite, the constraints upon them. Therein lies our belief in the importance of teaching as an exploration of alternatives and their consequences. Therein must rest our hope for better tomorrows.[32]

## FOOTNOTES

[1] William R. VanDersal, in a speech delivered at DeMatha High School, Hyattsville, Maryland (December 21, 1971).

[2] Dennis L. Meadows and Donella H. Meadows, *Towards Global Equilibrium: Collected Papers* (Cambridge, Massachusetts: Wright-Allen Press, Inc., 1973), p. 27.

[3] R. F. Dasmann, *Planet in Peril* (Paris: Penguin Books—UNESCO, 1972), p. 125.

[4] *Ibid.*, p. 26.

[5] *Ibid.*, p. 45.

[6] *Ibid.*, p. 37.

[7] Neil Jacoby, "Managing the Environment," *The Center Magazine* (January/February 1973): 65.

[8] VanDersal, *op. cit.*

[9] Robert Smythe, Ecologist, Environmental Impact Assessment Project, The Institute for Ecology, private conversation.

[10] Erich Fromm, *The Heart of Man* (New York: Harper and Row, Publishers, 1964), p. 183.

11 Henry Beston, *Northern Farm* (New York: Ballantine Books, 1972), p. 2.

12 William K. Reilly, editor, *The Use of Land: A Citizens' Policy Guide to Urban Growth* (New York: Thomas Y. Crowell Co., Inc., 1973), p. 3.

13 Charles E. Little, "The Environment of the Poor: Who Gives a Damn?," *Conservation Foundation Letter* (July 1973):1.

14 Joseph Wood Krutch, *The Great Chain of Life* (New York: Pyramid Books, 1956), p. 112.

15 Peter Harper, "Environmental Education as an Arena of Creative Conflict," *International Understanding at School* (April 1972): 7.

16 As quoted in Chas W. Williams, "A Nation Seeks Its Goals," *The Futurist* (August 1970): 115.

17 Edgar Faure, et al., *Learning To Be* (London: George C. Harrap and Co., Ltd., 1972), p. 104.

18 Chas W. Williams, *op. cit.*, p. 113.

19 Govan and Hadley, "Crisis of Cities, the Battle We Can Win," *Saturday Review* (February 24, 1968).

20 Richard M. Koff, "An End to All This," *Playboy* 18 (July 1971): 112, 114, and 206-208.

21 S. David Freeman, "The Energy Crisis," *Vital Issues* (November 1973): 3.

22 "Interview with the President of the Club of Rome," *UNESCO Courier* (January 1973): 12.

23 ENFO Newsletter, Florida Conservation Foundation, researched and edited by the Environmental Information Center, Winter Park, Florida. William R. Barada, editor.

24 James Noel Smith, *Environmental Quality and Social Justice in Urban America* (Washington, D.C.: The Conservation Foundation, 1974), p. 85.

25 Dennis L. Meadows and Donella H. Meadows, *op. cit.*, p. 167.

26 E. J. Farrell, "Choosing Values and Valuing Choices," *Association of Departments of English Bulletin* (March 1974): 52.

27 René DuBos, "The Biosphere, a Delicate Balance Between Man and Nature," *UNESCO Courier* (January 1969): 10.

28 Harper, *op. cit.*, p. 7.

29 "Environment and the Quality of Life," *Saturday Review* (May 2, 1970).

30 Nathan Hare, "Ecology, Black and White," *The Black Scholar* (April 1970): 31.

31 *Ibid.*, p. 31.

32 Farrell, *op. cit.*, p. 52.

# 8

# Should the Nation-State Give Way to Some Form of World Organization?

## William A. Nesbitt and Charles Bloomstein

### Introduction

EARTH'S people are presently organized into political units known as nation-states, each claiming absolute sovereignty over its territory. Sovereignty can be roughly defined as supreme internal power and freedom from external control.

It was not always so. Indeed, the nation-state system developed only within the last few centuries. Humankind's earlier history had tested many other forms of political organization—ranging from the family, the clan, and the tribe to the city-state, the feudal manor, the barony, the principality, the dukedom, the fiefdom, and so on. There is thus no reason to assume that the nation-state is the "natural" way humans should organize, or that it will last indefinitely into the future. Indeed, in its present form, it may not be able to solve the problems it faces, and its days may be numbered.

"The nation-state is obsolete," [1] wrote Richard J. Barnet. ". . . [The] nation-state has been rendered obsolete by the nuclear revolution in

WILLIAM A. NESBITT is Associate, Center for War/Peace Studies, New York, New York; Director, Studies in International Conflict Project, Center for International Programs and Comparative Studies, New York State Education Department; Teacher, Wooster School, Danbury, Connecticut.
CHARLES BLOOMSTEIN is Senior Director, Center for War/Peace Studies, New York, New York; Editor, Intercom.

the same way in which feudalism was made obsolete 200 years ago . . .," [2] said Hans J. Morgenthau. Norman Cousins argues that we must establish an authority "which takes away from nations, summarily and completely, not only the machinery of battle that can wage war, but the machinery of decision that can start a war." [3]

Others, with equally impressive credentials as students of world problems, no less desirous of peace and no less aware of the perils of the present international system of nation-states, disagree. John Burton of the University of London wrote, "The expectation of the development of a world order would be logical only if the world were under attack from another planet." He goes on to say in regard to an international force to keep the peace, "International enforcement is a form of tyranny and as such will never be accepted by states against which it is exercised." [4] Harvard's Karl Deutsch questions the value of a single world system and says:

A [world] government that had all control in one centralized place for decision making about the enforcement of law would have control over the law, much as the Roman Legions had control over the Roman Empire. Once such a government controlled all laws, it would be able to control all aspects of life.[5]

Even Maurice Strong, principal organizer of the Stockholm Conference of 1972 and a leader of the United Nations Environment Program, recently wrote:

. . . [The] development of new international machinery to deal with the complex problems of an increasingly interdependent technological civilization will not come about through the surrender of sovereignty by national governments but only by the purposeful exercise of that sovereignty. . . . The world is not likely to unite behind a common ideology or a super-government.[6]

## The Nature and Importance of This Issue

All students now in school were born into an already high-risk world environment. In a few years they will be participating, some in greater degree than others, in making or giving assent to decisions that will increase or reduce those risks—decisions that will lead toward more chance of war or more chance of peace. They may well decide that the nation-state, and its claims to absolute sovereignty, may be a form of world organization that nurtures war, while other forms nurture peace.

Clearly, this is an area of such transcending importance that our schools would be derelict if they did not give our students the most careful preparation possible for constructive participation in these awesome responsibilities. The next few years may well determine whether, and how, we shall move away from the present form of world organization.

John F. Kennedy said that we live under the Sword of Damocles of nuclear weapons. Hidden from view and/or carried in submarines and planes, hardened in silos—"every schoolboy knows" that these weapons, if used, mean the annihilation of attacker and attacked, and millions of others around the world. And the radioactive fallout in the aftermath of a nuclear war would mean not only lingering agony and death for many more of the human species but a pollution of the environment from which the earth might not recover. This possibility prompted economist Kenneth Boulding to write:

I believe the present international system [of nation-states] to be one which has a significant probability built into it of irretrievable disaster for the human race. The longer the number of years we contemplate such a system operating, the larger this probability becomes.[7]

With apparent detente with the Soviet Union, the probability of war may seem further away than it was in 1962. But from time to time events occur which remind us of the dangerous system in which we are still involved. For example, during the October, 1973 war between Israel and the Arab states, the United States went on a worldwide alert in the face of what appeared to be a possibility of direct Soviet intervention in the Middle East. After the crisis had subsided, Secretary of State Kissinger reminded us of the dangerous international system in which we still live. He commented:

I do not want to speculate what the United States would do if it should appear that instead of beginning an era of cooperation we were thrown back to the confrontations which sooner or later will have to be surmounted, because humanity cannot stand the eternal conflicts of those who have the capacity to destroy.[8]

Herman Kahn, a hardheaded realist, says that the most important problem the world is facing is war.[9] If a nuclear war were to erupt, all other problems would be meaningless. Obviously, in considering the future of the nation-state, no problem is of greater significance; indeed, the issue of war and peace has been the principal impetus for those who would radically change the nation-state system in favor of some other kind of world structure.

But even if nuclear war is avoided indefinitely, the cost of worldwide defense systems imposes heavy burdens. United States defense expenditures are now running well over $80 billion annually, and weapons costs are skyrocketing. For example, the B-1 bomber planes which the Pentagon now wants would cost over $60 million each, and building and maintaining the total fleet for ten years would exceed $50 billion. World military expenditures are already in the $200 billion range.

The magnitude of these expenditures seriously limits our capacity to tackle other problems, problems which do not respect national boundaries and whose combined effect may, all too soon, be as overwhelming, perhaps even more so, than war. Indeed, while most earlier efforts at supranational organization were motivated primarily by the need to contain war, it may now turn out that the overriding imperative to deal with these global problems may provide the key to reordering the nation-state system. The nation-state is not structured to cope with these newly perceived difficulties, and may have to give way. This could be viewed less as a failure and more as a necessary response to changing needs, much as earlier political structures which were superseded are now seen.

Let us take one day, chosen almost at random, as reported in *The New York Times*: March 11, 1974. And let us consider not only the news but its domestic and global implications for the future.

The lead story was about the Arabs postponing talks for ending the oil embargo. This item, not highly significant in itself, had underlying implications of historic proportions. Many Americans learned for the first time that actions affecting whether they would be able to get to work or not, if there was work, how warm their apartment or house would be, and how much they would have to spend for virtually every item in the family budget, were not taken solely in the United States but now also depended upon decisions made across the globe. Moreover, many Americans realized for the first time that their consumption of energy (about one-third of the world's total with only six per cent of the world's population) could not increase indefinitely. Oil supplies were finite, and production could not be increased to meet a doubling of demand every ten years.

Although the United States is the world's largest oil-producing country, it now must import oil and other energy sources at enormous cost. In 1972, the National Petroleum Council estimated that the net import of energy may cost as much as $30 billion by 1985. Robert McNamara of the World Bank predicted that the developed nations will have to pay an additional $53 billion in 1974 for the same amount of oil they used in 1973.[10] And it is estimated that world oil production will begin to decline sometime between 1985 and 2000.[11]

As the end of the hydrocarbon age looms, oil-producing countries naturally seek to make the best of what remains. Arab nations, with over half the known world reserves, have nationalized most of their oil production facilities, and other oil-producing countries may do the same. That same Monday, March 11, the *Times* reported that Venezuela, the third largest producer of oil in the world, was debating nationalization. Resource-rich Third World countries may follow these examples of higher prices for other raw materials, to gain the enormous increase in profits it will mean—all signifying higher costs to both rich and poor nations.

The oil crisis also highlighted the role of multinational corporations. Americans discovered that United States-based oil companies could not, certainly did not, make decisions from a national perspective; indeed, they had moved much of their activity outside the country. Companies such as Standard Oil of New Jersey, whose annual gross sales are larger than the Gross National Product of countries like Denmark, Austria, and Indonesia, viewed the United States as but one of many competitors for their product. Senator Henry Jackson is even looking into the allegation that the United States military forces were denied oil by American-based companies during the danger period of the October War.

Another article in that *Times* of March 11 dealt with a World Bank report on the critical food shortages and accompanying rising discontent in India, which is "among the developing countries most severely affected by the recent changes in the world energy situation." The relationship of food shortages to the energy problem is direct, for a part of India's problem is the high cost of fertilizers, which require large amounts of energy for production. John H. Knowles, President of the Rockefeller Foundation, said that the rising cost of oil may be the final straw for those nations which need to increase food production, and he foresaw possible mass starvation.[12] UN figures indicate that the developing countries need to increase energy consumption over eight times between 1970 and 2000 to continue growth, but the added cost for oil alone among the poor half of the world will be $10 billion in 1974. India's 1973 oil cost was $415 million in 1973 and over $1 billion in 1974. What will it be in 2000? Ward Morehouse, Director of the Center for International Programs and Comparative Studies, New York State Education Department, summed up these effects of the energy crisis:

. . . [The] oil-producing countries have set off a chain reaction which has affected in some measure all countries, East-West, North-South, rich-poor, and touched the daily lives of billions of individuals, ranging from the farmer in the Punjab in North India or Pakistan, who can no longer get the fertilizer he needs to sustain the modern agricultural technology which he has adopted in recent years through the "Green Revolution," to industrial workers, whose paychecks are diminished by the larger bite taken by the rising cost of petroleum products and a variety of natural resources, not just oil.[13]

One thing is clear; the higher cost of energy and raw materials will not help the developing nations, except those rich in resources. Careful estimates indicate that the poorer half of the world would have been doing well to bring average annual per capita incomes up to $300 (1965 dollars) by the year 2000, while the rich one-quarter will surely reach $5,000.[14] Because this rich-poor gap is increasingly evident, thanks to electronic communication and education both within and among countries, we may expect to see more conflict as rising expectations are disappointed. Barbara Ward and René DuBos asked:

Can we rationally suppose that they, the developing peoples, will accept a world "half slave, half free," half plunged in consumptive pleasures, half deprived of the bare decencies of life? Can we hope that the protest of the dispossessed will not erupt into local conflict and widening unrest? [15]

A front-page article in the *Times* brought the international food problem home, with the headline "Consumers in U.S. Face Competition for Nation's Food." It pointed out that Americans' food supplies and costs would be subject to "the demand of a hungry world, whose ever-increasing population has rising expectations and somewhat more affluence." We frequently hear that the number of people competing for enough to eat and for the limited raw materials for economic growth will increase from the present 3.9 billion to about 6.5 billion by the end of the century, extrapolating from present fertility trends. However "even if fertility decreases in the years ahead, world population in 2000 is not likely to be below 6 billion," [16] according to the Population Council. It scarcely need be pointed out that in the competition for food, as well as other resources, when prices rise the rich nations would outbid the poor.

Another March 11 article called attention to the scarcity of other resources and to a survey of several hundred top marketing executives, an increasing number of whom favor some form of allocation or rationing in the United States. The pressure for supplies has become so intense that "indications of bribery to get scarce materials is becoming common in industry. . . ." Too few Americans realize that our once resource-rich country is increasingly dependent upon imports of vital raw materials; for example, United States Department of Interior data indicate that by 1985 we will have to import 96 per cent of our aluminum, 55 per cent of our iron, 62 per cent of our lead, 47 per cent of our potassium, 87 per cent of our tungsten, and 72 per cent of our zinc.

We are the largest producer of copper ore in the world, but would have to import 34 per cent of our needs by then. Furthermore, according to Lester Brown, "The dramatic projected growth in dependence on imports also means the United States economy will become more vulnerable to external forces beyond its control. . . ." [17]

Scarcely a day goes by in the news without some attention to the problem of pollution, and an article in the *Times* reported a clash between the head of the Environmental Protection Agency and the White House over the Administration's proposal to revise drastically the Clean Air Act of 1970. At issue are efforts to maintain energy production through increased use of coal, strip mining, and nuclear power. Extensive extraction of oil from shale will pollute waterways in the West, with impact not only on Americans but Mexicans as well.

That water pollution often cannot be confined within national boundaries may now be too commonly realized to deserve detailed discussion. The runoff of DDT from rivers draining into the oceans has affected all wildlife. Oil from ocean tankers (some of which now hold 500,000 tons) and offshore wells washes up on remote beaches. Jacques Picard, the Swiss oceanographer, has estimated that five to ten million tons of petroleum, without considering accidents, go into the sea every year, affecting the marine plants that recycle most of the oxygen in the world.[18] Other pollutants going into the oceans are toxic metals, such as mercury, which has lodged in human brains through consumption of fish. And, as the use of nuclear energy increases, radioactive wastes may further threaten the earth's water system.

Nor can air pollution be considered solely a national problem. The burning of fossil fuels has added appreciably to the pollution of the atmosphere around the world. $CO_2$ has increased by .2 per cent a year and may eventually cause an increase in global temperature—the "Greenhouse Effect"—sufficient to melt polar ice enough to raise ocean levels. Dust and particulate pollution augment the cloud cover in areas, with incalculable effects upon weather.

One article in the *Times* that Monday suggests that these various problems in the news will lead to increased conflict. The Common Market's European Parliament in Strasbourg was meeting in an atmosphere of gloom. "The bold and noble dreams that galvanized the peoples of Western Europe after World War II appear to be disintegrating with the region's nations in increasing disarray individually and collectively." What had been held up as a model for the possible economic and political integration of other areas in the world—indeed, perhaps, the world itself one day—was in trouble; and one reason was the self-seeking, *sauve qui peut* behavior of some members, particularly France, during the October War and energy crisis. Holland, especially, suffered for her

pro-Israel stance through the Arab embargo, while France made unilateral deals with oil-producing countries. Of course, there are also
other reasons for the dimming hopes for a United States of Europe—
agricultural prices, monetary problems, and what the article called the
resurgence of "national egotism."

A classic source of conflict is struggle over scarce resources. (In conflict theory, resources also include nonmaterial items such as status.)
Right now, resources as a source of conflict* seem mostly to refer to
vital raw materials, as was land in the seventeenth and eighteenth centuries. (Will the seabed also become part of this conflict?) When he was
Minister of Finance of the Federal Republic of Germany, Helmut
Schmidt, who became Chancellor, foresaw such conflict:

It is a struggle for the distribution and use of the national product. . . . The
struggle over oil prices may be followed tomorrow by a similar struggle
over the prices of other important raw materials. And since what is at
stake is not just pawns on a chessboard, but the peaceful evolution of the
world economy and the prosperity of the nations of the world, we need a
politically sound philosophy if we are to win this dangerous fight.[19]

The key concept is interdependence. Our lives and our fortunes are
interrelated with those of the other residents of our earth. As our
biosphere is a single environmental system so are we part of a worldwide economic system. This the energy crisis should have brought home
to every American. What happens in another part of the globe directly
affects our well-being. As Barbara Ward said:

We have become neighbors in terms of inescapable physical proximity and
instant communication. We are neighbors in economic interest and technological direction. We are neighbors in facets of our industrialization and in
the pattern of our urbanization. Above all, we are neighbors in the risk
of total destruction.[20]

This brief overview of global problems is by no means exhaustive.
Not all problems have been touched upon (for example, human rights)
and none has been discussed sufficiently to indicate all possible ramifications. In focusing upon problems and not on those aspects of global
society that offer hope, if not solutions for the future, we should be
aware that we are in danger of adding to what Kenneth Boulding has
called the "doom boom." That focus is useful only if it leads to clearing
the way to constructive action.

---

* A recent work, also mentioned in Chapter 1, that emphasizes the future
conflict implications of world problems is Robert L. Heilbroner's *An Inquiry into
the Human Prospect*. He foresees "wars of redistribution" or "preëmptive seizure."

We are suggesting that there are global problems which will not disappear by themselves; that energy shortages, resource depletion, overpopulation, food shortages, and environmental deterioration all affect each other; and all in their combined impact have potentially dangerous implications for keeping conflict within tolerable bounds as we face the twenty-first century. Present conflicts may be worsened by competition for new sources of raw materials—the seabed tomorrow, the moon in due course. We are suggesting also that these interrelated problems at least call into question whether the nation-state as the focal point for most problem-solving is any longer adequate. Barbara Ward wrote:

The greatest institutional gap in our world is created by an inescapable, planetary, interdependence which breeds common grievances and creates common needs and opportunities, yet is matched by virtually no instruments of worldwide order and welfare. And it is through this gap that mankind can tumble into annihilation.[21]

And by implication this far, we are suggesting that an effective approach to teaching about the question of whether the nation-state should give way to another world system should deal with analysis and function. After examining the kinds of problems we face today and for the indefinite future, what sorts of institutional changes might work best for their resolution? Do global-national problems require a further reduction of sovereignty? Should we devote more attention to multiple loyalties?

### Should the Nation-State Relinquish Sovereignty?

Traditionally we have thought of the nation-state as a sovereign entity—proudly independent, a law unto itself, knowing no higher authority. The doctrine of sovereignty is embedded in international law; indeed, the United Nations Charter refers to "the sovereign equality of all members." The concept has been reinforced by our schools, especially through the teaching of history. Students learn, for example, that the United States became independent from Britain in 1776, henceforth able to determine its own destiny. Like students in other countries, Americans study about how their national government determined relations with "the outside world," how trade would be conducted and with whom, who could come into the country and leave, and above all, whether there would be peace or war. What went on inside the national boundaries was nobody else's business.

Various writers in the November, 1968 special issue of *Social Education* on "International Education for the Twenty-First Century" deplored the tendency of students to develop a view of the world from political maps, in which each country is indicated by a different color. From this image, frequently still in vogue in schools, each country is seen as an independent, separate, and sovereign unit. People see the nations of the world as differently colored billiard balls, large and small. They cannot be penetrated from the outside. When they do come into contact, through their governments, the smaller and lighter are pushed out of the way by the larger and heavier.

On the other hand, in recent years we have often been exposed to a very different view of the world. We have seen the earth from outer space as a beautiful, bluish, spherical planet, with swirls of white clouds, without political boundaries or different colors for different countries. The earth is seen as the habitat of all humankind—and the only one available. How prominent this image has become in the minds of Americans is hard to say.

It may be that the billiard ball model is all too common in the United States, even today. From birth we are still largely socialized from an almost unavoidable national perspective; we are bombarded daily in the national media primarily by local and national events. American history is often the only required course in social studies, usually in the 5th, 8th, and 11th grades. A casual reading of the news or watching of television might give the impression that almost the only interaction between countries is through governments; that Henry Kissinger's latest trip or the visit of some head of state to Washington *is* the international news. And many people think that power is a matter of size and military clout—that other countries of the world must get out of the way for the United States, the biggest and heaviest "ball" of all.

In what respects is this model in disagreement with reality? First, it ignores the unitary nature of the biosphere, a global system where damage to one part affects others. It ignores the common humanity of our species by suggesting that our differences are as great as those of the colors on a political map. The billiard ball image ignores maps other than the physical. It does not show that religions, ethnic groups, and tribes are not synonymous with political borders, that states are often a mosaic of cultures, and that such cultures cross state borders. It ignores the movement of peoples around the globe; indeed, a map of airline routes or shipping lanes may say more about the world than a political one. It ignores the activities of some 2,700 international organizations, about 90 per cent of which are nongovernmental. It ignores the operations of multinational corporations which are sharing research, materials, and profits with local companies and states. Above all, the billiard ball model ignores the realities of the weapons that can reach targets thousands of miles away, linking millions of humankind in their capacity for destruction.

We need more accurate models, as many educators have been saying; and we need them translated into techniques and a language that are meaningful to the young. John Burton has described a cobweb model— a mental map which would show the flow of communications and transactions, whether of words, people, or goods.[22] Perhaps a more attractive image than an earth spanned by cobwebs would be to imagine a giant map on which we could place a series of transparent overlays. Imagine that one overlay could be marked with every telephone call made across borders during, say, a month. Another, in a different color, shows every movement by tourists, or pilgrims to Mecca, Rome, and the Ganges. On another is every movement by businessmen; on another the journeys of government officials; on another is traced the comings and goings of UN personnel; and on still another, those of members of nongovernmental organizations. Similar transparencies could mark the flow of goods in trade, with perhaps a separate one for oil. Building such a mental map would give the student at least some idea that a global society has emerged, requiring a change in our world view as great or greater than what was required by people living in the fifteenth and sixteenth centuries, after the voyages of discovery.

Clearly, there is now a "fusion of the globe into one boundary-less field of human action. . . . There are no internal affairs left on our crowded earth!"[23] This increasing permeability of nation-states means that sovereignty has taken on a vastly different meaning from even a generation ago.

But while the imperatives of world society and the functional needs of states require a new definition of sovereignty, there is no denying that the nation-state is still the *actor* on the world scene. National decision-makers must be increasingly attentive to world society and they must operate under constraints that did not exist in the days of Bismarck or Theodore Roosevelt. But governments remain in control of what has been a fundamental aspect of sovereignty, the power to make peace and war. The question is not whether all sovereignty shall have to be surrendered to some international organization but rather whether the nation-state will have to be dragged, kicking and screaming, into a future where sufficient sovereignty will have to be relinquished so that global problems can be tackled and resolved.

### Should the Nation-State Receive Our Primary Loyalty?

The modern nation-state has been characterized not only by sovereignty but by strong devotion expected and received from its citizens. Generally in the past the claim of the state to fealty took precedence over all others—that of family, ethnic group, locality, even religion, although God was often invoked as being in full accord with the state's policies. We need to examine the nature of loyalty to the nation-state, especially in this nuclear age; and we need to consider whether that attachment is an insurmountable obstacle to the development of a broader vision beyond national borders, perhaps encompassing all humanity.

Why do people love their country? A meaningful analysis has been provided by Herbert Kelman of Harvard University, who points out that support for the nation does have a purely emotional side, what he calls a "sentimental attachment," more salient for some than others.[24] The nation-state may, in fact, satisfy a deep psychological need for identity with those of like kind—a "we-ness" with a larger group than the family. This loyalty is often stirred by national symbols, such as the flag, the anthem, shrines, etc.

But loyalty is not all sentimental, although too often it is thought to be. There is also an instrumental attachment; that is, the nation can be seen as providing many important functional needs, such as carrying mail, regulating transportation and utility rates, providing services, disaster relief, etc. Indeed, suppose we conceive of the nation-state as a social invention for accomplishing tasks. If we consider what well-organized states have accomplished in promoting economic development and the general welfare, they have performed remarkably well. But the question is increasingly being asked now whether they can continue to meet vital needs in the interconnected world in which we live, not least in providing the physical security that was a principal reason for their emergence.

A scientific study led by John DeLamater may be highly significant for educators in preparing people for the world of the future.[25] From 129 interviews, it discovered that individuals who were functionally committed to the national system and who derived rewards from participation in its institutions were less nationalistic and more receptive to what might be called global perspectives than people with other kinds of attachments, especially the emotional symbolic one. The former were less interested in military solutions to problems, more inclined to give foreign aid, even more willing to resume trade with Cuba. More important, they were "most likely to endorse strongly the establishment of world government," and "most favorable toward a strong international body and the United Nations, even at the cost of some US independence in decisions." They felt they could do something to prevent war. Significantly this group was better educated and had responsible positions in the "bureaucratic structure." They also had a low emotional response to national symbols, and supported "policies they viewed as instrumental to the national interest."

The study suggests the not surprising hypothesis that if people were better educated* and more successfully involved in the social system, they would be less chauvinistic and more tolerant of changes in foreign relations. But the study might be interpreted (although the researchers did not do so) to mean that people could be encouraged, through education for example, to recognize that the nation-state is not just a collection of symbols for which one feels an emotional loyalty, but also an instrument for meeting the functional needs of its citizens. Obviously, such people would more easily support necessary changes to get done another way things the nation-state on its own could no longer do.

If international organizations assume tasks heretofore belonging within national jurisdiction, does this mean a shift of personal attachment away from the nation-state? We must often remind ourselves of the crucial concept of multiple-loyalty in considering any question of transnational organization. Loyalty is not a finite pool of feeling, where if we take out some measure for one object there is less for another. That one loves one's family does not mean that one is less dedicated to the nation; and there may be nothing incompatible between commitment to the UN and to one's country, although conflicts are always possible where a difficult choice might have to be made between the two.

It is interesting to note that the German philosopher Herder in the eighteenth century developed a view, which sounds distinctly contemporary, of the compatibility of loyalty to one's group and the larger humanity. He saw mankind as an organic unity, with the various cultures in the world as but branches of the whole. The development to the fullest of any nationality's unique capabilities would add to the perfection of mankind. Thus, to be loyal to the nation could be an expression of loyalty to a humanity that all peoples shared.

### The Origin and Development of the Issue

The past is a rich mine of information for considering the issue of reconciling the nation-state with some kind of international authority. But in a quarrying of such vast dimensions, we obviously must be highly selective. We must find ways of processing the data produced by several thousand years of history. We need to develop a framework of relevant topics in which examples from history can be placed. Such a framework must be concept-oriented; and, because the issue is highly inter-

---

* Supporting evidence is provided by Daniel Yankelovich's study, preliminary findings of which were reported in the *New York Times* of May 22, 1974 (p. 45). On the question of whether patriotism is an important value, 40% of college-educated youth between 16 and 25 replied yes in 1969, and only 19% in 1973. Not immediate to this discussion, but perhaps most interestingly, the noncollege-educated youth saying yes declined at least as strikingly, from 60% to 35%.

disciplinary, we must borrow heavily from other social science disciplines. What are some of the concepts that might be at least briefly suggested here?

Much of what is taught in history is concerned with the consolidation of nation-states, in which the people and the state have been integrated. It may be fruitful to consider a broader concept of political integration, which can take us further into the past and be applied at various points in world history. As Karl Deutsch suggests, we might consider

the process by which villages become districts, counties, or baronies, which, in turn, are combined into duchies, or provinces, only to merge again into kingdoms. Kingdoms, in turn, have sometimes become consolidated into federations or empires.[26]

The study of this process can enable us to focus, for example, on why royal authority expanded in France during the Middle Ages. Languedoc, to take one example after the upheavals of the Hundred Years' War and the Cathar religious strife, accepted the rule of law and order under Louis IX as preferable to weak and contentious barons. Royal authority brought prosperity; it also brought protection from powerful neighbors like Spain. And, in the course of centuries, the peoples of this province, who initially spoke a different language, came to consider themselves Frenchmen.

Or, more recently, we can consider the unification of Italy or Germany. What was the process by which Germans or Italians came to feel some sense of belonging together, of nationalism? What was the role of language, religion, and the ideology of nationalism that preceded political unification? What part did the growing economic interconnectedness of these areas play in a willingness to form a state? To what extent was a common enemy a factor? After formal unification, what was still needed before Italy and Germany could be truly classified as nation-states? That is, what was the process by which already existing identifiable groups, some with proud histories, became amalgamated?

Study of the American experience can also raise questions about political integration. What factors helped the consolidation of the colonies into a union? Was a common enemy a necessary prerequisite? To what extent were functional economic needs and security forces for political integration? Was the Constitution a result of agreement upon basic values and feelings of identity? Did the Constitution then become an important element in the movement toward genuine integration? That is, to what extent do institutional arrangements follow from a long prior process of integration, and to what extent do they further that process? And what does the Civil War tell us about how the process may be interrupted? The South is, now more than ever before, an integrated part of the union. Is this the result of growing economic interdependence and prosperity?

Such a study of political integration will help students to understand that the formation of a nation-state is not the end of the process. Many Sicilians still do not consider themselves Italian. And even in that mother of parliaments, Great Britain, "nationalities" like the Welsh and Scots resent being thought of as Englishmen, which they are not. In many states that are thought of as unified, there are movements for autonomy or even independence.

The reasons for the disintegration of states surely deserves study in the context of international governance. Historically, what were the problems that multinational states, such as Austria-Hungary, faced? Why could no formula be devised that would satisfy felt local needs and at the same time continue the security and economic development advantages that a larger unit could bring? Contemporary states with nationality problems need also to be considered. Nigerian and Ugandan tribalism is a prime case in point. Belgium has been facing a strong independence movement from the Flemish-speaking people. Pakistan broke up, and we now have an independent Bangladesh. Will we face increasing tensions within multinational states such as Canada? For example, Alexander Solzhenitsyn has called for the disintegration of the Soviet Union into a number of states, an appeal that is not likely to be heeded, at least for the foreseeable future.

When we say that the creation of a political system does not necessarily mean that political integration has been completed, we are referring, as John Burton says, to a fundamental distinction between legal and legitimized authority.[27] Britain was the legal authority over the colonies at the eve of Lexington Green, but she had lost her legitimacy in the eyes of too many colonists, especially the political élite. Force of arms under a dictatorship may for a time keep authority, but people increasingly value participation in decision-making, and want to be able to consent willingly to the laws they are expected to obey. In examining the growth of international institutions, we must not only consider legal arrangements and authority, but legitimacy through consent.

The question of legitimacy leads to a caution about using the nation-state as a case study for the emergence of a world government. It is commonly thought that the historic process of integration of small political units into larger ones logically will result in a world state, that bringing law and order to a Languedoc or the American frontier by a central authority demonstrates that what is needed to curb international violence is worldwide government. But domestic examples of law and order also tell us that the well-ordered community does not have a policeman on every corner; there are never enough policemen. Effective government is based on widespread voluntary compliance, which means people assist the government in its functions, as did the deputy sheriff in the movie *High Noon,* not oppose it. In essence, it means that the state must be accepted as legitimate, with the sentimental and functional loyalty that goes with that.

Domestic disorder invites outside intervention, and future threats to peace may well result from opposing great powers carrying forward their conflicts in turbulent countries which have failed to legitimize their statehood. But some societies have been able to achieve a healthy measure of internal stability, and we need to find out why. What are the characteristics of the peaceful society, both within its borders and in its relations with other societies? A study by Matthew Melko of *52 Peaceful Societies* suggests a number of factors, only a few of which can be treated here.[28] He considers societies as far apart in time and geography as the Phoenicians, Byzantines, North Americans, English, and Swedes, and finds that, while there are exceptions, periods of peace usually go hand in hand with prosperity. This is supported by other studies which indicate there has been far more internal violence in the Third World in the recent past than in the industrialized societies of the West. Melko also finds that there is a correlation between domestic peace and a prosperity that is at least fairly well distributed, that is, there must not be too great wealth among the few and too great poverty among the masses. The tendency of peaceful societies to bring new members into the political élite is a function of income distribution and economic change. The failure of Old Régime France to accept the wealthy middle class into the governing system is a prime case in point. Significantly, he further found a correlation between trade and peace with other societies, for dangerous foreign adventures interfere with good markets. Contrary to a common assumption about the well-ordered society, a homogeneous population in terms of language, ethnic background, and religion did not help to preserve peace. The American and French Revolutions, as well as frequent war among Arab States, are but a few examples.

The acceptance of social change is necessary to both internal and external peace. States that accepted the necessity, in the nineteenth and twentieth centuries, to widen the franchise, support public welfare and education, and go along with nationally-oriented aspirations, etc., were more peaceful than those which did not. Such societies realized that a people's notion of what should be theirs as a matter of right had to be recognized; that "people will die for their rights, once they have become defined as such." [29]

Melko also points out that peaceful societies are often tolerant of other ideas and outside cultures. Such toleration "presumes that there is merit in all viewpoints and that some of these may contribute to solving . . . problems." Toleration encourages the view that "you do not fight outsiders because of their ideas" [30] and is associated with a universalist attitude, which, he says, ". . . [does] not make peace any more than nationalist attitudes [do], but [its] existence is a prerequisite to long periods of peace covering an extensive area." [31]

In teaching history we often devote large amounts of time to the causes of war, but very little to the causes of peace. The Melko study suggests that a society at peace with itself tends to be at peace with others. And countries now very much at peace with each other were often in conflict in the past. This is especially true of Western Europe; indeed, much of the history of Europe since the fall of Rome is concerned with war. Yet war between Western European powers is now almost unthinkable. Scandinavia is another case in point. And, while it is hard for Americans who know no history to believe, the United States and Canada were at war in the early nineteenth century.

Karl Deutsch calls these peaceful clusters pluralistic security-communities;[32] that is, the nation-states retain their independence but have created an environment of cooperation that is as binding as if they had drawn up a constitution and formed a confederation. What were the factors that produced peace after war? Do they tell us something about the possibility of such communities growing over large areas of the globe?

From a study of the North Atlantic area, Deutsch and colleagues found two conditions essential—major values must be compatible, and members must be mutually responsive. For example, the North Atlantic countries, with some exceptions, share a basic political ideology that embraces constitutionalism and democracy. They also developed "perpetual attention, communication, perception of needs, and responsiveness." [33] Deutsch particularly emphasizes the importance of communication and transactions, including "transmission of messages [mail, electronic media, etc.], personal contact through travel and foreign residence, and the exchange of ideas, goods, and services." [34] Among other useful but not essential factors for forming pluralistic security-communities were a "distinctive way of life that the units share," "superior economic growth," and "expectation of joint economic reward." [35]

The "cobweb" model suggests that, at least in the frequency and intensity of communications and transactions, much of the world is now a community. And even if basic political values are by no means in harmony, nations are increasingly realizing that they have a common interest in survival on a planet that is endangered by environmental deterioration, overpopulation, and food and resource shortages. They also realize that their security is no longer assured by the staggering military expenditures of the nation-state system.

Schools need to teach about the emergence of the "global village" in which we now live. They need to examine the background of interdependence and its exponential explosion in modern times. As historian C. Vann Woodward put it, we need to contrast America's relative self-sufficiency and "free security" during the nineteenth century with the contemporary world. The traditional topic is the emergence of the United States as a world power, but this should include its development as an interdependent power—with dependence upon others for security and for the means of economic growth.

## Stages in Considering This Controversial Issue

We need to devote more attention in the social studies to the history of institutional arrangements for promoting peace. At least from the time of Athens and the Delian League, man has tried to find ways to avoid war through some system of collective security. The study of the successes and failures of the Church in the Middle Ages, the Concert of Europe in the nineteenth century, and the League of Nations may shed some light on how to keep the peace when the political units to be controlled were essentially independent. Some discussion of various plans, such as the Grand Design of Henry IV, that of the Abbé de St.-Pierre, William Penn, and others, may be useful, as would be the efforts to draft international law to control war, such as at the Hague Conferences, the Washington and London naval conferences, and Geneva.

Above all, the United Nations and its related agencies and activities deserve serious discussion in our classrooms. Its peacekeeping role is important; indeed, it was said when the cease-fire was being arranged at the time of the October, 1973 war in the Middle East, that if the UN had not existed, it would have had to be invented, so important was it to have neutral troops to station between the two forces. However, students need to realize the limitations of the UN in keeping the peace when sovereign nations retain control over the world's military power. They also need to recognize that the International Court of Justice can play only a limited role in arbitrating disputes when some nations, including our own, refuse to use its services and abide by its decisions.

The functional activities of the UN and related agencies are also very important, and too often neglected. Students need to recognize that the economic, social, and environmental pre-conditions of peace are being laid down by the work of the Food and Agriculture Organization, the World Health Organization, UNESCO, UNICEF, and others. They need to study the UN efforts to further economic development in Third World nations, and the work of the Commission on Human Rights. Increasingly valuable are UN operations in pollution control. And they should understand that all of these activities are being carried on with funds that are insignificant in comparison with what is being spent by national governments on arms.

The United Nations should be studied as one model for international organization, considered along with other models proposed for coping with problems which have now reached crisis level—and threaten to get worse in the future. The UN may be placed along a spectrum of models in defining international structures, to which we now turn.

### Defining the Issue

There is a choice to be made between the status quo—in which the strongest nation-states retain the sovereign power to wreak annihilating damage upon each other and seriously disrupt life elsewhere; in which any disorder or instability in the Third World threatens to involve the nuclear powers; in which an interdependent world faces an array of interrelated problems, including competition for scarce resources—and some alternative. "The plain truth is," wrote Barbara Ward, "that if we cannot, as a human community, create the institutions of civilized living, our chances of carrying on the human experiment are just about nil." [36]

What are the alternatives to the present international system of nation-states? What institutional arrangements are not only desirable but feasible? What can work?

*All-Purpose World Government.* Such a world government is the nation-state writ large. Its proponents argue that as the nation-state has brought peace within its borders, so would the world state. Emery Reves wrote, "Wars between groups of men forming social units always take place when these units . . . exercise unrestricted sovereign power. . . . Wars between these social units cease the moment sovereign power is transferred from them to a larger or higher unit." [37] In addition to its function of providing security, the world government would also be responsible for global general welfare—guaranteeing protection against the worst natural and social calamities, promoting economic development, providing for health, education, and welfare, etc.

Today even the wealthiest and best-ordered large states are having difficulties in delivering these services to their peoples with efficiency, humanity, and attention to local needs. Futurist Herman Kahn foresees that technologically advanced states, because of their complexity, face the possibility of collapse by the mid-1980s. Indeed, nations, including the communist, are looking for ways to bring government closer to localities in order to function more effectively. Clearly, an all-purpose world government could be a bureaucratic nightmare. Even if the administrative problems were surmountable, financing would be extremely difficult, if not impossible, especially if poor areas of the world were to receive benefits from the rich. And, as Archie Bunker once put it in one of his most acute malapropisms, "There is no taxation without regimentation." Indeed, the principal reason world government is no longer given serious attention is the widespread fear that it might turn into tyranny.

And how to keep peace among billions of peoples who live in a quilt-work of cultures—rich and poor, literate and illiterate, large and small? Who should decide, and by what criteria, what would be a proper grievance, requiring intervention by the world authority? How should delegates be chosen and vote in the world parliament? Is it to be on the basis of power and wealth? In such case, the majority of the world's peoples would be subjects. Is it to be by population? Then the wealthy would be governed by the poor. Would representatives to the world government think only of their own "national" interests? Above all, how would the monopoly of power in the central authority be exercised? There are fears that the dominant group—whether the rich or the poor, whether white or non-white—would become a tyranny against the rest.

Nations now sovereign do not want to expose themselves even to the possibility of such dangers. As Bernard Brodie summarized such views, "The most important weakness of world government is that, apart from a very few persons . . ., no one seems to want it. That is, no one seems willing even to begin paying the price for having it." [38]

*Limited World Government.* But is there not some way by which nations may retain necessary control over domestic functions, but be deprived of the power to make war? Most plans which try to accomplish this fit under the general rubric of federalism. There is no precise definition of that formula, but it can be generally described as a situation where the constituent units, in this case nation-states, maintain their identity and structures and voluntarily surrender certain limited and specified powers to an overarching body in which they participate with the other members. The United States became a federation with the adoption of the Constitution, and a number of other nation-states now describe themselves as federations—like the (West) German Federal Republic. It is also possible to have regional federations, as well as a global one.

One critical feature in the structure of a federation is the decision whether the central body has the authority to act directly on the individual citizens of the member nation-states or must work through each nation-state's own organs. After great debate, the United States opted for direct power, and this now appears to be generally accepted as essential to a successful federation. But it is also true that this direct power helps create a dynamic through which the central body steadily expands its authority, so that more and more functions fall within its mandate. We have certainly seen this happen in the United States, especially during the past 40 years, as major problems were recognized as beyond the resolution capacity of the individual states.

Because the federal principle is capable of almost infinite variation, we shall elaborate here on only one plan, a carefully drawn proposal for a limited world government, by Grenville Clark and Louis B. Sohn, men with long experience both in international law and as advisers to the United States government. This is developed in detail in their book, *World Peace Through World Law,*[39] and is outlined clearly for high-school-age students in *Peacekeeping,** by Jack R. Fraenkel, Margaret Carter, and Betty Reardon, who are well-known to social studies teachers concerned with world order.

In the Clark-Sohn model there would be a General Assembly with national membership proportional to population; however, the largest states would be limited to thirty members, while the smallest would have at least one. At first, the members of the Assembly would be chosen by national governments but eventually they would be elected by direct vote of the people of each nation.

Fundamental to the plan is universal disarmament, to proceed in phases supervised by the General Assembly. Nations would maintain only light arms for the exercise of police functions.

An Executive Council of seventeen representatives (with no more than one from each state) from large and small nations elected from the Assembly would have among its responsibilities the enforcement of laws passed by the Assembly, and would decide on the use of the international police force to keep the peace. On important matters, such as the use of the peace force, at least eight of the large members and four from the smaller must agree. The peace force would be made up of full-time professionals with a limit on the number from any one nation. It would be deployed throughout the world to avoid concentrations in special areas and to enable quick dispatch of forces to any trouble spot.

There would be an International Court of Justice with compulsory jurisdiction. Judgments handed down by the court would be enforced

---

* See Methods and Materials Section.

by the General Assembly, with the peace force brought in as a last resort. Not only nations but individuals could be brought into court and tried for violations of the peace.

The Clark-Sohn proposal envisions a greatly expanded economic and social development program under a World Development Authority, financed through savings from the well over $200 billion dollars now expended globally each year for national defense. Nations would be taxed according to wealth, but Americans would pay far less than the $400 per capita now going to defense.

The plan also includes a Bill of Rights which provides that "all powers not delegated by express language or clear implication" are reserved to the member nations and their peoples. It further states that the world organization shall not violate the basic rights of any individual, including freedom of speech, press, and assembly. This Bill of Rights, however, does not protect individuals against their own government, for to do so would mean that the world organization could intervene in the internal affairs of states and nations, a Pandora's box which would almost surely prevent the plan's acceptance.

The Clark-Sohn model for a limited world government has great value in enabling us to consider alternatives to the present system. But it also raises many questions and some of the same fears as does an all-purpose world government. Would it create an imperium of the powerful nations, which would have effective control over the use of the peace force? Would the necessity for large-nation agreement in the Council paralyze peacekeeping activities? Would the great powers submit to being outvoted by well over 100 small countries in the General Assembly? And, of course, there is the key question—would nation-states ever relinquish their armed forces to a central authority, whatever checks and balances are established against abuses by the world organization, especially when national decision-makers associate their role and status with military power?

The Clark-Sohn plan assumes that there need not be more worldwide progress toward integration before the establishment of institutional arrangements that include an all-powerful armed force and a system of courts with compulsory jurisdiction. On this point, Chadwick F. Alger emphasizes that national integrations examined indicate that "governments are as much a result of *already* existing peaceful conditions as a *cause* of such conditions." [40] In fact, courts and armed forces are "of minor importance in the early stages of national integration. . . ." And "Excessive military commitments tended to destroy already integrated political units." [41] On the other hand, the looming world problems and events now unforeseen may make "a great leap forward" toward strong international institutions not only desirable but feasible in the long-range future. The study of Clark-Sohn and other models may at least prepare us to be open-minded about such alternative possibilities.

*Regional Institutions.* It is thought that regional organizations, such as the European Common Market, could become a stepping stone to world organization. The difficulties in moving ahead toward a United States of Europe do not negate the, argument for such a process, and there is not now sufficient practice or theory to discount that possibility. Certainly, movement in that direction should not be discouraged.

But while the European experience is a useful case study for exploring the factors in political and economic integration, some doubt that the creation of a strong regional organization among once competing nation-states will move the world closer to peace. Such a unit may become simply another superpower, competing with existing power blocs, and tending to become exclusive of non-members in the competition for world resources and markets. Bruce Russett fears that:

. . . the political integration of several large "regions," with a sharpening of the boundaries between groupings, implies a weakening of the worldwide cement that joins nations across regions. This would almost surely produce rigidities and heightened conflicts between groupings.[42]

*Functionalism.* The functional approach, which the authors support, is gradual, in the belief that any giant steps toward political integration are not only presently unrealistic but might even be dangerous, if premature. It takes the position that viable and legitimate transnational institutions result from a process during which limited and specific tasks are assigned to limited and specific organizations to meet particular problems. Necessity will be the mother of world political invention. As the head of the United Nations Environmental Program wrote:

It is only when nations find themselves incapable of exercising their sovereignty effectively or advantageously on a unilateral basis that they will agree—reluctantly—to exercise it collectively by agreement with other nations.[43]

There have been functional international organizations to meet specific needs at least as far back as 1874, when the Universal Postal Union was established. As the world became increasingly interconnected and interdependent, "rules of the road" and arrangements to regulate "traffic" were established with greater frequency. The advent of electronic communications, for example, necessitated new agreements and machinery for handling transoceanic messages and now satellite television. A great deal of work can be done on "old" problems, such as the development of a global system of measurement, on traffic signs and regulations, and even on currency—without violating national sovereignty. Non-governmental organizations, many of them already either transnational or possessing such connections, can be asked to develop proposals for these and a long list of other fields, including education.

We are confronted today with new problems, such as worldwide pollution, requiring transnational arrangements of a greater dimension, staffed by highly trained people with dependable funding—and, ultimately, with the authority to enforce regulations under some kind of international body. And a fair and nonviolent exploitation of the ocean bed may now require different and even more extensive institutional arrangements.

The functional approach would avoid forcing the issue between the continuation of the nation-state system, leading to conflict and perhaps nuclear war, and the creation of world government, presumably leading to cooperation and peace. It would eschew head-on attacks on national sovereignty. Rather, it would ask what needs to be done to solve problems not amenable to national solutions. As a leading scholar of the functionalist approach wrote ten years ago:

In a world of a hundred and more states sovereignty can in simple fact never be dismantled through a formula but only through function, shedding national functions and pooling authority in them; unless we are to give up all purpose of wide all-round international sharing in the world of peace.[44]

A functional approach would ask nations to consider the advantages of cooperative efforts in promoting the security and welfare of their own peoples. While nations may not yet share a common ideology and do fear world government, they can appreciate the universal need for survival and improvement in the quality of life. Maurice Strong summarizes our plight and opportunity:

The only practical hope is that the world will now respond to the common concern for its own survival, an acknowledgement of the essential interdependence of its peoples and an awareness that cooperative action can enlarge the horizons and enrich the lives of all peoples.[45]

### Using Data on Global Problems To Form Hypotheses

Students need data if they are to understand global problems. A particularly effective way to present basic data is to make transparencies of graphs and show them with an overhead projector. With the graphs visible on a screen in the classroom, the teacher can conduct a line of inquiry and help students raise questions leading to hypotheses. What follow are a few examples of this technique. For many other examples, see *Data on the Human Crisis: A Handbook for Inquiry,* which comes with a Teacher's Guide. (See footnote 14 for full reference.)

*World Population throughout History.* Before 1650 it took an average of 3,500 years for world population to double. Now, newborn children will see our present population double before they have reached middle-age, and quadruple before they die. Even if the birthrate decreases over the next 25 years, world population is apt to exceed 6 billion by that time, because of the increasing number of women reaching child-bearing age and who will be having children.

HYPOTHESIS: Population growth means people living closer together, and crowding will lead to more violence. (Students need to consider

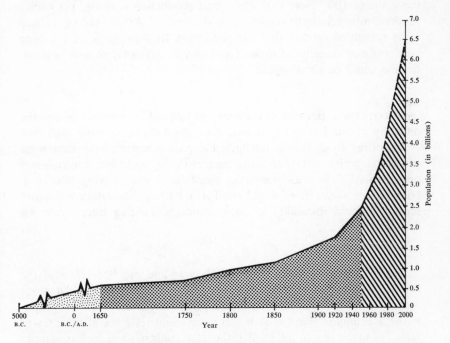

SOURCE: "World Population: Status Report 1974," *Reports on Population/ Family Planning,* Number 15, Population Council, 245 Park Avenue, New York, N.Y. 10017. Page 4.

whether there is a close correlation between crowding and violence. Are there more crimes of violence in cities? But what about the fact that crowded countries like Holland and Japan have much lower violent crime rates than the relatively uncrowded United States?) More people will also mean more demand for food and other resources. (Will this increase the potential for violent conflict?)

*Food Production.* Despite the "Green Revolution" and the resulting vastly improved crop yields, per capita food availability has not increased in the Third World, largely because of population growth. The new methods depend on huge quantities of fertilizer, which require large amounts of energy for production. Costs are skyrocketing, and developing nations are hard-pressed to afford increasing agricultural production. At the same time climate changes have resulted in mass starvation in north-central Africa. Other areas are threatened, including India.

The graphs on page 287 show changes in total and in per capita food production as compared to a base year, which was arbitrarily assigned the value of 100. Note that while total production is rising, per capita production is relatively stable or, in the case of Africa, falling. There is no reason to assume that the per capita food available in the base year was nutritionally adequate (generally it was not), so even a slight decline could be catastrophic.

HYPOTHESIS: Because of the continued growth of population, and the difficulty of continuing to increase food production, and the high cost of importing food, before too long the poor countries may face mass starvation, which will mean more conflict in the world between rich and poor nations. (Is mass starvation inevitable? Will starving masses in poor nations mean more world conflict?) Perhaps starvation will mean serious internal instability in such countries, inviting intervention by the superpowers.

*Growing Gap Between the Rich Quarter and the Poor Half of the World.* The recent growth rates for GNP per capita have been much higher in the rich countries than the poor. Even under the very optimistic assumption that the rich and poor countries grow at the present rates (as in the graph, page 288), the poor countries will be fortunate to reach an average per capita GNP of $300 by the year 2000. It is estimated that only about 900 million people lived in countries with average

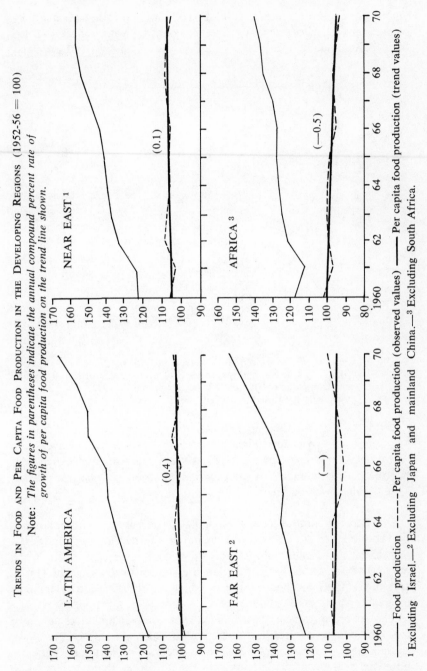

TRENDS IN FOOD AND PER CAPITA FOOD PRODUCTION IN THE DEVELOPING REGIONS (1952-56 = 100)

Note: *The figures in parentheses indicate the annual compound percent rate of growth of per capita food production on the trend line shown.*

—— Food production ----- Per capita food production (observed values) —— Per capita food production (trend values)

[1] Excluding Israel.—[2] Excluding Japan and mainland China.—[3] Excluding South Africa.

SOURCE: *The State of Food and Agriculture 1971,* The Food and Agriculture Organization of the United Nations, Rome, Italy. 1971. Page 4.

annual per capita incomes of at least $1000 in 1965 (the rich quarter); whereas over half of humanity lives in countries where income is less than $100 annually.

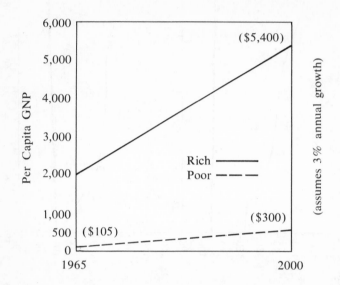

SOURCE: *Data on the Human Crisis,* The University of the State of New York, The State Education Department, Center for International Programs and Comparative Studies, Albany, New York. 1972. Page 28. Data provided by Bruce M. Russett.

HYPOTHESIS: As the gap between the rich and poor continues to widen, we can expect to see increasing conflict between the "haves" and "have nots." (Will the poor increasingly envy and resent the rich? Or will the poor be content if their economic position is at least somewhat better than it was before?)

*Depletion of Natural Resources.* Total world energy consumption has been doubling every 15 years. Demand in the developing countries is now also rising rapidly and is expected to multiply by 8.5 times in the next 30 years. Other basic materials are subject to the same pressures, and all resources are becoming increasingly costly as countries compete to acquire them.

The following table is based on known reserves and does not take into account new discoveries. There undoubtedly will be such new finds, so that these figures cannot be taken as accurate predictions. They do, however, provide some insights into the pressures that are bound to develop.

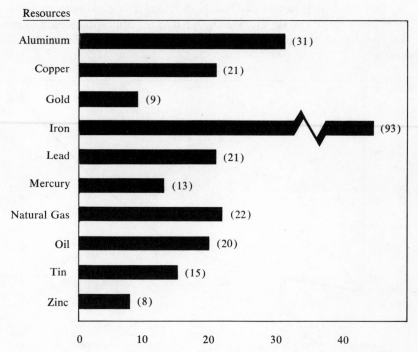

SOURCE: Data based on Dennis L. Meadows, et al., *The Limits to Growth,* A
Potomac Associates Book, Universe Books, New York, 1972.

*Further Data:* Maurice Strong of the United Nations Environment
Program said, "From the beginning of mankind to the end of World
War II, *all* the world's industry totaled less than will be produced by
the next three years of industrialization." He also said, "in one decade,
1959-1968, the United States used more resources than all the world's
people in all previous history." The U.S., with 6% of the world population, is consuming more than 40% of the irreplaceable resources.

The present known supplies of many basic natural resources will be
exhausted within the lifetime of students now in school if consumption
is not reduced.

HYPOTHESIS: As countries compete for scarce resources, there will
be increasing conflict in the world. (How might conflict be avoided?
Would some kind of transnational authority be able to allocate resources? Will the seabed, with its vast mineral wealth, be an area over
which nations will struggle? Could new institutional arrangements prevent such struggle?)

*Increase of Carbon Dioxide in the Atmosphere.* Fossil fuels (oil, natural gas, and coal) account for 97% of the energy used by industry. Burning these fuels in automobiles, homes, and factories, releases some 20 billion tons of carbon dioxide ($CO_2$) into the atmosphere each year. The buildup of this pollutant could affect the earth's temperature and weather.

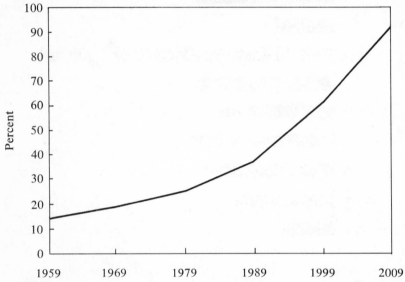

SOURCE: Graph based on data from John McHale, *World Facts and Trends,* Macmillan, Inc., New York, 1972.

HYPOTHESIS: Atmospheric pollution—as well as oceanic—cannot be solved by individual nations acting alone; there must be a world organization strong enough to set and enforce standards. (Could countries solve this problem without international organization? Could such an organization be effective without a degree of power that most nations would fear and oppose? Will the developing countries be able and willing to pay the costly price of controlling pollution as they industrialize?)

*World Military Expenditures.* At present prices, world military expenditures exceed $200 billion per year. The aggregate spent on arms is equivalent to the entire income of all the people in the poorest half of the world, with NATO and the Warsaw Pact countries accounting for more than 80% of all military spending. The fastest rates of increase in military spending, however, are in Africa, where many new nations have been building up their own forces since independence.

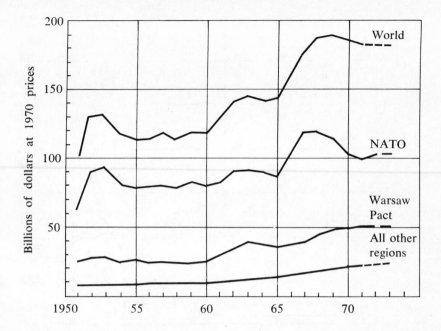

SOURCE: Stockholm International Peace Research Institute, *Yearbook of World Armaments and Disarmament*, Humanities Press, New York, 1973. Page 206.

HYPOTHESIS: Even though more and more is spent on arms, there is less security; moreover, arms expenditures make headway against other world problems almost impossible. (Do arms buildups increase tensions: for example, between the United States and the Soviets? What if even 10% [$8 billion] of the amount the United States spends on arms each year could be spent fighting pollution or urban problems?)

*Tourism and the United States.* The number of Americans traveling to foreign countries has increased by almost 20 times during this century. The number of foreign visitors to the United States has increased twelve-fold in the same period. (See table page 292)

HYPOTHESIS: The more people who get to know other cultures through travel, the less the likelihood of war. (Does travel always produce a favorable impression of another country? Even if most people return home with a positive image of another country, how might this affect the policy of government? What about students studying abroad and foreign students in the United States? Should this be encouraged as promoting peace in the world?)

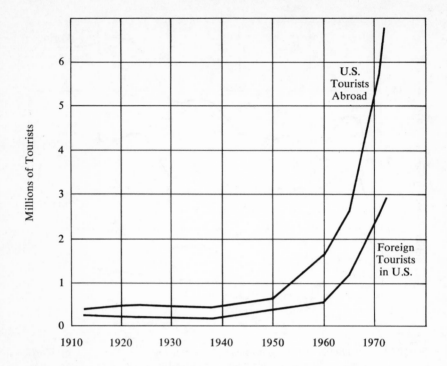

SOURCES OF DATA: Bruce M. Russett, *Community and Contention: Britain and America in the Twentieth Century,* MIT Press, Cambridge, 1963. Page 231. And the U.S. Bureau of the Census, *Statistical Abstract of the United States,* U.S. Government Printing Office, Washington, D.C., 1973. The data exclude travelers to and from Canada and Mexico.

*Increase of International Organizations.* Intergovernmental organizations result from agreements between countries and involve the establishment of some kind of staff and headquarters on a permanent basis. Some organizations are global, such as the United Nations, and its affiliated agencies, UNESCO, WHO, UNICEF, etc. Some are regional, such as the Organization of American States or the Organization for African Unity. Many are for specific purposes or functions, such as the International Whaling Commission or the Desert Locust Control Organization for Eastern Africa. Size usually varies with function and scope.

International non-governmental organizations include individuals and groups but not governments. There are organizations for businessmen, churches, labor unions, professional associations, international sports competition, hobbies, etc. The number of such organizations went from less than 200 in 1909 to nearly 2,500 in 1972.

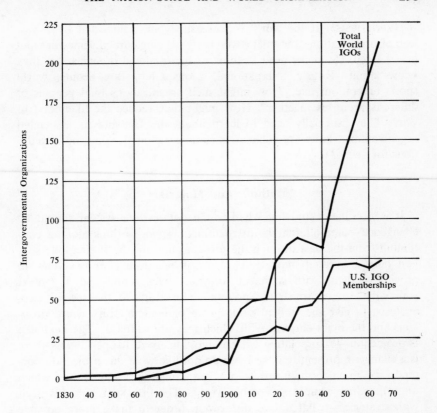

SOURCE OF DATA: Michael Wallace and J. David Singer, "Intergovernmental Organization in the Global System, 1815-1964," *International Organization* 24, #2, 1970.

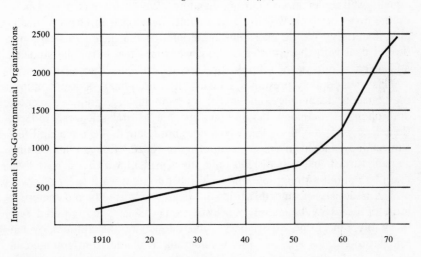

SOURCE OF DATA: Robert C. Angell, University of Michigan.

HYPOTHESIS: If the world is increasingly interconnected by a vast web of organizations, national sovereignty is being curbed somewhat and peace aided. (Students need to think of international organizations they know about—Rotary International, Lions Club, Boy Scouts, world sports federations, etc. How might such organizations bind peoples of different countries together? How might they reduce the likelihood of war? They especially need to learn about the UN and its associated organizations. How are such organizations helping to lay the foundations for peace?)

## Methods and Materials

It is useful, in studying whether the nation-state system should be changed to some alternative international system, to think along a continuum from the past through the present and into the future. We suggest here a five-step model. The first is perspective or overview, to provide students with sufficient historical background and a context with which to approach the present. This leads to the second step, analysis, to give the student some grasp of contemporary world problems and the main currents with which they are suffused. The next step is projection—extrapolating what is most likely to happen unless there is a change in present trends. If we do not like what this projection portends, we go on to the fourth step, an examination of alternatives which might produce a more acceptable world. The fifth step concerns itself with strategies—what do we do now in order to make more possible the preferred alternatives? The materials which follow have been organized under these rubrics, although many of them cross over and fit equally well under more than one heading. We have concentrated here on the first two steps, which are more fully developed in terms of available materials. We do cite some materials for the next two steps, but do not deal with the last step, action, which we feel is for the student, and teacher, outside of school—and for all citizens.

This methodology presumes a highly interdisciplinary study, employing concepts, techniques, and materials from history, political science, anthropology, sociology, psychology, and the natural sciences. Indeed, there is scarcely any discipline which does not relate to this issue, and few subjects now taught in schools cannot be included. Education can, and should, furnish us with insights into the world in which we now live, and ideas about a preferable one in which we might want to live.

The issue is vast, and this brief discussion of methods and materials must of necessity be merely suggestive. The selectivity required will inevitably reflect the experiences—and biases—of the authors. What follow are various kinds of useful materials available from commercial publishers or educational institutions or organizations. At the end of this chapter the reader will find a list of organizations which can be helpful.

## Overview or Perspective

We may begin with two books which concentrate on the problem of war. The more recent, by Joseph and Roberta Moore, *War and War Prevention* (Rochelle Park, N. J.: Hayden Book Co., Inc., 1974), is aimed at high school students and takes up the causes of war, from human nature to factors intrinsic to the nation-state system. It is especially helpful in discussing alternative models for preventing war, including the United Nations, a world federation of states, world government, and limited world government. Students are aided in their involvement in the issue through scenarios for testing the models and suggestions for classroom activities. Another overview, designed more for teachers, is *Teaching about War and War Prevention,* by William A. Nesbitt (N.Y.: Thomas Y. Crowell, Co., 1971). Using a framework of man, the nation-state, and the international system, it examines the causes and prevention of war and offers the history-oriented teacher practical suggestions along with examples of units and courses on war and peace. Both books provide bibliographies and suggestions about where to get more information, and help from organizations.

Almost all world or modern history texts include some study of the emergence of the nation-state, although the concept of political integration is usually not explicit. Teachers may therefore wish to consult *Nationalism and Its Alternatives,* by Karl W. Deutsch (N.Y.: Alfred A. Knopf, 1969) for a succinct and clear explanation of this concept. There are now also many non-text materials dealing with nationalism, such as: *Nationalism* in the Current Affairs Case Study series (*Newsweek*), with visuals and spirit masters; *Nationalism Kit* (free from the Center for Teaching International Relations); and *Nation-State* (Doubleday & Co., Inc.), a multimedia kit with two filmstrips and cassettes or records. A filmstrip in the audio-visual kit that accompanies *The Shaping of Western Culture* in the Fenton series (Holt, Rinehart and Winston, Inc.) makes a hard-hitting comparison of nationalism with religion. A 20-minute film entitled *Nationalism* (Encyclopaedia Britannica Educational Corp.), with Hans Kohn as a consultant, defines the concept and traces its stages, pointing out the constructive as well as destructive effects. The question of the utility of the nation-state is raised directly in "The Nation State, Obsolete or Dominant?" by James M. Becker in *Teaching About Collective Security and Conflict* (Atlantic Information Centre for Teachers, 37a High St., Wimbledon, London SW195BY, England, 1971). Robert M. Hutchins has an excellent chapter on the nation-state and world community in his book, *The Learning Society* (N.Y.: Praeger Publishers, Inc., 1968). There is also Doris Faber's *Nationalism* (N.Y.: Harper & Row, Publishers), in the *New York Times* Issues Series.

## Analysis

Many teachers are turning to case studies in order to focus on concepts in concrete circumstances, whether for term papers or classroom work. A case study that directly addresses itself to the problem of the nation-state as a source of conflict is the *July 1914 Crisis: A Case Study in Perception and Misperception*. This interdisciplinary unit includes readings for inquiry into misperception among national leaders in 1914 and into the intense nationalism that encouraged such misperception. *The Alpha Crisis Game: Origins of World War I* is a simulation game designed to introduce the subject in an experimental way. Both are available free from the Center for International Programs, N.Y. State Education Department.

Another such case study is *The Cuban Missile Crisis: Confrontation* (Social Studies School Service, 10,000 Culver Boulevard, Culver City, CA 90230). This multimedia set includes filmstrips and a simulation game, as well as other materials, and can be effective in demonstrating the problems of the nation-state system in avoiding war in the nuclear age. An interesting study would be to have students compare what happened in July, 1914 with October, 1962—one resulting in war and the other not.

Another simulation game kit uses historical perspective in considering dangers in the international system. *The State System Exercise* developed by William D. Coplin, (Markham Publishers) actually contains three simulations, one for understanding the eighteenth century system, a second for the pre-World War I period, and a third that of the post-World War II system with nuclear weapons. While the materials were developed for college undergraduate courses in international relations, the games are simple and suitable for high school. They can be completed in one class period, although more time must be allowed for post-game discussion and making comparisons of the games with the real world.

Any diagnosis of the condition of present-day world society runs the difficulty of being overwhelmed by the number of problems and concepts and the plethora of materials. Also in the case of most of the materials, it is impossible to separate diagnosis from prognosis since they deal with current problems and project them into the future. This is certainly true of Lester Brown's *World Without Borders* (N.Y.: Random House, Inc., 1972), perhaps the single best source for "putting it all together" conceptually for the teacher. Students will also find it valuable, since the author writes clearly and without difficult words or jargon. The first part, an "Inventory of Mankind's Problems," takes up such problems as the environment, the rich-poor gap, urbanization, and hunger, and shows the interrelationships with population trends, resources shortages, and the arms race. His description of global interdependence and the meaning of multinational corporations is vivid; and his suggestions for a better future, including the role of supranational institutions and how the quality of life might be improved, are balanced and hopeful. *This Endangered Planet: Prospects and Proposals for Survival* by Richard Falk (N.Y.: Random House, Inc., 1971) is too difficult for all but the most verbally able students, but extremely useful for teachers who want a conceptual framework for looking at global problems and the changes needed for survival. Falk believes this means moving toward strong international institutions away from the nation-state system.

Still another book encompassing the broad issue is *World Society* by John Burton (N.Y.: Cambridge University Press, 1972), written for British pre-university students and not easy. In some 170 pages Burton provides a keen analysis of world society, dismisses ideas of world government as neither feasible nor desirable, and comes out for the necessity of retaining much of the nation-state system, which he believes can keep peace by accurate decision-making and through existing means of resolving conflicts. René DuBos, in *A God Within* (N.Y.: Charles Scribner's Sons, 1972), has a chapter on the curious persistence of place as an important symbolism for humans. His inference is that smaller rather than larger political units are preferable. Also supporting these views, from another perspective, is Theodore Roszak, whose *Where the Wasteland Ends: Politics and Transcendence in Post-Industrial Society* (N.Y.: Doubleday & Co., Inc., 1972) expresses the conviction that the "one world" idea is coming too rapidly, that people are not ready and will not accept it, and that, in the meantime, it helps erode authentic cultural localism.

Lester Brown also wrote a 76-page booklet in the Foreign Policy Association's *Headline Series,* "The Interdependence of Nations," which is one of the most useful, if not the single most useful, books that schools could use for introducing the issue. A helpful supplement to the Brown booklet is *Data on the Human Crisis: A Handbook for Inquiry* (available free from Center for International Programs of the N.Y. State Education Department) with separate *Teacher's Guide.* The Handbook contains graphs and additional data on the major world problems in an 8½ x 11 format for making overhead projector transparencies. A useful annotated bibliography in the general subject area is "Multicultural and Worldminded Teaching," by Frank A. Stone (World Education Project, School of Education, University of Connecticut, Storrs, CT 06268).

The key problem, as has been emphasized above, remains the threat of nuclear war, and students should be under no illusions about the nature and meaning of all-out war today. There are many materials in various media for developing some affective vicarious experience with this problem. One is a kit with a filmstrip with cassettes, *The Age of the Megaton,* in the Doubleday Multimedia series. There are many useful films; for example, *The War Game* and *Hiroshima and Nagasaki* (rental: Indiana University Audio-visual Center, Bloomington, IN 47401). The best source of information about these and other films is the *War/Peace Film Guide* by Lucy Dougall (World Without War Council). A case study, *Hiroshima: A Study in Science, Politics, and the Ethics of War* in the Amherst Series (Reading, MA: Addison-Wesley Publishing Co.), can be used in the context of many courses, including American History. Two books, among many, which can help the teacher or the student put modern war into perspective are: *From Crossbow to H-Bomb* by Bernard and Fawn M. Brodie (Bloomington: Indiana University Press, 1973) and *War and Politics* by Bernard Brodie (N.Y.: Macmillan, Inc., 1973). See also the annotated bibliography by William A. Nesbitt, "Teaching About War and Its Control" (Center for International Programs, N.Y. State Education Department).

Materials for dealing with the major interrelated problems—population, resource depletion, environmental deterioration, poverty, and the rich-poor gap—and their conflict potential are now numerous. Several publications of the Center for War/Peace Studies are a good starting point and suggest other materials: *So You Want To Teach About . . .* includes guidelines and brief lessons on such subjects as conflict in United States history, interdependence, survival, and misperception; *The Quality of Life* has a futuristic approach to life styles, environment, etc.; and *Guides to Selected Curriculum Materials on Interdependence, Conflict and Change* contains teachers' comments and evaluations, after classroom use, on commercially available units.

CW/PS' publication series, *Intercom,* has some good material on this, with two issues, *Education on War, Peace, Conflict, and Change* (#65), and *Teaching About War, Peace, Conflict, and Change* (#67) providing an overview of the field. Then there is *Development: New Approaches* (#69), with suggestions, including role-play, for dealing with the rich-poor gap and economic development in the classroom; *Teaching About Population* (#72) has a teaching unit with lesson plans; *Teaching Toward Global Perspectives* (#73), which has practical lesson suggestions for 4th grade through 12th, employing various techniques, including simulation games.

The "great debate" about whether economic growth will have to be limited because of its environmental impact and diminishing irreplaceable natural resources is well developed in *The Ecology Controversy,* in paperback in the *Opposing Viewpoints Series* (Anoka, MN: Greenhaven Press). An issue of *Intercom, Multinational Corporations: The Quiet Revolution?* (#74), also has material on this. An excellent background piece to the whole question of global development and the role of the global corporation is Raymond Vernon's *Sovereignty at Bay: The Multinational Spread of U.S. Enterprises* (N.Y.: Basic Books, Inc., 1971). Also E. F. Schumacher's book *Small Is Beautiful: Study of Economics As If People Mattered* (N.Y.: Harper & Row, Publishers, 1973) presents arguments for limiting growth and brings up the relevant question of whether the nation-state is a suitable vehicle for handling such limitation.

A 1973 booklet, #5 in the *Teaching Social Studies in an Age of Crisis* series, *Teaching Youth About Conflict and War* (National Council for the Social Studies, 1201 Sixteenth Street N.W., Washington, D.C. 20036), by Nesbitt, Abramowitz, and Bloomstein, contains chapters designed to provide the teacher with a theoretical perspective for conflict and war, practical teaching suggestions, and annotated bibliographies. Schloat Productions has issued a number of sound filmstrips on various problem areas such as ecology, pollution, the ocean and its bed, and conflict. (See *Patterns of Human Conflict,* developed by CW/PS for Schloat Productions.) The annual catalog of the Social Studies School Service (address cited page 296) is an excellent annotated source for readings and other media on world problems and their future implications.

For teaching about the United Nations, a helpful starting point is a *Headline Series* booklet, "The UN at Twenty and After" by Lincoln P. Bloomfield (Foreign Policy Association). This publication, especially in the chapter "The 'Functional' United Nations," helps the student recognize the important work of the UN in other areas than peacekeeping. Also useful here is an issue of *Intercom* entitled *The UN At Twenty-five.* But perhaps the best current single source for social studies teachers and students is a recent paperback from UNESCO, *World Problems in the Classroom,* which has information and study suggestions on peace and security, disarmament, human rights, social justice, development, population, and environment, to name a few. Also, the United Nations Association of the U.S. has available for teachers an annotated bibliography of books, films, and other materials from and about the UN.

The American Association of University Women has developed a simple role-playing exercise on the UN and the future control of resources lying on and under the seabed, titled "A Scenario for a Model United Nations Conference on the Law of the Sea." For further information on the scenario one should write to UNA-USA, 833 United Nations Plaza, New York, NY 10017. Helpful supplemental background materials for this are: "The Law of the Sea," a film produced by UN/TV and available from Journals Films, Inc., 909 West Diversey Parkway, Chicago, IL 60614; "U.N. Debate on Ocean Control Moves into Choppy Seas," an article by Michael J. Berlin in the May/June 1973 issue of *War/Peace Report* (single copy $1.25) available from Gordon and Breach, One Park Avenue, New York, NY 10016; and "The Ocean Crisis: The Struggle to Protect, Manage, and Exploit the World's Oceans," by John J. Logue, in the April 1974 issue of *Vital Issues* (1-9 copies, 35¢ each, 10-49, 20¢ each), available from the Center for Information on America, Washington, CT 06793.

For experiential learning, simulation games have demonstrated their worth to an increasing number of teachers. One game that helps the student understand the interrelationship between various problems is *The Planet Management Game* (Boston, MA; Houghton Mifflin Co.), in which the players must manage an earthlike planet and make decisions about such variables as population, pollution, food and income. Another game, *Baldicer* (Richmond, VA: John Knox Press), effectively involves students in thinking about and looking for solutions to the world's food shortages in the context of a population explosion, unequal distribution of resources, and inflation. These and other games relating to international affairs are described in a 1974 issue of *Intercom* titled *Teaching Global Issues Through Simulation* (#75).

### Projection

Students need to think about alternative ways in which conflict can be controlled in the future through changes in the present international system, and the adoption of some better system of world organization. A well-conceived booklet in the *Perspectives in World Order Series* (N.Y.: Random House, Inc.), "Peacekeeping" by Jack Fraenkel, Margaret Carter, and Betty Reardon, uses models and scenarios enabling students to consider the League of Nations, the UN, and a future limited world government based on the Clark-Sohn proposal.

*World Order* (Chicago, IL: Rand McNally & Co.) by Byron G. Massialas and Jack Zevin, while at times heavy reading, is designed to have high school students consider the changing nature of war and what can be done about it. *World Order* is both historical and futuristic, requiring students to consider alternative models for world political organizations.

## *Alternatives*

A few simulation games are available to aid affective learning in this area. *Guns or Butter* (SIMILE II, P.O. Box 1023, La Jolla, CA 92037) places students in an international system like the present, with nuclear weapons, and raises questions about how the system can be changed to be less war-prone and satisfy human needs for more "butter." In the game of *Conflict* (SIMILE II), students play decision-making roles in a future disarmed world with a limited world government under which the amount of force that can be brought to bear to cope with a threat to peace depends upon the degree of consensus in the world organization. Also, "Peace Games," an article that originally appeared in the May, 1970 issue of the American Association of University Women's *Journal* and is available as a reprint from the Institute for World Order, enables students to test out models of international organizations through scenarios.

## *Organizations Which Can Provide More Information and Materials*

Center for International Programs and Comparative Studies, The State Education Department, Albany, NY 11224

Center for Teaching International Relations, Graduate School of International Studies, University of Denver, Denver, CO 80210

Center for War/Peace Studies, 218 East 18th Street, New York, NY 10003

Federalism Seventy-Six, 1280 Twenty-First Street, N.W., Washington, D.C. 20036

Foreign Policy Association, 345 East 46th Street, New York, NY 10017

Institute for World Order, 1148 Avenue of Americas, New York, NY 10036

International Association for Federal Union, 7705 Georgia Avenue, N.W., Washington, D.C. 20012

United Nations Association of U.S.A., 833 UN Plaza, New York, NY 10017

World Federalists USA, 2029 "K" Street, N.W., Washington,D.C. 20006

World Without War Council of the U.S., 1730 Grove Street, Berkeley, CA 94709

## Summary

The process of political integration on earth has been going on since human beings' earliest beginnings, and our assumption is that it will continue indefinitely. On this basis, the present nation-state form of organization is viewed as simply one stage, evolved in order to meet problems that preceding forms could not handle.

Supra-national organizations have been posited often in the past, primarily to eliminate the threat of war. That threat, the single greatest immediate danger to humankind, has now been joined by a whole series of other interrelated problems, each of which could be just as disastrous. The nation-state was not set up to cope with these other global problems, which do not respect, and indeed have no relation to, national boundaries. These include environmental deterioration, population, and exhaustion of limited resources, all of which have serious implications for international conflict. Newly accessible resources, such as those on the seabed, may also provide bases for conflict, as will price increases by resource-rich but hitherto powerless nations now anxious and able to exploit the scarcity of critical materials.

Some form of political integration larger than the nation-state is needed. It is as yet undetermined what that form is. Here it has been proposed that it be approached on a functional level, with the nation-state retaining sovereignty in those areas where it remains competent, and yielding power to new international or global organizations where such a larger arena is needed. It is postulated that such functional co-operation can be acceptable to the present nation-states, and that success in such cooperation can pave the way for increased political integration.

Since today's high school students will be tomorrow's governors of the world, this is an area which needs to be studied in the schools to prepare them for that awesome responsibility. Teachers need to have background knowledge, and to be acquainted with the materials and methods that will help them in the classroom.

## FOOTNOTES

[1] Richard J. Barnet, *The New York Times* (June 19, 1971).

[2] Hans J. Morgenthau, speech at Pacem in Terris Convocation (February 1965).

[3] Charles R. Beitz and Theodore Herman, eds., *Peace and War* (San Francisco: W. H. Freeman, 1973), p. 188.

[4] John W. Burton, *World Society* (New York: Cambridge University Press, 1972), p. 8.

[5] Karl Deutsch, *Nationalism and Its Alternatives* (New York: Alfred A. Knopf, 1969), p. 169.

[6] Maurice Strong, "One Year After Stockholm: An Ecological Approach to Management," *Foreign Affairs* 51 (July 1973): 707.

[7] Kenneth Boulding, "The Prevention of World War III," *Virginia Quarterly Review* (Winter 1962): 2.

[8] Henry Kissinger, *The New York Times* (October 26, 1973).

[9] Herman Kahn, "An Interview with Herman Kahn," *The Humanist* 33 (November/December 1973): 47.

[10] James Reston, "McNamara Looks Ahead," *The New York Times* editorial (March 20, 1974).

[11] Harry Lustig, "Our Dwindling Energy Resources," *UNESCO Courier* 27 (January 1974): 8.

[12] Harold M. Schmeck, Jr., "World Seen Near a Food Disaster," *The New York Times* (March 15, 1974).

[13] Ward Morehouse, "The Energy Crisis and Man's Future," a foundation draft proposal (New York State Education Department, Winter, 1974).

[14] William A. Nesbitt, ed., *Data on the Human Crisis: A Handbook for Inquiry* (Albany: The University of the State of New York, The State Education Department, and Center for International Programs and Comparative Studies, 1972), p. 29.

[15] Barbara Ward and René DuBos, *Only One Earth: The Care and Maintenance of a Small Planet* (New York: W. W. Norton & Co., 1972), p. 211.

[16] The Population Council, *Reports on Population/Family Planning* (New York: The Population Council, January, 1974), p. 4.

[17] Lester R. Brown, *Interdependence of Nations,* Headline Series (New York: Foreign Policy Association, 1972), p. 45.

[18] Noel Mostert, "Supertankers," *New Yorker* (May 13, 1974): 89.

[19] Helmut Schmidt, "Struggle for the World Product," *Foreign Affairs* 52 (April 1974): 442-443.

[20] Barbara Ward, *Spaceship Earth* (New York: Columbia University Press, 1966), p. 14.

[21] *Ibid.,* p. 17.

[22] Burton, *op. cit.,* pp. 35-45.

[23] *New Yorker* (March 4, 1974): 27.

[24] Herbert Kelman, "Education for the Concept of a Global Society," *Social Education* (November 1968): 662.

[25] John DeLamater, Daniel Katz, and Herbert C. Kelman, "On the Nature of National Involvement," *The Journal of Conflict Resolution* 13 (September 1969): 320-357.

[26] Deutsch, *op. cit.,* p. 4.

[27] Burton, *op. cit.,* p. 3.

[28] Matthew Melko, *52 Peaceful Societies* (Oakville, Ontario: Canadian Peace Research Institute, 1973).

[29] *Ibid.,* p. 183.

[30] *Ibid.,* p. 122.

[31] *Ibid.,* p. 125.

[32] Karl Deutsch et al., *Political Community and the North Atlantic Area: International Organization in the Light of Historical Experience* (Westport: Greenwood Press, Inc., 1957), p. 129.

[33] *Ibid.,* p. 129.

[34] *Ibid.,* p. 130.

[35] *Ibid.,* p. 130.

[36] Ward, *op. cit.,* p. 16.

[37] Robert Pickus and Robert Woito, *To End War* (New York: Harper & Row, Publishers, 1970), p. 49.

[38] Bernard Brodie, *War and Politics* (New York: Macmillan Company, 1973), p. 317.

[39] Grenville Clark and Louis B. Sohn, *World Peace Through World Law: Two Alternative Plans* (Cambridge: Harvard University Press, 1966).

[40] Chadwick Alger, in James M. Becker and Howard D. Mehlinger, eds., *International Dimensions in the Social Studies* (Washington, D.C.: National Council for the Social Studies, 1968), p. 76.

[41] *Ibid.,* p. 75.

[42] Bruce Russett, in Beitz and Herman, *op. cit.,* p. 235.

[43] Strong, *op. cit.,* p. 706.

[44] David Mitrany, in Beitz and Herman, *op. cit.,* p. 227.

[45] Strong, *op. cit.,* p. 707.

# Permissions

## 1. Some Thoughts on Controversial Issues

Page 26

Excerpt from *The Challenge of the Passing Years: My Encounter with Time* by R. M. MacIver. Copyright © 1963 by Pocket Books, Inc. Used by permission.

Page 27

Excerpt from *Education and Human Relations* by Ashley Montagu. Copyright © 1958 by Ashley Montagu. Published by Grove Press, Inc. Used by permission of the author.

Page 30

Excerpted from *End of the Road* by John Barth. Copyright © 1958, 1967 by John Barth. Reprinted by permission of Doubleday & Company, Inc.

Pages 30-31

Excerpt from *A Guide to Rational Living* by Albert Ellis and Robert A. Harper. Copyright © 1961 by Institute for Rational Living, Inc. Used by permission of the publisher, Prentice-Hall, Inc.

Page 31

Excerpts from *I'm OK—You're OK: A Practical Guide to Transactional Analysis* by Thomas A. Harris. Copyright © 1967, 1968, 1969 by Thomas A. Harris. Used by permission of Harper & Row, Publishers, Inc.

Pages 31-32

Excerpt from "Community Pressures and Education," Chapter 8 by Alan F. Griffin, in *Educational Freedom in an Age of Anxiety* edited by H. Gordon Hullfish in the Twelfth Yearbook of the John Dewey Society. Copyright © 1953 by Harper & Row, Publishers, Inc. Used by permission of the publishers.

Page 32

Excerpt from *Reflective Thinking: The Method of Education* by H. Gordon Hullfish and Philip G. Smith. Copyright © 1961 by Dodd, Mead & Company. Used by permission of the publisher.

Page 33

Excerpt from *Minority Report: H. L. Mencken's Notebooks* by H. L. Mencken. Copyright © 1956 by Alfred A. Knopf, Inc. Used by permission of the publisher.

Page 33

Excerpt from *Reconstruction in Philosophy* by John Dewey. Copyrights © 1920 original edition by Henry Holt and Co., 1948 enlarged edition by Beacon Press, 1950 (Editor's Note) by Eduard C. Lindeman. Third Printing, July, 1952 published as a Mentor Book of The New American Library of World Literature, Inc. by arrangement with Beacon Press. Used by permission of Beacon Press.

Pages 34-35

Excerpts from *Johnny Got His Gun* by Dalton Trumbo. Copyrights © 1939, 1959, and 1970 (Introduction) by Dalton Trumbo. Printed 1939 by J. B. Lippincott, Co., 1946 by Monogram Publishers, 1952 by The Liberty Book Club, 1959 by Lyle Stuart, Inc., 1967 and 1970 by Bantam Books, Inc. by arrangement with Lyle Stuart, Inc. Used by permission of Lyle Stuart, Inc.

Page 35
Excerpts from *The Bamboo Bed* by William Eastlake. Copyright © 1969 by Simon and Schuster, Inc. Used by permission of the publisher.

Page 36
Excerpt from "Logical Reasoning: An Educational Goal," by Alan R. Osborne and Gerald M. Reagan, in *Theory Into Practice,* 12:5, December, 1973, published by College of Education, The Ohio State University. Used by permission of the publisher and the authors.

Page 37
Excerpts from *Education for a New Morality* by Agnes E. Meyer. Copyright © 1957 by Kappa Delta Pi. Published by Macmillan Publishing Co., Inc. Used by permission of the publisher.

Page 40
Excerpt from *Minority Report: H. L. Mencken's Notebooks* by H. L. Mencken. Copyright © 1956 by Alfred A. Knopf, Inc. Used by permission of the publisher.

Page 40
Excerpts from *An Inquiry into the Human Prospect* by Robert L. Heilbroner. Copyright © 1974 by W. W. Norton & Company, Inc. Used by permission of the publisher.

Pages 41-42
Excerpt from "My Pedagogic Creed: A Statement of Personal Beliefs Regarding Secondary Social Studies Education," by Raymond H. Muessig, in the *Southwest Journal of Social Education,* 1:1, Fall, 1970. Used by permission of the *Southwest Journal of Social Education* and the author.

Page 42
Excerpt from *The Recovery of Confidence* by John W. Gardner. Copyright © 1970 by W. W. Norton & Company, Inc. Used by permission of the publisher.

## 2. Teacher Preparation and Models for Teaching Controversial Social Issues

Pages 47-49
Excerpts from *How To Handle Controversial Issues* (How To Do It Series, No. 14) by Richard E. Gross. Copyright © 1964 by the National Council for the Social Studies. Used by permission of the publisher.

Pages 54-55
Excerpts from "Family Planning Is Inherently Genocidal, True-False," by Carl Pope, in *Environmental Action,* May 15, 1971. Used by permission of *Environmental Action* and the author.

Page 56
Excerpts from "Thoughts on Feeding the Hungry," by Wayne H. Davis, in *The Arizona Republic,* 1970. Used by permission of the author.

Page 72
Excerpt from *Values and Teaching* by Louis E. Raths, Merrill Harmin, and Sidney B. Simon. Copyright © 1966 by Charles E. Merrill Publishing Co. Used by permission of the publisher and Sidney B. Simon.

Pages 74-75
Excerpts from *Helping Students Think and Value: Strategies for Teaching the Social Studies* by Jack R. Fraenkel. Copyright © 1973 by Prentice-Hall, Inc. Used by permission of the publisher.

Page 79
Excerpts from *Thinking with Values* (Teacher's Edition) by V. Clyde Arnspiger, James A. Brill, and W. Ray Rucker. Copyright © 1973 by Steck-Vaughn Company. Used by permission of the publisher.

Pages 80-82
Excerpts from *Principles and Practices in the Teaching of the Social Sciences: Concepts and Values* by Paul F. Brandwein, et al. Copyright © 1970 by Harcourt Brace Jovanovich, Inc. Used by permission of the publisher.

## 4. Should the Study of Death Be a Necessary Preparation for Living?

Pages 125-126
Excerpt from *Loss and Grief: Psychological Management in Medical Practice* by Bernard Schoenberg, Arthur C. Carr, David Peretz, and Austin H. Kutscher, editors. Copyright © 1970 by Columbia University Press. Used by permission of the publisher.

Pages 126-127
Excerpt from *Griefs and Discontents* by Gregory Rochlin. Copyright © 1965 by Little, Brown and Company. Used by permission of the publisher.

Pages 129-132
Excerpt from *The American Way of Death* by Jessica Mitford. Copyright © 1963 by Jessica Mitford, published by Simon & Schuster, Inc. Reprinted by permission of the publisher.

Pages 133-135
Excerpt from "The Dying Patient's Point of View," by Elisabeth Kubler-Ross, in *The Dying Patient* by Orville Brim, Jr., Howard Freeman, Sol Levine, and Norman Scotch, editors. Copyright © 1970 by Russell Sage Foundation. Used by permission of Basic Books, Inc.

Page 139
Excerpt from *Loss and Grief: Psychological Management in Medical Practice* by Bernard Schoenberg, Arthur C. Carr, David Peretz, and Austin H. Hutscher, editors. Copyright © 1970 by Columbia University Press. Used by permission of the publisher.

Pages 148-149
Excerpts from *Euthanasia and the Right to Death* by A. B. Downing, editor. Copyright © 1969 by Nash Publishing Corporation. Used by permission of the publisher.

Pages 154-157
Poem "A Flat One" in *After Experience* by W. D. Snodgrass. Copyright © 1968 by Harper & Row, Publishers. Reprinted by permission of the publisher.

## 6. Should Integration Be a Societal Goal in a Pluralistic Nation?

Page 210
Figure adapted from *Teaching Strategies for the Social Studies: Inquiry, Valuing and Decision-Making* by James A. Banks (with Ambrose A. Clegg, Jr.). Copyright © 1973 by Addison-Wesley Publishing Company. Reprinted by permission of the author.

Pages 220-223
Reprinted by permission of Hart Publishing Company, Inc., from its copyrighted volume *Values Clarification: A Handbook of Practical Strategies for Teachers and Students* by Sidney B. Simon, Leland W. Howe, and Howard Kirschenbaum.

## 7. Should We Believe That Our Planet Is in Peril?

Pages 233, 238
Excerpt from a speech delivered at DeMatha High School, Hyattsville, Maryland, December 21, 1971 by William R. VanDersal. Reprinted by permission of William R. VanDersal.

Page 234
Excerpt from *Towards Global Equilibrium: Collected Papers* by Dennis L. Meadows and Donella H. Meadows. Copyright © 1973 by Wright-Allen Press, Inc. Reprinted by permission of the publisher.

Pages 236, 237
Excerpts from *Planet in Peril: Man and the Biosphere Today* by R. F. Dasmann. Copyright © 1972 by UNESCO. Reprinted by permission of UNESCO.

Page 238
Excerpt from "Managing the Environment" by Neil Jacoby. Copyright © 1973 by *The Center Magazine*. Reprinted by permission of the publisher.

Page 239
Excerpts from a conversation with Robert Smythe, Ecologist, Environmental Impact Assessment Project, The Institute for Ecology. Reprinted by permission of Robert Smythe.

Page 241
Excerpt from *The Use of Land: A Citizen's Policy Guide to Urban Growth* edited by William K. Reilly. Copyright © 1973 by The Rockefeller Brothers Fund, with permission of Thomas Y. Crowell Company, Inc., publisher.

Page 243
Excerpt from "Environmental Education as an Arena of Creative Conflict," in *International Understanding at School* by Peter Harper. Copyright © April, 1972 by UNESCO.

Page 244
Excerpt from *Learning To Be* by Edgar Faure, et al. George G. Harrap and Co., Ltd., London, 1972. Reprinted by permission of the publisher.

Page 245
Excerpt from "An End to All This" by Richard M. Koff. Originally appeared in *Playboy* magazine, copyright © July, 1971 by *Playboy*. Reprinted by permission of *Playboy* magazine.

Pages 245-246
Excerpt from "The Energy Crisis" by S. David Freeman. Copyright © November, 1973 by *Vital Issues*. Reprinted by permission of Center for Information on America.

Page 247
Excerpt from *Environmental Quality and Social Justice in Urban America* edited by James Noel Smith. Copyright © 1974 by The Conservation Foundation. Reprinted by permission of the publisher.

Page 255
Excerpt from "The Biosphere, a Delicate Balance Between Man and Nature"
by René DuBos in *UNESCO Courier*. Copyright © January, 1969 by
UNESCO.

Pages 256-257
Excerpt from "Environmental Education as an Arena of Creative Conflict"
by Peter Harper in *International Understanding at School*. Copyright ©
April, 1972 by UNESCO.

Page 258
Excerpt from "Choosing Values and Valuing Choices," by E. J. Farrell, in
the *Association of Departments of English Bulletin*. Copyright © March,
1974 by ADE. Reprinted by permission of the publisher.

## 8. Should the Nation-State Give Way to Some Form of World Organization?

Page 265
Excerpt from "The Energy Crisis and Man's Future," a foundation draft
proposal by Ward Morehouse. Published by the New York State Education
Department, Winter 1974. Used by permission of the publisher.

Page 268
Excerpt from "Struggle for the World Product," by Helmut Schmidt, in
*Foreign Affairs* 52 (April 1974). Used by permission of the publisher.

Page 285
Graph from "World Population: Status Report 1974" from *Reports on
Population/Family Planning*, Number 15, published by Population Council,
New York City. Used by permission of the publisher.

Page 287
Graphs from *The State of Food and Agriculture 1971*, published by the
Food and Agriculture Organization of the United Nations, Rome, Italy.
Used by permission of the publisher.

Page 291
Graph from the Stockholm International Peace Research Institute, *Yearbook
of World Armaments and Disarmament*. Copyright © 1973 by Humanities
Press, Inc. Used by permission of the publisher.

## THE ILLUSTRATIONS

COVER, *The Prisoner*, 1968, Juan Genoves (acrylic and oil on canvas); PART I,
*Chess Set*, 1962, Man Ray (enamel and brass on wood board); page 2, *Man
Pushing the Door*, 1966, Jean Ipoustéguy (bronze); page 44, *The Prophet*, 1933,
Pablo Gargallo (bronze); PART II, six bronzes by Honoré Daumier, 1832-1835—
Top left, *Lefebvre (The Fine Trenchant Spirit)*, Center left, *Fulchiron (The Hypo-
crite)*, Lower left, *Girod de L'Ain or Admiral Verheul (The Simpleton)*, Top right,
*Dupin (The Orator)*, Lower right, *Harlé Père (The Old Fool)*; page 86, *Family
Group*, 1946, Henry Moore (bronze); page 122, *The Avenger*, 1914, Ernst Barlach
(bronze); page 166, *The Great Warrior of Montauban*, 1898, Emile-Antoine Bour-
delle (bronze); page 196, *Column of Peace*, 1954, Antoine Pevsner (bronze); page
230, *Dog*, 1951 cast 1957, Alberto Giacometti (bronze); page 260, *Sphere Number 6*, 1963-65, Arnaldo Pomodoro (bronze).

BOOK DESIGN AND PRODUCTION BY *Willadene Price*